The Moral and
Political Thought
of
Mahatma Gandhi

THE MORAL AND POLITICAL THOUGHT OF
Mahatma Gandhi

Raghavan N. Iyer

OXFORD UNIVERSITY PRESS
Oxford   London   New York

OXFORD UNIVERSITY PRESS
Oxford London Glasgow
New York Toronto Melbourne Wellington
Ibadan Nairobi Dar es Salaam Lusaka Cape Town
Kuala Lumpur Singapore Jakarta Hong Kong Tokyo
Delhi Bombay Calcutta Madras Karachi

**The Library of Congress Cataloged the First Issue of
This Work as Follows:**

Iyer, Raghavan Narasimhan.
The moral and political thought of Mahatma Gandhi [by]
Raghavan N. Iyer. New York, Oxford University Press,
1973.

xiii, 449 p. 22 cm. $12.50
Bibliography: p. [419]-421.

1. Gandhi, Mohandas Karamchand, 1869-1948—Political science.
2. Political ethics. 3. Nonviolence. I. Title.
JC273.G28 I 9 181'.4 72-96613
ISBN 0-19-501692-0 MARC
ISBN 0-19-502357-9 PBK
Library of Congress 73 [4]

Printed in the United States of America

to
NANDINI
exemplar of *tapas*

Every man should expend his chief thought and attention on the consideration of his first principles: are they or are they not rightly laid down? and when he has sifted them, all the rest will follow.

PLATO, *Cratylus*

PREFACE

The chief aim of this work is to elucidate the central concepts in the moral and political thought of Mahatma Gandhi, with special attention to the connection between his presuppositions and his precepts. Despite the vast and fast accumulating literature on Gandhi, scant justice has been done to the solid conceptual foundations of his thought. Without honest effort in this direction, the subtlety and potency as well as the open texture of his political ethic cannot be grasped either in theory or in practice.

I am grateful to G. D. H. Cole and B. P. Wadia for sage advice in November 1956 when I was first shown the need for such a study. Professor James Joll, Dr. Percival Spear and Mr. John Mabbott made valuable suggestions on several chapters. Professor John Plamenatz of Oxford was enormously helpful with his probing comments at different stages of my work.

I am indebted to Professor K. Swaminathan, Chief Editor of the Collected Works of Gandhi, as well as the Librarians of the Sangrahalaya at Delhi and at Ahmedabad for general assistance in consulting the complete files of Gandhi's extensive correspondence. I am also happy to acknowledge the kindness of Navajivan Press in allowing citations from copyright material.

This work has intangibly benefited from conversations with the Dalai Lama and Vinoba Bhave in India, with Albert West and Lord Pethick-Lawrence in England, and with a wide variety of colleagues and students in Oxford and Oslo, Accra and Chicago. I have, above all, been inspired by the authentic efforts of young people in Santa Barbara and elsewhere to evolve fresh applications of Gandhian concepts to the daily round and the common task.

R.N.I.

1975 Old San Marcos Road, Santa Barbara
(25th anniversary of Gandhi's assassination)
January 30, 1973

CONTENTS

1. INTRODUCTION   *3*

2. THE INDICTMENT OF MODERN CIVILIZATION   *23*

3. THE PURIFICATION OF POLITICS   *37*

    Religion and Politics   *38*
    The Concept of Power   *53*
    The Doctrine of Double Standards   *58*

4. THE NEED FOR ABSOLUTE VALUES AND
    FOR VOWS   *63*

    Moral Commitment   *64*
    Absolute Values and Eternal Principles   *67*
    The Need for Vows   *73*
    Pledges and Contracts   *81*

5. HUMAN NATURE, PROGRESS, AND
    PERFECTIBILITY   *87*

    The Concept of Human Nature   *88*
    Original Goodness and Human Perfectibility   *96*
    The Interpretation of History   *101*
    Assessment   *106*

6. INDIVIDUAL CONSCIENCE AND HEROISM
   IN SOCIETY   *113*

   The Individual and Society   *114*
   The Exaltation of Conscience   *119*
   The Socratic *Daimon* and Gandhi's Inner Voice   *125*
   The Concept of Conscience in the West and in India   *129*
   The Heroic Ideal   *133*
   Political Leadership and the Masses   *139*
   Conscience and Heroism   *144*

7. *SATYA*
   ABSOLUTE AND RELATIVE TRUTH   *149*

   The Concept of *Satya*   *150*
   "Truth Is God"   *155*
   Absolute and Relative Truth   *158*
   The Vow of Truth   *164*
   Truth in Politics and Society   *167*
   The Significance of *Satya*   *173*

8. *AHIMSA*
   NONVIOLENCE AS A CREED AND A POLICY   *177*

   The Meaning of *Ahimsa*   *178*
   Ahimsa in Politics and Society   *184*
   Ahimsa as a Creed and as a Policy   *192*
   Unavoidable *Himsa*   *204*
   Critics of *Ahimsa*   *207*
   Assessment   *212*
   Appendix: Attitudes Toward Nonviolence before
   Gandhi   *218*

9. *SATYA* AND *AHIMSA*
   THE RELATION BETWEEN TRUTH AND
   NONVIOLENCE   *223*

   Satya and *Ahimsa*   *224*
   Moksha and *Tapas*   *234*
   Tolerance and Civility   *239*

10. *SATYAGRAHA*
    ACTIVE AND PASSIVE RESISTANCE   *251*

       The State and the Citizen   *252*
       The Doctrine of Passive Resistance   *260*
       The Doctrine of *Satyagraha*   *269*

11. THE SCOPE AND SIGNIFICANCE OF
    SATYAGRAHA   *293*

       The Scope and Application of *Satyagraha*   *294*
       The Limits and Abuse of *Satyagraha*   *310*
       Criticisms and Assessment   *323*

12. *SWARAJ AND SWADESHI*
    SELF-RULE AND SELF-RELIANCE   *345*

13. MEANS AND ENDS IN POLITICS   *359*

14. ASSESSMENT   *373*

    Notes   *389*

    Bibliography   *419*

    Glossary   *423*

    Index   *429*

The Moral and
Political Thought
of
Mahatma Gandhi

1

INTRODUCTION

I have no desire to found a sect. I am really too ambitious to be satis-fied with a sect for a following, for I represent no new truths. I en-deavour to follow and represent truth as I know it. I do claim to throw a new light on many an old truth.

MAHATMA GANDHI

Political thinkers are properly studied without undue reference to their personalities. Plato's political experiences, Spinoza's singular saintliness, Rousseau's personal torments, the complex character of Marx, the public career of Kautilya, may all throw some light upon their theories but need not affect our appraisals of them. Biographical evidence is often dubious and firm judgments about remote figures are hazardous. No doubt it is sometimes useful to know about the declared purposes or practical intentions of abstract theorists, and especially of social critics. For example, our awareness of Saint-Simon's strong personal messianism may be relevant to our grasp of his *Nouveau Christianisme* and even of his *Du système industriel*.

When we turn to Mahatma Gandhi's moral and political concepts, we find it peculiarly difficult to ignore his personality and his activities. No saint or politician before our century could have achieved in his lifetime the world-wide attention that Gandhi received. He had his detractors but made no enemies, and he won the deep affection of vast numbers of people as well as of his eminent contemporaries. He has been classed with the Buddha and Christ, Socrates and the *Bhakti* saints of medieval India. He has been celebrated as perhaps the greatest man of our century by men as different as the Dalai Lama, E. M. Forster and Lord Samuel. Einstein has surmised that generations to come "will scarcely believe that such a one as this, ever in flesh and blood, walked upon this earth." In India he is venerated by the masses as a *Mahatma*. At the same time he has been called a poseur and impostor,[1] a masochistic moralist,[2] a deluded crank. But his critics have been uncomfortable in their contempt for the man, while some admirers have conceded that his conduct was at times apt to be enigmatic.

Gandhi's nearness to us in time, and the immense power of his radiant goodness, have obscured the fact that he is too untypical of our age to be understood as a person by his contemporaries. His personality, rare in any century, but unique in ours, has had so intense an impact that it has diverted attention from his claims to be regarded as a political thinker. In India the tribute now paid to him as "Father of the Nation" and as saint or prophet is often a compensation by the intelligentsia for its failure to study his writings and to consider seriously his political insights. It is hastily assumed in India and elsewhere that Gandhi's moral greatness as a man and his remarkable role as a charismatic leader are more crucial than his contribution to moral and political thought. His own beliefs certainly required him to scrutinize his acts more than his ideas and theories. This does not, however, reduce the value of a close examination of his ever-refining exposition of his basic concepts and his theoretical standpoint in relation to politics and society.

More books and essays have already been written about Gandhi than about any other figure in world history except the founders of the great religions. No one else has ever been compared to such a wide range of historical personages. He has been likened not only to Krishna, Rama, St. Francis, St. Joan and Wesley, but also to Cromwell, Jefferson, Cobbett, Mazzini, Lincoln, Lenin and Sun Yat-sen, and yet again to Rousseau, Thoreau, Marx and Tolstoy. Such comparisons could be more confusing than helpful. Gandhi certainly combined multiple roles in his life and was active in many different spheres. He was the heroic champion of human rights in South Africa; the revolutionary leader of a mass movement for political freedom; a crusader against untouchability; an experimenter in nature cure, dietetics and education; a reformer much concerned with alcoholism, the exploitation of women and cruelty to animals; a student of comparative religions and a powerful advocate of their doctrinal and practical unity; a skilled lawyer and draftsman of petitions and memoranda; a prolific correspondent who gave moral guidance to thousands of people in many countries; the founder of several *ashram*s and communal settlements; the author of a few books and pamphlets and thousands upon thousands of articles on a great variety of subjects; something of a mystic and monk—definitely an ascetic figure, pledged to several exacting vows, including the vow of non-possession; a daring though not a systematic political thinker.

Of the many images that have been presented of Gandhi, two have been predominant—the saint and the politician. He has been vividly portrayed as a saint by Romain Rolland, Carl Heath and Stanley Jones, a portrait confirmed by those who were closest to him. Gandhi himself disclaimed the appellations of "saint," "ascetic," *sannyasi* and *Mahatma*,[3] and described himself simply as one "who claims only to be a humble searcher after Truth, knows his limitations, makes mistakes, never hesitates to admit them when he makes them and frankly confesses that he, like a scientist, is making experiments about some of 'the eternal verities' of life, but cannot even claim to be a scientist. . . ."[4] He regarded his "Mahatmaship" as an oppressive burden[5]—"there is not a moment I can recall when it may be said to have tickled me."[6] He was concerned to disclaim the position of a prophet because of his conviction that the moral values he sought to translate into his personal and political acts could be applied by one and all so as to transform human relationships and the very nature of social and political activity.

Whether he was or was not a saint or *Mahatma,* to view him as such will hinder rather than help us in grasping his moral and political thought. In his autobiography he stressed that he was an ordinary man who evolved by setting himself seemingly impossible standards. Reginald Reynolds has pointed out that those who set him apart from humanity are unwittingly implying that he was a hypocrite. "If they are right, then Gandhi's demands on frail human nature were as fraudulent as those advertisements which show pictures of muscular giants with the assurance that anyone can develop the same muscle-bound torso by taking a few pills."[7] This analogy could be misleading insofar as a moral genius may be genuinely mistaken in overlooking his rare gifts in comparing himself with ordinary men. On the other hand, it is reasonable to assume that men are less unequal in their innate moral capacities than in their mental or aesthetic faculties. Although Gandhi has been regarded by a few contemporaries such as C. F. Andrews, as a new religious teacher, his appeal lay chiefly in that he became for many people in different countries a living symbol of the moral power and goodness in man. He seemed to be the conscience of humanity. He identified himself completely with the poor and the weak, with *Daridranarayan* (God as manifested in the meek and the wretched).

The image of Gandhi as a politician is even more puzzling than the image of him as a saint. He has been aptly described as "a hyphen connecting the middle classes and the people which transferred energy from each to the other."[8] And yet, his simplicity and directness confounded the modern politician, parliamentarian and publicist. Lala Lajpat Rai spoke for many politicians of his generation when he said:

They suspect him of some deep design. He fears no one and frightens no one. . . . He recognizes no conventions except such as are absolutely necessary not to remove him from the society of men and women. He recognizes no masters and no *gurus*. He claims no *chelas* though he has many. . . . He owns no property, keeps no bank account, makes no investments, yet makes no fuss about asking for anything he needs. Such of his countrymen as have drunk deep from the fountains of European history and European politics and who have developed a deep love for European manners and European culture, neither understand nor like him. In their eyes he is a barbarian, a visionary and a dreamer. He has probably something of all these qualities because he is nearest to the verities of life and can look at things with plain eyes, without the glasses of civilization and sophistry.[9]

If this is how he struck the older Indian politicians, it is hardly surprising that he seemed strange—too exotic to be real, too good to be true—to some of his Western opponents; and he was wholly unacceptable to the westernized Jinnah. The greatest of his political antagonists, Smuts and Halifax, came to respect a man whom they found difficult to deal with. Smuts said that "while he was prepared to go all out for the causes which he championed, he never forgot the human background of the situation, never lost his temper or succumbed to hate. . . . His manner and spirit even then, as well as later, contrasted markedly with the ruthless and brutal forcefulness which is in vogue in our day."[10] But he also struck Lord Linlithgow as slippery, and Lord Pethick-Lawrence as inflexible.

Contradictory statements have often been made about Gandhi as a politician, and some of his critics have pointed to the contradictions in him. The Reverend W. H. Holmes, a missionary deeply hostile to Gandhi, contended that there were really two Gandhis, that the humble humanitarian and Hindu monk was almost overnight transformed into a political revolutionary completely obsessed with a worldly aim.[11] On the other hand, even George Orwell, who confessed to an aesthetic distaste for Gandhi and who felt that politics by its very nature is inseparable from corruption and fraud, conceded that there was almost nothing in Gandhi's "extraordinarily mixed" character that "you can put your finger on and call bad."[12] Still others have contented themselves with the view that Gandhi was a saint among politicians and a politician among saints. What is undeniable is that as a saint he was all too human and as a politician he possessed a charisma that seemed to be superhuman. He was patently good but also extremely astute,[13] a combination that is normally believed to be impossible. In the Indian tradition, the sage, unlike the saint, is required to combine the wisdom of the serpent with the gentleness of the dove. An Indian critic of Gandhi pointed out that "behind his politics there was always the touch of the old Indian tradition of leadership, entirely different from what you understand in Europe. We in India understood it."[14]

Gandhi himself claimed that the politician in him had never dominated a single decision of his,[15] that he had sacrificed no principle to gain a political advantage,[16] that he was used to misrepresentation all his life,[17] that there was a consistency running through his seeming inconsistencies,[18] that his leadership was not of his seeking but "a fruit of faithful service,"[19] that he was a "practical dreamer"[20] but not a visionary.[21] He once remarked to Polak: "Most religious men I have met are politicians in disguise. I, however, who wear the guise of a politician, am at heart a religious man."[22] Gandhi was not a politician in the sense that he might well have failed in the practical business of government and that he never sought or held any political office—not even the official leadership of any party.[23] Politics was to him not a profession but a vocation, and he was a politician only in the sense that he was conscious of a mission to serve the masses in the political and social sphere and to inspire them with a love of the common ideal.

In order to grasp Gandhi's moral and political thought, it is not necessary to come to a firm view about Gandhi's personality, as a saint or a politician, a saintly politician or a political saint. The different images of Gandhi merely show how difficult it is to assess his character and personality. It is, however, necessary to accept his profound integrity as a thinker and as a seeker of truth. If we do not, we shall be constantly tempted to explain away his political statements and concepts entirely in terms of his psychological make-up or the historical conditions which shaped his thought. Even if we could find the causes of particular statements, these would be logically independent of the reasons he gave for them, the grounds on which he defended them or characterized their importance. It is most apposite to regard Gandhi as a *karma yogi* in the Indian tradition, as a religious man of action in the political and social sphere. He sought to apply those moral values which are regarded as precious in personal life—truth and love—in the difficult domain of political and social action. As early as 1903 he studied Patanjali's *Yoga Sutra*. No Indian before him had made this book the basis of the ethical discipline of people engaged in politics and social work as Gandhi did in the Satyagrahashram at Sabarmati.

Gandhi's personal integrity as saint, politician and thinker may be seen not only from his life and his writings but also from the intimate accounts given of him by two people who knew him well but never became his disciples—the Reverend J. J. Doke who knew Gandhi during his early life in South Africa, and Reginald Reynolds who knew him during the last phase of his life in India. To accept Gandhi's integrity does not mean that he was infallible or made no mistakes or even that there were no contradictions in his character and his thought. It does, however, imply the rejection of what Chesterton called "the principle of the curate's egg," a principle all too often employed by writers about Gandhi. Either he was a man of integrity or he was not; he could not be both saint and trickster. A man of integrity can have moral lapses or deceive himself at times, but he will freely admit to lapses which he recognizes and he will do what he can to mitigate or avoid self-deception by ruthless self-examination. Gandhi admitted his errors and "Himalayan blunders" and he was always severe with himself. If we still doubt his integrity,[24] it is a reflection upon us and not upon him.

There are several reasons why Gandhi has not been regarded as a moral and political thinker by many who have written about him, and especially not by most Indian intellectuals. First of all, the personality of the man has attracted so much attention that his voluminous writings have been neglected. Secondly, there has been a natural but undue concentration upon the image of the politician and reformer formed during his active phase of over thirty years in India, from 1914 to 1948. On his return to India he was a mature man of forty-five who had done his essential thinking on morals and politics in South Africa between 1903 and 1914. All his important concepts—*satya, ahimsa, satyagraha, sarvodaya,* even *swaraj* and *swadeshi*—had been formulated in his mind and in his writings before he embarked upon the political activities which brought him into the limelight. The image of Gandhi held by almost all who knew him in India is markedly different from the image that the Reverend J. J. Doke, H. S. Polak and Albert West had of him.

Thirdly, Gandhi was not an intellectual in the conventional sense —an erudite and sophisticated man, with academic qualifications, who writes books or speaks in the jargon of the lecture room and the *salon*. He said of himself: "I am not built for academic writings. Action is my domain."[25] He did not write any systematic treatise on morals and politics, not even a systematic booklet in the Indian tradition like Vinoba Bhave's *Swarajya Shastra*. The only books he wrote in Gujarati were *Hind Swaraj*, a tract in the form of a dialogue; *Ethical Religion (Niti Dharma)*,[26] a collection of talks; *Satyagraha in South Africa*, a full account of the movement he launched; *The Story of My Experiments with Truth*, an unfinished autobiography; *From Yeravda Mandir* and *Ashram Observances in Action*, both collections of letters to the members of Sabarmati Ashram; and lastly, a pamphlet in English entitled *Constructive Programme*. Besides these books, there is his paraphrase into Gujarati of Plato's *Apology*, later translated under the title *The Story of a Satyagrahi*, his paraphrase of Ruskin's *Unto This Last*, his collection of articles on sexual morality entitled *Self-Restraint versus Self-Indulgence,* his *Guide to Health,* his *Economics of Khadi* and *Cent Per Cent Swadeshi*, both collections of articles on village industries. There is also the important work entitled *The Gita According to Gandhi*, an English rendition by Mahadev Desai of Gandhi's Gujarati translation and commentary, with much supplementary material written by Desai.

Fourthly, Gandhi's moral and political thought is so closely bound up with his religious and ethical beliefs that several writers have concentrated upon the latter to the exclusion or the detriment of the former. Gandhi was not a philosopher in the sense in which the word is understood today in the West. He was not interested in abstract theoretical speculations about the universe and man, and he was not concerned with epistemological or logical enquiries. He was not even a moral philosopher in the strict sense; he was not concerned with the nature of moral appraisals or with the logical status of imperatives, principles and concepts. As a result of the mistaken emphasis on Gandhi as a religious figure, other writers have tended to set aside his moral concepts and to consider his political ideas almost entirely in relation to the practical problems that faced Gandhi as a politician and reformer in the Indian context.

Lastly, most of the few serious attempts to study Gandhi's moral and political ideas have largely tended to concentrate upon his "techniques." Many people in India and especially in the United States believe that Gandhi's originality lay in his formulation of a totally new technique of social and political action. It is claimed that this technique is superior to others which are commonly employed, not merely in its moral rightness but also in its practical effectiveness, in almost any context. Such a claim is not easy to justify in the abstract, and it serves only to obscure the richness of Gandhian concepts.

These five reasons may help to explain, but they cannot be used to justify, the widespread neglect, especially in India, of the importance of Gandhi's moral and political thought. It is necessary to consider each of these reasons in order to establish the view that Gandhi's thought is worthy of serious study, showing at the same time the other factors to be taken into account in such a study.

The view that the man is far more important than his writings is misleading in at least one respect. The fact that Gandhi was an exceptional human being does not necessarily mean that his writings are unimportant. People often feel, perhaps without being aware of it, that a man of exceptional goodness cannot also be a significant thinker, especially if he did not write a single major treatise. Even in the case of the religious prophets, an excessive emphasis is sometimes given to their personal qualities by those who have a psychological need to devalue the importance or immediate relevance of their recorded sayings. The crucial question here is how morally exceptional men meant their sayings and writings to be taken by others.

It is, of course, possible that remarkable individuals like Gandhi could be mistaken in their view of their own writings. As a matter of fact, Gandhi was inclined to underrate rather than to overstress the significance of his written words owing to his deep dislike of the idea of fathering a sectarian cult. Just as he disdained the title of

Mahatma, he also disowned the notion of anything like "Gandhism." He once told the Gandhi Seva Sangh:

> Let Gandhism be destroyed if it stands for error. Truth and *ahimsa* will never be destroyed, but if Gandhism is another name for sectarianism, it deserves to be destroyed. If I were to know, after my death, that what I stood for had degenerated into sectarianism, I should be deeply pained. . . . Let no one say that he is a follower of Gandhi. It is enough that I should be my own follower. . . . You are no followers but fellow students, fellow pilgrims, fellow seekers, fellow workers.[27]

Even more specifically, Gandhi was well aware that some people would swear by his statements in his innumerable articles in *Young India* and *Harijan.* In 1933 he went so far as to say:

> I have often said recently that even if all our scriptures were to perish, one *mantra* of *Isopanishad* was enough to declare the essence of Hinduism. . . . Even so what I have said and written is useful only to the extent that it has helped you to assimilate the great principles of truth and *ahimsa.* If you have not assimilated them, my writings will be of no use to you.[28]

Gandhi, like the religious prophets but unlike most political thinkers, was concerned that after his death some would ascribe a literalness and finality to his entire body of statements that he never intended. He made disclaimers which, for example, Marx never did. Although Marx is reputed to have said at the end of his life that he was not a Marxist, he did think that his writings contained a system of scientific truths which could be taken literally and to which finality could be ascribed.

It would be un-Gandhian to attach a scriptural status to the pronouncements of Gandhi. It would also be at variance with his intentions to treat his writings as embodying a system of scientific truths. As he pointed out in 1939:

> At the time of writing I never think of what I have said before. My aim is not to be consistent with my previous statements on a given question, but to be consistent with truth as it may present itself to me at a given moment. The result has been that I have grown from truth to truth; I have saved my memory an undue strain; and what is more, whenever I have been obliged to com-

pare my writing even of fifty years ago with the latest I have discovered no inconsistency between the two. But friends who observe inconsistency will do well to take the meaning that my latest
writing may yield unless, of course, they prefer the old. But before making the choice they should try to see if there is not an
underlying and abiding consistency between the two seeming
inconsistencies.[29]

Whereas Marxism rapidly acquired for its followers the revelatory
status of the Semitic religions and was meant from the first, like
Comte's positivism, to possess the authority of science, the half-
formulated and unsystematic nature of "Gandhism" is somewhat
similar to that of Hinduism and even more to that of Buddhism. If
we must talk of "Gandhism," we must not forget that it stands for
a distinctive attitude toward politics and society rather than a specific political and social creed. It is a particular ethical standpoint
rather than a fixed formula or definite system. There can be no
claims to Gandhian infallibility, no authoritative body of apostolic
interpreters, no set ritual involving *khadi* and the *charkha*.

The upshot of all this is that there is no system of propositions
and imperatives that we can associate with Gandhi, no wholly new
truths, no patented innovations of technique, no proven conclusions. This does not mean, however, that his writings are not to be
carefully examined and sorted out into testable statements and unverifiable (or unfalsifiable) presuppositions, involving fundamental
concepts with ancient antecedents, fresh formulations and original
applications. Gandhi meant his statements to be taken seriously.
He did not want them to be taken as constituting a system, let
alone a complete one.

It is worthwhile to concentrate upon Gandhi's concepts of conscience and heroism, tolerance and civility, *satya* and *asatya, ahimsa*
and *himsa, moksha* and *tapas, satyagraha, swaraj* and *swadeshi*.
All these concepts are based upon metaphysical presuppositions,
but they have important ethical and political implications. Although
Gandhi did not write any conventional treatise—nor did most classical Indian thinkers, except Kautilya and Sukra—he wrote a vast
number of articles in which he expounded his concepts, explained
their implications, defended them against criticisms and misconcep-
tions, and suggested applications. His collected writings, when

published in their entirety, will be contained in over eighty large volumes. Almost all of these writings are inconclusive and many are fragmentary, but among them there are important essays embodying his political thought. Far from regarding all of them as ephemeral, he thought that his central convictions and crucial statements would come to be accepted in the decades after his death.

It is a common error to think that most of Gandhi's life in South Africa and even in India was taken up entirely with political activity. There were, in fact, significant pauses between the various movements he launched, and the time for thought and for writing that he gave himself in his *ashram*s was considerable. Most of his visitors were preoccupied with his political activities or with his religious beliefs or with relatively minor matters concerning his views on health and asceticism. Professor Charles Sisson of Elphinstone College, Bombay, however, was concerned with Gandhi's moral and political ideas. He had long sessions with him in the 1920's before he returned to England and concluded that Gandhi was more of an intellectual and original thinker than most other Indian scholars. He felt that at the time Gandhi was very much as he imagined Rousseau to have been.[30]

The view often held, especially by those in India, that Gandhi was not a well-read man, is misleading. He was himself partly responsible for this mistaken view, perhaps owing to his distrust of academic "intellectuals" with little experience of the problems and the daily lives of the masses. In his autobiography, written in jail, he gave the unintended impression that he did not read many books. As a matter of fact, very few people could claim to have read, as he did, almost all the works of Tolstoy, or to have studied carefully a variety of classical Indian texts. In his autobiography he merely mentions Tolstoy's *The Kingdom of God Is within You* and the *Gita* among the few books which had a profound influence on his life. Similarly, he stresses the crucial role in his development that was played by Ruskin's *Unto This Last*. In the years after his autobiography was written, he read *Fors Clavigera* regularly. He said at the time: "We may read this book a number of times and yet never be tired of it. And each time we shall learn from it something new."[31] He was at ease more with writers of the late nineteenth century—English moralists like Carlyle and Ruskin, Edward

Carpenter, Max Nordau and Henry Wallace, or Americans like Emerson, Thoreau and Lloyd Garrison—than with twentieth-century thinkers like Freud.

During his first internment in 1907, Gandhi was glad to have a free run of the prison library. He borrowed the works of Carlyle, and the Bible. He was lent, by a Chinese interpreter, an English translation of the *Koran*, the speeches of T. H. Huxley, Carlyle's *Lives of Burns, Johnson and Scott,* and Bacon's *Essays.* He also studied the *Bhagavad Gita*, several Tamil works, an Urdu book which he does not name, and some of Plato's Socratic dialogues. He planned translations of Carlyle and Ruskin and regretted that his release prevented him from completing them.[32] During his third internment, in Pretoria, he read several Sanskrit, Tamil, Hindi and Gujarati works, including the Upanishads, *Manusmriti,* the *Ramayana*, Patanjali's classic on yoga, the *Sandhya Gutika* and several books by his friend Kavi Rajchandra, who had a profound influence on him.[33] He was struck by the Upanishadic injunction: "Whatever thou dost, thou shouldst do the same for the good of the soul."[34] He also read Emerson. He felt that Tolstoy's writings inspire great confidence because Tolstoy tried to practice what he preached. Gandhi did not know that Tolstoy's practice fell far short of his preaching. In later life he pointed out that Ruskin, unlike Tolstoy, did not attempt to apply his ideas to his daily life and "rested content with the expression of ideas."[35] During the period of his imprisonment in Pretoria he was much influenced by Carlyle's writings on the French Revolution and thought that they confirmed Mazzini's opinions.[36]

Gandhi's reading was wide-ranging and substantial. It was not planned and was chiefly determined by accident in that he chose from among the books that came his way rather than read for any set course. Even as a student in London qualifying for the bar, the legal textbooks that he read carefully—then standard works on equity, common law, Roman law and real property—interested him far less (with the exception of Mayne's *Hindu Law*) than *The Song Celestial* and *The Light of Asia* of Sir Edwin Arnold, the New Testament, *The Key to Theosophy*—which he counted among the few crucial influences on his life—and Henry Salt's defence of vegetarianism.[37] When a friend urged on him Bentham's *Introduc-*

tion to the Theory of Morals and Legislation to change his views on meat-eating, Gandhi, who was then nineteen, found it hard to follow. He simply said: "These abstruse things are beyond me. I admit it is necessary to eat meat. But I cannot break my vow."[38] His instinctive suspicion of utilitarianism remained with him all his life, and he explicitly criticized it when he expounded his doctrine of *ahimsa*.

Far from losing his taste for selective reading or from being at a disadvantage for not completing his university education in India, he continued to educate himself and to read diligently during his later periods in jail. In 1923 in Yeravda Jail, although a man of fifty-four (an old man by Indian standards), he accounted for every minute of his time and read about 150 books on a wide variety of subjects.[39] He read the whole of the *Mahabharata* and a Gujarati account of the six systems of Indian philosophy, besides *Manusmriti* and the Upanishads. He read the commentaries on the *Gita*—often the starting point of ethical and even political enquiries in modern India, fulfilling the function both of Plato's dialogues and the New Testament—by Shankara, Jnaneshwar, Tilak and Aurobindo. He also read extensively on the different religions practiced in India, as well as *The Varieties of Religious Experience* by William James. He did not confine himself to religious literature. He read Gibbon, Goethe, Buckle, Haeckel, Guizot, Benjamin Kidd, Lecky, Geddes, Shaw, Kipling, Wells, and Motley's *Rise of the Dutch Republic*.

Among the books that Gandhi studied carefully were Butler's *Analogy* and Henry Drummond's *The Natural Law in the Spiritual World*. When, before he was quite thirty, he first read Drummond in South Africa, he felt that if he had that writer's "facile pen," he would demonstrate even better that there was a natural law in the spiritual world.[40] In 1928 he compared Drummond's classification of natural laws to the exposition in the fourteenth chapter of the *Gita* on *sattva, rajas* and *tamas*, the threefold division of the qualities of nature, affecting the "ascent of man" through three stages to the position of the Perfect Man, *Purushottama*.[41] In 1934 Gandhi also indicated that he was influenced by Adam Smith's discussion in *The Wealth of Nations* on the interaction between natural and human factors in economic growth.[42]

The sporadic and accidental nature of his reading continued to the very end of his life. In 1937 he was much influenced by Armstrong's *Education for Life*, especially the chapter "Education of the Hand."[43] In 1938 he was impressed by Roth's study of *The Jewish Contribution to Civilization*.[44] The fortuitous nature of much of his reading affected the steady but unsystematic development of his moral and political thought, but he always exercised his strong personal judgment in letting a book influence him. It is interesting to note that while he read Bentham too early in life to understand him, he read Marx and Engels too late in life for his views to be affected even in the slightest. And yet, his rejection of Bentham was hasty but instinctive, and his dismissal of Marx (rather like the dismissal by Keynes) was based upon a quick but firm assessment. When in 1944 he read *Das Kapital*, together with books on anatomy, grammar and economics, he expressed surprise that it was badly written despite the leisure that Marx had had for his studies. At the same time he said: "I do not care whether Marxism is right or wrong. All I know is that the poor are being crushed. Something has got to be done for them. To me this is axiomatic."[45] In 1946, when asked about Marx, he said that he had a high regard for Marx's great industry and acumen, but he could not share the view that the use of violence could usher in nonviolence. He also felt that world thought was rapidly moving beyond Marx, but this did not detract from the merit of Marx's labors.[46]

Gandhi never claimed to be, and certainly cannot be regarded as, a well-trained intellectual, but this does not mean that he was not an original thinker. His reading, especially on morals and politics, was greater and wider than is usually realized, though less systematic than that of the other leading Indian intellectuals of his generation. And yet, it was far more critical because of his willingness to give his whole attention to anything he decided to read, and the fresh, original, deep-rooted approach he brought to it. Gokhale, Ranade, Tilak, Aurobindo, Tagore and Nehru were more sophisticated "intellectuals" than Gandhi, or at least much better educated, but they were also more uncritical. Subhas Bose and M. N. Roy were intellectually gifted but also singularly uncritical in their response to fashionable Western *isms*. Certainly, no other influential Indian intellectual was as steeped as Gandhi was in the religious and philosophical texts of the classical Indian tradition as well as in the writings of daring Western moralists of the nineteenth century like Tolstoy, Thoreau, Ruskin, Emerson and Carlyle. It is hardly surprising that no other Indian politician or religious man became as original in his thinking as Gandhi. His earnest study of ancient Indian texts enabled him to view politics and society *sub specie aeternitatis*. His ready response to unorthodox and subsequently neglected moralists of the nineteenth century in the West helped Gandhi to bring a pre-1914 standpoint—individualistic, heretical, heroic and humane—to the civic life of the twentieth century.

Gandhi distrusted reason more than most modern moral and political thinkers in the West. He stressed the limits of reason, regarded *ahimsa* as "a matter not of the intellect but of the heart"[47] and felt that in general men are ultimately guided not by the intellect but by the heart: "The heart accepts a conclusion for which the intellect subsequently finds the reasoning. Argument follows conviction. Man often finds reasons in support of whatever he does or wants to do."[48] This does not mean that Gandhi's mind was always made up before he considered the facts; he was too much of a disciple of Gokhale to do this. Dr. Zakir Husain, an erudite scholar of Gandhi's time, thought that Gandhi was "one of the most rational thinkers I have come across."[49] It was not incompatible with his rational outlook to be conscious of the extent to which the emotions color and determine seemingly intellectual attitudes to practical questions. He was, of course, not a rationalist—he distrusted reason too much for that—and he placed a religious reliance upon faith on the ground of the inadequacy of any man's personal experience and mental faculties. In the last analysis, Gandhi stands outside the modern tradition of political reasoning because of his unwillingness to follow a strictly logical route in coming to conclusions. He had a logical mind but felt that:

> The Jains are apt to carry things to their logical conclusion. But mere logic sometimes leads to wrong conclusions and is disastrous in results. This is not the fault of logic, but all the data needed in order to arrive at a proper conclusion are not available at all times. Again one who hears or reads a word does not always understand it in the speaker's or writer's sense. Therefore the heart,

that is devotion, faith and knowledge grounded in experience are invested with greater importance. Logic is a matter of mere intelligence, which cannot apprehend things that are clear as crystal to the heart. On the other hand the intellect often believes in certain things, but if they do not appeal to the heart, they must be rejected.[50]

Despite his growing distrust of unaided reason and mere logic, it must be noted that Gandhi as a young man, when his essential thinking was done, had a strong skeptical streak, which in later life he never wholly lost in regard to the cruder beliefs in all religions. J. J. Doke has remarked that "a strong natural tendency in analytical study made him question the why of everything."[51] As a result, he brought to the books he read in early life a burning passion to find the truth. When he felt convinced by Ruskin or Tolstoy or Thoreau, his response was also total, which is not unknown among earnest-minded skeptics. Being conscious that he had "no university education worth the name" and of his intellectual limitations, he claimed that the limited reading that he did enabled him thoroughly to digest what he did read.[52] As a result, the books he regarded as most important had an enormous influence over his life as well as his entire outlook. The *Gita* became for him a "dictionary of daily reference."[53] In 1932 he made a deep study of the *Isopanishad*, together with various commentaries, and its verses became for him the basic verities underlying his concept of non-violent socialism.[54]

The enormous importance of Gandhi's metaphysical presuppositions to a grasp of his moral and political ideas imparts a classical flavor to his thought. He is reminiscent of the Stoics and somewhat of Plato, but also of Christian thinkers like Aquinas and Acton, and of the Christian socialists. Yet his intense moral concern, which dominates his thinking, makes him rather resemble Rousseau and Tolstoy, though he has less to say about the business of government than even Rousseau, and more to say about the problems of political morality facing the citizen than Tolstoy. Just as he stands closer to pre-Machiavellian writers in the West, so too he is in the tradition of pre-Kautilyan attitudes toward politics and society. And yet both these assertions have to be qualified. He is pre-Machiavellian in his refusal to segregate religion from politics, but he is also post-Asokan in his emphasis upon *dharma* rather than *moksha*, the Moral Law rather than personal salvation through political disengagement.

Even if we stress Gandhi's religious outlook, its highly eclectic nature has definite political implications. He, no doubt, called himself a Hindu, but went further than any other modern Hindu in saying that his Hinduism included the best in all other religions. No Hindu since Ram Mohan Roy was as eager as Gandhi to respond to the *Koran,* and even Roy did not stress, as much as Gandhi did, Jain and Buddhist notions. Even as a Hindu, Gandhi was a Vedantin as well as a Vaishnava—a Vedantin in his transcendental monism and a Vaishnava in his faith in the grace of God as a Person. Similarly, in South Africa he came under the influence of Esoteric Christianity[55] as expounded in the writings of Maitland and Kingsford, but he was also affected by the stress of Protestant clergymen upon the notion of divine grace. Above all, he emphasized the doctrine of *Karma*, which is even more dominant in Buddhism than in Hinduism, and he clearly endorsed the universalism of the Theosophists early and late in life. In 1947 he told Louis Fischer: "In the beginning, the leading Congressmen were theosophists. Mrs. Annie Besant attracted me very much. Theosophy is the teaching of Madame Blavatsky. It is Hinduism at its best. Theosophy is the brotherhood of man."[56]

The difficulty of pinning down Gandhi's religious affiliation was mentioned by the Reverend J. J. Doke as early as 1909:

> A few days ago I was told that "he is a Buddhist." Not long since, a Christian newspaper described him as "a Christian Mohammedan," an extraordinary mixture indeed. Others imagine that he worships idols. . . . I question whether any system of religion can absolutely hold him. His views are too closely allied to Christianity to be entirely Hindu; and too deeply saturated with Hinduism to be called Christian, while his sympathies are so wide and catholic, that one would imagine he has reached a point where the formulae of sects are meaningless.[57]

Similarly, all sorts of political labels have been applied to him— individualist, anarchist, socialist, communist, liberal, reactionary, revolutionary, nationalist, cosmopolitan and so on.

Gandhi's political concepts possess a variety of meanings ranging from religious purity to political expediency, but he was neither a pure absolutist nor a mere opportunist in his interpretations of the terms he used. It would be a failure to grasp the man or his ethical preoccupations to explain away his concepts entirely in terms of political expediency. He certainly evolved his concepts and elaborated them in the context of practical problems that he faced as a politician and social worker. This does not entitle us to regard the concepts of *satya, ahimsa* and *satyagraha*, for example, simply as rationalizations of political passions or physical weakness. It is far more appropriate to consider his concepts in terms of their metaphysical and moral presuppositions than to regard them as techniques justified solely by their results. On the basis of his presuppositions Gandhi was convinced that *ahimsa* would certainly triumph, but he would have held to it even if its immediate application was likely to meet with failure. Many of his followers, especially in the United States, have stressed the effectiveness rather than the rightness of his concepts, whereas he himself was far more concerned with the latter although he had a sanguine faith in the former.

Professor Morris-Jones has suggested[58] that Gandhi's claim to be regarded as a political thinker lies in that he did give an account of the nature of political activity, presented a relationship between the activity and the moral nature of man, and gave a sketch of a set of criteria for the judgment of politics. But none of these attempts can be understood without descending into the depths of what Romain Rolland called the vast religious crypt below the edifice of his moral and political thought. To pursue Rolland's metaphor, we must pay careful attention to the pillars—Gandhi's concepts—resting on the floor of the crypt and firmly supporting the entire edifice.

2

THE INDICTMENT OF MODERN CIVILIZATION

Never has the individual been so completely delivered up to a blind collectivity, and never have men been less capable, not only of subordinating their actions to their thoughts, but even of thinking. Such terms as oppressors and oppressed, the idea of classes—all that sort of thing is near to losing all meaning, so obvious are the impotence and distress of all men in the face of the social machine, which has become a machine for breaking hearts and crushing spirits, a machine for manufacturing irresponsibility, stupidity, corruption, slackness and, above all, dizziness. The reason for this painful state of affairs is clear. We are living in a world in which nothing is made to man's measure; there exists a monstrous discrepancy between man's body, man's mind and the things which at the present time constitute the elements of human existence; everything is disequilibrium. There is not a single category, group or class of men that is altogether exempt from this destructive disequilibrium, except perhaps for a few isolated patches of more primitive life; and the younger generation, who have grown and are growing up in it, inwardly reflect the chaos surrounding them more than do their elders.

SIMONE WEIL

The *point d'appui* of Gandhi's moral and political thought was provided by what he himself called "a severe condemnation of modern civilization" in *Hind Swaraj*. This polemical tract, written in 1909, was hailed by Middleton Murry in 1938 as a spiritual classic, and even more extravagantly, as the greatest book written in modern times.[1] Yet, in 1912, Gokhale, whom Gandhi esteemed as his political *guru*, thought *Hind Swaraj* to be so crude and hastily conceived that the author himself would destroy it after spending a year in India. But even thirty years after he wrote it, Gandhi held that he had seen nothing to make him alter the views expounded in it, though he might change the language here and there.[2] Lord Lothian thought that "all Gandhism" was to be found in this dialogue of about thirty thousand words. When it was first published in Gujarati, it was proscribed by the government of Bombay. Gandhi responded by issuing a translation, for he felt he owed it to his "English friends" that they should know its contents. *Hind Swaraj* was also sent to Tolstoy, who recorded in his diary on April 20, 1910: "Read Gandhi about civilization, wonderful."[3]

Hind Swaraj was written with terse directness and solemn fervor for the comparatively few readers of the Gujarati section of *Indian Opinion*. It was barely two years since Gandhi had initiated passive resistance in South Africa, but he had already been actively engaged in fusing and clarifying in his own mind his ethical convictions and political ideas. *Hind Swaraj* marks a crucial phase in crystallizing his thought. His conversations in London with Indian proponents of violence moved him to issue a warning against their "suicidal policy," and to assign the iniquities of imperialism to modern civilization rather than to the English as a people:

> I have written because I could not restrain myself. . . . These views are mine, and yet not mine. They are mine because I hope to act according to them. They are almost a part of my being. But, yet, they are not mine, because I lay no claim to originality. They have been formed after reading several books. That which I dimly felt received support from these books.[4]

Gandhi referred his readers to the list of books recommended in his appendix, which included the writings of Plato, Mazzini, Ruskin,

Thoreau, Maine, Naoroji, Edward Carpenter and Max Nordau and several works of Tolstoy.

Hind Swaraj must not be seen merely as a heartfelt response to the doctrine of violent revolution or as a declaration of convictions chiefly derived from books that deeply affected Gandhi. The bold assertions in the booklet were really the logical extension of a line of thinking that had begun at least fourteen years earlier. Even as a young man of twenty-five, he wrote in South Africa that, despite its dazzling surface, its material attractions and madly feverish activity, modern civilization was a hindrance rather than a help to the needs of the human soul and the craving for a better life.[5] A decade later, he reacted almost as strongly to a disastrous fire in Paris as Voltaire did to the Lisbon earthquake. He felt that a grim tragedy lay behind all the tinsel splendor of modern civilization, that the ceaseless rush of living left no time for contemplation and the dead were soon forgotten, that the marvels of science, the claims of civilization and the gospel of progress could offer neither stability nor certainty, nothing substantial to struggling humanity. The moral he drew was, however, very far from Voltairean—the conviction that on this earth we are merely sojourners, and consolation could come only from a firm faith "not in the theory, but in the fact, of the existence of a future life and real Godhead."[6] If men could only see themselves as pilgrims on earth, immortal spirits on their probation, they would view everything in the earthly kingdom *sub specie aeternitatis*.

It was not just the moral inadequacy and extravagant pretensions of modern civilization, but its treacherously deceptive, hypnotic and self-destructive tendency that was the theme of *Hind Swaraj*. Gandhi did not simply adopt the method of *doute absolu*, of questioning every single achievement of civilization, its excellence and permanence. He went much further in holding that a man laboring under the delusions engendered by modern civilization is like a dreamer who revels in the seeming reality of his dream. Man today is an emasculated—a favorite word of Gandhi—victim of a vast humbug that is kept alive by schools, legislatures, armies, churches, prisons and hospitals.[7] Our civilization has the seductive color of a consumptive who clings to life but is doomed to die. This analogy is reminiscent of Fourier's comparison of civilization to a sick

person yearning to be healed by some miracle and seizing fever-
ishly upon every fresh panacea, or of Tawney's image of a hypo-
chondriac who is so absorbed in the processes of his own digestion
that he goes to his grave before he has begun to live. In our own
time, Eric Fromm has argued that just as there is a *folie à deux*, so
there is a *folie à millions*; "the fact that millions of people share
the same forms of mental pathology does not make these people
sane."[8]

Even in the era of Renaissance humanism, it was thought by
Erasmus that it was natural for good men to lament this corrupt
world. Gandhi's critique of modern civilization, however, was not
the typical response of theological pessimism or of despairing
world-weariness. Its relentless severity is bound up with his chosen
standpoint which was closely similar to that of Tolstoy. Both felt
that the consciousness of the common people was frustrated by a
system of "life-corroding competition" which resulted in bondage
rather than freedom. Both held that the fundamental guidance of
the life of man can be only internal, and in no wise external, arising
from the will of other people. Gandhi referred explicitly to the
teachings of all religions that we should remain passive about
worldly pursuits and active about godly pursuits, that we should
set a limit to our worldly ambition. He went so far as to maintain
that humbugs in worldly matters are far worse than the humbugs in
religion, that the dire cruelties committed in the name of sectarian
religion cannot compare with the endless victims destroyed in the
fire of civilization, that religious superstition, though repugnant, is
harmless compared to that of modern civilization. All these judgments are disputable, but they are crucial to a comprehension of
the Gandhian critique in *Hind Swaraj*:

> This civilization takes note neither of morality nor of religion. Its
> votaries calmly state that their business is not to teach religion.
> Some even consider it to be a superstitious growth. Others put on
> the cloak of religion, and prate about morality. But, after twenty
> years' experience, I have come to the conclusion that immorality
> is often taught in the name of morality. . . . Civilization seeks
> to increase bodily comfort, and it fails miserably even in doing so.
>   This civilization is irreligion, and it has taken such a hold on
> the people in Europe that those who are in it appear to be half

mad. They lack real physical strength or courage. They keep up their energy by intoxication. They can hardly be happy in solitude. Women, who should be the queens of households, wander in the streets or they slave away in factories.[9]

If Gandhi's attack appears to be rather extreme and bizarre in places, this is partly because contemporary industrial society and bourgeois civilization have become more sophisticated though no less vulnerable than the callous factory system. There is no doubt much dissimilarity between nineteenth- and twentieth-century capitalism. But the essential relevance of *Hind Swaraj* is perhaps even more poignant today owing to the deepening and spreading sense of alienation, especially among the young, from the beliefs and values of an acquisitive if affluent society.

Similarly, if Gandhi used what he himself called "harsh terms" in depicting the political institutions of representative democracy more than half a century ago, present-day accounts of that period are often no less harsh. Although no one but Gandhi would characterize "the Mother of Parliaments" as "a sterile woman and a prostitute,"[10] recent attacks on the Establishment—what Cobbett called "The Thing"—and on the contemporary working of representative democracy are no less unsparing.[11] Gandhi's knowledge of Western political systems was perfunctory at best, but as the intensity of his criticism derives from his moral judgments rather than from detailed knowledge of matters of fact, he would not see any reason to tone down his indictment, though he might vary his epithets and examples, if he wrote it today. He upheld the belief, steadily undermined since the eighteenth century, that social institutions and political and economic activity are subject, like personal conduct, to ethical appraisals. This belief is based on the assumption that social institutions are the visible expression of the scale of moral values that mould the minds of individuals, that it is impossible to alter institutions without affecting those valuations.

Most of the twenty short chapters of *Hind Swaraj* continue in an uncompromisingly critical vein about the political and social institutions of modern civilization, the glaring gap between its lofty claims and its unedifying conduct, and the destructive impact of an imperialistic commercial system upon a traditional rural culture. It is only too easy to plead the case for the defence, and to point out that the former lawyer had by no means told the whole story about modern civilization. If so, we can hardly blame an earnest prosecutor of social evils for not displaying the mind of a cross-bencher, still less for not providing a judicial statement of the pros and cons. Gandhi was religiously convinced from the first—as he insisted later on in a controversy with Tagore—that the rejection of untruth is as much of an ideal as the acceptance of truth. "All religions teach us that two opposite forces act upon us and that the human endeavour consists in a series of eternal rejections and acceptances."[12]

Gandhi's strong indictment of the self-doomed materialism of modern life must, at least in part, have owed its impassioned assurance to H. P. Blavatsky's castigation of Victorian cant in her imaginary dialogue with a Christian, which Gandhi counted among the few books that had a decisive impact on his life. *Hind Swaraj*, which also took the form of a dialogue, is reminiscent of passages in her book condemning the educational system and competitive ethos of "Christian" civilization. In her article on "Civilization, the Death of Art and Beauty," she warned Asian societies in 1891 not to imitate the will-o'-the-wisp of modern European civilization or to sacrifice their individuality for an empty show and shadow, or to exchange the original and the picturesque for the vulgar and the hideous.

> Truly and indeed it is high time that at last something should be done in this direction, and before the deceitful civilization of the conceited nations of yesterday has irretrievably hypnotized the other races and made them succumb to its upas-tree wiles and supposed superiority. Materialism and indifference to all save the selfish realization of wealth and power, and the over-feeding of national and personal vanity, have gradually led nations and men to the almost entire oblivion of spiritual ideals, of the love of nature to the correct appreciation of things. Like a hideous leprosy our Western civilization has eaten its way through all quarters of the globe and hardened the human heart. . . . It is canting and deceitful from its diplomats down to its custodians of religion, from its political down to its social laws, selfish, greedy and brutal beyond expression in its grabbing characteristics.[13]

Under the influence of this indictment of the Victorian age, Gandhi also compared modern civilization to the "deadly upas tree."

One writer has linked the whole modern system to the Upas tree. Its branches are represented by parasitical professions . . . and over the trunk has been raised the axe of the true religion. Immorality is the root of the tree. So you will see that the views do not come right out of my mind but they represent the combined experiences of many.[14]

It is not at all surprising that *Hind Swaraj* has evoked a wide variety of responses which necessarily reflect the presuppositions of the reader as well as the moral authority of Gandhi. *Hind Swaraj* has been called a seminal book,[15] a disturbing book,[16] a revolutionary message,[17] the vision of a New Order comparable but superior to Rousseau's *Du contrat social* and Marx's *Das Kapital*.[18] All these responses were made about thirty years after the book was written. Even though the warmest admirers of Gandhi could not endorse *Hind Swaraj* in its entirety, it was still possible for Delisle Burns to conclude, after reading *Hind Swaraj*, that

> . . . It would be a very great advantage in English and American politics as well as in the conduct of industry and common life in the West, if the influence of such a man as Gandhi were to spread among us. It would reinforce moral principles which tend to be obscured by the pursuit of wealth and power.[19]

Similarly, G. D. H. Cole commented at the same time on *Hind Swaraj*:

> Across thirty years it has, to me who belongs to the West, deep power to disturb—much deeper power than it could have had when it was written. . . . Gandhi's case against the West looks . . . infinitely stronger than it looked, to us Westerners, thirty years ago. For it does seem as if all our material advances in machine mastery were unloosing upon us, not the plenty for which we had hoped, but an overmastering capacity for destruction. . . . We have also grown more cruel—or some of us have; and those of us who are untouched by the recrudescence of cruelty know not how to prevent its spread without dire risk of falling ourselves under its spell. . . . If our civilization is radically wrong, it will destroy itself. . . . The Gandhi of this book could not be, in the West, a leader, but only a martyr at most. If,

however, the fault in our civilization is but superficial, however pervasive and disastrous; if our men are men underneath the veneer, . . . then we need not despair. We shall need leaders who are masters of themselves, as Gandhi is. . . .[20]

On the other hand, an acquaintance of Gandhi remarked that he went off the rails in *Hind Swaraj* and indulged in the emotions of a machine-smashing Luddite, that "it is all fine Ruskin-Tolstoyan rodomontade by a lawyer with a printing press, a good prize essay as unreal as Rousseau's *Discours sur les sciences et les arts.*"[21] It is true that *Hind Swaraj* was rapidly written.[22] Gandhi's attack, delivered more in anguish than in anger, may seem at times to be similar to the outbursts of Russian rebels like Belinsky. But the book clearly shows that he was deeply committed, in a way that was not open either to the youthful Rousseau or to the venerable Tolstoy, to a public demonstration and a political embodiment of his ethical and social principles. If Gandhi's concern is like that of a long line of constructive social critics ranging from Saint-Simon to Tawney, he was, even more, like Mazzini and Lenin, a man of action and a revolutionary in dead earnest. To explain away the challenge delivered by Gandhi at the age of thirty-nine as a rhetorical indulgence in Luddite emotions would be unfair and smug.

It is true that insofar as *Hind Swaraj* is a manifesto of moral condemnation, it contains imagery of compelling power rather than a closely reasoned statement. It might profoundly disturb the doubter but it cannot convert the convinced believer in the *mystique* of modern civilization. Gandhi did not provide a rigorous social analysis from which his political conclusions could be logically derived. He did not even attempt this in *Hind Swaraj*. He was more concerned to declare and define his position to those in South Africa and in India who were willing to listen. In a way the impact of *Hind Swaraj* is not dissimilar to that of the *Communist Manifesto*, despite the latter's greater reliance on a seemingly scientific argument. Both were written by mature young men whose thinking was governed by a total value judgment, but more so in the case of Gandhi than of Marx. Both manifestoes provide dismal portraits of a world they felt to be self-contradictory in its basic assumptions and institutions, a world self-doomed to destruction. For Marx, the villain is the capitalist system, history the judge and its executioner the proletariat. For Gandhi, the villain is the creed of hypocritical materialism, the judge is the individual who frees himself from the collective hallucination, and the executioner is the Moral Law (*Karma*) that inexorably re-adjusts disturbed equilibrium in the cosmos and in the affairs of men.

Gandhi's diagnosis of modern civilization was Tolstoyan in its moral tone and, like Marx, he also prophesied doom. Yet his view of humanity and history was fundamentally optimistic owing to the certainty of his personally tested but unprovable faith. He was not prepared, like Mazzini, to accept the social structure of the world as merely an external manifestation of the moral and intellectual condition of humanity. Modern civilization was for Gandhi a positive menace to the moral growth of man rather than simply a magnifying mirror of his moral deficiency. Even *Hind Swaraj* conceded that "civilization is not an incurable disease," that people are not bad at heart and their mode of thought is not inherently immoral.[23] Civilization stands self-condemned, but it is possible for courageous and compassionate men to adopt a massive program of action rather than resign themselves, like Spinoza's wisely silent philosophers, to a stoical philosophy of apparent submission. Nor is it necessary to turn society violently upside down or vainly to attempt to reduce it to a primordial *tabula rasa.*

There is no clearer or surer statement of Gandhi's central standpoint than in his letters to Henry Polak in 1909 and to Albert West in 1910. Shortly before embarking on *Hind Swaraj*, he wrote to Polak:

> As a passive resister, I am unconcerned whether such a gigantic reformation, shall I call it, can be brought about among people who derive their satisfaction from the present mad rush. If I realize the truth of it, I should rejoice in following it, and, therefore, I could not wait until the whole body of people had commenced. All of us who think likewise have to take the necessary step; and the rest, if we are in the right, must follow. The theory is there: our practice will have to approach it as much as possible. Living in the midst of the rush, we may not be able to shake ourselves free from all taint. . . . I . . . feel that I should no longer withhold from you what I call the progressive step I have taken mentally.[24]

After his completion of *Hind Swaraj* and his return to South Africa, he wrote from Johannesburg to Albert West:

> . . . For me I am going through many a battle. Circumstances surrounding me just now are not at all congenial. But I think my mind is at peace. My mind as you know is extremely active— never at rest. I am trying bold experiments. . . . The more I observe, the greater is the dissatisfaction with modern life. I see nothing good in it. Men are good. But they are poor victims making themselves miserable under the false belief that they are doing good. I am aware that there is a fallacy underneath this. I who claim to examine what is around may be a deluded fool. This risk all of us have to take. The fact is that we are all bound to do what we feel is right. And with me I feel that modern life is *not* right. The greater the conviction, the bolder the experiments.[25]

Between them, these two crucial letters of Gandhi suggest how similar his theoretical position was to that of Rousseau and yet how different were their conceptions of the relation between theory and practice, let alone their temperaments and their conduct. Both felt deeply at odds with modern society, but the alienation expressed in Rousseau's writings was desperate and total. Both had a Socratic eye for the falsity of prevailing dogmas and the dangers of popular apathy. But, unlike Gandhi who was humble before his hero, Rousseau proudly placed himself with Socrates: "It cost Socrates his life because he said precisely the same things as myself." Both were tragic figures, tormented by self-analysis, misunderstood by their followers, misrepresented by their critics, but their perceptiveness put them beyond the ken of their clever contemporaries, and their critical relevance transcends the bounds of space and time. Gandhi, like Rousseau, thought that with its inducement to ambition and rivalry, modern society induces man to put on a mask which stifles his authentic self. Our civilization stunts what it has not stifled and leaves behind a gross caricature of the godlike potentialities of man. Civilized man is born and dies a slave. All his long life he is imprisoned by his institutions, what Veblen calls the "bias of settled habits." Political life reflects the same gulf between the potential and the actual, the same estrangement between man and his environment. Reason is deployed in the service of deception, and conscience either connives at collective crimes or is extinguished by external pressures. Civilized man has fabricated endless complications to existence, but he merely uses what he has acquired to make his condition miserable. By transforming reason into cunning and adopting stratagems of dissimulation and hypocrisy, by worshipping at the altar of wealth and happiness, he wholly upsets the delicate balance between wants and needs, craving and fulfillment. In short, modern man is perverted, undermined and even depraved by society. There is a continuous contradiction between our deepest convictions and those considerations upon which our institutions are founded, maintained and justified.

Gandhi never swerved from his initial rejection of the values and institutions of modern civilization, and the tragic view he took of it was finally confirmed by the First World War. In his lecture to Muir College at Allahabad in December 1916 he propounded, for the first time, the proposition that material progress is in inverse relation to moral progress. He elaborately defended the view that there is a well-marked tendency in the rise and fall of civilizations, confirming a compensatory law connecting material affluence and moral turpitude. At the least, he held, there is no basis for the opposite and popular belief that material advancement induces moral progress. "Increase of material comforts, it may be generally laid down, does not in any way whatsoever conduce to moral growth."[26]

In order to put Gandhi's view of progress into proper perspective, it must be noted that the early apostles of progress—Turgot, Condorcet, Herder, Kant—did not actually formulate a law of automatic progress, despite their abounding optimism. In the first phase of the idea of progress, it was chiefly a moral ideal toward which humanity was thought to be moving. It was not until the latter half of the nineteenth century that efforts were made to formulate a general law of progress with some precision, as a result of the artifacts of applied science and the Darwinian doctrine of evolution. The culminating point was reached toward the turn of the century long after Fourier and Marx wrote. It was natural for Gandhi, as earlier for Wallace, to challenge the concept of unilinear or automatic progress. Even in the West the feeling was emerging that progress is neither simple nor continuous, that advance in one direction is often accompanied by retrogression in another, that factual claims could be conceded and yet challenged in terms of moral values. Péguy regarded the view of automatic progress as a cosmic generalization of bourgeois capitalism, with its *mystique* of savings.

Gandhi's indictment was much less extreme than the assumption of latter-day theories of progress that intellectual and material advance would necessarily be reflected in better human relations or in moral and cultural elevation. Earlier, even Condorcet had stressed the importance of the right use of new knowledge and Renouvier had attacked predestinarian or necessitarian views of progress. Then, as now, there was no religious or economic warrant for the belief in the inherent stability and spontaneous productive expansion of the competitive, capitalist system. But none of these doubts entered the minds of those who took for granted the permanency of their political universe in an era of advancing imperialism and European ascendency.

In the 1920's Marxists strongly reacted against the complacency of capitalist Europe, though they talked about the encirclement of Bolshevik communism by world capitalism. And yet, Communists took over from western Europe the bourgeois faith in ever-increasing progress through material and scientific development. Gandhi was the first thinker to see clearly what was common to European capitalism and Communist Russia. He easily extended his attack on modern civilization, the gospel of material progress and the glorification of violence to cover Soviet civilization as well as the capitalist countries. He told Saklatwala, a Communist M.P. who came to see him in 1927, that he detested the multiplication of wants and machinery, the mad desire to destroy distance and time, to increase animal appetites and go to the ends of the earth for their satisfaction. He expressed his deep distrust of the schemes of amelioration of governments.[27] Since modern civilization is one tissue of intertwined evils, no plan of partial and gradual reform from within the system could produce a lasting remedy. He was concerned with the destruction of systems, not of persons; those who tried to destroy men adopted their manners and became worse. The "soulless system" of modern civilization, based on mutual suspicion and fear, had to be destroyed without our becoming soulless ourselves.

If Gandhi condemned what he called the pseudo-civilization of capitalist and communist systems of industrialization, what was then his own conception of true civilization? In his definition, civilization is that mode of conduct which points to the path of duty. "Performance of duty and observance of morality are convertible terms. To observe morality is to attain mastery over our mind and our passions. So doing, we know ourselves. The Gujarati equivalent for civilization means 'good conduct.' "[28] This may seem an unusual definition of civilization, but Mirabeau, who was the first person in the West to employ the word, similarly gave a moral criterion. "Civilization does nothing for society unless it is able to give form and substance to virtue."[29]

Gandhi's rejection of the cult of material progress by no means meant any lack of concern with the problem of mass poverty. He went so far as to say that for the poor the economic is the spiritual[30] and that to them God can appear only as bread and butter.[31] The cause of poverty was, in his view, the covetousness of the rich and the exploitation of the needy by the greedy. The redistribution of income is more important than the raising of output, and the fulfillment of the basic needs of the masses requires the limitation of the wants of the richer classes. If the masses were prepared to shun the evils of capital accumulation, "they would strive to attain a juster distribution of the products of labour."

> Under the new outlook multiplicity of material wants will not be the aim of life, the aim will be rather their restriction consistently with comfort. We shall cease to think of getting what we can, but we shall decline to receive what all cannot get. It occurs to me that it ought not to be difficult to make a successful appeal to the masses of Europe in terms of economics, and a fairly successful working of such an experiment must lead to immense and unconscious spiritual results.[32]

If Gandhi's solution to the problem of world poverty is to be feasible, it will require nothing less than a revolutionary change in prevailing attitudes to consumption and to wealth in affluent societies as well as in the poorer countries now caught up in "the revolution of rising expectation." Most critics of Gandhi's view would argue that even if it were intrinsically defensible, it would be wholly utopian. His own defence would be that the only alternative to his utopian-seeming solution is an explosive encounter between the richer and poorer nations which would destroy modern, industrial civilization.[33]

When Gandhi wrote *Hind Swaraj*, it was not fashionable in the West or in India to condemn outright modern, industrial civilization. Even now it may be tempting for the complacent to respond blandly to Gandhi's attack in the words of the World-Controller in *Brave New World*: "So you don't much like civilization, Mr. Savage." It would, in any case, be wrong to dismiss Gandhi as a literary Luddite, as a fanatical opponent of all machinery, wealth and power. He was not against these so much as ruthless mechanization, the Midas-complex and power-mania. It may be readily conceded that *Hind Swaraj*, like Ruskin's *Fors Clavigera*, contains passages which are severe and exaggerated in their shocking solemnity. In general, the typical prophets of righteousness—Isaiah, Jesus, Paul, Dante, Milton—did not mince their words. They felt that strong evils needed strong names, and sought, by scorching instances, to brand these into the hearts and understanding of their hearers. *Hind Swaraj* was, however, written not so much by a prophet of righteousness as by a righteous revolutionary. Gandhi's profound discontent led him to a daringly sanguine view of how politics may be purified, how absolute standards may be upheld in all human relationships and how individual conscience may be combined with heroism in society.

3

THE PURIFICATION
OF POLITICS

La politique se moque de la mystique, mais c'est encore la mystique qui nourrit la politique même. . . . Ce sont les mystiques qui sont même pratiques et ce sont les politiques qui ne le sont pas. C'est nous qui sommes pratiques, qui faisons quelque chose, et c'est eux qui ne le sont pas, qui ne font rien. C'est nous qui amassons et c'est eux qui pillent. C'est nous qui bâtissons, c'est nous qui fondons, et c'est eux qui démolissent. C'est nous qui nourrissons et c'est eux qui parasitent. C'est nous qui faisons les œuvres et les hommes, les peuples et les races. Et c'est eux qui les ruinent.

CHARLES PÉGUY

Gandhi's severe indictment of modern civilization can be better understood if it is placed in the context of alternative attitudes that he either rejected or ignored. It is possible to adopt a pessimistic attitude toward human life and modern civilization in terms of its supposedly inherent sinfulness and propensity toward evil, a condition that is deplorable but irremediable. To deny this would be blind and to rave against it would be futile and silly. A variant of this view would stress folly and error rather than sin and evil, and it would be couched in the idiom of rationalist cynicism rather than of religious pessimism. Alternatively, it is possible to take an essentially optimistic view of human life and of modern civilization in terms of its innate possibilities for good and to formulate some form of doctrine of Progress or Redemption in society. This view could also be worked out along religious or secular lines and might even be made the basis of some form of millennial and apocalyptic quest. Daring and often dogmatic political thinkers have generally tended toward either a pessimistic or an optimistic position. On the other hand, there are those cautious and moderate theorists who have regarded human life and modern civilization as an inevitable mixture of good and evil, enlightenment and error, capable of pragmatic and utilitarian justification. This view could also be supported either on rational or on religious grounds.

All these three paradigmatic standpoints (which could be put in secular language or in a religious form, whether in the Judaeo-Christian or the Hindu-Buddhist traditions) were of no use to Gandhi. He chose neither an Augustinian nor a purely Pelagian standpoint, and he could not compromise in the manner of Aristotle or Aquinas. Nor did he follow in the wake of a messianic revivalist like Vivekananda, a patient reformist like Ranade, a militant realist like Tilak, or a romantic universalist like Tagore.

Gandhi's standpoint was peculiarly his own and may be regarded as another of the major alternatives available. He derived his outlook from the traditional Indian doctrine of *maya*, or illusion, and he also stressed the notion of *moha*, delusion or glamour. The evident evil in this world and in modern civilization is enormous and deep-rooted, while what seems to be good is merely delusive and ephemeral. The apparent good is almost worse than the admitted evil because it has a hypnotic and narcotic effect on the moral perception and will of man. If this spell could be lifted for the individual, he could then proceed to purify human society of its dross, and restore the natural strength and activity of the spiritual and moral faculties. The answer to apathy or acquiescence in evil does not lie merely in Stoic detachment or in political disengagement, but even more in heroic action both in regard to changing the opinions of others and to applying the truth as one sees it to the conditions of society.

In *Kali Yuga*, the age of darkness in which we now live, the conditions of life and the pace of living are peculiarly obstructive to the fulfillment of the highest ends of men, but we are tested as sojourners on earth by the extent to which we refuse to compromise with, or become victims of, the surrounding forces of materialism. *Rama Rajya*, the Golden Age, is unattainable at present or in the forseeable future, and, in any case, its advent cannot be achieved through a violent repudiation of such of our fellow men as are deceived and tainted even more than we are. But recognizing *Kali Yuga* and "satanic" civilization for what they are, the servants of society must live like cenobitic monks,[1] and work like crusaders, so as to capture more and more of the atmosphere of *Rama Rajya*, the Golden Age. At the least, they should be willing to alleviate the evil of *Kali Yuga* for those of our fellow men who are not ready or willing to seek first the Kingdom of Heaven.

The Gandhian indictment of modern civilization represents a moral and spiritual standpoint that is seen even more clearly in his attitude to politics. For him, the sickness of our "satanic" civilization is closely connected with the "soullessness" of present-day politics.[2] In a materialistic society, regardless of its religious or humanistic professions, the State and the entire system of government become corrupt. All political institutions become merely instruments for the pursuit of power, whether directly or by the indirect manner in which they maintain and foster the ownership of property and provide the psychological incentives that are connected with power. "Man has always desired power. Ownership of property gives that power. Man hankers also after posthumous fame based on power."[3] Gandhi had no illusions about the possi-

bility of purging the State of power-striving and the egoistic pursuit
of its own interests. However, while he recognized, like Hobbes and
Machiavelli, that the pursuit of power is a basic human characteristic, perhaps even an animal drive, he was also convinced that just
as power creates its own normative rules, moral values also create
power and enhance the possibility of individual effectiveness and
collective survival.

The interplay of power and moral values is at the center of the
problem of politics, but is usually understood solely in terms of
moralizing the conduct of the State. Gandhi was, however, far more
interested in challenging the conventional view of the nature and
domain of politics, in widening the concept of power, and, above
all, in destroying the dichotomies between private and public morals, religious values and political norms, ethical principles and political expediency. In a materialistic civilization this requires nothing less than an assault on deeply rooted and widely held notions
of realism and self-interest, narrowly defined, that flow from the
segregation of true religion and power politics. In an acquisitive society the State is doomed to remain a sorely inadequate and not
merely imperfect instrument, and its power a standing inducement
to social corruption.

As early as 1915, Gandhi declared his aim "to spiritualize" political life and political institutions. Politics is as essential as religion, but if it is divorced from religion it is like a corpse, fit only for
burning.[4] As a result of the segregation between political and religious life, the masses seem merely to render unto Caesar what is
Caesar's and for the rest do much as they like. In traditional India,
the vast organization of caste answered not only to the religious
wants of the community but also to its political needs.[5] Politics, divorced from religion, has absolutely no meaning, according to Gandhi. Politics is a part of our being and not separable from the rest
of life.[6] We need to understand political institutions, but we also require the steady light of religious faith, appealing to the heart as
well as to the intelligence.

In the preface to his autobiography, Gandhi declared that his devotion to truth had drawn him into politics, that his power in the
political field was derived from his spiritual experiments with himself, and that those who say religion has nothing to do with politics

do not know what religion means.[7] He was concerned with the purification of political life through the introduction of the *ashrama* or monastic ideal into politics. He repeatedly insisted that politics cannot be isolated from the deepest things of life. When he visited London in 1931, Laurence Housman said at a reception at Friends House that in churches we are all sinners while in politics everyone else is a sinner, and that Gandhi had shown the way of unification of politics and religion through constant heart-searching and the concern to define and declare one's private faith.[8] In an address at Guildhall, Gandhi spoke about the vow of voluntary poverty for a politician. He said that when he found himself drawn into the political coil, he asked himself what was necessary to remain untouched by immorality, untruth and political gain, and decided that a servant of the people must discard all wealth and private possessions.[9] Later on, in India, he pointed out to his colleagues that there is a close connection between politics and social reform, that he who is not ready for small reforms will never be ready for great reforms, that one must forget the political goal in order to realize it and that to think of it at every step is to raise unnecessary dust.[10] "Our little doings and little systems will disappear, but truth and non-violence will endure forever."[11]

Gandhi was from the first determined to approach politics, as everything else, in a religious spirit, while he had no doubt that his own fundamental concern was with the religious life. He told a group of missionaries in 1938:

> I could not be leading a religious life unless I identified myself with the whole of mankind and that I could not do unless I took part in politics. The whole gamut of man's activities today constitutes an indivisible whole. . . . I do not know of any religion apart from activity. It provides a moral basis to all other activities without which life would be a maze of sound and fury signifying nothing.[12]

He was certain that he could never be a votary of principles which depended for their existence upon politics or anything else.[13] While even social work is not possible without touching politics, political work must ever be looked upon in terms of social and moral progress.[14] Power resides in the people, not in legislative assemblies.[15]

If people help themselves, politics will take care of itself. At the same time Gandhi could call politics an unavoidable evil.[16] But he could not go as far as Thoreau in regarding politics not merely as "the gizzard of society," but also as "infra-human, a kind of vegetation," an activity which should be unconsciously performed.[17]

In order to understand Gandhi's position, we must, first of all, see that he both narrowed and broadened the connotation of "politics," and secondly, that he used the word "religion" in a special sense quite different from its common sectarian implications. When he spoke disparagingly of politics, he referred to the politics of power and regarded it as an overestimated segment of politics as a whole. "To me political power is not an end but one of the means of enabling people to better their condition in every department of life."[18] He did not merely distinguish between power politics and what Huxley, in *Grey Eminence*, called "goodness-politics." He went further in denying that power politics is ultimately detachable from the rest of politics, which he regarded as co-extensive with the whole of life, the entire range of human activity in society. If politics were artificially separated from everything else, especially from religious values and faith, it would either become a game played according to its own amoral rules that might be given a moral disguise, or else it would become an illegitimate usurper of the religious emotions and needs of men. He felt that much mischief had been done throughout the world by the divorce between public and private conduct.[19]

When Gandhi spoke of religion, he was more concerned with religious values than with religious beliefs, with the fundamental ethics that he believed to be common to all religions, rather than the formal allegiance to received dogmas that becomes a barrier to religious experience. Religion does not mean sectarianism. It means a belief in "the ordered moral government of the universe."[20] He referred to "the religion which transcends Hinduism, which changes one's very nature, which binds one indissolubly to the truth within and which ever purifies. It is the permanent element in human nature which counts no cost too great in order to find full expression and which leaves the soul utterly restless until it has found itself."[21] It sustains a person as nothing else does. It is "rock-bottom fundamental morality." When morality incarnates itself in a living man it becomes religion, because it binds, it holds, it sustains him in the hour of trial.

Gandhi was wholly against state religion, even if a country had only one religion. Sectarian religion, he felt, is a purely personal matter and has no place in politics. A society or a group which depends partly or wholly on state aid for the existence of religion does not deserve or have any religion worth the name. In reality, there are "as many religions as there are individuals."[22]

It was really Gandhi's intention to protest against the compartmentalization of human life that had been brought about in the name of the segregation of politics from religion.[23] Politics, like the whole of civilization, must always be viewed *sub specie aeternitatis*. If most people today fail to see it as such, the blame must lie with theologians as well as politicians. Politics, like religion, is ever concerned with "the happiness of the toiling masses, a means to the realization of the highest realizable in life."[24] Public life is a testing-ground, like communal and family life, for the highest spiritual qualities in man. Social thinkers in the West, who have stressed the close connection between religion and politics, have usually thought in terms of a state religion. Lamennais, for example, argued that the unity of morality is lost through a multiplicity of religions. The French traditionalists—de Bonald, de Maistre and Lamennais—were convinced that the State and society could neither come to be, nor continue, without an official religion. Lamennais regarded religion as the source of law and the foundation of social organization. The basic dependence of the State on religion means that the undermining of religion results in the destruction of society.

Rousseau, unlike Lamennais, distinguished between private and civic religion. He pointed out in *Du contrat social* (*iv.viii*):

> Now it is very important to the State that each citizen should have a religion which makes him love his duties; but the dogmas of that religion are important neither to the State nor to its members except in so far as they have a bearing on morals and on the duties that he who professes it is bound to fulfil towards others. . . . Whenever theological intolerance is allowed, it cannot fail to have some civil consequences; . . . now that there no longer

is, nor can be, any exclusively national religion, you should tolerate all those which tolerate others, in so far as their dogmas
contain nothing contrary to the duties of the citizen.

In his view of politics and religion Gandhi comes closer to Acton
than to Newman, to Rousseau and Mazzini than to Lamennais or
de Maistre. Politics is the art of doing on the largest scale what is
right, and, as an affair of principle, it touches eternal interests and
religious sentiments. He would have agreed with Acton's attack on
the attempt to make morality wholly independent of the sanctifying
power of religion; he respected reason but distrusted any appeal to
the universal voice of reason to the exclusion of the response of the
heart. On the other hand, he could not possibly show Cardinal
Baronius's contempt, shared by Acton, for political notions that
limit the ecclesiastical domain. Gandhi's attitude was liberal and
radical rather than conservative toward religious as well as social
and political institutions. He, therefore, invoked religion against all
authority and not in support of Church or State. He combined an
absolutist sense of sanctity toward religious values with a flexible
and critical attitude toward religious institutions, and he was wholly
critical toward existing social ideals, though less so toward traditional social institutions. There was an anarchist and even revolutionary element in Gandhi's thought in these matters, but although
he extended this especially toward the "weighted fetters of the
State," he could not go as far as Proudhon's attack on "the inherent materialism of the group and the inevitable hypocrisy of association" in social life. He could have agreed with Blanqui that
social transformation is inseparable from fundamental political
changes, but he would not place his faith in the primacy of politics
per se and the need to capture power at any cost.

Gandhi's attitude toward politics and religion reveals the influence of Emerson and of Mazzini. In his essay "Politics," Emerson
argued that all social institutions are vulnerable and alterable. Society may seem to be immovably fixed in a condition of rigid repose, but it is more fluid than we realize and "any particle may suddenly compel the system to gyrate around it, as Pisistratus and
Cromwell did for a time and as every man of truth, like Plato or
Paul, does for ever."[25] Politics, in Emerson's view, rests on neces-

sary foundations and cannot be treated with levity. Every actual
State is corrupt, but it is impossible to fix in advance the boundaries of personal influence, especially of those who base themselves
on eternal truths and become "organs of almost supernatural force."
Existing parties are parties of circumstance, not of principle. We
pay unwilling tribute to governments founded on force. There are
not enough men in our "barbarous society" with sufficient faith in
the power of rectitude to inspire them with "the broad design of
renovating the State on the principles of right and Love."[26]

Emerson's stress on contemplation was acceptable to Gandhi but
it appealed to him less than Mazzini's emphasis on action. Like
Mazzini he believed that life is a mission, that it is not ours to
squander. Man should not isolate himself in sterile contemplation
of his own individuality; the mind must not mislead the heart; and
true religion is a gospel of duty toward society requiring political
action. But to Gandhi, the hope of leading a whole national community along a political short-cut into the Kingdom of Heaven on
earth is illusory, so long as the human instruments and the material
of political action remain untransformed. Politics of the proper type
is far from easy, for it is in political life that the most intractable
moral problems occur, especially to men of deep religious faith.

The core of Gandhi's position lies in his belief that while "politics today encircles us like the coils of a snake from which one cannot get out no matter how one tries,"[27] the only way of wrestling
with the snake is to introduce religion into politics. Even the struggle for the civil rights of Indians in South Africa became for
him a religious struggle. "By religion I do not mean formal religion or customary religion but that religion which underlies all religions. . . ."[28] Religion, for Gandhi, means a spiritual commitment which is total but intensely personal. He firmly believed in the
fundamental unity of life, and rejected the distinction between public and private, secular and sacred.

Social reform, even more than "purely political work," is a
means to self-purification, and, in the long run, both must have
their rise in a boundless love of mankind. Gandhi's standpoint
comes closest to that of Saint-Simon, who believed that religion has
always served and will always serve as the enduring basis of social
organization, and that humanity has always found itself in a scien-

tific, moral and political crisis, whenever the religious idea was undergoing modification. Of course Gandhi's conception of religion was different from that of Saint-Simon, but both agreed that religion and politics must alike embrace all walks of life and that neither can be merely a set of pragmatic precepts for a limited sphere of action. Both discarded the division between spiritual pursuits and secular interests.

Gandhi was not so much challenging the modern notion of a secular (i.e., non-sectarian) State as that conception of secular or profane politics which goes back to the Augustinian distinction between the political and religious orders. To the early Christians one of the main reasons for this distinction was that the religious order alone regulated the rites and ensured the possibility of redemption. St. Augustine sharply contrasted the holy society sustained by Christian *caritas* and the "minimum society" imperilled by human *cupiditas*. The political and the spiritual were non-competing orders; neither could protect the other and each had to be seen and respected on its own terms. The Augustinian contrast meant that the political order could never be elevated, but could only be endured. The political community contained individuals typifying the antithetical ways of life associated with the *civitas terrena* and the *civitas dei,* the State and the Church. Aquinas, unlike St. Augustine, stressed the vital role of the political order as necessary for the attainment of the highest earthly good; it could not, however, effect the supreme good. It was not until Machiavelli that politics came to be emancipated entirely from the encumbrances of a theological world-view. Meta-politics, to use Coleridge's term, was replaced by *Realpolitik,* but the older forms of religious emotion and language were carried over into the newer imagery of the nation-state. A political society, according to Machiavelli, could escape atrophy or corruption only by a certain ritual of self-redemption. This notion of a revivifying principle, strangely reminiscent of the eucharistic usages, was carried into later political theory, particularly among early English constitutionalists. Harrington, for example, argued that a republic which adhered to its basic laws would be assured of the power of collective self-perpetuation. In general, the secularization of politics, that eventually resulted from the doctrine of segregation between politics and religion, has obscured the fact that a religious fervor and flavor was introduced into the political vocabulary and thinking of nationalistic states.

In Indian political thought there was a clear allocation of functions between *regium* and *sacerdotum, Kshatriya* and *Brahmin,* but there has never been a sharp demarcation between religious and political discourse or conduct. The notions of *ṛta* and *dharma* helped to knit the political into a cosmic whole, a gradually ascending hierarchy of ends reflected in successive phases of the life of every man. In Aurobindo's words:

> It was a marked feature of the Indian mind that it sought to attach a spiritual meaning and a religious sanction to all, even to the most external social and political circumstances of its life, imposing on all classes and functions an ideal, not, except incidentally, of rights and powers but of duties, a rule of their action and an ideal way and temperament, character, spirit in action, a *dharma* with a spiritual significance.[29]

The closeness between religion and politics did not mean that there was a subordination of the State to any church. In fact, Indian political thought was not affected by anything like the Church-State struggle in the West. It was Asoka who brought in the notion of a non-sectarian, "secular" State in which all religions were respected and all men fused their religious and political concerns through the notion of *dharma.*

Gandhi was in accord with Indian tradition in rejecting the modern dichotomy between religion and politics, but he went much further than most classical Indian thinkers in dispensing entirely with notions of *raison d'état* and social necessity and in holding that the propensity of politics to become corrupt can be effectively countered. He rejected the possibility of any conflict, in the ultimate analysis, between political expediency and moral principles derived from religious conviction. He did not deny the difficulty or the complexity of political choices and decisions, but in this they were not really different from what we call religious or moral dilemmas. The important thing in either case is to distinguish between essentials and non-essentials, between what we know to be true and what we believe to be desirable, between *sreyas* and *preyas* as distinguished in the Upanishads. We cannot compromise between truth and falsehood, for "all incompatible mixtures are bound to explode."[30] Life is made up of compromises in regard to matters of lesser importance and concerning the good that we may seek to achieve, but these compromises must bring us nearer our ultimate goal.[31]

Gandhi thought that the saint and the revolutionary are not incompatible, although the former is more concerned with his inward integrity and the latter with his outward effectiveness. The saint must not become a self-deceiving escapist who refuses to act, while the revolutionary politician must not become a self-seeking opportunist who is ever ready to sacrifice his declared principles. The true saint must be effective in society, while the true revolutionary must be possessed of the deepest integrity; in the end, the two categories merge into each other. In this way Gandhi upheld what Archbishop Temple called "the error of medieval monasticism,"[32] the belief that it is possible to live a life in society that is altogether at variance with its prevalent moral standards.

Gandhi's view of politics was the consequence of, and not independent of, his view of morality. He would have entirely agreed with Kant's essay "On the Discordance Between Morals and Politics." Kant argued that there could be a conflict between morals and politics if ethics is itself regarded as a general doctrine of prudence or expediency, a view that he wholly rejected in favor of the view that it was a system of unconditionally authoritative laws in accordance with which we always ought to act. "I can easily enough think of a moral politician as one who holds the principles of political expediency in such a way that they can co-exist with morals: but I cannot conceive of a political moralist who fashions a system of morality for himself so as to make it subordinate and subservient to the interest of the statesman."[33]

In this Kantian sense Gandhi could be seen as a "political moralist"; he was certainly not a "moral politician." His moral standpoint was absolutist in all spheres and was based upon the conviction that true religion and true morality are inseparably bound up with each other, that "so long as the seed of morality is not watered by religion it cannot sprout,"[34] and that "if we take out the essence of all moral laws, we shall find that the attempt to do good to mankind is the highest morality."[35]

Gandhi also believed, like Kant, that the seeming antagonism between political prudence and moral convictions arises only when moralists are deficient in practice and therefore inclined to despotism. A political good must not be desired for its own sake but as a practical consequence of the realization and performance of one's primary moral obligations. Further, political as well as private morality becomes purer the less it depends upon the proposed physical or moral advantage the individual sets as his end. Political and moral evil are alike self-destructive. In theory, there cannot be any objective opposition between politics and morals, while the subjective conflict between them that exists for the individual is merely a consequence of selfishness, and will continue to serve as a stimulus to virtue, assuming the sincerity of the individual.

Gandhi was not a student of Kant, any more than he was familiar with the thought of Saint-Simon, but derived his position from the *Bhagavad Gita* and his own religious study and experience. In his attempt to make politics religious and religion practical, he based himself upon a neglected strand of Indian tradition— the path of *karma yoga,* or spiritual realization through social action, that is associated with classical heroes like Rama and Janaka and has been re-affirmed in modern India by Vivekananda[36] and Aurobindo.[37] Gandhi believed strongly, unlike either Vivekananda or Aurobindo, that the time had come for the purification of politics and the reformation of formal religion in India. He pointed to the corrupting nature of politics, while at the same time he declared his faith in the possibility of its purification. Politics is dangerous but it is not sinful or beyond redemption. It could become a means to spiritual perfection as legitimate and sacred as any other spiritual path because it should, in principle and in practice, be possible to enter it without losing one's soul. Politics, as usually understood, cannot be morally justified or spiritually utilized, but it has a potential legitimacy of the highest order if its corrupting nature is understood and continually countered through a process of spiritual self-purification.

Gandhi was, in fact, following in the footsteps of the Buddha in showing the connection between the service of suffering humanity and the process of self-purification. He rejected the distinction between the mundane and the ultramundane, the natural and the supernatural. Neither *artha* (politics) nor *moksha* (salvation) could be separated from *dharma* (social and personal morality). He did not merely contend, like Vijneswara, that *artha* must be subordinated to *dharma* in the case of conflict but went further and, as in the *Dharmasutra* literature, regarded politics as a branch of ethics; *artha* was an aspect of *dharma.* Gandhi was more concerned with the *dharma* of the citizen than that of the ruler, and did not therefore take his stand on the concept of *rajadharma* (royal duty) in ancient Indian religious literature. He shared the view of the Jain writer, Jinasena, that *rajadharma* could not provide real happiness. He would also have agreed with Bana's attack on Kautilya's illusions about enlightened self-interest. But unlike Jinasena, and like the Jain writer Hemachandra and Somadeva, he regarded politics as a necessary feature of daily life which must be justly conducted and properly controlled. Politics is also a means of enforcing and promoting morality, although to be "pure" it must rely on persuasion rather than on coercion. This notion of "pure" politics was regarded in classical Hindu political thought as significant only in *Satya Yuga,* the Golden Age; in *Kali Yuga* the use of *danda* or legitimate coercion was regarded as unavoidable and could be justified in terms of the recognized obligation of the ruler to preserve the social system and uphold the citizen's performance of his traditional *dharma.*

Gandhi declared once that the distinction drawn by Vivekananda between religion and politics does not hold and that Vivekananda was often led by his emotion, which obscured his understanding.[38] Gandhi also firmly disagreed with Tagore about the extent to which political methods hindered the religious pursuit and the highest moral and spiritual ends. But his main controversy was with Tilak who held that politics could not be regarded solely from a religious standpoint. In order to appreciate the significance of Gandhi's views about politics in the Indian context, it is necessary to read this controversy. In January 1920 Tilak wrote to Gandhi:

Politics is a game of worldly people, and not of *sadhus,* and instead of the maxim *"akkhodhenajine kkhodham"* [conquer anger by non-anger] as preached by Buddha, I prefer to rely on the maxim of Shri Krishna, *"ye gatthaa mam parapadyamthe thaams-*

> *thatthaiva bhajaamyaham"* [in whatever way men resort to me, even so do I render to them]. . . . Both methods are equally honest and righteous but the one is more suited to this world than the other.[39]

Gandhi replied:

> For me there is no conflict between the two texts. . . . The Buddhist text lays down an eternal principle. The text from the *Bhagavad Gita* shows to me how the principle of conquering hate by love, untruth by truth, can and must be applied. If it be true that God metes out the same measure to us that we mete out to others, it follows that, if we would escape condign punishment, we may not return anger for anger but gentleness even against anger. And this is the law not for the unworldly but essentially for the worldly. With deference to the Lokamanya, I venture to say that it betrays mental laziness to think that the world is not for *Sadhus*. The epitome of religions is to promote *Purushartha*, and *Purushartha* is nothing but a desperate attempt to become a *Sadhu*, i.e., to become a gentleman in every sense of the term.[40]

Gandhi did not refute Tilak but merely met his assertions with counter-assertions. If they differed in their conceptions of politics, this was because they also diverged in their views of religion.

On another occasion, Tilak said in connection with a political campaign of Gandhi's:

> A ship on the seas makes progress towards the Polar star keeping it in view as a guide, but it does not wish to reach the Polar star. Similarly, a religious ideal may be a very high guide but there must be a practical ideal in our political activities. A mere high religious ideal does not prove very useful in practical politics. By all means keep the Polar star in view, but remember that you are not going to get on to the star.[41]

Gandhi appreciated the difference between the ideal and the immediately practicable, but he differed from Tilak about what was immediately practicable and what should be regarded by us at any time as immediately practicable, which is not merely an empirical matter but ultimately a question of faith. The real point for Gandhi was the refusal to distinguish between religious and political ideals.

He felt that he was entitled to expect as much in politics as in religion from those who shared his beliefs. He once told a visitor to his *ashram,* "Every act . . . has its . . . spiritual, economic and social implications. The spirit is not separate. It cannot be."[42]

There is a very revealing passage about Tilak's view of Gandhi in one of Ajgaonkar's reminiscences:

> Tilak asked me: "What is Gandhi's caste?" I replied, "Gandhi is a Vaisya by caste and a Vaishnav by religion." Tilak looked surprised and replied: "It is strange that up to now I did not know Gandhi's religion. People will laugh at my ignorance about such a great man. I was under the impression that Gandhi was a Jain, because all his opinions and teachings savour of the Jain religion —Non-Violence, *Satyagraha,* fasting, etc. All these are more in keeping with Jain teachings than the Hindu religion. But these means are of no use in politics, which is required to change its attitude from time to time. Exalted religious principles or abstract doctrines about truth are not of much value in the present political game. I don't think that *Satyagraha* and fasting will have the least effect upon the mind of our rulers who are adepts in political warfare. We must use against them the same means as they use against us and as their tactics change, so must ours."[43]

Gandhi and Tilak did not merely disagree; they also misunderstood each other to some extent. This is not uncommon in practical politics. For example, in argument with a Marxist, a Conservative may be amazed to find that actions of his, to which he had never thought of giving a political significance, are endowed with a political significance by his opponent. A Conservative and a Marxist, or a relativist like Tilak and an absolutist like Gandhi, distinguish the purview of politics by different criteria reflecting wholly different ways of thinking about political questions. Each of them, adopting his own method of identifying a political situation confronting him, might easily fail to distinguish correctly between political and non-political actions in the conduct of the other. Thus what seems to be disagreement is really a failure in communication. Furthermore, Tilak especially did not grasp, as a result of Gandhi's ambiguous use of the word "politics," the distinction that was fundamental to Gandhi between "sattvic"[44] politics and "so-called politics" centered on power.[45]

THE CONCEPT OF POWER

Apart from the fact that at different times Gandhi narrowed and broadened the connotation of politics, there was also an ambivalent element in his attitude to the place of power in politics, whether purified or corrupt. This was because he always looked at politics more from the standpoint of the rebel than of the ruler, of freedom than of authority, of the individual than of the State. He was not merely suspicious of all power, like Jinasena in India or d'Holbach and Acton in the West, but he also rejected the normal notion of power. He believed that true power resides in the people and not in governments or legislatures,[46] and he hoped that political power, in the ordinary sense, would not enter Indian villages. "Power is of two kinds. One is obtained by the fear of punishment and the other by acts of love."[47]

In December 1947, a few months after India attained independence, Gandhi told his closest colleagues, the members of the Hindustani Talimi Sangh:

> By abjuring power and by devoting ourselves to pure and selfless service of voters, we can guide and influence them. It would give us far more real power than we shall have by going into the government. But a stage may come, when the people themselves may feel and say that they want us and no one else to wield the power. . . . Let us not be in the same cry as the power-seekers. . . . It is my firm view, that we should keep altogether aloof from power politics and its contagion. . . . To set our own house in order is the first indispensable requisite, if we want to influence political power . . . to regard adult suffrage as a means for the capture of political power, would be to put it to a corrupt use. . . . Today, politics has become corrupt. Anybody who goes into it is contaminated. Let us keep out of it altogether. Our influence will grow thereby. The greater our inner purity, the greater shall be our hold on the people, without any effort on our part.[48]

A few days before his assassination, he said at a prayer meeting: "I wonder if we can remain free from the fever of power politics or the bid for power, which afflicts the political world in the East and the West."[49]

As a politician who regarded politics and religion as inseparable,

Gandhi showed, especially at the time of Indian independence, an extreme suspicion of political power as ordinarily understood—the power over the lives of the people that is vested in governments and is sought by legislatures. He did not believe it was possible for power to be so organized as to ensure that those who seek it for its own sake or from selfish motives nevertheless use it, to a considerable extent, for the public good. As a political thinker, however, Gandhi was really trying to challenge the very notion of power, which has acquired in the modern world the kind of importance and autonomous character that some medieval philosophers gave to the universal essences which they believed to constitute reality.

It is interesting in this connection to notice the transition in the ancient world from the Greek view of power to that of the Roman Empire, from Aristotle to Polybius. Plato and Aristotle had appreciated the phenomenon of power as necessary to coordinate and direct human activities in order that basic needs be satisfied. But they did not consider power to be the main mark of a central association composed of contributing parts. With the declining significance of popular participation, the losing struggle to maintain republican institutions, and the growing importance of bureaucracy, power assumed an all-embracing role while the other factors in political society were being reduced to secondary significance. Polybius, in his *Histories,* reflected on the nature of power in accounting for the rapid emergence of Roman supremacy. Similarly, in India we witness a transition from the subordination of *artha* to *dharma* in the early republics (Hindu and Buddhist) to Kautilya's apotheosis of *artha* in the Mauryan Empire. *Danda* or coercion ceases to be merely a regulative device in the interests of social harmony and becomes the very pivot of governmental activity in the maintenance of imperial stability in an era when traditional moral codes have lost their former compelling force. Kautilya's obsession with the coercive power of government is really paralleled in the West by the new and total significance given to power by Machiavelli and Hobbes.

Pre-modern thinkers in the West, and pre-Kautilyan writers in India, rarely faced up to the problem of the cumulative effect on society of the consistent application of coercion. It was assumed that once affairs were set in motion along the prescribed paths, once proper education, the spread of knowledge or of faith, the improvement of social morality, and all the other pressures flowing from a rightly ordered environment had begun to operate, there would be progressively less need for the systematic application of coercion. Machiavelli and Kautilya were, however, convinced that the inherent instability of the political world could be countered, and then only partially, by resolute governmental action. In corrupt societies violence is the only means of arresting decadence. Hobbes's theory of sovereignty went even further, and was based on the belief that from an atomistic society of warring units effective political power could be generated. A political union is achieved when power is concentrated instead of diffused among various agencies.

The Hobbesian sovereign stood, in a sense, outside his society without any real leverage except that supplied by fear and self-interest; his power lacked the sustaining support of society, which was itself a loose connection of discrete individuals. The contrived nature of society excluded any natural dependence among the members. A political machine, by definition, is devoid of any subtle connecting tissue of needs and affections which blends the parts into an organic whole. It is this modern notion which Tagore attacked in his essay "State and Society." There is a basic element missing in the modern monistic view of State power, which the classical Indian and Greek thinkers never neglected. Gandhi in India, like Rousseau in the West, was anxious to reassert the idea that the stuff of power is not to be found in the passively acquiescent subject, but in the "engaged" citizen, with a capacity for public involvement and active political participation.

The State has a distinct power of direction but its effectiveness depends on the ability to elicit other forms of power to support its own. For Gandhi the corollary to this statement is that if individuals recognize the power in their hands and use it constructively to secure the social good (*sarvodaya*), or to engage in non-violent resistance (*satyagraha*) against unjust laws and repressive measures of the State, the monopolistic effectiveness of State power would be reduced and its coercive authority would be morally and materially undermined. In this way the purification of "power politics" would become possible. Hence the enormous importance that Gandhi gave to what he called the "Constructive Programme" launched by the voluntary servants of the people—dedicated missionaries and conscientious revolutionaries bound by vows, willing to introduce the monastic as well as the heroic ideal into political and social life.

Since the time of Montesquieu and Locke in the West, and of Kautilya in India, political power has often come to be regarded as a finite quantity of storable and distributable force residing at the apex of the political and social system. When it is evenly divided between the crucial agencies of decision-making, or when its concentration at a single point is prevented by a complicated machinery of checks and balances at the apex, the stable equilibrium of the system is said to be achieved. The stress in politics—as in science—is said to be on regularity and reliability, predictability and practical manipulation. The holders of political power are seen as active agents, and society as a collection of victims or beneficiaries. The supreme power-holders seem to possess a God-like standpoint and to be uniquely free since no one in the hierarchy stands above them; the difference between liberal and despotic systems (and between the theories justifying them) is mainly concerned with the extent to which the Leviathan can be influenced and restrained from below. The arena of conflict has been transferred from society to politics, or apparently so, and the politician has been sometimes described as an adjuster of interests whose job it is "to seek arrangements of persuasion and compromise which will enable society to proceed without too much delay and confusion."[50] Given this view, the charismatic leader is seen as a man who explodes irreverently upon the political scene, changes its whole character, and "makes a new heaven and a new earth for politics to flourish in";[51] nonetheless he is the exception rather than the rule, ephemeral if explosive, and lacking the staying power of the politician. Such leaders may be regarded as abusing political power in the narrow sense implicit in conventional usage. Gandhi, however, argued—sometimes as inconcretely as the Populists—that the source of power is always to be found much less in the struggles and inclinations of politicians as a body than in the nature of the society in which they operate.

In the Gandhian as in the Marxist view, the evil lies in society, not in the politicians as such, although Gandhi thought that the politicians were also blameworthy insofar as they fostered or encouraged certain social attitudes. Further, it is not in the mere alteration of the class structure, but in the purification of politics in its relation to social attitudes and moral values, that the hope of men of vision must lie. While Hobbes asserted the unqualified primacy of the political over the social at a time when society seemed to be dissolved in the State, Gandhi regarded power, like welfare, as wholly a by-product of social activity and the complex web of human relationships, as expressed through a variety of groupings, from the family upward. The more that political power which is based on coercion and hierarchy seems important, the greater the spiritual poverty of the society in which this is allowed to happen. But society can and must be changed through the efforts of its most morally developed members. The disease of political power in excess may be caused by the withdrawal of such men from society, a process which Durkheim took to be an index of social disorder.

Power-holders are by no means free and impartial agents, commanding the actions of others by means of coercion, crude or subtle. Their range of choice is not as great or almighty as is often believed, and they are more the victims of movements and social attitudes than they know. As Meinecke recognized, "the subject people allows itself to be governed because it receives some compensations in return and . . . through the medium of its own latent impulses towards power and life also nourishes the similar impulses on the part of the rulers. . . . The ruler is transformed into the servant of his own power."[52] The ruled, however, do not realize the extent of their power as they are overawed by the apparent omnipotence of State power. They come to conceive power as narrowly as their rulers; in this lies their real slavery, a product of ignorance rather than of inherent weakness, of self-deception rather than self-denial. Therefore, in challenging the notion of "political power," Gandhi meant to assert the primacy of the social over the political (in the narrow sense), but expressed himself ambiguously by regarding the social as identical with the political (in the broad sense).

THE DOCTRINE OF DOUBLE STANDARDS

Above all, it is Gandhi's notion of power and of the relation between politics and society, or between politics (in the narrow
sense) and politics (in the broad sense), that accounts for his tenacity in holding to the view that politics and religion (in his un-
sectarian, almost mystical, conception) are inseparable, and in challenging the common contention that there are two levels or types
or standards of morality, one for the individual in his private life
and in his immediate surroundings, the other for political life and
collective conduct. This standpoint has been stated plausibly over
and over again, from Aquinas to Maurras, Kautilya to Tilak, Jowett
to Niebuhr. *Prudentia politica* or *niti* is held to be the charioteer of
the other virtues, and adapts the natural law or *dharma* to *raison
d'état* or *artha*. Politics may be subordinated, but it must not become
subservient, to morals.

Aristotle pointed out that the distinction between the single good
of a person and the common good of his group is not merely one of
degree but also of kind; *non secundum et paucum sed secundum
formalen differentiam*. Aquinas distinguished between the common
good and the divine purpose, between two orders of reality in the
universe, *bonum intrinsecum* and *bonum extrinsecum*. Similarly
Kautilya had argued that *artha* had priority over everything else
in practical affairs, although it cannot be pursued to the exclusion
of *dharma*; he also held out against abstract, canonical interpretations of *dharma*. This reminds us of Richelieu's view that a man
who is governed by abstract maxims is more dangerous to the
State than anyone else and that moral precepts provide few clues
to what is politically advantageous. In his *Trois idées politiques,*
Maurras wrote that the "order of politics and the order of conscience are distinct" and referred to the superior necessities of nations (a phrase strikingly similar to Disraeli's).

The doctrine of double standards has been elaborately defended
by Reinhold Niebuhr. He criticizes the total Augustinian dichotomy
between the religious and the secular, the tendency in all "rigorous
religion" to contrast sharply the absolute moral ideal and the injustices of society, resulting in defeatism. But he thinks that we can-

not completely eliminate "certain irreconcilable elements in the two types of morality, internal and external, individual and social. These elements make for constant confusion but they also add to the richness of human life. . . . It would . . . seem better to accept a frank dualism in morals than to attempt a harmony between the two methods which threatens the effectiveness of both."[53] It is tragically unavoidable that the human spirit is unable to conform its collective life to its individual ideals. The standards we recognize in our relations as individual to individual are attenuated in collective actions within our society, and vanish in relations between societies. This is a statement of fact, but in Niebuhr's view it justifies and necessitates political policies which a purely individualistic ethic must always find embarrassing. The collective and the individual both have "organic reality," but the former must lack the "self-transcendence" of the latter.

It was absolutely and continually fundamental to Gandhi to reject this dominant doctrine of double standards, with its varying sources of support, types of formulation and methods of justification. It is not that Gandhi failed to distinguish between fact and value, or even between what men must ideally do and what they can practically achieve. He recognized that in politics as in life, we continually search for a middle term in our attempt to mediate between the desirable and the possible. Nor did he fail to see that politics, like medicine, requires immediate action based upon incomplete knowledge. Every act, according to the *Gita*, inevitably contains an element of error in this imperfect world. This may be truer of politics than of personal life, though this is by no means self-evident. What Gandhi denied was that in politics we must make more allowances, or even need more elbow room, than in the personal moral quest in the company of men of varying and even conflicting human aspirations. It was because Gandhi took very seriously, and regarded as highly complex and dilemma-ridden, the process of moral growth, choice and decision for the sensitive individual that he regarded politics as altering the sphere, but not the moral value or validity or culpability, of human action.[54]

Gandhi would agree that political puritanism which concentrates on demonstrations and provides alibis or excuses for decisions and choices, risks and sacrifices, is immoral. But he believed that it is our duty to cling to what we regard as right in the face of the facts, and this may require the readiness to suffer for one's beliefs or to withdraw into oneself to find a basis for actions; it can never justify the abdication of one's responsibility or a passive resort to continued inaction. He would not regard the morality of the intention, as Nietzsche did, as only a "pre-morality." He was convinced of the closeness between firm and pure intentions, and the capacity for effective choices and decisions on the basis of what is held to be right and necessary. The will to believe (in the phrase of William James) is bound up with the capacity to act. The spiritual or religious hope and faith must be realized in political terms, but this cannot require, or at any rate justify, the use of morally ambiguous means to attain political ends. In this sense, there can be no distinction between the secular and the sacred, and political integrity is as sacred as personal integrity.

Gandhi's rejection of prevalent political morality is founded on the belief that it is based upon a narrow, temporary and false view of the interests, needs and ends of man—a view that derives from the doctrine of double standards. He was influenced by the line of reasoning defended by Hobhouse's essay "The Useful and The Right," which he read.

> Indeed, it may be said that questions of right run up into questions of fact, since the question whether a given right should be recognized by society is ultimately settled by the question whether its refusal is in the long run compatible with the principles on which that society is based and which it desires to maintain. If not, no self-deception will prevent the working out of the process whereby the refusal to apply a principle in a given case makes a breach in the ethical constitution of society that can only be made good by repentance and reparation.[55]

Whereas Marx contended that a society governed in terms of class interests is self-destructive, that exploitation (engendered by and augmenting hypocrisy) cannot last, Gandhi held that a society governed in terms of double standards is self-destructive. Political and personal morality must coincide and extend to all human beings in all walks of life. The purification of politics requires the removal of the taint of double standards by men of courage and integrity.

As with Gandhi's views of civilization, so with his views of politics. He rejected the view that politics is inherently sinful and irremediably so, whether for reasons of theological or secular pessimism. He also rejected the view that politics is intrinsically moral *in its own way* and that this political morality could be perfected, whether through religious or worldly institutions or leaders. He further rejected the view that politics is characteristically pragmatic and that some form of prudential or utilitarian justification, whether put in religious or sociological terms, is adequate in the long run. Gandhi's own view is that politics is inherently impure and involves pollution and could never be ideal in any sense, but that it can and must be purified, and this requires, as a first step, the repudiation of any distinction between public and private, political and personal, morality. This notion of pollution, in one form or another, seems to be common to the whole Indo-European stock of people.[56] But whereas pollution in Homer is the presence of a substance (even physical) which hampers man's relations with the supernatural, Gandhi's moral notion of pollution refers to the contagion of power-seeking that hampers man's relations with his fellow men in politics and society.

It could be contended that Gandhi was not in his own life always right about the facts, despite the sincerity and thoroughness of his search for the truth regarding morals and politics. He may also have failed to distinguish properly between individual and social psychology, between the behavior of the individual and that of the crowd, between the facts that must be taken into account in personal and political morality. But this does not in the slightest affect the validity and value of Gandhi's attack on the doctrine of double standards, an attack which is really based upon a Platonic and Kantian rather than an Aristotelian or Humean view of morality. If Gandhi refused to distinguish between political expediency and personal morality, this was due to his concern for absolute standards.

4

THE NEED FOR ABSOLUTE
VALUES AND FOR VOWS

*The property of a value is to assume a certain function in relation to
life and, as it were, to mark it with its seal. . . . Fidelity to oneself is
both difficult to achieve and discern. . . . Fidelity cannot be separated
from the idea of an oath; this means that it implies the consciousness
of something sacred. . . . A code of ethics centred on fidelity is ir-
resistibly led to become attached to what is more than human, to a
desire for the unconditional which is the requirement and the very
mark of the Absolute in us.*

GABRIEL MARCEL

It is impossible to grasp what Gandhi really had in mind when he spoke about the purification of politics or about the spiritual poverty of modern civilization without considering his own view of morality and the imperative need for moral commitment to self-chosen values. True morality consists, for Gandhi, not in following the beaten track, but in finding out the true path for ourselves and in fearlessly following it.[1] No action which is not voluntary can be called moral.

> So long as we act like machines, there can be no question of morality. If we want to call an action moral, it should have been done consciously and as a matter of duty. Any action that is dictated by fear, or by coercion of any kind, ceases to be moral. It also follows that all good deeds that are prompted by hope of happiness in the next world cease to be moral.[2]

In his *Ethical Religion* (*Niti Dharma*), published in 1912 on the basis of lectures given by him, Gandhi had stated simply that he alone can be called truly religious or moral whose mind is not tainted with hatred or selfishness, and who leads a life of absolute purity and of disinterested service.[3] Without mental purity or purification of motive, external action cannot be performed in a selfless spirit.[4] Goodness does not consist in abstention from wrong but in abstention from the wish to do wrong; evil is to be avoided not from fear but from a sense of obligation.

Consistency was less important to Gandhi than moral earnestness, and rules were less useful than specific norms of human excellence and the appreciation of values. He often quoted with relish Emerson's time-worn dictum that "a foolish consistency is the hobgoblin of little minds." He had also read, early in life, Butler's *Analogy* and in all probability used the original edition which included his *Dissertations on Virtue*. Butler had argued that it was of limited (if not of little) importance to look for general rules of conduct and general formulations of right and of good ends to be pursued.

> The enquiries which have been made by men of leisure after some general rule, the conformity to or disagreement from which

should denominate our actions good or evil, are in many respects of great service. Yet let any plain honest man, before he engages in any course of action, ask himself "Is this I am going about right, or is it wrong? Is it good or is it evil?" I do not in the least doubt but that this question would be answered agreeably to truth and virtue, by almost any fair man in almost any circumstance.[5]

Butler also believed in the "uniformity of interest" and of conscience, and therefore in the "uniformity of duty."

Gandhi, unlike Butler, was concerned to stress the complexity rather than the simplicity of the moral life. The fact is that "the path of duty is not always easy to discern amidst claims seeming to conflict one with the other."[6] "Life is governed by a multitude of forces. It would be smooth sailing, if one could determine the course of one's actions only by one general principle whose application at a given moment was too obvious to need even a moment's reflection. But I cannot recall a single act which could be so easily determined."[7] He would not go as far as Godwin and regard every case as a rule to itself, but he would have concurred that no action of any man was ever entirely the same as any other action. Gandhi shared Butler's distrust of a single general principle as the criterion to all conduct, and he also shared, perhaps borrowed, Butler's notion of conscience. But he was also deeply influenced by the *Gita*, which asks "What is action? What is inaction?—here even the wise are perplexed."[8] If he could not accept the idea of uniformity of duty, it was because of his positive suspicion of formal and mechanical consistency as being an impediment—rather than an index—to moral growth. He made his position very clear:

> Consistency, as I have often said, is not an absolute virtue. . . .
> I may even take poison as medicine. It is poison for you, but for
> me it is nectar. . . . Consistency lies in living up to the truth as
> one sees it from moment to moment, even though it may be in-
> consistent with one's own past conduct. There can be, there ought
> to be, no uniformity in the actions of a man whose life undergoes
> a continual growth and who goes on rising in the spiritual scale.[9]

Gandhi's view of moral growth not merely allows for the inevitability of inconsistencies between moral decisions made at different times and in different situations, but also for the impossibility of achieving at any time or in any situation the entirety of what one sets out to do. The goal ever recedes from us. The greater our progress, the greater the recognition of our unworthiness. "Satisfaction lies in the effort, not in the attainment. Full effort is full victory."[10] This was why he ever held to the maxim, "One step is enough for me,"[11] even if he seemed at times to be guilty of spiritual ambition in his willingness to widen his immediate aim in any political campaign. He conceded that there was usually ample room for compromise. "I ever compromise my own ideal even in individual conduct not because I wish to but because the compromise was inevitable. And so in social and political matters I have never exacted complete fulfilment of the ideal in which I have believed."[12] However, he believed that there are always times when one has to say "thus far and no further," and on every issue the limiting line has to be determined on the merits of the case.

Although Gandhi tried to introduce a large element of flexibility and experimentation into his view of moral conduct, he was insistent that this should not be at the expense of the intensity and fullness of moral commitment to chosen ends either in individual or in political life.

> All action in this world has some drawback about it. It is man's duty and privilege to reduce it, and while living in the midst of it, to remain untouched by it as much as it is possible for him to do so. To take an extreme case, there can perhaps be no greater contradiction in terms than a compassionate butcher. And yet it is possible even for a butcher if he has any pity in him. In fact I have actually known butchers with gentleness that one would hardly expect from them. The celebrated episode of Kaushik the butcher in the *Mahabharata* is an instance in point.[13]

Gandhi's real concern was that men generally hesitate to make a beginning if they feel the object cannot be had in entirety. Such an attitude of mind is in reality a bar to progress.[14] He felt that there was no reason why in the moral as in the scientific sphere men should not grant the possibility of things undreamt of being realized.

ABSOLUTE VALUES AND ETERNAL PRINCIPLES

It was because of his desire to combine urgency with flexibility and faith with humility that Gandhi pleaded that every individual must uphold in a spirit of sanctity what he considers to be the highest human values. There can be neither moral discipline nor moral authority—without which no real revolution can be achieved in politics and in society—unless we are prepared to recognize certain values as ultimate and supreme. An essential assumption for Gandhi was that at the critical moment the individual could, by reason of his moral discipline, be relied upon to come forward in accord with his deepest and most cherished ideals. This assumption is directly opposed to Hume's belief that in politics we must assume that all men are knaves even if we do not believe this to be borne out by the facts. Gandhi believed that men become knaves or *goonda*s mainly because they have not been helped by society to see the need to pursue consciously worthy ends reflecting the highest human values.

Traditional Indian ethics distinguished between the basic needs that belong to all sentient creatures—such as *artha* (interest) and *kama* (pleasure)—and those human values (*purushartha*) which are specifically pursued by self-conscious beings. *Dharma* (duty) was regarded as a regulative principle, an instrumental value that is designed to govern the pursuit of *artha* and *kama,* according to certain schools of thought. Others, especially some *Mimamsaka*s of the *Prabhakara* school, regarded *dharma* as an instrumental value in a higher sense than in the formal regulation of *kama* and *artha*; these "theological utilitarians" held that *dharma* is superior to *kama* and *artha* insofar as it is uniquely conducive to *moksha* or salvation.

Gandhi, however, followed the *Mimamsaka*s and the Buddhists in regarding *dharma* as the highest human value, an end in itself, to which even *moksha* is secondary during life on earth. *Dharma,* in his view, has no meaning apart from *lokasangraha*, the welfare of the whole world. Self-conquest is not just a means to self-realization as they both must be valued in terms of their contribution to the common good of humanity. The crucial point for Gandhi, as for some traditional Indian schools, was that *dharma* must not be taken in a formal sense, as laid down by scripture or by custom, but rather as the object of discovery, the self-chosen means of self-discipline of every human being who wishes to qualify as a moral agent. Like Gautama, one of the oldest of the Indian law-givers and moralists, Gandhi placed the virtues of the soul (*atmaguna*) above mere ceremonial or precedent. Further, he believed that the "primary virtues" are cultivable by "the meanest of the human species,"[15] and that man would cease to grow the moment he ceased to discriminate between virtue and vice.[16] In fact, Gandhi almost regarded as the identifying mark of man's moral status his capacity to hold certain values (chosen and interpreted by his own reason and intuitions) as absolute, sacred and inalienable.

It has often been pointed out that anyone who is profoundly committed to transforming society by political action, or to the purification of politics through moral means, must self-consciously maintain an order of priorities among human activities, and therefore presuppose definite standards of human excellence. The hierarchical system of values that embodies the ethical continuity of commitment of a political culture would be reflected in its social structure, its allocation of resources and its legal system. The ends of human endeavor, political action and social policy need not be regarded as fixed with a static finality at any stage of human history. We do not have to be either teleologists or theologians in order to accept the necessity for moral commitment.

In general, the decision-makers in a political society may be pushed to make evaluations that could be shown to presuppose judgments of ultimate significance, even if not explicitly formulated. Such crucial preferences could also be inferred from typical behavior as the values upon which leaders fall back in the last resort when their political decisions are persistently challenged. The more explicitly leaders formulate the larger purposes and the deeper grounds upon which their decisions rest, the more they can self-consciously make consistent choices between clear alternatives, choices for which they could assume definite responsibility. This is relevant to the level of moral maturity of a political community. Changes in practical application need not violate the sanctity of shared values for different individuals over a period of time in which there is no fundamental ethical reformation. In a society in which there is a stable consensus in regard to the ultimate ends of conduct, there could still be a variety of different conceptions of the way of life in which these ultimate ends could be fruitfully and feasibly embodied. Men could still disagree about the priorities in specific contexts, about secondary principles, and the moral complexities in the balancing of short-term and long-term considerations.

The ethical problem, especially for the political revolutionary and social reformer, does not merely involve making difficult decisions but also requires adoption of a breadth and height of perspective which ranges beyond what is immediately practicable and perhaps beyond what will ever be wholly practicable for anyone. Positive exhortations to oneself become more significant than negative commandments to others. To set an example is no less vital than to formulate a moral code. Consistent indifference to self-examination is certain to undermine the moral credibility needed to induce others to make sacrifices on behalf of shared values. Of course, one strictly need not have an explicit set of values to make self-examination more important than exhortation, or personal example more meaningful than the external enforcement of formal rules. The connection between the self-conscious adoption of specific moral values and the authenticity of moral exemplification is not logical but psychological.

The crucial thing for Gandhi, as for Kant, is not to teach people what is right, nor to lead them to examine and criticize their convictions (though this is more important to Gandhi than to Kant), but to get them to do what they know they ought to do. In this way, Gandhi tended to assimilate all the virtues to that of moral courage. He did recognize the need to show men what they could usefully regard as moral norms in political and social life, but his practical concern was with *akrasia* or weakness of will. He was against offering inducements or threats, theological incentives and sanctions. "If virtue has no attraction in itself, it must be a poor thing to be thrown away on the dung heap."[17] The distinctiveness as well as the difficulty in Gandhi's ethical thought lies in the fact that he was both something of a Stoic and an existentialist.

Like Vedanta, the classical tradition of Western metaphysics saw in rational thought and first principles the guide to all action and the basis of all wisdom. Action is not so much opposed to thought as to passion. True knowledge and free action consist in conformity with an order existing prior to all human action. The disagreements of men and their moral discrepancies throughout history are taken as equal proof of the imperfection of their knowledge of moral principles, and of their conduct. A preliminary asceticism is required to repel everything which will estrange them from the universally valid order. Everyone must free himself from his passions and prejudices, from everything that carries the stamp of his personality and environment. The best way of guiding our reason consists principally in a purificatory discipline, which leads us to attach ourselves to clear and distinct conceptions of moral ends. Man is alone in the presence of the universe. In its extreme form, this standpoint involves the view that we can observe and contemplate and arrive at a knowledge of moral truths without getting involved in action. In practice, we may have to act but even if we do not, we might come to these truths, just as we might come to recognize excellence in some art without practicing that art.

On the other hand, the activist tendency of our time stresses the need to commit oneself to something concrete as a basis of personal action, to subject eternal truths to temporal tests, to check and change our thoughts and our intuitions by their results and repercussions. We can discover moral truth or come to have stable and consistent moral principles which we find satisfying only by acting ourselves and reflecting upon our actions. This was Hegel's position and perhaps also that of the existentialists—though they also hold something more than this. For some existentialists, moral principles are not truths that we come to know but values that we come to accept and find satisfying in daily life.

As a political thinker and actor, Gandhi belonged more to the latter school of thought; as a religious believer and an inheritor of the Indian tradition, he belonged to the classical tradition. "A man is but the product of his thoughts, what he thinks he becomes," he said in his *Ethical Religion*. He assumed that man often becomes what he believes himself to be.[18] "A man who broods on evil is as bad as a man who does evil if he is not worse."[19] At the same time Gandhi's stress on absolute values, which we come to choose as the basis for commitment to political and social activity directed toward moral and religious ends that are the product of contemplation, is also connected with his reliance on moral principles based upon the Moral Law. In the end commitment to certain fundamental moral convictions involves the acceptance of certain non-moral beliefs, but the ultimate abstract premises of our ethics must stand unsupported by reasons and can be confirmed only through action requiring us sometimes to take sides on concrete issues.

Gandhi is wholly Kantian, owing to his adherence to the *Gita,* in his belief in the universalizability of the Categorical Imperative of Duty. Men must perform their *dharma* for its own sake if *dharma* is to have any meaning at all. The very virtue of *dharma* is that it is universal, that "its practice is not the monopoly of the few but must be the privilege of all." "He who is not prepared to order his life in unquestioning obedience to the laws of morality cannot be said to be a man in the full sense of the word."[20] At the same time, "moral authority is never retained by any attempt to hold on to it. It comes without seeking and is retained without effort."[21]

Gandhi told his followers in 1937 that "an eternal principle, as the Jains say, has no exceptions."[22] He recognized that between the ideal and practice there must ever be an unbridgeable gulf.[23] "An ideal will cease to be one if it becomes possible to fulfill it."[24] He refused to believe that there is one single universal principle which could serve as a criterion to all moral decisions, or that morality is mainly rule-governed. "One virtue does not lead, at any rate all at once, to all the other virtues and a particular quality ceases to be a virtue when it solidifies into a custom."[25]

Gandhi firmly held to the view that there are fundamental principles based upon the Moral Law. He wrote to an inquirer in 1932: "When we have grasped fundamental principles, we should be able to apply them to any given set of circumstances. If we cannot do this, it means that our grasp of first principles is feeble. . . . It is like geometry, in which we can solve all problems based on a theorem we have mastered."[26] Further, he repeated that whatever a man sows, that shall he reap. The law of *Karma* is inexorable and impossible to evade.[27] But, "although I believe in the inexorable law of *Karma* I am striving to do so many things, every moment of my life is a strenuous endeavour, which is an attempt to build up more *karma* to undo the past and add to the present."[28] Again, "I firmly believe in the law of *Karma,* but I believe too in human endeavour. I regard as the *summum bonum* of life the attainment of salvation through *karma* by annihilating its effects by detachment."[29] This does not mean that a detached person can nullify the working of the law of *Karma* (the law of ethical causation and moral retribution), but he can mentally rise above the plane of effects so that he is not psychologically bound down by the consequences of his past actions.

The supremacy of the Moral Law in the universe makes it necessary for us to grasp the fundamental principles of morality. According to Gandhi "a principle is a principle and in no case can it be watered-down because of our incapacity to live it in practice. We have to strive to achieve it, and the striving should be conscious, deliberate and hard."[30] And yet he conceded that a principle is the expression of perfection, and as imperfect beings like us cannot practice perfection, "we devise every moment limits of its compromise in practice."[31]

Early in life, Gandhi had been deeply influenced by Thoreau's essay "Life without Principle." Thoreau contended that most moral prophets were employed in excusing the ways of men instead of encouraging them to become morally self-supporting. "We select granite for the underpinning of our houses and barns; we build fences of stone; but we do not ourselves rest on an underpinning of granitic truth, the lowest primitive rock. Our sills are rotten."[32] In the lives of men, a sense of direction is lacking, a feeling of purpose. As a result, they are vulnerable to the evil influence of unprincipled politicians who are ruthless and casuistical in their pursuit of selfish ends. Coleridge similarly argued that whole nations have been so far duped as to regard with constipated loyalty instead of loathing the "molochs of human nature." These politicians and leaders "are indebted for the far larger portion of their meteoric success to their total want of principle, and surpass the generality of their fellow-creatures in one act of courage only, that of daring to say with their whole heart, 'Evil, be thou my good!' All system so far is power."[33] It was a similarly uncompromising stance that made Gandhi talk of the "soullessness" of politics in a "satanic" civilization. We get the leaders and rulers we deserve and their successful and consistent scorn of principle is allowed to prevail by our general lack of purpose and by our indifference to the fundamentals of morality.

THE NEED FOR VOWS

The practical recommendation that follows from Gandhi's view of morality, with its profound political and social implications, is his unique advocacy of vows. Absolute values cannot be cherished or upheld in society and politics unless an increasing number of social workers and political crusaders accept the monastic ideal and introduce it into public life. This involves the taking of vows as the necessary means to self-purification and self-discipline, without which the purification of politics and the revolutionary transformation of society would be impossible. As Gandhi's reliance on vows has been the subject of much controversy, it is necessary to state his own position in full.

He believed that a life without vows is like a ship without an anchor or like an edifice that is built on sand instead of rock. A vow is a deliberate commitment to a moral principle. A vow imparts stability, ballast and firmness to one's character. What reliance, he argued, can be placed on a person who lacks these essential qualities? An agreement is nothing but a mutual interchange of vows; simultaneously one enters into a pledge when one gives one's word to another. In fact, our entire social fabric rests on the sanctity of the pledged word.

> The world would go to pieces if there was not this element of stability or finality in agreements arrived at. The Himalayas are immovably fixed for ever in their place. India would perish if the firmness of the Himalayas gave way. The sun, the moon and other heavenly bodies move with unerring regularity. Were it not so, human affairs would come to a standstill. . . . The same law, which regulates these heavenly bodies, applies equally to men. A person unbound by vows can never be absolutely relied upon. . . . To shirk taking of vows betrays indecision and want of resolution. One can never achieve anything lasting in this world by being irresolute. For instance, what faith can you place in a general or a soldier who lacks resolution and determination?

. . . No general ever won victory by following the principle of "being vigilant so long as he could." . . . A vow is like a right angle. An insignificant right angle will make all the difference between ugliness and elegance, solidarity and shakiness of a gigantic structure. Even so stability or instability, purity or otherwise of an entire career may depend upon the taking of a vow.[34]

He conceded that the taking of vows that are beyond one's capacity would betray thoughtlessness and want of balance, and also that a vow can be made conditional without losing any of its efficacy or virtue. The essence of a vow does not consist in the difficulty of its performance but rather in the unflinching determination to stick to it in the teeth of difficulties. He felt that pledges and vows should be taken on rare occasions, that "a vow is a purely religious act which cannot be taken in a fit of passion."[35]

The advantage of vows lies, according to Gandhi, in the fact that acts which are not possible by ordinary self-denial become possible with the aid of vows which require extraordinary self-denial. Vows are both a recognition of the fickleness of human nature and an additional aid to even the strongest of minds. "A vow is to all other indifferent resolves what a right angle is to all other angles. And just as a right angle gives an invariable and correct measure, so too a man of vows, rightly followed, gives of himself an invariable and correct measure."[36] He felt that rules of general application do not serve the purpose of keeping a man straight and warning him when he is going wrong as an individual vow can. "We find therefore the system of declaration followed in all large and well-conducted institutions."[37] Ministers, legislators, soldiers have all to take an oath.

A man who breaks a pledge he has deliberately and intelligently taken forfeits his manhood and becomes a man of straw. Gandhi went so far as to believe that a vow, far from closing the door to real freedom, opens it. To be bound by a vow is like passing from libertinism to a real monogamous marriage. The refusal to bind oneself with vows shows a weak mentality.[38] If there is any doubt that one's views may change or that one will fail to carry out a vow, this only betrays a lack of clear perception that a particular thing must be renounced—wealth or property, violence or cowardice or falsehood.

It is obvious that Gandhi's conception of a vow cannot be seen apart from his entire view of morality. If the only purpose of a vow is utilitarian and self-disciplinary, the problem still remains of overcoming weakness of will in carrying out the vow that was intended to remedy it. Must one make vows to carry out one's vows, and so on in an infinite regress? Gandhi was really as much concerned with the dependability of men in society as with their self-discipline for its own sake. "Your capacity to keep your vow will depend on the purity of your life. A gambler or a drunkard or a dissolute character can never keep a vow."[39] Such people could not be disciplined by the mere taking of vows. The social and political reformer needs self-discipline if he is to be dependable and if he is to promote the habits of reliability and self-restraint in society, and he must take vows that commit him completely. Vows are thus a sign of the fullness, intensity and authenticity of personal commitment to chosen ideals and social ends. Vows must not merely be adopted as crutches or psychological stimulants that aid the arduous process of self-discipline.

Gandhi's attitude toward vows was challenged by two of his closest admirers, C. F. Andrews and J. C. Kumarappa. As soon as he returned to India from South Africa, Gandhi set up the Satyagrahashrama, a monastic community, in Ahmedabad. The members of this *ashram* were expected to take the vows of truth, non-violence, celibacy, control of the palate, non-stealing, non-possession, self-sufficiency (*swadeshi*), fearlessness and the elimination of untouchability in the caste system. A few years later, Andrews, after much thought, argued that Gandhi's position had a strength of its own but not that of the highest truth. He quoted his own experience with vows that he had taken as a member of the Irvingite sect and later on of the Anglican priesthood, and felt that it is not good to bind one's whole life by vows which pledge the future. He felt that the *Ramayana* is less suitable today as a guide to conduct than the *Mahabharata*. Similarly, the New Testament's admonition not to swear at all must be preferred to the examples in the Old Testament of drastic vows with inhuman consequences.

It is especially wrong, argued Andrews, to encourage immature and growing people to take vows. "Verbal consistency may be only a lower form of truth, not truth itself. It may even overshadow the truth and obscure it. For life is always a growth into something new and unexpected and original."[40] A vow is a form of self-mutilation or a refusal to do something new and unexpected and original. Andrews conceded that Gandhi in his own life had been benefited by the vows he took, particularly at moments of moral crisis and breakdown. Though vows might be useful as temporary expedients, they are dangerous as life-long pledges. Life goes on and if we stand against its current we merely get drowned. It is by our response to the new and the unforeseen that we must be judged, not by uniform conformity to our self-appointed standard. Gandhi conceded that moral growth would be hampered by making a fetish of consistency, but he was convinced that moral growth would be impossible in practice if men did not take vows and keep to them to the best of their ability.

In 1930 Kumarappa wrote that he was unable to see eye to eye with Gandhi as regards the importance of vows. He argued that spiritually and morally all men are not alike and that consequently men need different methods of guidance, a fact acknowledged by most religions and especially by Hinduism. Just as idols are legitimate aids at lower stages of development, so too vows are psychological expedients for leaders who strive to hold up to the highest resolve the actions of their followers. The general run of men are not always constant in their spiritual strength and vision and cannot maintain a high level of conduct and discipline for long. A vow is a device or a religious observance calculated to keep such persons up to their highest light.

> When a man reaches a high pitch of emotion he declares to the world what his intentions are and this brings to bear upon his actions a certain amount of public opinion which keeps him to his resolve. Vows have also been conceived as a bargain with God. I feel a vow is a helpful crutch, it is a protective hedge; it is a dam to raise the level but it is not the end nor is it of the highest.[41]

Further, Kumarappa felt that a person who has taken a vow ceases sooner or later—and more often sooner than later—to appeal to his ideals every time a difficult situation arises. He acts in a particular way, not because his ideals dictate that course but because he has taken a vow to do so.

A vow emphasizes the deed rather than the ideal behind it. The vow-maker is on a moral plane, not on the spiritual. Vows make us mentally lazy. We decide once and for all and we lose our moral exercise and in time our moral sense gets palsied. It is a short cut to get people to act in the way leaders will have them act, but it ultimately leads to cultural degeneration.[42]

Kumarappa also contended that vows and blind obedience to custom and authority had their share in causing the present degeneration in India, and that in the West the Christian churches (especially the Catholic Church) were not in accord with Christ's teaching in that they resorted to vows as concessions to the weakness of man. A vow is a decided falling off from spiritual grace to moral expediency—a substitute for determination rather than a stimulus to it. Kumarappa further pointed out that he had never felt the need for a vow or a pledge and that his reliance on his inward strength and determination carried him through. Finally, he wondered whether Gandhi was really forming a new concept midway between determination and vow, in which case another word had to be coined to express it.

Gandhi did not enter into any written controversy with Andrews on the subject of vows but he replied in full to Kumarappa. He felt that Kumarappa had misunderstood his meaning and this was in part because the word "vow" is an unsuitable equivalent for the original Sanskrit term *vrata* (a solemn resolve or a spiritual decision) or for the term *yama* (a spiritual exercise or self-imposed disciplinary rule or restraint) that is used in Patanjali's *Yoga Sutra*. He wrote to Kumarappa:

You seem to think of vows publicly administered to audiences. This may not be good. The vow I am thinking of is a promise made by one to oneself. We have to deal with two dwellers within, Rama and Ravana, God and Satan, Ormuzd and Ahriman. The one binds us to make us really free, and the other only appears to free us so as to bind us tight within his grips. A "vow" is a promise made to Rama to do or not to do a certain thing, which if good we want to do but have not the strength unless we are tied down, and which if bad we would avoid but have not the strength to avoid unless similarly tied down. This I hold to be a condition indispensable to growth. I grant that we are higher than the sun, how much more necessary for us to be at least as true and faithful as the sun, if not truer and more faithful? If in matters of commerce, a man who vacillates is useless, why should he fare otherwise in matters spiritual, which carry with them infinitely greater consequences? If you hold that I must speak and do the right thing at any cost, you grant my whole position and so you also do if you grant that at the peril of my life I should be faithful to my wife or friend. You can easily multiply such instances. For me Jesus was preeminently a man of unshakable resolution, i.e., vows. His yea was yea for ever. A life of vows is like a marriage, a sacrament.[43]

In another letter, he wrote that if a man makes an unalterable decision to do or not to do a particular thing, it is to be regarded as a vow.

The strongest men have been known at times to have become weak. God has a way of confounding us in our strength. Hence the necessity of vows, i.e., invoking God's assistance to give us strength at the crucial moment. But I must not strive with you. It seems to me that we mean the same thing but express it differently—you in Spanish and I in Italian, shall we say?[44]

To Gandhi a vow really means unflinching determination, without which progress is impossible; this could appear as inflexibility in our relations with others. He felt that our respect for each other in society must be based upon and can come only through the cultivation of firmness in adherence to carefully formulated and freely chosen ideals. In an atmosphere of moral flabbiness and general unreliability there could be no real basis for mutual respect amid both disagreements and concord. All men are tested precisely at those moments when they are most tempted to deviate from their declared purposes. "Determination is worth nothing if it bends before discomfort. The universal experience of humanity supports the view, that progress is impossible without inflexible determination."[45]

Gandhi denied that there could be a vow to commit a sin, for he believed that if such a vow is sincerely made, there arises in time a clear and compelling necessity to give it up. Vows should not be taken about dubious matters. They can be taken only on the basis of universally recognized principles. The example of a man who gives up his life rather than his vow to uphold a generally accepted principle is likely to wean the weak from their ways, and thus becomes a great power for good in the world.

To do at any cost something that one ought to do constitutes a vow. It becomes a bulwark of strength. Gandhi felt that a man who says that he will do something as far as possible betrays either his pride or his weakness. The limitation "as far as possible" provides a fatal loophole. All business depends upon men fulfilling their promises with a certainty that can be counted upon except under entirely unforeseen conditions, and if possible even under great strain or what may seem to be extenuating circumstances. "The sun is a great keeper of observances; hence the possibility of measuring time and publishing almanacs."[46] Similarly, Gandhi felt, in a society in which at least a few men set the example of impeccable adherence to generally cherished ends, and in which most men recognize the need for the utmost dependability in social relationships and in political life, there is the maximum possible stability, harmony and the assurance of moral advance.

In order to understand Gandhi's position regarding vows, it is necessary to put it in the context of Indian tradition and especially of his active faith in the truth of the doctrine of re-birth. For a believer in re-birth, it is impossible to lay down in advance the extent of moral development and spiritual resolve of which any man is capable. Gandhi believed that we must regard all men as potentially divine, that moral failure is less blameworthy than the lowering of ideals or the general levels of mutual trust in human society. The willingness of the spirit is more important than the weakness of the flesh.

One of the oldest meanings of *vrata*, as found in the *Rigveda*, is "divine will or command." The order (*rta*) observable in nature was considered to be the consequence of the *vrata* of the gods, and it could be reflected in human society through the deliberate and vigilant performance of *dharma*. The instinctual behavior of the lower kingdoms and the motions of natural objects have a rhythm and a reliability that men must consciously emulate if they are to become conscious embodiments of the divine power that pervades the universe. Any conscious or unconscious infringement of the divine order is to be expiated by imposing on oneself some sort of self-denial. Such a resort to *vrata* was supposed to purify the performer and elevate him spiritually. In course of time, *vrata* was made to connote any observance or activity raised to the position of sacrosanctity and unquestionable authority and thus came to refer also to social obligations.[47] The observance of vows was even more necessary for the aspirant to a life of complete renunciation or for a seeker after mystical attainment as in Patanjali's *Yoga Sutra*. The Jains, for their part, distinguished between *anuvrata*s and *mahavrata*s, minor and major vows.

To Gandhi, as to the Buddha, the pursuit of salvation is a form of exalted selfishness unless it means the detached, dedicated service of humanity for its own sake. All of us are obliged to place our resources at the disposal of humanity. The social and political reformer requires a rigorous discipline no less than the mystic or the recluse; in fact, he needs it even more insofar as he has chosen the more exacting task of introducing the monastic ideal into politics and society. Gandhi was more concerned with the elevation of his fellow men through his own example and teaching than with his own salvation or self-realization. He thought that each man must discover his own *dharma* for himself, as taught in the *Gita*, and he has to discipline himself through his own self-chosen vows rather than through the duties of his station as determined by social convention and custom. Whether a man resorts to minor or to major vows depends entirely on himself and not on his mode of pursuit of moral ends as laid down by tradition in terms of his caste or vocation. Gandhi also refused to distinguish sharply between minor and major vows as in the long run they are seen to be interdependent and indivisible.

The Jains stressed that "he who conquers one thing [egoism] conquers many things [the various known vices]," that he who becomes truly selfless ceases to bother about any of the familiar desires of men. Gandhi too taught that all the disciplines are of equal importance; if one is broken, all are broken. Spiritual and social life were indivisible for him and he, therefore, gave an original and daring formulation to the traditional Indian doctrine of *vrata* in its application to daily life. He discarded the distinction between recluse and rebel, mystic and moralist, religion and politics, monastic and mundane life. He defended his concept of a vow both in religious and in social terms, on absolutist and on utilitarian grounds, thus confusing some of his followers while at the same time confounding his critics. His practical intention was to exalt disinterested action over passive detachment and human service over personal salvation among Indians, while at the same time showing that the path of active participation in human society and in politics did not preclude the cultivation of inward detachment and the pursuit of salvation.

PLEDGES AND CONTRACTS

To say that vows are impractical in our day and age because they would be unwisely taken by impetuous idealists and pushed to fanatical extremes, or because they could become the means through which religious organizations or authoritarian leaders hold their followers, is to mistake effects for causes and to miss the main point of Gandhi's stand. A promise does not preclude the right to change one's course if one's moral growth requires the repudiation of ill-considered pledges. A man's solemn promise to himself to try at all times to live up to the best that he knows, is not given to anyone else, nor is it subject to changes of place and time. Such a promise would increase in value to the extent that external contracts and guarantees are no longer needed. Through the misuse of a vow, men bind themselves to partialities, often to blindness and a blunting of the ever-growing moral sense. But through the proper use of a vow, a man may be able to identify himself unconditionally with the noblest principles of morality as understood by him. In modern society the validity of a contract rests upon the reasonableness of its terms. In Western law contracts are good when they define relations within reasonable limits of uncertainty. Understanding of the legitimate functions of contracts and pledges brings a greater tendency to enforce the fulfillment of those that are inherently reasonable.

Durkheim has thrown much light on the process by which reciprocal pacts as well as "unilateral contracts" and oaths came to acquire a solemn, binding and even sacred character. Human wills can bind themselves only by being projected outwardly. Juridical formalism is only a substitute for sacred formalities and religious rites. Individual wills have to become known so that society may attach a moral significance to them.

This declaration or outward manifestation is done by the aid of words. Now, there is something in words that is real, natural and living, something that can be endowed with a sacred force thanks to which, once pronounced, they should have the power to bind and to compel those who pronounce them. It is enough for them to be uttered according to a certain ritual form and in certain ritual conditions. Henceforward, they have become sacred. We can well imagine that words, once they have assumed this sacred quality, impose respect on those who have uttered them. They carry the same prestige as those persons and things which are themselves the object of rights and duties. They too, therefore, may be a source of obligations. . . . In these circumstances, once the words have left the lips of the contracting party, they are no longer his own, they have become something exterior to him, for they have changed in nature. . . . He can no longer change them and he is bound to carry them out. The oath, too, is a means of communicating to words, that is, to the direct manifestations of the human will, the kind of transcendence we see in all moral things.[48]

Hume contended that a man who promises anything subjects himself to the penalty of never being trusted again in case of failure. "Interest is the first obligation to the performance of promises."[49] Very little experience of the world is needed to make us perceive the consequences and advantages of promises. "The shortest experience of society discovers them to every mortal; and when each individual perceives the same sense of interest in all his fellows, he immediately performs his part of any contract, as being assured that they will not be wanting in theirs."[50] He further contended that since every new promise imposes a new obligation of morality on the person who promises, and since this new obligation arises from his will, "it is one of the most mysterious operations that can possibly be imagined, and may even be compared to transubstantiation or holy orders, where a certain form of words, along with a certain intention, changes entirely the nature of an external object, and even of a human creature."[51] And yet, to Hume, because the obligation of promises is an invention in the interest of society, it is "warped into as many different forms as that interest requires, and even runs into direct contradictions, rather than lose sight of

its object."[52] Promises carry no natural obligation and are mere artificial contrivances for the convenience and advantage of society.

Gandhi was prepared to urge the utilitarian advantages of vows
for human society, but this was by no means enough or even in-
nocuous in itself. If every member of society bases his reliance on
promises purely on the trustworthiness of others and makes the latter a pre-condition of his own promise, the level of social and political morality would gradually sink to a standard of safety that
cannot be conducive to heroism and sacrifice and the willingness to
hold to one's own word of honor without counting the cost in times
of trial. Hence Gandhi was more concerned with promises made to
oneself than with those made to others. A vow is a way of binding
oneself to help oneself, a means of measuring the trust one can
place in oneself.

The sanctity of vows was more important to Gandhi than their
utility. The utilitarian standpoint brings promises made between
the members of society to the same plane of pragmatic considerations as the laws of the State. It is not easy to appeal against the
laws of the State, however unjust, on the basis of one's pledge to
oneself if the pledge is itself taken wholly from prudential and in-
ferential considerations. No doubt, a principle accepted on purely
utilitarian grounds can be used to justify disobedience to law, and
such a principle might be the subject of a vow. But this, though
quite conceivable, is much less likely to be common or effective
than a pledge taken on non-utilitarian grounds. The purification of
politics requires that we get beyond pragmatic tests to absolute
values.

Gandhi's view comes close to that of Proudhon, who regarded
the concept of compacts as a commandment of morality rather
than a legal or a social norm. "That I may remain free, that I may
be subjected to no law but my own, and that I may govern myself,
the edifice of society must be rebuilt upon the ideas of contract."[53]
Every man is free to accept or to refuse the rules of fair play and
to form part of the society of savages, or to join the fellowship of
the human race.

When I bargain for any object with one or more of my fellow-
citizens, it is clear that then my will alone is my law; it is I my-

self who, in fulfilling my obligation, am my government. If then I could make that contract with all, which I do make with some, if all could renew it with each other; if every group of citizens, commune, canton, department, corporation, company, etc., formed by such a contract and considered as a moral person, could then, always on the same terms treat with each of the other groups and with all, it would be exactly as if my will was repeated *ad infinitum*. I should be sure that the law thus made on all points that concern the republic on the various motions of millions of persons, would never be anything but my law; and, if this new order of things was called government, that this government would be mine. The regime of contracts, substituted for the regime of laws, would constitute the true government of man and of the citizen, the true sovereignty of the people, the *REPUBLIC*.[54]

Gandhi, like Proudhon, held to an anarchist vision of a society in which coercion would be replaced by concord and the laws of the State would increasingly become unnecessary in view of the certainty of the reciprocal relationships of trust and obligation into which all men enter. Proudhon, however, put his faith in the magic of a simultaneous act of collective will to give mutual agreements the flavor of complete freedom. Hume, on the other hand, talked in terms of the mysterious process of transubstantiation by which sanctity is seemingly given promises entered into on the basis of mutual advantage and the recognition of common interest over a period of time. Both of them were eager to stress the contrived and deliberate human character of the achieved concord and interdependence. They did not rely on an act of God or any form of divine authority for the attainment of a social and political end. And yet they could not, any more than any of the propounders of a social contract in the West, dispense with some form of magical or fortuitous and spontaneous concurrence of common sense or free action.

The very word "sanction" is derived from the verb *sancire*, which is related to *sacer* (holy), and means to sanctify, to make inviolable through religious consecration. Those things which are by their nature unstable and precarious, whose functioning depends on the insight and will of men, tend to establish themselves more firmly through the appeal to religious sanction. No doubt Bentham thought we could dispense with the notion of the conscience, the *forum internum*, and every religious sanction. For him, only the principle of pleasure meets "the two essential requirements of an ethical formula"—it should be incontestable or self-evident and it should be incapable of being misused. All higher forms of sanction are subject to error and misuse. There is, however, no reason to assume that the physical sanction or the pleasure principle is unambiguous and reliable. It is also dependent on a being endowed with free will and variable understanding and is decisively influenced by other sanctions. Human societies embody evolving systems of sanctions. In the course of history, systems of sanctions compete for the dignity of being regarded as the ultimately valid and determining forces of life. Gandhi felt—like the anarchist Proudhon but unlike the conservative Hume—that the system of sanctions in modern society suffers from the lack of absolute authenticity and authoritative force at a time of moral disintegration. He thought it necessary and possible to bring all social relationships to the level of sanctity of our individual contract with our deepest self and with God.

Gandhi did not believe that before a reform of the social order can be made effective all men must first be converted to a life of exemplary virtue and strenuous vow-keeping. This would be merely a pharisaical pretext for avoiding any effort at radical social reform, an excuse for apathy arising out of intellectual distortion. Revolutions are the work of comparatively small groups of men who consecrate all their energies to the task. It is to these men that Gandhi addressed himself, while also hoping to disturb the complacency of a much larger section of society. He was convinced that we can only transform the social order of the modern world by affecting at the same time, and first of all, a renewal of moral and spiritual life in responsive individuals, by digging down to the moral and spiritual foundations of human existence, by awakening a new impulse in the hidden depths of social life. He felt that it is high time that sanctity should descend from the cloistered life to the world of secular culture, and labor in social and political affairs so as to reform the temporal order of mankind. Will not sanctity suffer in the process? If it remains inviolable, will it be sufficiently effective? Such questions are not new and could be asked by sympathetic critics as well as confirmed cynics. Gandhi's answer could only be that the world has known leaders of the people who were saints, that if the good society is ever to be achieved on earth and replace a civilization he regarded as "satanic," it will be the work of such moral leaders whose lives are sanctified by vows and immersed in the continual service of their fellow men.

5

HUMAN NATURE, PROGRESS, AND PERFECTIBILITY

What has for centuries raised man above the beast is not the cudgel but an inward music: the irresistible power of unarmed truth, the attraction of its example.

BORIS PASTERNAK

The term perfectible . . . not only does not imply the capacity of being brought to perfection, but stands in express opposition to it. If we could arrive at perfection, there would be an end to our improvement.

GEORGE GODWIN

Gandhi's indictment of modern civilization, his view of politics and especially of social and individual ethics, are firmly based upon his assumptions regarding human nature and human perfectibility. He started with a very definite conviction about what man is in his essential nature and of what he becomes through a false view of himself, of what he should be and can become, and of his place in a law-governed cosmos. All political theory must begin with some coherent view of the psychology of man, at least insofar as it affects his moral aims and conduct in society. This does not necessarily mean that human nature must be seen as a static and permanent, uniform and unvarying, substratum underlying all human activities. No empirical studies of social relationships can answer the more fundamental questions, involving assumptions and theories regarding human nature, that moral and political philosophers have raised.

Marx's failure to formulate a clear conception of human nature makes it easier for us to regard him as a crusader and a powerful propagandist rather than as a political thinker, in the strict sense. It is, of course, true that Marx did ask and attempt to answer questions about human nature in his early philosophical writings, but he entirely ignored them in his later works in which Marxism, as a system, was elaborated. Hobbes, on the other hand, began his political theory with a psychological theory, apparently empirical but essentially *a priori*; his mechanistic, authoritarian picture of the State was devised for a fear-driven, self-seeking humanity that could be manipulated. Locke, and later on Mill, advocated a mild and minimal role for government on the assumption that man was naturally a harmless and self-improving creature and that his economic aims and activities were automatically helpful to society.

Political theory which does not start from a theory of human nature tends to become either pretentious or trivial. The choice between an optimistic conception (from Plato to Kant) and a pessimistic view (from St. Augustine to Hobbes) of human nature is logically independent of the choice between an open and a closed view of human nature, or again, of the choice between the acceptance and the rejection of the perfectibility of man, or finally, the degree of power and autonomy that is granted to man in relation to Nature (or God) and his material and social environment. Since the seventeenth century many political thinkers in the West have taken for granted that human nature possesses a characteristic and constant structure, the essential features of which could be formulated as a result of introspective insight and detached observation, or as the necessary corollary of a coherent rational theory of the universe. Even Hume, who had no use for the idea of natural law or transcendental order, did not doubt that there are "the constant and universal principles of human nature." This assumption has been questioned or set aside in our own agnostic and skeptical age. In Vedic India and in Pythagorean Greece, man was regarded as a microcosm of the macrocosm. In order to understand man we must contemplate the cosmos. Any theory of human nature, as Feuerbach recognized more clearly than perhaps anyone else, must not only point to the essential difference between man and the brute but also between man and God (or Nature). Man is both an observer, standing apparently outside the world, and an agent affecting and affected by the world. Man converses with himself but can also put himself in the place of another, and his essential nature is an object of thought. A human being, unlike an animal, can formulate and articulate his intention to act for his own benefit or for the good of others, according to his own conception of himself in relation to others as well as his view of the world around him and his expectation of an order of events in the future.

Political philosophy involves a search for "a definition of man" and the major political thinkers differ in the accounts they give of the powers essential to men. This means both description and prescription; the facts are verifiable but cannot be conclusively settled, the values and choices commended may be defended or disputed in terms of moral principles and common experience, but must in the end be left for each individual to test for himself. Man first of all sees his nature as if out of himself, before he finds it in himself. Man also denies to himself only what he attributes to God or Nature. Alternatively, what a man declares concerning God or Nature, he in truth declares concerning himself. Augustinianism puts God in the place of man; Pelagianism puts man in the place of God. The denial of the divinity of man is usually accompanied by the humanization of God in the image of what man would like to be but could never become. The denial of God often leads to the deification of man.

In secular philosophies, the elevation of man is usually achieved through a mechanistic conception of nature and the belief that human reason is capable of comprehending and manipulating the world. On the other hand, it is possible to stress the impotence and the irrationality of man in relation to a determinist view of the world or a historicist view of society as an objective and independent reality in time. In any case, it is not easy to dispense with "the para-political myth" regarding man, for it is deeply embedded in our language.[1]

Where does Gandhi stand in relation to all this? Human nature, he repeatedly asserted, will find itself only when it fully realizes that to become human it has to cease to be bestial or brutal.[2] He claimed, in 1921, to be a fairly accurate student of human nature and "vivisector of my own failings. I have discovered that man is superior to the system he propounds."[3] In his autobiography, he declared that the brute by nature knows no self-restraint, and man is man because he is capable of, and only insofar as he exercises, self-restraint.[4] Elsewhere, he states that the duty of renunciation differentiates mankind from the beast.[5] Man becomes great exactly to the degree to which he works for the welfare of his fellow men.[6]

The differences between men are merely those of degree, not of kind. "We were, perhaps, all originally brutes. I am prepared to believe that we have become men by a slow process of evolution from the brute."[7] To the extent of this Darwinian element in his thought, Gandhi was more a Victorian than a Hindu. Again, "man must choose either of the two courses, the upward or the downward, but as he has the brute in him he will more easily choose the downward course than the upward, especially when the downward course is presented to him in a beautiful garb."[8] The "downward instinct" is embodied in all men. Gandhi claimed that he was not a visionary but a practical idealist, and that non-violence is the law of our species as violence is the law of the brute. The moment a man awakens to the spirit within he cannot remain violent.[9] The essential difference between man and the brute is that the former can respond to the call of the spirit in him, can rise superior to the passions, to selfishness and violence, which belong to brute nature and not to the immortal spirit of man. "This is the fundamental conception of Hinduism, which has years of penance and austerity at the back of the discovery of this truth."[10]

Fundamentally, Gandhi believed in what he called the absolute oneness of God and therefore also of humanity. "The rays of the sun are many through refraction. But they have the same source."[11] He was fond of quoting the Mohammedan saying: "Man is not God; but neither is he different from the light (or spark) of God— *adam khuda nahin, lekin khuda ka nur se adam juda nahin.*" The essence of his position is contained in his statement that "we were thus born with brute strength but we were born men to realize God who dwells in us. That indeed is the privilege of man and it distinguishes him from the brute creation."[12] Man is bestial in origin but he is human precisely because he is potentially and essentially divine. It is not that Gandhi offers a simple dualistic view of man, but rather that man is neither brute nor God and is human insofar as he uniquely possesses the power of choice that determines either the increasing brutalization of his nature and a reliance on instinctual violence (reinforced by intellectual violence), or his increasing awareness and manifestation and consequent realization of his innate divinity. To become divine is to become attuned in thought, feeling and act to the whole of creation. More specifically, human nature at its best is seen when "it acts equally towards all and in all circumstances it approaches the divine."[13]

Gandhi declared explicitly that he was a believer in *Advaita* (the Indian doctrine of monism), "the essential unity of God and man and for that matter of all that lives."[14] This is similar to the Stoic idea of the universe as a divine whole and of mankind as an essential unity in which the individual can realize himself. Man alone is made in the image of God.

That some of us do not recognize that status of ours, makes no difference, except that then we do not get the benefit of the status, even as a lion brought up in the company of sheep may not know his own status and therefore does not receive its benefits; but it belongs to him nevertheless, and, the moment he realizes it, he begins to exercise his dominion over the sheep. But no sheep masquerading as a lion can ever attain the leonine status.[15]

He argued that to prove the proposition that man is made in the image of God, it is surely unnecessary to show that all men admittedly exhibit that image in their own persons.[16] It is enough to show that one man at least has done so. "And, will it be denied that the great religious teachers of mankind have exhibited the image of God in their own persons?"[17] At the same time, the *hubris* of man needs to be corrected by a contemplation of nature. "When we look at the sky, we have a conception of infinity, cleanliness, orderliness and grandeur which is purifying for us. . . . When once we are in tune with the sky, the nature of our environment on earth ceases to have any significance for us."[18] Man must adopt a correct mental posture, neither too high nor too low, as was taught in the *Gita*.

The doctrine of man's oneness with God and humanity has several implications. First of all, this doctrine is incompatible with the belief that an individual may gain spiritually and those that surround him suffer. Gandhi believed that if one man gains spiritually, the whole world gains with him and if one man falls, the whole world falls to that extent.[19] There is not a single virtue which aims at, or is content with, the welfare of the individual alone. Conversely, there is not a single moral offence which does not, directly or indirectly, affect many others besides the actual offender. Hence, whether an individual is good or bad is not merely his own concern, but really the concern of the whole community, indeed of the whole world.[20] Secondly, the monistic doctrine implies that all human beings are working consciously or unconsciously toward the realization of that identity.[21] Furthermore, "I believe that the sum total of the energy of mankind is not to bring us down but to lift us up."[22]

Thirdly, what one man is capable of achieving is possible for all to attain.[23] "All mankind in essence are alike. What is therefore possible for me, is possible for everybody. . . ."[24] Gandhi did not go so far as the Stoics did in regarding man as "cosmopolitical," designed to form by deliberate effort a single community with one common law, a "City of Zeus" or universal *communis deorum et hominum civitas.* To Gandhi the moral solidarity of mankind was an ever-present fact rather than merely a contrived political ideal that remains to be realized. Further, "I have been taught from my childhood, and I have tested the truth by experience, that primary virtues of mankind are possible of cultivation by the meanest of the human species. It is this undoubted universal possibility that distinguishes the human from the rest of God's creation."[25]

Fourthly, it is quite proper to resist and attack a system, but to attack and resist the author is tantamount to resisting and attacking oneself. "For we are all tarred with the same brush, and are children of one and the same. Creator, and as such divine powers within us are infinite. To slight a single human being is to slight those divine powers, and thus to harm not only that human being, but with him the whole world."[26]

Fifthly, man's ultimate aim is the realization of God, and all his activities, social, political, religious, have to be guided by the ultimate aim of the vision of God. The immediate service of all human beings becomes a necessary part of the endeavor, simply because the only way to find God is to see God in creation and be one with it. This can be done only by service of all. "I am a part and parcel of the whole, and I cannot find Him apart from the rest of humanity."[27] Again,

> . . . true individuality consists in reducing oneself to zero. The secret of life is selfless service. The highest ideal for us is to become *vitaraga* (free from attachment). Ethical rules were framed by *rishis* (seers) on the basis of personal experience. A *rishi* is one who has realized for himself. *Sannyasa* in the *Gita* is renunciation of actions inspired by desire (*kama*). He is a man who is the ruler over his body.[28]

Clearly, then, the divinity of man manifests itself according to the extent to which he realizes his humanity, i.e., his oneness with his fellow men. For Gandhi, as for Spinoza, men must unite themselves "by bonds that make all of them as one man." The unity between all men, though veiled from common sight, is in fact as "real" as the idea of separateness is to a man still under the spell of his senses. Although at times Gandhi spoke of God as a person and the ideal man as a servant (*dasa*) of God, he really regarded God, as the Stoics did, as an indefinable and universal Power that cannot be conceived apart from humanity or from the whole of nature. Each man is a ray or a part (*amsha*) of that divine Power that underlies all change, that is changeless, that holds all together, that creates, dissolves and re-creates[29] all forms of life.

Every man is born into the world with certain natural tendencies that are variable and alterable, while at the same time he is born with certain definite limitations that he cannot overcome. While admitting that man usually lives by habit, Gandhi held that it is better for him to live by the exercise of the will.[30] Men are capable of developing their will to an extent that could reduce exploitation by others to a minimum and make them capable of self-rule. Man's triumph consists in replacing the struggle for existence by a struggle for mutual service.[31] Man is a thinking no less than a feeling animal. To renounce the sovereignty of reason over the blind instincts is, therefore, to renounce a man's estate.

> Man's estate is one of probation. During that period he is played upon by evil forces as well as good. He is ever prey to temptations. He has to prove his manliness by resisting and fighting temptations. He is no warrior who fights outside foes of his imagination, and is powerless to lift a finger against the innumerable foes within, or what is worse, mistakes them as friends.[32]

In man, reason quickens and guides the feeling; in the brute, the soul ever lies dormant. To awaken the heart is to arouse the dormant soul, to awaken reason and to inculcate discrimination between good and evil.[33] "The rule of all without the rule of self is deceptive and disappointing, as a painted toy mango."[34]

Gandhi recognized that in spite of the greatest effort to be detached, no man can altogether undo the effect of his environment or his upbringing. But he believed that man is essentially capable of self-direction. It is "man's privilege to overcome adverse circumstance."[35] Manliness consists in making circumstances subserve ourselves. Those who will not heed themselves perish. To understand this principle is not to be impatient, not to reproach fate, nor to blame others. "He who understands the doctrine of self-help blames himself for failure."[36] He argued that while in *Kali Yuga* the level of practice had deteriorated, the mind of man in history had progressed a great deal. Man's practice has not been able to keep pace with his mind.

> Man has begun to say, "This is wrong, that is wrong." Whereas previously he justified his conduct, he now no longer justifies his own or his neighbour's. He wants to set right the wrong, but he does not know that his own practice fails him. The contradiction between his theory and his practice fetters him. His conduct is not governed by logic.[37]

Self-direction, for Gandhi, involves passing moral judgment on one's own behavior, justifying or condemning it. But man mistakenly believes he has set right what was wrong; he tries, fails and does not always recognize that he has failed. Yet, he progresses at least insofar as he recognizes as wrong what he once regarded as right, and he tries to avoid it, even if he cannot always assess correctly his level of effort and the extent of his failure. What distinguishes man from the brute is his ceaseless striving to rise above the brute on the moral plane. "Mankind is at the cross-roads. It has to make its choice between the law of the jungle and the law of humanity."[38]

Gandhi had thus a frankly optimistic view of human nature. "I am an irrepressible optimist. . . . My optimism rests on my belief in the infinite possibilities of the individual to develop nonviolence."[39] And yet in practice Gandhi was often more inclined to deny a pessimistic view than to uphold a positively optimistic view of human nature. "I refuse to believe that the tendency of human nature is always downward,"[40] he declared in 1926, and stated the next year, "Men like me cling to their faith in human nature . . . all appearances to the contrary notwithstanding."[41] In fact, it is in moments of trial that human nature shows itself at its best.[42]

> I know that people who voluntarily undergo a course of suffering raise themselves and the whole of humanity, but I also know that people, who become brutalized in their desperate efforts to get victory over their opponents, or to exploit weaker nations or weaker men not only drag down themselves but mankind also. And it cannot be a matter of pleasure to me or anyone else to see human nature dragged in the mire. If we are all sons of the same God, and partake of the same divine essence, we must partake of

the sin of every person whether he belongs to us or to another
race. You can understand how repugnant it must be to invoke
the beast in any human being.[43]

Though we have the human form, without the attainment of the
virtue of non-violence we still share the qualities of "our remote
reputed ancestor the orangoutang."[44] In 1938 Gandhi again declared, "man's nature is not essentially evil; brute nature has been
known to yield to the influence of love. You must never despair of
human nature."[45]

ORIGINAL GOODNESS AND HUMAN PERFECTIBILITY

Gandhi's greater concern for the rejection of a pessimistic view
than the dogmatic assertion of an optimistic view of human nature
can be better understood in the light of Kant's essay "On the Radical Evil in Human Nature." Kant distinguishes between the frailty,
the impurity and the depravity of human nature. To Gandhi as to
Kant, frailty is an inevitable result of the weakness of the will,
which could in principle be remedied; impurity is the unfortunate
consequence of the fact that even our purest motives are not wholly
untainted by considerations other than the highest; while depravity
points to the corruption rather than the inherent evil of the human
heart.

Kant contended that every bad action, when we inquire into its
rational origin, must be viewed as if the man had fallen into it directly from a state of innocence through a free exercise of his elec-
tive will. Man may fall into evil by seduction, yet the original constitution is adapted to good and it could not be corrupted by any
other than man himself, if he is to be held to be accountable for his
corruption. We must presuppose that a germ of good has remained
in its complete purity, indestructible and incorruptible, and in this
way the propensity to evil is compatible with a high view of human
nature and a belief in the original capacity for good.

The moral culture of man must begin not with improvement of
morals but with a transformation of the mind and the training of
the will. This is why Gandhi insisted: "Man and his deed are two
distinct things. Whereas a good deed should call forth approbation and a wicked deed disapprobation, the doer of the deed,

whether good or wicked, always deserves respect or pity as the case may be."[46]

When Mencius said that human nature is good he was in some degree speaking tautologically, because in the last analysis he seems to have meant by the "good" that which is in harmony with human nature. Gandhi gets round this difficulty by bringing God into his account, God taken as equivalent to the oneness of all life. Man is good because he is divine, i.e., capable of realizing his kinship with the whole of creation and especially the rest of humanity. For Gandhi, as for the Confucians, an evil man is one who does not change, not one who cannot be changed. To Mencius a man's nature is naturally good just as water flows naturally downward; this is attested by the fact that man is teachable. The consequence of this doctrine of original goodness is that humanity cannot be divided into good and bad; there are only evil acts, no wholly evil men. Gandhi, however, felt that it was more important at times to combat the doctrine of original sin than to argue for the doctrine of original goodness.

At times Gandhi confined himself to pleading for an open rather than a closed and fixed view of human nature and of human possibilities. Human life is a series of compromises, but although it is not always easy to achieve in practice what one holds to be true in theory,[47] it is both unwise and unjustifiable to lower the theoretical ideal of human development. "Let us be sure of our ideal. We shall ever fail to realize it, but shall never cease to strive for it."[48] The ideal will cease to be one if it becomes possible to realize it. The pleasure lies in making the effort, not in its fulfillment.[49] Yet, "ideals must work in practice, otherwise they are not potent."[50] When a man works for an ideal, he becomes irresistible.[51] We must believe, if we are to be truly human, that it is more natural to be good than it is to be evil, "though apparently descent is easier than ascent."[52] "Who can predict the future?" he asked.[53]

The virtue of an ideal lies in its boundlessness. But although religious ideals must thus from their very nature remain unattainable by imperfect human beings, although by virtue of their boundlessness they may seem ever to recede farther away from us, the nearer we go to them, still they are closer to us than our very hands and feet because we are more certain of their reality and truth than even our own physical being. "This faith in one's ideals alone constitutes true life, in fact it is man's all in all."[54] Man does not become divine when he personifies the innocence of faith in himself. Only then does he become truly man. In our present state, no doubt we are in part man and in part beast, but in our ignorance and even arrogance we say that we truly fulfill the purpose of our species when we behave like beasts.[55] It is not easy to efface the old *samskaras* or acquired tendencies of thought and character,[56] but we must reject "the theory of permanent inelasticity of human nature."[57] In the last analysis, Gandhi supported his view by his belief, so essential to the Buddha, that "nothing in this world is static, everything is kinetic. If there is no progression, there is inevitable retrogression."[58] Man has the supreme knack of deceiving himself,[59] and of failing to see that "human nature is such that man must either soar or sink."[60] We are the makers of our own destiny. "We can mend or mar the present and on that will depend the future."[61]

Thus Gandhi challenged all lukewarm theories of human nature that stress the possibility and the necessity of achieving an equilibrium or a balance between good and evil tendencies, just as he challenged all lukewarm theories of social equilibrium based upon a balance between the fears and the dreams, the bestial instincts and the moral aspirations of men. To stress the good or the evil is to become inevitably involved in a cumulative process of increasing good or of increasing evil; there can be no stability or certainty or reliability in any intermediate position. If no man is irretrievably evil, it is because it is in principle never too late to reverse gear or to alter one's course.

In support of Gandhi's view of human nature it could be argued, as the philosophers of the Enlightenment were apt to do, that man's naturally good (or rational) urges are vitiated not so much by irrational urges, instincts and passions, as by the false and even dangerous teaching about man's inherently evil nature; vested interests and tyrannical ambitions find in that theory a justification for their politics of oppression, exploitation and enslavement. To insist on the inherent evil of human nature only serves the evil purposes of cunning and greedy power-seekers.

It might be argued that it is odd to contend that anyone should want to teach what is false and corrupting in a world where men are naturally good. The doctrine of human goodness does not, however, imply that all men are good or that there are no selfish and evil tendencies in human nature. The very notion of original goodness would have no meaning if it wholly excluded the existence of any evil. In a sense, the advocates of the doctrine of original goodness are suggesting that in existing societies human nature has been prevented from retaining its natural virtue or from coming into its own. This could, however, be pushed too far, as Marx did in holding that we could know what human nature is really like only in the classless society of the future. In this case the doctrine of human goodness is emptied of any immediate significance, and it is not surprising that Marx neither held to such a doctrine nor explicitly to its opposite. The thinkers of the Enlightenment believed in the inherent goodness of man and at the same time thought that ignorance and error give birth to passions which restrict the free flow of the finer tendencies in human nature.

Alternatively, it is possible to take a less dramatic view and to argue that a river cannot rise above its source, that it is better to believe in the original goodness than in the original evil of human nature if we wish to transform men and to change society, that an excessive emphasis on the weakness of the flesh could render inert and inoperative the inherent willingness of the spirit. A man's image of himself can, and in fact does, affect him, and therefore even if it is not based on a provable theory, it can, within limits hard to define, produce its own verification. However, in the end it must be admitted that it would be unsatisfying though not self-contradictory to believe in human reason or human goodness without also believing in the rationality and progressive tendency of the universe or of human society if not of the entire course of human history. It is not strange that de Maistre, for instance, who at times refused to admit to there being a human nature as such (although he was prepared to believe in the dubious category of national character), also repudiated the basic assumption of the Enlightenment—the rationality of the universe. It is also not surprising that although Gandhi appeared at times to be pleading for an open view of human nature, he was really unable to support his doctrine of original goodness or his castigation of the doctrine of original sin without advancing also a theory of human perfectibility, divine grace and the upward tendency of cosmic and human evolution. *Dharma* or morality cannot be ultimately divorced from *ṛta* or cosmic order.

Man, according to Gandhi, will ever remain imperfect but "it will always be his part to try to be perfect."[62] There is nothing at a standstill in nature; only God or the ultimate, transcendental Reality, could be motionless, perfect and beyond evolution. Man is characteristically a progressive being, and yet, through mental inertia, is unable to see that the universally valid rules of conduct are fundamentally simple and easy to carry out.[63] Man believes and lives,[64] and no one dare be dogmatic about the capacity of human nature, in any particular instance, for degradation or exaltation.[65] No human being is so bad as to be beyond redemption; no human being is so perfect as to warrant his destroying him whom he wrongly considers to be wholly evil.[66] We must believe that every man can think for himself.[67] The rationality of human nature is the precondition of its theoretical perfectibility. Every individual must be regarded as an end and none as a means. We must assume that every man can understand his own powers through the head and that he has the heart to affirm in practice his faith in himself. Being necessarily limited by the bonds of the flesh, we can attain perfection only after the dissolution of the body.[68] Besides, "where would be room for that constant striving, that ceaseless quest after the ideal that is the basis of all spiritual progress, if mortals could reach the perfect state while still in the body?"[69] By perfectibility on earth, therefore, is meant the possibility of growing toward total awareness of our true nature, which is fundamentally identical with that of everything that lives.

Gandhi's belief in perfectibility is, in the final analysis, dependent upon his belief in rebirth. There is, of course, no necessary logical connection between the two doctrines. The species could be perfectible even if there were no rebirth as it may seem easier to hold to a notion of collective perfectibility than to believe that a man is perfectible in a single lifetime. Gandhi was concerned with individual, not collective, perfectibility. For him time was no consideration. If it takes time then it is but a speck in "the complete time cycle."[70] "I am a believer in previous births and rebirths. All our relationships are the result of the *samskara*s we carry from previous births."[71] Further, ". . . If for mastering the physical sciences you have to devote a whole lifetime, how many lifetimes may be needed for mastering the greatest spiritual force (non-violence) that mankind has known? For if this is the only permanent thing in life, if this is the only thing that counts, then whatever effort you bestow on mastering it is well spent."[72]

Thus Gandhi's faith in human perfectibility is not merely a moral conviction but is ultimately based upon metaphysical beliefs that not all men are ready to accept. But he was not so naïve as to think that men could be transformed overnight. "All men are imperfect, and when imperfection is observed in someone in a larger measure than in others, people are apt to blame him. But that is not fair. Man can change his temperament, can control it, but cannot eradicate it. God has not given him so much liberty. If the leopard can change his spots, then only can man modify the peculiarities of his spiritual constitution."[73] In fact, not only must we recognize that man is born to make mistakes, but we should magnify our own errors so as to be deterred from falling into them again.[74] We must be conscious of the fallibility of human nature and this must make us humble, without destroying our confident conviction in the truth as we see it.[75]

THE INTERPRETATION OF HISTORY

Gandhi's view of human nature is dependent on his interpretation of history as well as his view of cosmic evolution. "Life is an inspiration. Its mission is to strive after perfection, which is realization."[76] He believed in the power of the spirit of man to shape its environment to some extent and thus affect the course of history. He explicitly rejected the Marxist interpretation of history. He could not agree that our ideologies, ethical standards and values are altogether a product of our material environment.[77]

> The Marxist regards thought, as it were, as a "secretion of the brain" and the mind, "a reflex of the material environment." I cannot accept that. . . . If I have an awareness of that living principle within me, no one can fetter my mind. The body might be destroyed, the spirit will proclaim its freedom. This to me is not a theory; it is a fact of experience.[78]

When Gandhi said that he did not believe that it is *prakriti* (matter) which originates and governs the thought-processes of *purusha* (spirit),[79] he was clearly enunciating a faith and a belief that are not susceptible to proof any more than is the opposite view.

Gandhi was convinced that what was good in Marxism was not original or exclusive to it, and what was exclusive to it was not necessarily good.[80]

> My quarrel with the Marxists is that even if the paradise of material satisfactions, which they envisage as their final goal, were realized on earth, it would not bring mankind either contentment or peace. But I was wondering whether we cannot take the best out of Marxism and turn it to account for the realization of our social aims.[81]

He believed that what had made the teaching of Marx dynamic was that he regarded mankind as a whole and, transcending class divisions, identified himself with the cause of the poor oppressed toilers of the world. "But in that he is not alone. Others besides him have done the same."[82] While conceding the vision and dynamism of Marx, Gandhi explicitly rejected his reductionism.

> I do not consider economic factors to be the source of all the evils in the world. Nor is it correct to trace the origin of all wars to economic causes. What were the causes of the last war? [1914] Insignificances. . . . Was not Helen the cause of the Trojan War? but why go so far? The Rajput wars, which belong to modern history, had never their origin in economic causes.[83]

Gandhi's criticism of this Marxist interpretation of history was more just than profound, but he put his finger on the basic weakness of Marxism. "These people have concentrated their study on the depths of degradation to which human nature can descend. What use have they for the study of the heights to which human nature could rise?"[84]

The virtue of Gandhi's view of history lay for him in its being dynamic, hopeful and universal, but "ultimately it is the Unseen Power that governs the course of events—even in the minds of men who made those events."[85] Although he had a transcendentalist view of history, he could not, like Newman, ask "When was the face of human society . . . other than evil?"[86] To Newman

> . . . the whole visible course of things, nations, empires, states,
> politics, professions, trades, society, pursuits of all kinds . . .
> come of evil; they hold of evil, and they are instruments of evil;
> they have in them the nature of evil; they are the progeny of sin-
> ful Adam, they have in them the infection of Adam's fall; they
> never would have been as we see them, but for Adam's fall.[87]

Gandhi could not possibly regard the whole world as a "confeder-
acy of evil." On the other hand, he was a theological teleologist[88]
who believed that just as God has a purpose for the universe as a
unit, God has a purpose for every particle of life too—for man as
well as the ant.[89] Gandhi wanted the lesson of humility to be
learned from the futile wars and crumbling empires of history. Man
is nothing when he sets himself up against the stream of life and
the divine purpose of the universe. "Napoleon planned much and
found himself a prisoner in St. Helena. The mighty Kaiser aimed at
the crown of Europe and is reduced to the status of a private gen-
tleman. . . . Let us contemplate such examples and be humble."[90]
And yet the role of the individual was central to Gandhi's view of
history. "Supposing Hitler were to die today, it would alter the
whole course of current history,"[91] he declared during his detention
at Poona in 1942.

Gandhi really wavered between the cyclical theory of historical
development current among the ancient Greeks and Hindus, and
the Augustinian conception of history as a kind of drama whose
central plot has been conceived prior to its enactment by human
beings. His view of history comes close to that of Herder, who
thought that history teaches us to act according to God's eternal
laws, that this earth is an inn for travelers, but also that "nothing
in nature stands still; everything exerts itself and pushes on,"[92] and
man is unique because, as essentially the most perfect of beings, he
is also the most perfectible. Gandhi would not have gone as far as
Pasternak, who said that "there are no nations, but only persons,"[93]
but he refused to believe, as Hegel did, that human societies and
nations have a character or soul even as the individual has. History
is not a cataclysmic affair and its internal dynamic is not one of
self-perpetuating conflict. Nor did Gandhi argue that everything is
inherently and inevitably progressive, that no event is wasted as it
contributes somehow to the realization of perfection. He held that

historical events constitute not merely a meaningful pattern but also conform to causal laws discoverable by man. No doubt he believed that "human society is a ceaseless growth, an unfoldment in terms of spirituality,"[94] but it is in relation to the mind of man and not in the field of knowledge or the realm of morals or in the sphere of social relations that we must look for the key to progress. Of course, the fact that mankind persists shows that "the cohesive force is greater than the disruptive force, the centripetal force greater than centrifugal."[95]

Our real source of hope lies in the progressive awareness by human beings of the need to replace brute force by deliberate non-violence, coercion by consent, paternalism by self-dependence. "History is really a record of every interruption of the even working of the force of love or of the soul. . . . History, then, is a record of an interruption in the course of nature. Soul-force, being natural, is not noted in history."[96]

The secular trend of improvement in mental awareness applies only to *Kali Yuga*, the age of darkness that began 5000 years ago, an age which must be fitted into a larger cyclical span. Human history is, for Gandhi, neither a unilinear trend of progress nor a static picture of eternal recurrence, but, rather, a spiral-like movement that is determined by the power of spirit over matter within the limits of the course plotted out by *Karma*, the compensatory law of ethical causation. There is a divine guarantee that good will ultimately triumph over evil, but he explicitly rejected the unilinear view of human progress, individual or collective. "Life is not one straight road. There are so many complexities in it. It is not like a train which, once started, keeps on running."[97] Although Gandhi, like Kant, believed that the end and purpose of human life is to achieve moral autonomy and freedom under self-imposed laws, he did not share Kant's basically unilinear conception of history in which mankind marches by slow degrees but inexorably toward an infinite end.

Gandhi did not base his confidence in the perfectibility of man either on human reason or on the progress of knowledge. He could not, like Helvetius, believe that "ignorance is always compelled before the immense power of the imperceptible progress of enlightenment."[98] Like Turgot, he implicitly repudiated the notion of mechanical progression; evil and error are necessary for the realization of progress and "the entire mass of humanity, by alternations of calm and agitation, good and evil, proceeds continuously, if slowly, towards a greater perfection."[99] In 1922 Gandhi wrote, "History is more a record of wonderful revolutions than of so-called ordered progress."[100] But he could not go so far as Turgot and regard "the tumultuous, dangerous passions" as a principle of action, and consequently of progress. Nor could he believe, like Condorcet and others, in any law of automatic progress which would necessarily guarantee that the future of humanity would be immeasurably brighter than the past. He was, of course, a teleologist to the extent that he regarded the cosmic and the historical process as a developmental series of events through which the true nature of man's perfection is destined to be realized, but this is secured by the triumph of spirit over matter in nature rather than by any independent historical law of social progress. Of course, if most human souls or monads progress from life to life more than they regress, then, assuming that new monads are not always coming into the world, society must make progress though there is no law of social progress, i.e., there is no tendency for an earlier social order to generate a higher social order out of itself. Society improves only because most of the souls that it includes continually make some progress. And yet, Gandhi did not pretend that the whole course of history and of evolution had reached its end station in our own times, still less did he hold, like Comte and Marx, that the present happens to fall into a unique category in the succession of ages.

It might be argued that, if Gandhi believed in a cosmic and historical process through which man's nature is perfected, he did implicitly believe in a law of social progress. There could, however, logically be a doctrine of perfectibility (i.e., a doctrine asserting not only that man is capable of improvement but tends to improve) unconnected with a law of social progress. It could be held (though implausibly) that on the whole, individuals tend to get better as they get older, or (and more plausibly) that they live many lives and on the whole tend to get better the more lives they have lived. The first alternative, though logically possible, is implausible because we have plenty of evidence that it is not true; the second alternative is more plausible because it is unfalsifiable. Whoever adopts it cannot be proved wrong by a single appeal to the facts. It is true that Gandhi did not believe merely that man is capable of improvement or merely that as a matter of fact he has improved but also that there is an inherent tendency to improve. Insofar as this tendency reveals itself through a historical process, we could say that there is an implied law of social progress. This very notion, however, is logically unsound. It is odd to talk of the collective progress of societies with the same ethical significance that belongs to the idea of individual self-improvement. Even Saint-Simon and Marx did not formulate precisely a law of social progress. They never made a clear and self-consistent statement whose truth could be tested by an appeal to the facts.

ASSESSMENT

Apart from the belief in rebirth (or palingenesis), Gandhi's views come closest to those of Godwin. He did not state explicitly that "mind, in a progressive view at least, is infinite,"[101] but he would have agreed with Godwin that if we could arrive at perfection at a future date, there would be an end to our improvement.[102] By perfectible is not meant the capability of being brought to final and total perfection on earth, but rather the possibility of being continually made better and receiving perpetual improvement, in the sense of coming closer to a realization of the oneness of humanity and of all life. Universal benevolence is an ideal toward which we can strive, and which if it can never be reached, can always be brought a little nearer. It is certainly always possible to widen the area of our sympathies, even if we cannot successfully remove all the barriers between men.

However, like Kant and Rousseau and unlike Godwin, Gandhi believed that the goodness of man is grounded not in some instinctive inclination of sympathy, but in man's capacity for self-determination. Its real proof lies not in the impulses of spontaneous affection but in the deliberate recognition of an ethical law to which the individual will surrenders voluntarily. What distinguishes man from all other beings is the gift of perfectibility so that he does not tarry in his actual condition but strives beyond it. Whereas Voltaire's pessimism remained playful, Gandhi's optimism, like Rousseau's, was filled with and sustained by tragic seriousness, despite his abundant fund of humor. He constantly demanded that men, instead of losing themselves in a passive acceptance of the miseries of existence, must understand their destiny and master it themselves. All his political and social ideals grow out of this demand.

The stress on human perfectibility is always related to the demand for a new society and a new vision of humanity. Gandhi was ever in dead earnest as a radical reformer although he never became an iconoclast. He always assumed that men would, simply because they could, avail themselves of the capacities that distinguished them from animals. He underestimated man's powers of self-destruction, as he despairingly realized toward the end of his life. Although Gandhi pleaded for an open view of human nature and stressed its variability and capacity for transformation, he sometimes tended to regard it as a constant, marked by a goodness in which we must not merely believe but which we can take as something ever-present. And yet, Gandhi's conception of human nature was essentially dynamic, and derived its urgency especially from the context of passivity, procrastination and cynicism which he found both in South Africa and in India.

In order to appreciate the full significance of Gandhi's view of human nature and human perfectibility, it is necessary to place it in the context of Indian thought and tradition. The Indian concern has always, in theory, been with transformation rather than information, with the radical reconstruction of man's nature, a renovation of his understanding both of the outer world and of his own existence—a transformation as total as possible, amounting to a complete conversion or a "second birth," the state of the true Brahmin, the "twice-born." All the classical schools of Indian philosophy include disciplines (*sadhana*), practical means for the attainment of the goal of self-transformation. The aim is not so much the perfection of reason or of virtue as the realization of the essential nature common to oneself and to all men, and also to God or the ultimate Reality. The essence of man is beyond reason and beyond all human relationships—a doctrine that is sometimes misunderstood to mean that the nature of man is wholly beyond all rational inquiry and wholly beyond all ordinary human relationships and ties.

In the Vedas we find no questions asked about human nature. It is taken for granted that man is the meeting point of the gods of the universe, the controlling forces of the cosmos. The world is a world of action, meant for action and sustained by action. Human action, when based upon a comprehension of the cosmic forces, can transform the nature of the universe. In the Upanishads man is viewed as being the imperfect or incomplete reproduction of the divine nature; as the seat of desire, which is to be eventually satisfied or destroyed; as controlled by the law of *Karma* and transmigration, which fixes one's condition after death, and one's inherited tendencies in the next life; and lastly, as capable of salvation, which he can hope to attain in the end, but also full of ignorance or false knowledge, which hinders that salvation. Each man is the manifestation on a small scale of what is manifested on a large scale in the whole world. The Upanishadic stress is, however, on contemplation rather than on action.

In *Kaushitaki* we have the trial of the soul, corresponding to the Egyptian judgment in the Hall of Osiris, or to the Persian test at the Bridge of the Separator. The myth given here describes the journey of a soul that goes out on the way of the Gods, after having learned the truth. The *Gita* is less explicitly concerned with cosmology; selfish desire, *kama*, is counted as the enemy of man and the root of all evil. The perfect man is both capable of absolute detachment and of disinterested action.

In the Buddhist tradition, man is considered specifically as a wayfarer, a *margayayin*, and the way is the way of the development of inwardness. "Look inward; thou art Buddha."[103] Jain metaphysics classifies the world into two categories, *jiva* (spirit) and *ajiva* (matter). Man is the *jiva* bound by matter and in his pure state is unconditioned and omniscient. For Buddhists and for Jains the world is a world of *Karma* or causality, which must be comprehended and transcended. The perfect man does not seek private salvation but works for the emancipation of the whole of humanity. The Indian epics also preach mainly the life of action for imperfect men, and the performance of daily duties is regarded as a more suitable path for ordinary men than the way of contemplation.

In all these different Indian schools men are bound together either by human *karma* (action) or by *prakriti* (matter) or by *purusha* (spirit), or by all three. The descent into matter is involuntary because it is beyond the powers of man, but once he emerges upon the cosmic scene, the ascent back to the primeval spirit depends upon man himself and upon voluntary effort. The universe is not hostile to man's spirit but he becomes misguided as to his true nature, due to ignorance and passion. Man is a peculiarly privileged creature with the choice between spiritual inwardness and extreme involvement into matter, but he cannot wholly avoid either the cycle of *pravritti* or outgoing, or the cycle of *nivritti* or withdrawal. Involvement in the world can be effective and not destructive only if it is based upon the strength that comes through inwardness; inwardness, on the other hand, can be fruitful and not escapist only if it is seen in the context of the world around us and of the true nature of things. Without inwardness, our involvement in the world can never rise to the level of universal conceptions of duty and of service to humanity. Without involvement, our inwardness can never rise to the stature of impersonality that characterizes the divine principle of life. Self-mastery and the service of others are interdependent aspects of moral and spiritual growth.

What Gandhi wished to stress was the potency in society of what he called "soul-force." While brute-force is based on egotism, which creates conflict and misery, soul-force is based on love, trust and humility, which create harmony and true happiness. To live egoistically, whether by pursuing self-conquest for its own sake or by seeking the conquest of power and consequent control over the lives of others, is simply to fly against the facts of cosmic and human interdependence and to be finally, if not periodically or even perpetually, frustrated. "I believe in the existence of a beneficent power that overrides and upsets all human plans. It even produces order out of chaos, and redresses wrongs in spite of the tyranny of tyrants."[104] We are living in the midst of death. "What is the value of 'working for our own schemes' when they might be reduced to naught? . . ."[105] But we may feel as strong as a rock, if we can truthfully say we work for schemes that are in accord with the Moral Law and the fundamental fact of universal solidarity. Then nothing perishes.

I have found that life persists in the midst of destruction and therefore there must be a higher law than that of destruction.

Only under that law would a well-ordered society be intelligible and life worth living. And if that is the law of life, we have to work it out in daily life. Whenever there are jars, wherever you are confronted with an opponent, conquer him with love. In this crude manner I have worked it out in my life. That does not mean that all my difficulties are solved. Only I have found that this law of love has answered as the law of destruction has never done. . . . The more I work at this law, the more I feel the delight in life, the delight in the scheme of the universe. It gives me a peace and a meaning of the mysteries of nature that I have not power to describe.[106]

Gandhi really reaffirmed the position of the Buddha, who taught that "by rousing himself, by earnestness, by restraint and control, the wise man may make for himself an island which no flood can overwhelm."[107] At the same time, he based himself upon the doctrine of action upheld in the *Gita*, and also wished to find a new meaning for the heroic ideal of the *Ramayana* in the context of *Kali Yuga*, the age of darkness in which we find ourselves at this stage of cosmic and human evolution. "A life of service must be one of humility. . . . True humility means most strenuous and constant endeavour entirely directed towards the service of humanity."[108] The God of the *Gita* is continuously in action without resting for a single moment. We learn from the God of the *Gita*, as from the angel voices in Goethe's *Faust*, that he who is ever striving in the world wins his salvation in the end, though only with the help which comes from the highest spiritual world—what, in fact, is termed "grace" in the language of Christian "theology" and "divine favour" (*prasad*) in the final chapter of the *Gita*. If we would serve God or become one with the universal life-principle, our activity must be as unwearied as that of Krishna. "This restlessness constitutes true rest. This never-ceasing agitation holds the key to peace ineffable."[109]

Gandhi was insistent that men must not be daunted from the path of action by the danger of the contamination of the marketplace and the political arena. Like Goethe, he mistrusted everything which might lead men away from activity in the outside world to a false inward contemplation that suggests the self-sufficiency of the recluse. If he invoked the heroic ideal of the Indian epics, it was because he wished those to whom integrity is precious in India and elsewhere to take greater risks than they are usually prepared to take. There is little value in cloistered virtue or the pursuit of truth in the privacy of personal life. It is necessary for the saint and the revolutionary to abjure all violence and, even more, to seek and uphold what they regard as the truth in the challenging context of political activity and the complex relationships of society.

The ultimate significance of the Gandhian doctrine of human perfectibility is the preparedness for error in our endeavors and the readiness to take large risks, checked only by a continuous exercise of self-analysis and the willingness to make amends for mistakes made through mere good intentions or weakness of will. Such a course of daring involvement in the affairs of the world, combined with the discipline that comes with the cultivation of inwardness, may even postpone the attainment of individual enlightenment and salvation. And yet, the attempt to merge the ideal of personal fulfillment and salvation with the common ideal of collective salvation and the welfare of all may be seen in the long run to be a worthier way to attain our own spiritual ends. In any case, an alternative course of conduct was unacceptable for Gandhi.

> Theoretically when there is perfect love there must be perfect non-possession. The body is our last possession. So a man can only exercise perfect love and be completely dispossessed, if he is prepared to embrace death and renounces his body for the sake of human service. But that is true in theory only . . . so that perfection in love or non-possession will remain an unattainable ideal as long as we are alive, but towards which we must ceaselessly strive.[110]

To affirm human perfectibility in the context of politics and of society is to invert Hobbes and to discard the fear of death, to accept the risk of political and physical martyrdom, a worthwhile risk for the true revolutionary.

6

INDIVIDUAL CONSCIENCE
AND HEROISM IN SOCIETY

Reason may be stamped by Opinion. And, therefore, though vicious times invert the opinions of things, and set up a new Ethick against Virtue, yet hold thou unto Old Morality; and rather than follow a multitude to do evil, stand like Pompey's Pillar conspicuous by the self, and single in Integrity. And since the worst of times afford imitable Examples of Virtue, since no Deluge of vice is like to be so general but more than eight will escape; eye well those Heroes who have held their Heads above water, who have touched Pitch and not been defiled, and in the common Contagion have remained uncorrupted.

SIR THOMAS BROWNE

The people are no bad judges of sincerity. It is the enthusiast who inspires them with enthusiasm; whatever else he may be, their man of destiny is at least a man of faith. . . . Because he believed he was believed. We smile at the simplicity of the believers. We no longer hope that any individual, however heroic, will make all things new. . . . But if men had never promised more than it was possible they should perform, society would be the poorer; for the achieved reform is the child of the unachieved ideal.

H. W. C. DAVIS

The crucial consequence of Gandhi's indictment of modern civilization as well as his plea for the purification of politics and the need for vows based upon absolute values, his view of human nature and human perfectibility, is twofold. First of all, the continual term of reference is the infinite importance and immeasurable potency of the individual in society, his moral autonomy and his status as a moral agent and an ever-evolving entity. Secondly, there is the decisive shift in emphasis and valuation from thought to action, the replacement of the *via contemplativa* by the *via activa* as the supreme and most immediate consideration, a standpoint that may truly be regarded as revolutionary in the Indian context, comparable to the decisive turning-point that is rightly ascribed to the seventeenth century in Europe. It would not be extravagant to consider Gandhi as one of the most revolutionary of individualists and one of the most individualistic of revolutionaries in world history. This does not make it any easier to interpret him as a thinker or to emulate him as a man. He could never wholly extricate himself from the difficulties of his position as a person and as a thinker who wished to bridge the glaring gap between the saint and the politician. To castigate him on this account would be to display a shallow insensitivity; it would be facile to confront the temerity of his undertaking with the timidity of the unimaginative critic.

Gandhi declared in 1924 that "the individual is the one supreme consideration"[1] and held to this belief until the very end of his life. His basic affirmation stands in direct contrast to Schopenhauer's allegedly Oriental view that "the individual is nothing and less than nothing." His distrust of the machine, his suspicion of the power of the State, his repudiation of capitalism and imperialism as also of Marxism, his attitude toward all institutions, were all consequent upon his faith in the supremacy of the individual person. If the individual ceases to count, what is left of society, he asked.[2] Individual freedom alone, he argued, can make a man voluntarily surrender himself completely to the service of society; if freedom is wrested from him, man becomes an automaton and society is ruined.

> No society can possibly be built on a denial of individual free-
> dom. It is contrary to the very nature of man. Just as a man will
> not grow horns or a tail, so will he not exist as man if he has no
> mind of his own. In reality even those who do not believe in the
> liberty of the individual believe in their own.[3]

At the same time Gandhi did not lose sight of the fact that man is
essentially a social being who has risen to his present status by
learning to adjust his individualism to the requirements of social
progress.

> Unrestricted individualism is the law of the beast of the jungle.
> We have learnt to strike the mean between individual freedom
> and social restraint. Willing submission to social restraint for the
> sake of the well-being of the whole society, enriches both the
> individual and the society of which he is a member.[4]

Gandhi's middle position is a deliberate reconciliation between romantic naturalism and social determinism. He could not, like Turgenev, for example, regard life itself as an eternal struggle of the
centrifugal and centripetal tendencies. In Turgenev's essay on
"Hamlet and Don Quixote," Hamlet's egoism is contrasted with
Don Quixote's enthusiasm. Carried to extremes, the Hamlets are
tragic figures lost in thought and the Quixotes appear as crack-
brained men of action. This dichotomy was transcended in Gandhi's view of the relation between introspection and action. His
ideal was that of the *karma yogi* who values introspection chiefly
as the basis and guide to effective action, who desires to change society rather than to contemplate the universe.

Gandhi's individualism was not at all like that of Herbert Spencer and the classical economists, and is somewhat closer to the position of Kant and Rousseau. He did, of course, believe that society
is no more than an aggregate of individuals and can have no other
aim than the development of those individuals. Self-development as
an egoistic ideal, though, is a morally empty notion in Gandhi's view
of ethics. Whereas Western individualism emerged in modern ur-
ban society and is bound up with the doctrine of natural rights,
Gandhi's individualism derived from the concept of *dharma* or natural obligations which held together the traditional rural communities of ancient Indian civilization. The agency of the State is re-

quired to watch over the maintenance of individual rights. The *dharma* of different people is not dependent upon State intervention; it is ultimately a matter for self-discovery although it may be initially indicated by social custom and local tradition. It presupposes *rta* or cosmic equilibrium, the harmony of nature, but it is not necessarily teleological and it certainly excludes the Hegelian idea that every society has a predetermined purpose superior to individual ends and unrelated to them.

Gandhi recognized that there was no justification for the *hubris* of the arrogant and self-isolated individual, defiant of social conventions and every form of authority merely because of their conventional or authoritative character. "The power to stand alone till the end cannot be developed without extreme humility. Without this power a man is nothing worth."[5] And yet Gandhi wanted every man to become "a full-blooded, fully developed member of society."[6] Against the Soviet system he quoted to Friedman the Biblical dictum: "What shall it avail a man if he gain the whole world and lose his soul?"[7] It is beneath human dignity for any man to lose his individuality and to become a mere cog in the machine. Men should live and work for the common good, and they must look not to political parties but to their own souls for direction.

Gandhi believed that no power on earth can make an individual do anything against his own will.[8] An individual becomes irresistible and his action becomes all-pervasive in its effect when he voluntarily "reduces himself to zero."[9] Such bold assertions of Gandhi were merely expressions of unprovable faith. Today it would seem that many powers on earth can make the individual act against his will (unless *voluntary action* is defined as Hobbes defined it); and an individual who is selfless is not irresistible unless we mean and believe that his inner resistance can never be wholly crushed. What Gandhi wished to stress was that every act contains its own propaganda and needs no other. Movements, societies and sects waste their time and energy saying what everyone ought to do, whereas the individual must act without waiting for others.[10] The man of peace may appear to be out of place in a society full of strife, yet he can work and act among his fellow men, refusing to surrender to the spirit of evil.[11] In a well-ordered society industrious and intelligent men can never be a menace; if they have any defects, the very order of society corrects them.¹² The only effective sanction against the evil-doer in any society is enlightened public opinion. Gandhi reversed the ancient Indian maxim "As the king, so the people," and declared, "As the people, so the king."¹³ If, however, the masses are carried away by the passions of the moment, it is possible for the conscientious individual to stand apart.

Gandhi refused to believe, like some conservatives and some revolutionaries, that society is governed by laws of growth which are beyond the ability of any individual to alter. He sometimes used organic analogies, but he refused to recognize any irreversible social laws. The individual can show his superiority to any system. He recognized that the hypostatization of the State and of society arises out of a failure to distinguish between what exists now and what we think ought to be. The distinction between the State and society must ever be made, but not at the cost of regarding either as being logically and morally prior to the individual. Those who, like Hegel, hold that society and the State are prior to the individual use the word "individual" in a special sense—to mean a self-conscious moral person. They argue that men become self-conscious and moral only in society, where they can acquire the concepts which enable them to be objects of thought and criticism to themselves. To Gandhi, on the other hand, the human soul is autonomous in society because it is an integral part of the rational and moral order of nature.

Traditionally, Vedic thought bequeathed the belief that man lives in a wider society that embraces all the creatures and deities of the universe, and consequently a strong individualism developed in the context of Indian society. There has been a repeated exhortation in the Indian tradition that man should rise above society, and while social virtues are necessary in social life, they must be ultimately transcended in the individual. In early Greek thought, the radical individualism of the Sophists was opposed by the metaphysical idea of society as the macrocosm. Man is, Protagoras insisted, "the measure of all things," but even this is not to be taken as referring to the individual but rather to the universal man, attuned to nature, corresponding to the Indian concept of *purushottama*.

The word "social" is itself Roman in origin and has no exact equivalent in Greek or Indian thought. The Latin usage of the word *societas* indicated an alliance between people for a specific purpose. It is only with the later concept of a *societas generis humani*, "a society of mankind," that the term "social" began to acquire the general meaning of a fundamental human condition. In modern times the ancient distinction between public and private has become extremely thin, if not practically non-existent; both have been subsumed under the social. Even privately cherished values have become dependent upon social valuations. When Nietzsche spoke about the trans-valuation of values (*Umwertung aller Werte*), he merely meant an alteration in our valuations. Gandhi was, however, concerned to allow in all situations for an appeal to ultimate values that are wholly independent of, and transcend, all social valuations affecting public and private conduct. No doubt it is possible to hold that it is only as social beings that men acquire values, including the values they appeal to when they condemn accepted values. Gandhi, on the other hand, belonged to the school of classical thinkers, Indian and Greek, who believed in the existence of eternal verities in nature from which men may derive the ethical values they choose to regard as absolute.

Everything that contributes toward giving those who are at the bottom of the social scale, or who feel oppressed by their social environment, the feeling that they possess an inherent value and are capable of appealing to ultimate values that transcend social valuations, is bound to be subversive. Gandhi's thought is deeply subversive, in a Socratic sense. Every genuine appeal to ultimate values has a corrosive action on the established order. No one in our time has more strongly stressed this than Camus in *L'Homme révolté*:

> In every act of rebellion, the man concerned experiences not only a feeling of revulsion at the infringement of his rights but also a complete and spontaneous loyalty to certain aspects of himself. Thus he implicitly brings into play a standard of values so far from being false that he is willing to preserve them at all costs. . . . An awakening of conscience, no matter how confused it may be, develops from any act of rebellion and is represented by the sudden realization that something exists with which the rebel can identify himself—even if only for a moment.[14]

Camus identifies the appeal to ultimate values exclusively with the act of rebellion. It is, no doubt, possible to hold that the conservative could make a genuine appeal to ultimate values in support of the established order. In practice, however, it seems easier to appeal to nature against existing society than to justify an imperfect system by appealing to an ideal conception of nature.

Gandhi proclaimed two values as ultimate—*satya* and *ahimsa*, truth and non-violence. These could be invoked by every individual in every situation. Like the Stoics, he believed that the good man will not live in solitude as a hermit, for he is naturally sociable and active. Virtue is a disposition or capacity of the ruling "principle" of the soul, assured and unchanging, worthy of choice for its own intrinsic quality, and its exercise is a continuous activity, i.e., never interrupted by lapses and omissions because it can never be lost. The appeal to intrinsic, eternal values could be used to reject conservative as well as meliorist creeds that justify the present by appealing to the past or the future and also the means employed by the distant ends they are supposed to subserve.

To Gandhi it is necessary to do what seems to be right in scorn of consequences, and every single act must be independently justified in terms of the ultimate and unchanging values rather than by the results that are expected to emerge. The appeal of the individual must in the last resort be to his own conscience rather than to reason, to what Adam Smith called "the ideal man within the breast." Preoccupation with reason can be a hindrance to action whereas conscience is kept alive by concern for right action rather than for pure thought. Turgenev, Bakunin, Herzen, Belinski were convinced that analytical thought is the very source of inner division, atrophy of will and inability to act. This Schopenhauerian suspicion of thought was never consciously shared by Gandhi, and even if it was present in him, it was never carried to extremes or rationalized in any way.

THE EXALTATION OF CONSCIENCE

Gandhi's belief in the supremacy of the individual and of his role in society cannot be grasped without turning to his fundamental concept of conscience. In this respect he is more Socratic than Stoic. One of the earliest and most abiding influences on his thought and life was Plato's account of the defence and the death of Socrates, which Gandhi paraphrased into Gujarati under the title *The Story of a Satyagrahi*. This provided for him a practical demonstration of Bishop Butler's view in *The Analogy* that life in this world is a state of probation, involving trials, difficulties and danger, and intended for moral discipline and improvement. Owing to Gandhi's identification of the religious with the moral—a religious man is one who incarnates in his life an exacting moral ideal[15]—his justification of conscience was essentially ethical although couched in theistic language.

He declared in his *Ethical Religion* that conscience is the voice of God, the final judge of the rightness of every deed and thought. He wrote in 1919 that "there are times when you have to obey a call which is the highest of all, i.e., the voice of conscience, even though such obedience may cost many a bitter tear, and even more, separation from friends, from family, from the State to which you may belong, from all that you have held as dear as life itself. For this obedience is the law of our being."[16] Further, in matters of conscience, the law of majority has no place. Repeatedly, in South African courts and subsequently in India, he appealed to a higher court than courts of Justice, the "Court of Conscience" that supersedes all courts.[17] "The human voice can never reach the distance that is covered by the still small voice of conscience. The only tyrant I accept in this world is the still small voice within."[18]

In August 1921 a correspondent complained that as a result of Gandhi's continual harping on conscience, youngsters and grown-up people were talking utter nonsense under cover of conscience. Youngsters have become impudent and grown-up people unscrupulous. "Can you not prevent this mischief? If you cannot, please withdraw the word from use and stop the drivel that is being said in the name of that sacred but much abused word. Pray tell us who has a conscience? Do all have it? Do cats have a conscience when they hunt to death poor mice?"[19] Gandhi conceded that the charge was not without substance. Every virtue has been known to be abused by the wicked but we do not on that account do away with virtue. We can but erect safeguards against abuse. "When people cease to think for themselves and have everything regulated for them, it becomes necessary at times to assert the right of individuals to act in defiance of public opinion or law which is another name of public opinion. When individuals so act, they claim to have acted in obedience to conscience."[20] He further contended that youngsters as a rule must not pretend to have conscience, which is a state properly acquired only through laborious training.

> Wilfulness is not conscience. A child has no conscience. The correspondent's cat does not go for the mouse in obedience to its conscience. It does so in obedience to its nature. Conscience is the ripe fruit of strictest discipline. Irresponsible youngsters therefore who have never obeyed anything or anybody save their animal instinct have no conscience, nor therefore have all grown-up people. The savages for instance have to all intents and purposes no conscience. Conscience can reside only in a delicately tuned breast.[21]

The important consequence of this clarification is that there is no such thing as mass conscience as distinguished from the conscience of individuals. Gandhi's position on this matter may be contrasted with that of Durkheim, who put forward a theory of "the collective conscience." The *mystique* which Rousseau and Durkheim wove about the group enabled them to legitimize coercion when employed on behalf of the moral purposes of the community. The "collective conscience" is said to embody something other than the totality of individuals that compose it. Gandhi could not believe in the moral priority of any collective agency over the individual.

At the same time he thought it safe to say that when a man makes everything a matter of conscience, he is a stranger to it. It is true that "conscience makes cowards of us all." "A conscientious man hesitates to assert himself, he is always humble, never boisterous, always compromising, always ready to listen, ever willing, even anxious, to admit mistakes."[22] Gandhi was thus led to idealize the conscientious man, reducing in this way the practical and universal force of his stress on conscience. He fortified himself with the thought that the world has no difficulty in distinguishing between conscience and an arrogant or ignorant assumption of it. The introduction of conscience into our public life is welcome even if it teaches only a few to stand up for human dignity and rights in the face of the heaviest odds. "These acts will live for ever, whereas those done under whims are like soap-bubbles enjoying a momentary existence."[23]

At times Gandhi took an extremely individualistic position, to the despair of some of his colleagues and the wrath of his cynical opponents. "I do not want any patronage, as I do not give any," he retorted. "I am a lover of my own liberty and so I would do nothing to restrict yours. I simply want to please my own conscience, which is God."[24] Some years later, he was mainly concerned to assert that what must count with a public servant is the approbation of his own conscience. He must not be like a rudderless vessel, a person who, leaving the infallible solace of his own conscience, ever seeks to please and gain the approbation of the public. Service must be its own and sole reward.[25] On a later occasion, he was asked whether in developing the new national spirit in India he would like to make patriotic feelings so strong that duty to one's country would be a higher good than obeying one's personal conscience. He replied that one's own inner convictions come first always, but in a nation where character is developed in all individuals, there can be no conflict between the dictates of one's own conscience and those of the State.[26] Just as he idealized the man of conscience, so too he rather readily envisaged an impossible condition for a nation as a whole, in which all men would be moved by the dictates of conscience, thus ruling out any real conflict between the moral and practical aims of the rulers and the ruled.

It is easier to uphold the sanctity of individual conscience if we can assume the continuing presence of a common outlook and similar moral response among the members of society. This would mean that men can know and understand each other and communicate by accepted moral signs. Gandhi held to such a notion of conscience as a common, unifying force, whereas in the West many since Locke have pictured conscience as a divisive force. Today conscience is denied any priority in political matters owing to the Lockean belief that society, unlike a state of nature, requires the surrender of private judgment to the "legislative." The trouble arises, however, when the distrust of individual conscience gives way to the notion of a social conscience, the internalized expression of external convictions. Individual conscience, unlike the notion of social conscience, is intended as a defence against the group rather than as a method for inducing individual conformity to the group.

Those who have tried to dispense with the concept of individual conscience in politics have merely invested the notion of individual "interest" with much of the same sanctity and immunity. Whereas the strength of conscience lies in its wholly internal character and is unaffected by material loss or physical injury, interests are closely involved with wealth and status which depend on outside occurrences. What is common to both conscience and interest is their individualistic character, the subjectivity of a judgment about it, and the impossibility of forcibly imposing it. The decline of individual conscience in liberal theory ushered in a new social world where men, no longer able to communicate on the basis of a common interior life, are reduced to knowing each other solely from the outside, on the basis of socially acquired responses and values. The estrangement of man from man is implied in Locke's terse description of the human condition where individual consciences are strangers to each other. Man becomes conscious of his fellows only when he and they collide; conflicts and friction become the chief sources of man's awareness of his fellows. Bentham regarded conscience as a "thing of fictitious existence" because of his belief that man has nothing to gain and finds no source of enjoyment in introspection and self-knowledge. Once man is stripped of his conscience and reduced to a mere series of external acts, it is easy to treat him as an object rather than a subject, an instrument rather than an intrinsic end. The notion of social conformity implies that the individual must adjust his actions and tastes, his style of life, to a social denominator. It assumes that individual adaptation will contribute to social cohesion and order and also that individual happiness can be attained only by observing social standards. The individual is invited to internalize social norms so that they may operate like individual conscience.

Gandhi was concerned with socializing the individual conscience rather than internalizing the social conscience. This can be understood in the light of his concept of human nature and perfectibility. Man is viewed not as a creature moved by self-interest but as a person who asserts his autonomy by recognizing obligations owed to himself in the quest for self-perfection. Gandhi perhaps underestimated the urgency of self-interest and the reality of conflicts of interest in society. But he was acutely aware of the tragic self-alienation of man in a society centered on material interests and relegating conscience to the margins of political and social life. He was deeply concerned to find the basis for social solidarity and authentic community life in action motivated and checked by conscience.

In practice, Gandhi urged the importance of "infinite patience and inward longing." Toward the end of his life, he told a sincere atheist who came to him:

> Every one who wants a true life has to face difficulties in life, some of which appear insurmountable. At that time it is faith in God that is Truth alone, that will sustain you. The fellow-feeling which makes you feel miserable because of your brother's misery is godliness. You may call yourself an atheist, but so long as you feel akin with mankind you accept God in practice. I remember clergymen who came to the funeral of the great atheist Bradlaugh. They said they had come to pay their homage because he was a godly man.[27]

Gandhi's belief in conscience led him to respect the conscience of those who disagreed with him. In the difficult days of negotiation that finally led to the partition of India, he wrote to Wavell, citing Wordsworth's Happy Warrior, and urging him "to dare to do the right."[28] He wrote in a similar vein to Lord Pethick-Lawrence, who was in turn anxious to assure him that his own empirical and rational attitude did not rule out faith, just as Gandhi's faith in conscience did not rule out reason.[29]

Gandhi's test of the presence and power of individual conscience was the willingness to suffer for one's beliefs to the point of spiritual isolation and even public ridicule, involving if necessary political martyrdom and even physical death. A man of conscience is put on trial in a time of crisis, the hour of danger for himself and for the entire society or State. Like Socrates in Plato's *Apology*, Gandhi would assert: "Wherever a man's place is, whether the place which he has chosen or that in which he has been placed by a commander, there he ought to remain in the hour of danger, taking no account of death or of anything else in comparison with disgrace." Gandhi's worldly critics may have felt that he invoked his conscience and the voice of God too often and too freely in the everyday business of politics, yet none could deny that toward the end of his life, just before and after the partition of India, he bravely accepted the consequences of his conscientious objections. He became, as he said, a voice in the wilderness, a figure of spiritual isolation, lonely amid the rejoicing crowds on Independence Day, but respectful to the last of the motives and the consciences of those who honestly differed from him.

THE SOCRATIC *DAIMON* AND GANDHI'S INNER VOICE

Acton's complaint against the deification of conscience by Socrates may also be leveled by the orthodox against Gandhi. "When Socrates declared that he would obey God rather than man, he meant God manifest within—with no oracle, no sacred book, no appointed minister—with no organ but within."[30] Gandhi, like Socrates, is seen more clearly in the light of the inspiration of his "divine something" (*daimonion ti*, as Plato calls it), which internalizes the influences external to the spirit and objectifies its inner demands, so keeping an equal balance between man and god. The belief in *daimones* as mediating spirits between gods and men was traditional in ancient Athens and not unfamiliar in Vedic India, but Gandhi, like Socrates, regarded the intervention of the *daimon*—what he repeatedly called his "inner voice," which sometimes spoke to him and remained silent at other times to his infinite despair—not so much as a command laid down on the human spirit by an external power as "an absolute law of the spirit itself," to quote Hegel's terms for the task of the Delphic oracle. On the other hand, to make this interior voice wholly subjective is to destroy its religious character and distort the position claimed by Socrates and Gandhi. In some pre-Socratic writers and to some Indian mystics, the *daimon* or *devata* was no more than the genius or overbrooding spirit personal to each man.

If we adopt a wholly rationalist attitude and take the *daimon* merely as a metaphor for a common psychological process, thus denying it all transcendence and regarding it simply as a pathological oddity, a hallucination or a hysterical symptom, we are, in fact, denying that it is an instrument of any communication and leaving

Gandhi and Socrates, and many of the great mystics, enclosed in themselves, in a sort of autarchy, a pathetic state of self-deception. Even if we wish to deny the objective reality of the mystic's experience, which is strictly no easier than to affirm it, it is both unnecessary and presumptuous to deny categorically its subjective validity, i.e., the veracity of the mystics. It may be that it is at the fire of exceptional and spiritually subtle egotism that many of the saints and mystics, like St. Theresa, St. Joan and Ramakrishna, have warmed their hands; it may well be likely that daily life in the company of such types would have been a burdensome experience, which would not have surprised them, to the extent that their intentions and exhortations were meant to be subversive of complacency and common sense; it also may be true that most of us would not willingly turn to such personages in moments of moral anguish, political and social crisis or physical catastrophe.

Above all, we cannot assume that a spiritual or moral authority is always right in his guidance, even if it comes from visions and inner voices, especially in political and social matters. Such men are also subject to ordinary human frailties, and even if they are not as liable as worldly leaders to be corrupted by power, they may well, like Becket in *Murder in the Cathedral*, be subject to spiritual temptations and peculiar forms of self-will, if not self-love, that arise at their stage of development. And yet men of conscience may win their battles because of their secret appeal to the spiritual element in their opponents, that humane element from which even cynics and doubters cannot quite shake themselves free. As Gilbert Murray wrote when Gandhi was still in South Africa and less than forty-five years old: "Be careful in dealing with a man who cares nothing for sensual pleasures, nothing for comfort or praise or promotion, but is simply determined to do what he believes is right. He is a dangerous and uncomfortable enemy because his body which you can always conquer gives you so little purchase over his soul."[31] His appeal to his conscience derives value from his appeal to ours.

It may indeed be inevitable, as Shaw suggests in his preface to *St. Joan*, that to appeal insistently to inner voices and private visions and to take an unrelenting stand on the compulsions of one's own conscience is in the end to invite martyrdom. But insofar as

Gandhi and Socrates, even more explicitly than St. Joan and Bruno, were claiming for themselves what they truly believed to be available to all, their own view of their *daimones* needs to be properly understood. The admonition of his *daimon* always comes as a surprise to Socrates, and it is only after the event that he understands the significance of the supra-rational injunction of his familiar spirit. The Socratic *daimon* has been described as Apollonian rather than Dionysian. It is at once external and internal to the soul, which it enlightens in order to govern; it is not an intermediary *being* but a mediating *utterance*. "When I speak of my *daimon* I am not introducing a new god. I believe in this divine *voice*."[32] The Athenians, who recognized no mean between conformist piety and intellectual atheism, could not understand this *mystique* of the clear conscience, which reconciles obedience with the self's possession of itself. Plutarch contended in his *De Genio Socratis* that the "familiar" of Socrates was not a vision, but the perception of a voice or the apprehension of something said which came to him in some mysterious way, similar to the intuitive apprehension sometimes secured in dreams, when the soul can be made "attentive to the voice of the higher powers."[33] Further, Apuleius suggested in his *De Deo Socratis* that the familiar spirit of Socrates used to stop him from doing some of the things he had undertaken, but never encouraged him in anything.[34] In the case of Gandhi, he actually claimed positive guidance and not merely negative warnings from his "inner voice."

As early as 1916, Gandhi declared that, "there come to us moments in life when about some things we need no proof from without. A little voice within us tells us, 'You are on the right track, move neither to your left nor right, but keep to the strait and narrow way.' "[35] In 1920 he wrote that there are moments in life when we must act, even though we cannot carry our best friends with us; the "still small voice" within us must always be the final arbiter when there is a conflict of duty.[36] He claimed that having made a ceaseless effort to attain self-purification, he had developed some little capacity to hear correctly and clearly the "still small voice within."[37] In 1925 he claimed that though many say they speak under the authority of the inner voice, not all will be able to substantiate the claim.[38] Before one is able to listen to that voice, one has to go through a long and fairly severe course of training, and when it is the inner voice that speaks, it is unmistakable. The world cannot be successfully fooled for all time.[39]

The nearest Gandhi came to giving a full account of this inner voice was in 1933. He wrote:

> For me the Voice of God, of Conscience, of Truth, or the Inner Voice or "the Still Small Voice" mean one and the same thing. I saw no form. I have never tried, for I have always believed god to be without form. But what I did hear was like a Voice from afar and yet quite near. It was as unmistakable as some human voice definitely speaking to me, and irresistible. I was not dreaming at the time I heard the Voice. The hearing of the Voice was preceded by a terrific struggle within me. Suddenly the Voice came upon me. I listened, made certain it was the Voice, and the struggle ceased. I was calm. The determination was made accordingly, the date and the hour of the fast were fixed. . . . I have no further evidence to convince the sceptic. He is free to say that it was self-delusion or hallucination. It may well have been so. I can offer no proof to the contrary. But I can say this, that not the unanimous verdict of the whole world against me could shake me from the belief that what I heard was the true Voice of God.[40]

He not only denied that there was any question of hallucination but even claimed to have stated a simple scientific truth, to be tested by all who have the will and the patience to acquire the necessary qualifications.[41]

> You must try to listen to the inner voice but if you won't have the expression "inner voice," you may use the expression "dictates of reason," which you should obey, and if you will not parade God, I have no doubt you will parade something else which in the end will prove to be God, for, fortunately, there is no one and nothing else but God in this universe.[42]

Finally, he was convinced that a person falsely claiming to act under divine inspiration or the promptings of the inner voice without having any such, will fare worse than one falsely claiming to act under the authority of an earthly sovereign, for the former may lose not only his body but also his soul.

THE CONCEPT OF CONSCIENCE IN THE
WEST AND IN INDIA

The important thing for us, is, of course, not the legitimacy of Gandhi's claims for his inner voice but the significance of his theoretical conception of conscience, identified with the infallible voice of Truth or God in man. This conception has had a long history in European thought. It was held by Bishop Butler, Kant and Vinet, and many others. The notion was fully developed only in the eighteenth century, although it goes back to Sophocles, Euripedes, Socrates, and the Stoics who held that the true guide is the Voice of Pure Reason which dwells in our souls, like the Logos in the cosmos. In the thirteenth century this Voice of God or conscience was held to be infallible, a voice which ought to be obeyed always, even if apparently wrong. With the decline of coercion the claims of conscience rose. "The soul became more sacred than the State, because it receives light from above, as well as because its concerns are eternal, and out of proportion with the common interests of government."[43]

It appeared to some seventeenth-century sects that governments and institutions are made to pass away, like things of earth, whereas souls are immortal, that there is no more proportion between liberty and power than between eternity and time, that the sphere of enforced command ought to be restricted within fixed limits, and that what had been done by authority and outward discipline and organized violence should be attempted by division of power and committed to the intellect and the conscience of free men. Some Puritans regarded a man's conscience as his castle, with kings and parliaments at a respectful distance. William Penn's doctrine of the inner light led him to proclaim liberty of conscience, which became the basis of the government of Pennsylvania, Voltaire's "best government." In the eighteenth century, conscience became not only judge but lawgiver for both men and nations. Kant argued that conscience proves God when reason cannot. Rousseau developed the idea so that he concluded from it that man is originally good and is corrupted only by outward influences, the inward influence being right and good. Toward the end of the eighteenth century, conscience was developed as a substitute for sectarian religion.

The arguments against conscience are that it is not infallible, that it is often obscure and misleading, that it is the echo of others and not the Voice of God, that it is incapable of being defined and that it negates free will. Conscience became in time the ally of rationalism and the great resource of unbelief. Acton, therefore, regarded it as a capacity that is capable of being extinguished in individuals and in entire nations.[44] On the other hand, Leslie Stephen regarded it as the utterance of the public spirit of the race, ordering us to obey the primary conditions of its welfare.[45] This view is, however, consistent with Acton's belief that conscience becomes more and more enlightened by experience and the discipline of history. It is enough for oneself, not for another, but it exists in each one of us until we smother it; it is the law of self-government. Benjamin Constant, who has been accused of "fetishism of the self," went so far as to regard man as sacred because he is a temple; he has a divine right because of his possession of a divine spark, conscience. The notion of the sovereignty of conscience was really needed to challenge the notion of legal sovereignty or at least its implication of a supreme moral authority in a community. The doctrine was naturally opposed most strongly by Hobbes, whom Marx called "the father of us all."

Acton wrongly contended that conscience is unknown in the religions of the East. This contention could be plausibly defended by distinguishing sharply between the notion of moral obligation and the concept of conscience. It is true that the two, though clearly allied, are not identical. For example, J. S. Mill had a moral philosophy which dispenses with the notion of conscience as we find it in Rousseau or Kant. He does not use the idea as they did and attempts an explanation of it which would not satisfy them or Luther or the medieval Christian moralist. Yet he does not (as James Mill and Bentham do) dispense entirely with the usual notion of moral obligation by treating it as if it were merely a fear of consequences. Though he does not give a satisfactory account of moral obligation, he uses the idea in the usual way. All this is true, but it does not provide any contrast which is peculiar to the West. Among the several schools of classical Indian thought, a similar distinction was made the subject of divergent views regarding the grounds of moral obligation as well as the moral promptings of the self-validating Imperative acting directly on human volition. Deussen's view, that while Christianity sees the essence of man in will Hinduism sees it in knowledge, is a gross over-simplification current in the cruder forms of Christian apologetics.

The notion of *vidhi* or the Moral Imperative has been elaborately analyzed by the *Prabhakara*s and attacked by the *Naiyayika*s. It was attacked insofar as it was regarded as anything more than a personal command which compels acceptance through *phalechcha* or desire for the consequence. It has been defended on the ground that without it there could be no firm and constant sense of moral obligation in man. According to one school of thought, *vidhi* is recognized as authoritative because it is conducive to good, while according to another school it is authoritative in itself. In the former view, the objective authority of the Imperative is due to the intrinsic worth of the end in view, while obligatoriness is due to the objective value of being subjectively appropriated through a particular desire. In the latter view, the moral authority of the Imperative is independent of the end or consequence. In an extreme formulation of this view, the Imperative constitutes the sanction, the motive as well as the moral authority of the *vidhi*. Consequential or prudential morality leads to an indefinite series of ends that has no end. A *vidhi* has absolute and independent authority; it is autonomous (*svatantra*). It is a positive, self-validating command. This Imperative is said to act on the agent's will through moral prompting (*prerana*), and, like the soul, it is known only through itself (*svasamvedya*).

A variety of interpretations of *vidhi* or conscience (authoritative suggestions to the will) is given by Vidyadandi in the *Ashtasahasri*. It could be considered objectively or subjectively, or as objective duty, supported by impulsion or as subjective impulsion modalized into objective duty. It could be regarded as self-validating through the projection of itself, or as a link between duty and subjective prompting. It could also be regarded as an organic complex consisting of the subjective factor, the objective factor and the nexus of concrete experience which is neither the one nor the other. It could also be regarded as something entirely transcendental, or it could be seen as the inward, progressive tendency of man as a moral agent. Finally, it could be regarded as an object which conduces to the self's fruition or as the agent himself, as both *sadhaka,* accomplisher, and *sadhya,* the accomplished. Similarly, there is controversy over whether *niyoga* should be regarded as an impersonal law without any personal source, or as the prescription of a superior to an inferior being.

For the Charvakas or materialists, *niyoga* is only the command of the earthly king and not of any perfect person. For the Jains and the Buddhists, however, *niyoga* represents the verdict of spiritual sages; their law is the declaration of the *apta*s or seers of the transcendental plane, who are possessed of spiritual insight as well as universal compassion. There is, however, nothing said explicitly about visions and voices that proclaim to man from outside or from within the dictates of his own conscience. There are, of course, many instances in the Indian tradition of saints and devotees (*bhaktas*) who hear voices and see visions, but these are not made the basis of any moral commands and are rather regarded as conferments of divine grace and even guidance.

Despite the traditional analysis of moral consciousness and of conscience and command in India, no thinker before Gandhi had laid so much emphasis on the notion of conscience as the basis of all social and political action. It could be safely contended that this notion really came to him from the West, although he put it to bolder and wider uses than had usually been the case in the West. Gandhi once complained to Tagore that Indians were in the habit of saying Yes to everything and needed to develop the power to say No to evil, injustice, untruth and violence. This power of rejection and of rebellion was something that modern India had to learn from the West.[46] Herein lay for Gandhi the crucial and practical significance of his concept of conscience as the Voice of Truth. To renounce conscience is to renounce the right to appeal to values that are not externally determined, and this amounts, as Camus said, to renouncing rebellion in order to accept the empire of slavery.

Once the possibility has been recognized of creating, by means of the forces of rebellion alone, the free individual of whom Romantics—notably Shelley—dreamed, it is tempting to incorporate freedom itself in the movement of history. It is then difficult to prevent man from taking refuge in the permanence of the party in the same way that he formerly prostrated himself before the altar. There is, no doubt, nothing to prevent men who believe that freedom is achieved gradually in the course of history from becoming docile members of an authoritarian party which justifies its clinging to power. In this case, however, the appeal to a historicist doctrine is accompanied with a drastic redefinition of the commonly understood concept of freedom.

There is nothing logically binding about the choice of either rebellion or conformity; this is rather a psychological truth about human beings, borne out by the history of our own time. The concept of conscience may seem to be irrational insofar as it is claimed to be unchallengeable. An important distinction must, however, be made. Those who regard conscience as only a conditioned response may wish to challenge the authority of a certain set of rules or imperatives that a person has adopted. But conscience in the proper sense gives authority to whatever set of rules one does in fact adopt. It could be said that a person has a conscience in so far as he has moral values or adopts moral rules at all. In this sense, the concept of conscience does not necessarily presuppose a belief in God or in the Voice of God. On the other hand, a believer in God or some ultimate and transcendental Reality cannot be blamed for couching his declaration of faith in his moral autonomy and primacy as a person in terms of his theistic or transcendental beliefs. The main point here is the internalization of authority, whether along religious or rationalistic lines. In either case, it may be claimed that the achievement of moral autonomy is the mark of moral and spiritual maturity. Instead of being guided by the commands and principles of other people, we must be guided by our own, if we are to be truly self-determining agents. This is the critical test of moral individuation.

THE HEROIC IDEAL

Although Gandhi based his faith in the supremacy of the individual on his view of conscience and of the duty that a man owes himself, his stress on action rather than thought led him to assert that the duty that a man owes himself is also owed by him to his fellow men. Society is the mirror in which we can look at ourselves and judge our actions with the eye of an impartial spectator. This is, as Adam Smith pointed out, the only looking-glass by which we can, with the eyes of other people, scrutinize the propriety of our own conduct. The concept of conscience may have ultimate significance on its own in a moral and religious sense, but its practical import for Gandhi lay in its connection with his plea for heroic and even rebellious action in society. Those who follow the heroic ideal are bound by obligations which they must fulfill, and are forbidden to perform certain actions which are shameful. Honor, unlike morality, is more positive than negative; its obligations are more to the fore than its prohibitions. Honor becomes what morality not always is—an incentive to rigorous action in many fields.

In most instances of rebellion, the individual, the Antigone, the Prometheus, even the solitary Just Man of Plato's Republic, is not really claiming to throw off entirely the yoke of the community and its *themis,* but appealing against them to a better community, a truer *themis,* which at the time he cannot see except by faith. Although Gandhi may have believed that the individual's worth is tested by his power to stand alone, he did not think that, in practice, the heroic individual who is sustained by his private vision of *Rama Rajya* stands absolutely alone even in *Kali Yuga,* the age of darkness. He attracts to himself a band of like-minded heroes, possessed of similar vision and also claiming to have a clearer light and to possess a deeper concord than is usually sought by most men.

The faith in the higher city is generally combined with an appeal to experience. The glorification of the Kingdom of Heaven is accompanied with an insistence on the enslavement of man in the existing kingdoms on earth. Antigone appeals from the mere modern law of Thebes to Zeus and *dike,* to the unwritten rules of the gods and to the cosmic order of transcendental justice. Plato chooses at the end of the *Republic* to make *dikaiosune,* or justice, the basis of a mythic restatement of the traditional concepts of *themis* and *moira.* Against the laws of prevailing and tyrannical groups, it is a primordial *themis* or *Rama Rajya* to which these rebels or reformers want to return, a *themis* which everyone can understand, a *Rama Rajya* in which every man can invoke if not become Rama. The heroic ideal exalts the individual, even the adventurer, and enables every brave spirit to feel that "the world is his oyster, which with his sword he'll prise open." For Gandhi this is the sword of *satya* or truth, which has to be used to combat every form of social and political injustice. Tyranny has to be fought, and the Kingdom of Heaven has to be taken by the sword of truth and nonviolence.

In reaffirming the heroic ideal Gandhi was vindicating the oldest tradition in India embodied in the two great epics that are still widely loved and vividly told in the countryside. The *Ramayana* and the *Mahabharata* have come down from the earliest times and were transmitted for centuries from generation to generation by an oral tradition. A similar tradition survives in the West in the Homeric poems. The Indian and the Greek epics exalted a conception of manhood in which personal worth held pride of place. The essence of the heroic outlook is the pursuit of honor through action. The hero, in Indian legend, uses the potentialities that lie dormant in all men to the utmost and wins the warm approbation of his fellows because he spares no effort and shirks no risk in his desire to make the most of his powers in the service of a supreme ideal. For him "the Ideal is only Truth at a distance" (in Lamartine's striking phrase). His honor is the center of his being, and any abdication from it calls for instant atonement. He faces danger fearlessly and regards it as a trial that gives him the necessary challenge to show what stuff he is made of. Such a conviction and its code of behavior are built on a man's conception of himself and of what he owes to it. It is the creed of the *karma yogi* pointing to the path of action. Gandhi infused this creed with the spirit of selfless detachment extolled in the *Gita* and he stressed its application to contemporary politics and society. His uniqueness lies in the fact that he combined the heroic ideal of the *satyagrahi* with a profound belief in the moral power and heroic response of the masses.

Early in life, Gandhi studied Carlyle's *Heroes and Hero-Worship*. During his first term in jail in 1908 in Transvaal, he read Carlyle's *Lives*. He commenced to do a Gujarati translation of a book by Carlyle but could not complete it during his short sentence. "I would not have become tired even if I had got more than two months,"[47] he said. We have no record of what he took from Carlyle's *Heroes and Hero-Worship*, but from his subsequent utterances on different occasions, it is not rash to assume that he was at least a bit influenced by Carlyle's essay "The Hero as Divinity" and probably more so by the essay "The Hero as King." He certainly indicated that he was impressed by Carlyle's study of Mohammed. During his third jail experience he read and commended Carlyle's "French Revolution," which he thought was written in a very effective style. It is clear from later remarks that he thought that any revolution which relied on violence could not really succeed in the long run; it could not secure a society based on new values if it flouted those values in the process of achieving its goals. The heroic ideal must stress courage rather than violence.

Carlyle's doctrine has been frequently mis-stated and misrepresented by hostile critics; it certainly sounds too fascistic for our comfort, but it must be seen in the context of some of the more naïvely egalitarian and mechanistic beliefs of his age. The phrase "hero-worship," which is now inseparably connected with Carlyle, was originally Hume's. Carlyle laid stress on the importance of recognizing and reverencing human greatness. He opposed the determinist's and the historicist's view that man is wholly the creature of circumstances and he pointed to heroic leaders as the exception which confutes rather than confirms the supposedly general rule. He recognized that a great man could sometimes be the "synopsis and epitome of his age," but he was concerned that the world was fast losing its religiosity and its reverence for human achievement through a literal and mechanical notion of the actual equality of all men. Men must have the power to discern human greatness and to emulate it, a doctrine that goes back to Plutarch. Carlyle went further and believed that a nation that can recognize its heroes partakes of their heroic nature. "If hero means *a sincere man,* why may not every one of us be a hero?"[48] There is in man an indestructible reverence for heroes, a share of heroism, which "no sceptical logic or general triviality" can ever take away. The hero sees into the heart of things, pierces beneath the "outer hulls and wrappings," brushes away appearances and hearsays, and beneath transient symbols retains a clear vision of eternal truths. It matters not under what symbol the hero has had knowledge of truth, it matters less what work circumstances may have given him to do —Odin with his Norse Paganism, Mohammed and Islam, Dante with his Medieval Catholicism, Cromwell with his Protestantism. It is by virtue of their sincerity, their goodness, the truth that was in them, that their work still lives, and must live forever. Such a definition must exclude evil-doers like Hitler, Mussolini and Robespierre, but it cannot overlook Napoleon or Bismarck.

The trouble, of course, is that Carlyle too readily assumed that might and right are identical in the long run, because of his basic belief that the universe is wholly managed by a just power. He was also too widely tolerant, all-comprehensive in his application of his doctrine. It is true he did not go so far as Callicles in Plato's *Gorgias,* whose doctrine of the superman leads to an extreme immoralism, the abolition of accepted law and the reversal of values that are hitherto respected. But Carlyle derived from his doctrine an authoritarian conception of government, like that of Callicles, owing to his extreme cynicism, and suspicion of a head-counting democracy. He recognized that many heroes are revolutionary anarchists, but even these men he regarded as ultimately "missionaries of Order." It is doubly tragical for a great man to be "image-breaking and down-pulling." Even seeming chaos must seek a center to revolve around. The true hero drives toward the practical and practicable; has "a genuine insight into what *is* fact."[49] Carlyle's wrath was reserved mainly for dilettantism, insincerity. "The heart lying dead, the eye cannot see. What intellect remains is merely the vulpine intellect."[50] If we reject true heroes, we are ruled by sham-heroes, lacking the sharp power of vision, the resolute power of action. "Virtue, *Vir-tus,* manhood, here-hood, is not fair-spoken immaculate regularity; it is first of all . . . Courage and the Faculty to do."[51] Carlyle recognized that sometimes even in a real hero "the fatal charlatan-element got the upper hand."[52] He apostatizes from his old faith in facts and takes to believing in semblances, yields to self-deception. In the end Carlyle's individualism that sometimes runs mad is the sign of the break-up of a whole system of conventional values which have become too weak to inspire respect or to enforce emulation.

Gandhi may have been influenced by some of these dangerous ideas to a greater extent than we can prove, but the essential fact remains that, unlike Carlyle, he reverenced the masses and genuinely disliked their deference to him as a *Mahatma,* or great soul.[53]

His main concern was always with the primacy of courage among the human virtues and his horror of helplessness. He wrote in 1929 that "it is only because we have created a vicious atmosphere of impotence round ourselves that we consider ourselves to be helpless even for the simplest possible things."[54] The courage which he advocated for himself and for others and as an essential requirement in politics and society was the courage of the soul. "Courage has never been known to be a matter of muscle, it is a matter of the heart. The toughest muscle has been known to tremble before an imaginary fear."[55] Virtue must be based on *virya,* the dauntless energy that fights its way to the supernal truth out of the mire of terrestrial lies. Gandhi pointed out that if you want to follow the vow of truth in any shape or form, fearlessness is the necessary consequence. "And so you find, in the *Bhagavad Gita,* fearlessness is declared as the first essential quality of a Brahmin."[56] We fear consequences, and therefore, we are afraid to tell the truth. A man who has overcome attachment will certainly not fear earthly consequences. "The trouble is that we often die many times before death overtakes us."[57] Above all, to Gandhi, "where there is fear there is no religion."[58]

As a consequence of Gandhi's emphasis on fearlessness and courage, hero-worship is ruled out, for it is open to all men to become heroes or at least to become more heroic than they might otherwise remain. He declared explicitly that "we must worship heroism, not heroes. The hero may later on disgrace himself and in any case must cease to exist, but heroism is everlasting."[59] He admonished some of his followers for being worshippers of a person and not a principle, and added that the worship of any person, far from elevating, only lowers one. Acceptance of principles without assimilation is the result and this is not enough.[60] The safest thing is not to worship any person, living or dead, but to worship perfection, which resides only in God, known as Truth. The danger of the individual's feeling of weakness is, according to Gandhi, that it is compensated for by a desire for power. The alternative and superior way for the weak man is to shelter behind a worthy cause rather than to seek power as a prop to self-confidence. "Measures must always in a progressive society be held superior to men, who are after all imperfect instruments, working for their fulfilment."[61] If we want to serve society, we must put measures before men. The latter come and go, but causes must survive even the greatest of them.[62]

POLITICAL LEADERSHIP AND THE MASSES

Gandhi's plea for heroism in society involved him in the recognition of the need for inspired leadership in political and social activity and the role of small groups as pioneers and pathfinders, but also in a stout refusal to distinguish sharply between the elect and the masses. "All cannot be leaders, but all can be bearers,"[63] he declared in 1921. Courage, endurance, fearlessness and above all self-sacrifice are the qualities required of our leaders. "A person belonging to the suppressed classes exhibiting these qualities in their fullness would certainly be able to lead the nation; whereas the most finished orator, if he has not got these qualities, must fail."[64] In well-ordered organizations, leaders are elected, he said, for convenience of work, not for extraordinary merit. A leader is only first among equals. Someone may be put first, but he is no stronger than the weakest link in the chain.[65] And yet the true leader shows his capacity to assume heavy burdens of responsibility by taking upon himself the errors and failings of those weaker than he is, and if necessary atoning for them and using them as the basis of his own self-examination.

A leader is useless when he acts against the promptings of his conscience. Furthermore, he proves himself and rises to the height of his position of responsibility, his Atlas-like burden, only when he is prepared to make an act of acceptance, a gesture of sacrifice, even an act of vicarious atonement. Naomi Mitchison has well described the persistence in politics of the idea of catharsis or conversion, an idea derived from religious mythology and to be found also in some primitive societies. Rationalists may chafe at the idea of the blood sacrifice, or washing in the blood of the lamb, and of the redeemer or mediator between man and God, but politics, as Sorel and Pareto have pointed out, is inevitably irrational insofar as it is concerned with the passions and not merely the rational purposes of men; it cannot dispense with myths.

It may be that leaders and led should always have this "tragic drama" relation between them: that no leader should be tolerable to the led unless he or she has made the act of acceptance, has experienced the change of focus ("rebirth") and is prepared if necessary to be the sacrifice. As it is, a certain number of leaders have done this, to some extent at least, but not all.[66]

Those who try to dispense with the notion of political charisma also tend to concentrate on the normal behavior of a stable society and to regard crises as aberrations and abnormalities insofar as they cannot be coped with by conventional procedures. The heroic and revolutionary conception of political and social action is, however, based on the view well expressed by Herzen. In order to influence and lead men, it is not enough to demonstrate political truths to them as geometrical theorems are demonstrated; it is necessary to dream their dreams. This view is at least as old as Philo Judaeus, who said in his *De Josepho*[67] that the true statesman is, like Joseph, the wise interpreter of the dreams of men, who can sit in judgment on the daydreams and fantasies of his fellows, who may imagine that they are awake.

In traditional India, the roles of the political leader and of the soothsayer were sharply demarcated; the Brahmin and the Kshatriya, the seer and the doer, just collaborate rather than usurp each other's functions. In modern times, the roles tend to be combined or the role of the seer is altogether abandoned. Hume, for example, put forward the familiar view that no leader can receive a general mandate or be universally recognized and accepted. The ascendancy of the ruler or of any leader is based primarily upon the approval of some limited group with specific interests; other groups with other interests are then in time subdued by force or persuasion. The picture of a society composed of different groups with clashing interests is dominant in political thought in the West, and the two-party system has been proclaimed as the paradigm of a tolerable competitive model, in which the rules of the game are equitable. In India competition is anathema and the supreme stress is on concord and social harmony, in which the holders and seekers of political power have to justify themselves in terms of the common needs and ends, the accepted values of society. Power must be diffused in such a way that the entire system is based on a conception of social virtue morally prior to the clashing claims of sectional interests. The appeal to individual conscience and obligation (*dharma*) must be combined with the recognition of the moral status of the heroic leaders who have proved themselves by acts of sacrifice (*yajna*) and fearlessness (*abhaya*).

As a result, Gandhi and even more his followers in contemporary India display an ambiguous and even ambivalent attitude to political power, in the conventional sense, and continually appeal to society against the State, to public opinion against the minimized role of government. The difficulty here has been well summed up by Joan Bondurant:

> The suggestion that, ideally, society would be best governed by a class that does not want to rule but agrees to do so for the good of society has been advanced more than once in the course of centuries of man's reflection upon political processes and institutions. But a system of extra-party, extra-institutional leadership, established through demonstration of sincerity, service, effectiveness, and direct appeal, and functioning as political conscience within a system of representative, democratic government, has not yet been formulated.[68]

Inevitably, Gandhi was too preoccupied with the problems of the rebel to pay enough attention to the tasks before a ruler. In view of the lethargy of his countrymen, his doctrines required a constant appeal to heroism, the heroism of martyrs rather than of conquerors, more capable of inspiring civil disobedience than of improving the quality of government.

Gandhi insisted that a living faith cannot be manufactured by a majority and that corruption is the bane of governments by majority. Some would argue that, while there is often corruption where there is a government supported by a majority, it is not necessary that such governments should be specially prone to corruption. Gandhi, however, took it for granted, like Plato, that in the midst of suspicion, discord, antagonistic interests, superstition, fear, distrust and the like, not only is there no safety in numbers but there may even be danger in them.

> Numbers become irresistible when they act as one man under exact discipline. They are a self-destroying force when each pulls

his own way or when no one knows which way to pull. . . . I am convinced that there is safety in fewness so long as we have not evolved cohesion, exactness and intelligent co-operation and responsiveness. One virtuous son is better than one hundred loafers. Five *Pandavas* were more than a match for one hundred *Kauravas*. A disciplined army of a few hundred picked men has time without number routed countless undisciplined hordes.[69]

Gandhi agreed that in a popular institution, it must be the opinion of the majority that must count. But he always held that when a respectable minority objects to any rule of conduct, it would be dignified for the majority to yield to the minority.

Numerical strength savours of violence when it acts in total disregard of any strongly felt opinion of a minority. The rule of majority is perfectly sound, only where there is no rigid insistence on the part of the dissenters upon their dissent and where there is on their behalf a sportsmanlike obedience to the opinion of the majority. No organization can run smoothly when it is divided into camps, each growling at the other and each determined to have its own way by hook or by crook.[70]

This could happen within any party, even more so in the whole of society.

The greatest obstacle to the incarnation of the heroic ideal in society, Gandhi felt, is that we have not yet emerged from the "mobocratic" stage. He was aware, like Mikhailovsky, that even strong and honest minds were ruined by surrendering to murky movements, springing from mass fear and mimicry, and moulded by the degrading herd instinct of collective mimicry. Mikhailovsky, in his essay "The Hero and the Crowd" (1882), recalled how easily medieval crowds were hypnotized by mass hysteria, but hoped that the lessons of history might push the nineteenth-century crowd a stage further along the road to self-command. Gandhi too had no illusion in this regard. He declared that his consolation lay in the fact that "nothing is so easy as to train mobs, for the simple reason that they have no mind, no premeditation. They act in a frenzy. . . . They repent quickly."[71] He insisted that we dare not reject a single member of the community, for we shall make progress only if we carry all with us. "My faith in the people is boundless.

Theirs is an amazingly responsive nature. Let not the leader distrust them,"[72] he declared in 1920. He felt that the masses are by no means so foolish, or unintelligent as we sometimes imagine.

> They often perceive things with their intuition, which we ourselves fail to see with our intellect. But whilst the masses know what they want, they often do not know how to express their wants and, less often, how to get what they want. Herein comes the use of leadership, and disastrous results can easily follow a bad, hasty, or what is worse, selfish lead.[73]

The "potential hero" in a democracy sees what others do not. His will to action is stronger, his knowledge of what must be done to realize what he sees is surer. For these reasons, he finds himself more often than not in a minority. His sense of his vocation impels him to fight for his insight, and his loyalty to the democratic ideal compels him to make this interest the common faith of the majority. So long as he does not renounce politics as a sphere of activity, his task is to get himself accepted by a majority. Insofar as he seeks to win popular support by patient methods of education, relying upon the inherent reasonableness of his vision, he runs the risk of failure. He may, therefore, be tempted to become a demagogue to cajole and cater to the majority. He thus acquires a contempt for the group he leads by virtue of the methods by which he corrupts them. If the majority is persuaded that he is right, he may be further tempted to press for greater powers and to usurp delegated power to secure his own ends. Gandhi safeguarded against these dangers by insisting, first of all, that the heroic leader must never hold office or occupy any formal position of power. Secondly, he must seek acceptance and maintain it not just through reasoning with the masses, and certainly not by appealing to their negative emotions. He must identify himself with the dreams, activities and sufferings of the people. His life must be a continual sacrifice of self in the immediate service of his fellow men. He must be a monk, striving to become a saint, willing to be a martyr, a non-violent revolutionary, a moral educator who can bring about a new political consciousness and creative social awareness among the masses.

Especially in India, Gandhi felt, the masses have no political consciousness. Their politics are confined to bread and salt and to communal adjustments. Politicians must represent the masses in opposition to government.

> But if we begin to use them before they are ready we shall cease to represent them. We must first come in living touch with them by working for them and in their midst. We must share their sorrows, understand their difficulties and anticipate their wants. . . . We must see how we like being in the boxes, miscalled houses, of the labourers of Bombay. We must identify ourselves with the villagers who toil under the hot sun beating on their bent backs and see how we would like to drink water from the pool in which the villagers bathe, wash their clothes and pots, in which their cattle drink and roll. Then and not till then shall we truly represent the masses and they will, as surely as I am writing this, respond to every call.[74]

Gandhi stressed the necessity of using our imagination when making moral decisions. To be capable of moral judgment and moral conduct on a significant scale, one has necessarily to put oneself in the place of other people and imagine sympathetically how they feel. Like Adam Smith, he pointed to the connection of conscience with sentiments of active sympathy and imagination. Gandhi recognized no God except the God that is to be found in the hearts of the "dumb millions." He said in 1939 that "I worship the God that is Truth or Truth which is God through the service of these millions."[75] Further, anything that millions can do together is, he believed, charged with a unique power, the magical potency of collective *tapas* or moral fervor, the cumulative strength of generally shared sacrifices.[76]

CONSCIENCE AND HEROISM

Gandhi was anxious to combine his stress on individual conscience with a program of mass action, requiring not merely an ardent and select band of heroic leaders but a contagious spirit of heroism in society. He was, however, inclined to underestimate the extent to which popular opinion could clash with the high purposes of heroic leadership. This brought him considerable disillusionment with the Indian masses, in whose capacity for non-violence and courage he had believed, toward the end of his life. The intentions of his followers may have been unmistakably good, but they tended to ignore the limits of heroic social action in a society of enslaved men who are not entirely capable of grasping the theoretical justification or the practical application of the heroic ideal.

In Homeric society or in the *Ramayana,* though the *agathos,* the warrior or the Kshatriya leader (the *satyagrahi,* in Gandhi's reformulation of the concept) may display *arete* or embody *satya* and *ahimsa,* and therefore deserve to succeed, it was inconceivable that no steps should be taken by society to ensure that its highest standards were generally maintained. Public opinion, the *demou phatis,* was recognized to be the most important standard. Appearances are no less important than facts, and intentions matter less to the generality of people than what they regard as attainable results. The Homeric hero could not fall back upon his own image of himself, for it only had the value which others put upon it. A feeling of pain and anger is the natural response to what seems to be failure, and thus the claims of society against the *agathos* or hero are enforced. The hero must continually prove himself in the eyes of the people.

We have the tragic spectacle of the noble hero at odds with an environment that is shown to be too strong for him through the weaknesses of his fellow men. The Hamlets of this world hurt themselves, and suffer intensely through their own inward cogitations and ceaseless, tortuous self-analysis. But the hero, like the valiant knight of La Mancha, is trounced by the prisoners whose liberty he secured and fares worse at the hands of the rough herdsmen. Neither can attain the serenity of spirit and transcendence of suffering that comes either through intense love of one's fellow men or the pure contemplation that helps to overcome the *principium individuationis.* The hero represents a revolutionary urge, a desire to defy the powers that be, a longing for absolute freedom from the necessities that press upon us in our ordinary lives. We recognize that this revolutionary, iconoclastic urge in ourselves is heroic; indeed all progress depends upon it, and yet when it exceeds itself or expects too much of others and of the world around it, it is visited by penalties which, however undeserved or excessive, are unavoidable.

The price that the hero must pay is ultimate neglect—even obloquy or hypocritical adulation or, at the most, posthumous canonization. To withdraw at the right time may be a way out, but it cannot be contemplated by the irrepressibly heroic leader. Hence the Greek or ancient Indian mistrust of the tendency to carry men too far and too fast from the common herd and from the beaten track, into that state of zeal and infatuation with individual ideals where the ordinary feelings of men and the conventions of society become irrelevant. Tragedy ensues against the background of immense forces, more powerful if less estimable than the best that the individual can produce. The heroic individual becomes irrepressibly anarchistic when, though he is conscious of the pressure of society upon him, he becomes too completely convinced of the capacity of himself and of his followers to break free from the limitations of their fellow men. The masses will use the heroic leader for their own purposes rather than enable him to realize fully his own. There is a deep sense in which it is true to say that it is the leader who is finally led or pushed along a path which may end in a fearful precipice. The hero is doomed, like the heroes of tragedy. He may welcome martyrdom, which may be admirable, but he could easily develop at the height of despair an unarticulated death wish, which represents his moment of disillusionment and involuntary abdication.

The difficulty becomes even more marked and poignant when the heroic individual, whose conscience is all-important to him, advocates and attempts to realize the fusion of the roles of the saint and the revolutionary. The saint declares that the only way to reform politics and society is to persuade and inspire masses of people to become far more reasonable and kindly than they are; the revolutionary insists that no such widespread change of heart can be created by mere exhortation or even by excellent example, and that we must begin by changing the conditions of society. To raise men to a higher degree of moral integrity without first improving their conditions would be to perform a miracle. To this the saint may reply that you cannot change conditions without first creating a widespread desire to do so, as we are nearly all too selfish or cowardly to risk much, even for the sake of a new society and a new political order. The saint feels that unless he learns to know himself in relation to God or the universe and gains self-mastery, he can neither know what is truly desirable nor have the strength to live in service of his fellows. The revolutionary, on the other hand, feels that to worry about his own soul is selfish and mean and to worry about the souls of others is presumptuous and sanctimonious. Furthermore, the saint may be led to deify the individual and belittle the aims and concerns of society, while the revolutionary may be led to disparage individuality and hypostatize society. Strength of will is gained and realized through heroic action, but it is combined with a capacity for silent suffering that is the product of thought and conscience.

Gandhi sympathized with both positions and hoped to resolve the apparent conflict between them by commending both conscience and heroism, thus combining honor and morality. He condemned spiritual sanctimoniousness and the obsession with private salvation; he also condemned the violence and impatience that produce a ruthless element in the revolutionary. He believed that a change of heart is neither genuine nor lasting if it does not result in changes in the social and political order. He was equally concerned to show that social meliorism and political messianism are self-destructive insofar as they ignore the values that they invoke in the process of achieving their ultimate aims. It is impossible to persuade people that a change in the existing order is desirable without the personal commitment to values that are held sacred. On the other hand, it is useless to cling to what one cherishes as being of absolute importance and not to care about its acceptance as a criterion of social action and the goal of political life. We may similarly contrast, following Turgenev, the introspective man of thought and the extroverted man of action, Hamlet and Don Quixote. The Hamlets of this world, with their passion for self-criticism and self-analysis, may envy at times the Don Quixotes for their enthusiastic commitment and their capacity for non-reflective, enthusiastic action. But the latter are sometimes characterized by a certain dullness and blind fanaticism. They are, in Turgenev's language, like flying cranes but also like obstinate rams.

In the end, Gandhi neither accepted the dichotomies between contemplative and crusader, saint and politician, private and public virtues, nor even allowed that there can be any real conflict of values or virtues that may be regarded as ultimate and absolute.

Like the Stoics, especially Diogenes Laertes, he thought that the different virtues involve one another and the true possessor of one must possess all and, further, that virtue is sufficient in itself to ensure individual and collective happiness, even if its attainment and its preservation involves a great deal of suffering. Also, like Cleanthes, he believed that virtue can never be lost. On the other hand, Gandhi did not go so far as the Stoics in their refusal to accept that there could be anything intermediate between virtue and vice. He believed that there could be degrees of truth and nonviolence, courage and self-restraint. In the Indian context, Gandhi was concerned with the integrity of the Indian tradition as well as the needs of a vast, revolutionary movement. He rejected the borrowed conception of terrorism as a legitimate instrument of a revolutionary program, and at the same time he discarded the prevailing notion of the spiritual life as a matter for monks in monasteries or peripatetic pilgrims and recluses. Above all, Gandhi was concerned to show that the sickness of industrial civilization and the "soullessness" of contemporary politics are as much the cause as the consequence of the spiritual poverty, moral impotence and apathy of the majority of mankind.

7

Satya

ABSOLUTE AND RELATIVE TRUTH

Every political theory absolutely depends on a theory of truth whether it makes it explicit or not. As a basis for a programme of action, it always conceals a theory of truth. In justifying any given type of State . . . we must know of whom the recognition of truth in a social body may be expected, and under what conditions it may be possible. The problem of authority in social and political relations is inextricably tied up with the problem of knowledge. Conversely, whatever the doctrine of truth may be, it has certain inevitable and determinable consequences for political theory . . . the difference between an absolute and relative theory of truth is . . . of decisive, constitutive importance in establishing institutions which form the public will. Man has always justified unlimited coercion by rightly or wrongly assuming and monopolizing the possession of some political truth.

HANS BARTH

From first to last, *satya*, or truth, was sacred to Gandhi—the supreme value in ethics, politics and religion, the ultimate source of authority and of appeal, the *raison d'être* of all existence. He regarded it as a "philosopher's stone," the sole talisman available to mortal man.[1] It is *Paramarthasatya*, the highest of human ends, transcending and endowing value to *artha*, or material welfare, *kama*, or human affections and happiness, *dharma*, or the moral law and cosmic order, and also to *moksha*, or eventual emancipation. This basic belief is an ever-present element in the Indian tradition and is common to the Hindu, Buddhist and Jain religions, though at different times *satya* has in practice been subordinated in emphasis—without making it wholly subservient—to *moksha, dharma, ahimsa* and even to *artha*. *Satya* has also been regarded at times as entirely equivalent to *dharma*. Gandhi declared that morality is the basis of things and truth is the substance of all morality.[2] *Satya* is the essence of *dharma*.

It must be noted at the very outset that the word *satya* does not correspond exactly to what we normally mean by truth or by veracity. It has a variety of connotations, of which the most important are: real, sincere, existent, pure, good, effectual, valid.[3] *Satya*, as Gandhi stressed on several occasions, is derived from *sat*, which means being. *Sat* also means abiding, actual, right, wise, self-existent essence, as anything really is, as anything ought to be.[4] The derivation of *satya* from *sat* was taken by Gandhi to imply that "nothing exists in reality except Truth, everything else is illusion."[5] Beyond and behind the illusory flux of fleeting phenomena there is an eternal substratum of noumenal reality, a single bedrock of supernal Truth. In the Indian tradition, *SAT* in its highest sense stands for the absolute, archetypal Reality and for the absolute, archetypal Truth. Although a clear distinction was made between knowledge and being, between epistemology and ontology—in fact, the main preoccupation of the classical philosophers in India was with strictly epistemological enquiries—this distinction was said to be transcended at the height of the human quest, when the knower and the known are united in a state of mystical communion owing to their essential identity with a single, if unknowable, Reality. Until this mystical communion, transcending

thought, is achieved, truth consists merely in the correspondence between the objective notion (*Begriff*) and the thing in itself (*Sache*),
in the language of Kant and Hegel, or between atomic propositions
and atomic facts, in early Russellian terminology. In fact, ancient
Indian philosophers went much farther than this and contended, like
Parmenides, that the known is the same thing that can be thought and
that can be.

The Rigvedic and Platonic notion of the ever-existent Absolute
Truth was essential to Gandhi for the purpose of endowing truth, as
normally understood, with indisputable and universal sanctity as the
highest moral value and the highest human end. Being chiefly concerned with individual integrity in human society, he appealed to the
ultimate, final and preordained integrity of the cosmic order. Furthermore, the moral order of the cosmos (*ṛta*) reflects *Sat* as the
Natural Law of Eternal Truth, which no man can ever elude. This
metaphysical and transcendental conception of truth, which is an integral part of Indian tradition, implies the transiency of falsehood,
the elusive but indestructible nature of Absolute Truth or Reality,
the sustaining power and self-subsistent energy of every intimation
of that which is ultimately real or true, the notion that repressed truth
acts like magic when revealed and possesses a therapeutic effect, that
truth is the only source of power in the long run, and that *asat*, or
untruth, is incapable of binding universal consciousness or the Life-
Force to the limitations of the individual. Further, whereas truth is
universifiable, falsehood cannot secure universal assent. *Satya*, derived from *Sat* or the one reality, is the source of eternal and universal values like truth, righteousness and justice—truth in the realm of
knowledge, righteousness in the domain of conduct and justice in
the sphere of social relations. Truth, in the narrow epistemological
sense of common usage, is only a part of the wider meaning of *satya*.

Not only was truth the most important and an all-inclusive principle to Gandhi, but it was also logically prior to all the other human
virtues and excellences. In daily life, we may gain only the faintest
glimpses of the mighty effulgence and indescribable luster of Absolute Truth, "a million times more intense than that of the sun."[6]
But as truth is the very breath of our life,[7] a man without even
a particle of it would be dead, and life without a modicum of
integrity would be not only worthless but also meaningless. If

everything is lifeless without truth, untruth is destructive and emasculating, despite apparent and temporary benefits that we may ascribe to it. We may never attain to the truth in its fullness, but it will suffice if we never turn our backs on it. All our activities must be truth-centered, for we are really alive only to the extent that we are truthful. "You feel vitality in you when you have got truth in you. . . . It is a permanent thing of which you cannot be robbed. You may be sent to the gallows or put to torture; but if you have truth in you, you will experience an inner joy."[8] It is the ability to determine truth for himself that distinguishes man from the brute,[9] and yet truth is not reached by reasoning alone but by immediate apprehension. There are degrees of apprehension, and although Absolute Truth is constant and complete in itself, human awareness of it is a continuous and dynamic process. To find truth completely is to realize oneself and one's destiny, to become perfect.[10] Every truth is "self-acting" and has inherent strength,[11] but it is latent until it is embodied in the actions as well as the thoughts of a human being.

The Gandhian apotheosis of *satya* is conceptually more in accord with the views of the ancient Greeks and of the Stoics than with the Cartesian conception of truth, but it is in practice closer to modern existentialist rather than classical notions of truth insofar as it stresses action rather than thought. The Greeks, among the greatest truth-worshippers in history, praised wisdom as the participation of human reason in the divine reason which pervaded the cosmos, whereas the Jews praised wisdom as the understanding and fear of the personal God who determined the course of history by His inscrutable will. Wisdom consists, said Heraclitus, in saying what is true and acting in obedience to Nature. Veracity for most Greeks was not something negative, not just an acute consciousness of the errors and stupidities of others, but a passionate sense of truth as something positive, admirable, desirable, beautiful. The pursuit of truth was not merely regarded as a good in itself but it was also regarded by Pythagoras, Plato and even Aristotle as the highest kind of life, comparable to the contemplative activity of God. The traditional view that truth was given in revelation by the gods was replaced by the conviction that men can find it out for themselves. Truth has its own appeal and makes its own claims on its servants, as Democritus saw when he said that he would rather find out a single truth than have the Kingdom of the Persians. The seriousness with which men then sought truth had indeed a religious earnestness as when Anaxagoras built an altar to Truth.

Truth was apostrophized and transcendentalized particularly by the Pythagoreans and the Stoics, but even the Cynics, who stood ideas on their head and deliberately falsified the currency (*paracharaxis*) of everyday language, were mainly anxious not to allow rules of convention such authority as they believed to belong only to the rules or laws of nature. Similarly, the Sophist Antiphon contrasted the adventitious rules of legislators with the inevitable and innate laws of nature. If a man transgresses the rules which are innate in nature, the injury which he incurs is not due to men's opinion but to the facts of the case. Later on even Aquinas, who denied that truth was the understanding of a bodiless essence, regarded it as the utterance of what exists and did not dichotomize what is instinctive and what is construed, what is found and what is enacted. The Stoics had identified *nature* with *ratio*, but for Aquinas this *ratio*, or meaning, was a shaping purpose, not just a logical essence.

The Encyclopedists of the eighteenth century returned to the Stoic notion that Nature, being Reason, has established rational interrelations between all things, and that evil implies ignorance of these relations and the consequent failure to obey them. There were, of course, differences between the Stoics and the Encyclopedists in their conception of nature. The Stoics saw nature, not as created by God, but as itself divine—they were monists but not monotheists. When the Encyclopedists spoke of nature as rational they meant only (a) that it is intelligible that everything that happens does so in accordance with a discoverable law and that there is a coherent system of such laws and (b) that it was created by a rational Being (i.e., a Being that reasons). The Supreme Being is also subject to that Truth which is the theoretic basis of morality, so that morality proceeds from a power higher still, from Eternal Reason. Early in the eighteenth century Vico held that society is founded on truth, the basic demand being that all action must be *bona fide* and founded on mutual trust. The law of society (*lex societatis*), which constitutes natural law, comprises two imperatives— *ex bona fide agito* and *ex vero vivito*. Cicero's dictum in *De officis* that truthfulness in word and promise (*fides*) is the basis of justice was amended by Vico into the maxim that truth itself, the mother of fidelity and all other virtues, is the foundation of justice in nature and society.

The Enlightenment also brought in the notion that truth could set men free and make them capable of emancipating their fellow men from traditional and respectable errors. In the nineteenth century, this Socratic notion was firmly rejected by Nietzsche, who held that truth is something to be created, not discovered, to be enacted and not to be found. With Kierkegaard we get the belief that truth lies only in action and can be experienced only through action. There is no union, no communion, no universality to contest the dominion of the individual, unique and isolated; truth is forever the outcome of his own decision and can be realized only in the free acts that spring from this decision.

Gandhi could not regard truth either as solely the object of reason or as simply the product of human decision. For him, as for Simone Weil, truth is nothing less than the splendor of reality and cannot be gained without an understanding of the Eternal Law of Nature, but when it is perceived and seized, it must be acted upon. In this sense, truth must be both discovered and created, found and enacted. Gandhi, who read Mazzini, would have agreed with him that truth is to be sought among the secrets of an intuition that defies analysis, in the rapid, intense concentration of every faculty upon a given point, and that having found the truth, the individual's duty lies in making it known and putting it into effect. The world is not merely a spectacle; it is a field of battle, upon which those who care for the truth must play their part, whether as victors or martyrs. In this activist view of truth, Gandhi went even further than Marx. It is not enough for thought to be based upon truth; the life of the thinker must express it, must represent it visibly in his actions.

In short, Gandhi's position is theoretically closer to that of the Natural Law School than to that of the existentialists, though he comes close to the latter in practical intention. There are moral truths to be discovered, and their truth does not depend on their being acted upon. Man is not (as for the existentialists) his own legislator, giving a meaning to his life by committing himself to principles which have no significance at all apart from such committal. He would not go so far as this, but he did stress that we could lay no claim to our independent truth unless we realize it by our own efforts in our daily life. Like Godwin, Gandhi believed that it is the property of truth to be fearless and to prove victorious, that truth must be sacred and inviolable. But he went even further and believed, like Thoreau, that any truth is better than make-believe, and that the individual and society must, like nature, rest on an underpinning of granitic truth, the lowest primitive rock. The universe reflects *Sat* or Absolute Truth and society must ultimately rely on the same foundation, which is possible only when its members become truth-worshippers, common votaries at a single shrine consecrated to the unattainable, but ever-existing and all-powerful, deity of *Sat*, revealed in the world as the Eternal Law of Truth.

TRUTH IS GOD

Gandhi's deification of truth was a deliberate decision. In 1928 he pinned his faith in the benevolence of God shown in the persistence of life in the midst of death, of truth in the midst of untruth and of light in the midst of darkness.[12] Although he regarded God as an impersonal, all-pervading Reality, he was also apt—in the tradition of Vaishnava theism, reinforced by his contact with Christian theologians—to anthropomorphize God. In 1931, however, Gandhi distinctly shifted his emphasis from God to Truth as the ultimate object of human worship and reliance. Truth alone exists; *satya* is derived from *Sat*. If there is God, Truth must be God.[13] Even if we do not wish to assume the existence of God, we must assume the existence of Truth if we are to evolve as human beings. God is difficult to define, but the definition of Truth is deposited in every human heart.[14] In 1932 Mahadev Desai, Gandhi's closest disciple, wondered whether truth could inspire men and conduct movements and possess a power of action in the sense in which belief in God could. Gandhi answered by pointing out that he used the word "truth" in a wide rather than a narrow sense, that the notion of an eternal Ruler (*Ishvara*) is inferior to *satya* defined as the eternal Truth.[15] "Indeed it is all the same whether we say that the universe is a function of Truth or that it is a function of Law." Gandhi held that the Moral Law is logically prior to the existence of God, that the obligatoriness of the law does not derive from God's willing his creatures to obey it. In an important discussion with Dr. Conger in 1933 he stated that the truth as men see it has only relative reality.[16] As no one could live without truth, there is an eternal Truth that permeates the world and unites all men in their essentials with the essence of Reality and of Nature.

Gandhi was concerned to find a common basis for a common quest in the company of atheists and agnostics as well as theists. He said to a friendly atheist: "Truth means existence; the existence of that we know and of that we do not know. The sum total of all existence is absolute truth or the Truth. . . . The concepts of truth may differ. But all admit and respect truth. That truth I call God. . . ."[17] This notion of truth as an objective, impersonal reality is historically prior to the atomistic, epistemological and scientific view of truth. As Russell recognized: "Truth, as conceived by most professional philosophers, is static and final, perfect and eternal; in religious terminology it may be identified with God's thought and those thoughts which, as rational beings we share with God. The perfect model of truth is the multiplication table, which is precise and certain and free from all dross."[18] To Gandhi, as for the Stoics, who identified God with the Logos of Eternal Reason, and for mystics like St. Augustine, Plotinus and Synesius, Truth in its most transcendental sense is identical with God or the Divine Reality and is a proper object of worship and total devotion. Gandhi's ultimate justification for the preservation of this transcendental notion of ultimate Truth was not intellectual but practical, and the same is true of his deification of Truth and even his faith in God. "A mere mechanical adherence to truth and non-violence is likely to break down at the critical moment. Hence I have said that Truth is God."[19] We cannot do without absolutes, felt Gandhi, and what better absolute can we afford than that of Truth?

As a result of his conception of Absolute Truth, identified with the existence and the reality of the totality of things, Gandhi was not merely able to regard *satya* as the necessary basis of all life and, therefore, of human society, but also to look upon every man as a "truth-seeker," by definition. In addition to this Comtean notion that all are seekers after truth, united in a common quest, he be-

lieved that all men inherently embody truth and are thus united in
the possession of a common inalienable inheritance of common
unquestionable potentialities. If no finite being could ever know or
possess truth in its fullness, equally none could be denied it or deprived of it completely. In March 1922, he wrote from prison to
a follower:

> As I proceed in my search for truth it grows upon me that Truth
> comprehends everything. . . . What is perceived by a pure
> heart and intellect is truth for that moment. Cling to it, and it en-
> ables one to reach pure Truth . . . the wonderful implication
> of the great truth *Brahma Satyam Jaganmithya* (*Brahma* is real,
> all else unreal) has grown on me from day to day. It teaches us
> patience. This will purge us of harshness and add to our toler-
> ance. It will make us magnify the molehills of our errors into
> mountains and minimize the mountains of others' errors into
> molehills.[20]

It is because every man inherently embodies truth that he is divine;
this is a more significant formulation for Gandhi than the converse
inference. To believe in Absolute Truth, which is God, implies
that every man embodies a portion of that truth, i.e., is a soul pos-
sessing "soul-force." As truth is the substance of morality, man is a
moral agent only to the extent that he embodies and seeks truth. By
truth is not merely meant the abstention from lies, not just the prudential conviction that honesty is the best policy in the long run, but
even more that we must rule our life by this law of Truth at any
cost.[21] We must say No when we mean No regardless of consequences.[22] He who ignores this law does not know what it is to
speak and to stand for the truth, is like a false coin, valueless.[23] He
has abdicated from his role and status as a moral being. Devotion
to truth is the sole reason for human existence, and truth alone
really sustains us at all times. Without truth it would be impossible
to observe any principles or rules in life. Abstract truth has no
value unless incarnated in human beings who represent it by prov-
ing their readiness to die for it.[24] "The truth of a few will count, the
untruth of millions will vanish even like chaff before a whiff of
wind."[25] If the observance of truth were easy, if truth cost one nothing and were all happiness and ease, there would be no beauty about

it. Even if the heavens should fall, we must adhere to truth. Untruth and dishonesty often seem to win, but in reality truth wins in the end. We do not always know wherein lies our good, and it is, therefore, best to assume that good always comes from following the path of truth. Those who observe it may be few but "they are the salt of the earth, it is they who keep society together, not those who sin against light and truth."[26]

ABSOLUTE AND RELATIVE TRUTH

Gandhi attempted to bridge the distance between his archetypal conception of Absolute Truth and his practical stress on a universal, common quest for truth by sharply distinguishing between absolute and relative truth. He was both somewhat of a pragmatist and something of a Platonist, a difficult combination but one that he did not regard as impossible. Owing to his subordination of contemplation to action as the supreme requirement, it is not surprising that he should attempt to show that an "aristocratic" notion of truth traditionally cherished by an élite or leisured class, could be combined with the relativistic and instrumentalist view of truth that is common in modern mass society. But there was nothing contrived about Gandhi's adherence to a dualistic concept of truth. It flowed naturally out of his metaphysical presuppositions which were part of the earliest Indian tradition. He contended that it is impossible for us to realize perfect Truth so long as we are imprisoned in this mortal frame. We can visualize it only in our imagination.[27] While we must have faith in the Absolute Truth that we can imagine but cannot attain, there is nothing wrong in every man following Truth according to his lights. Indeed, it is his duty to do so. Then if there is a mistake on the part of anyone so following Truth, it will be automatically set right. For:

> The quest of Truth involves *tapas* or self-suffering, sometimes even unto death. There can be no place in it for even a trace of self-interest. In such selfless search for Truth nobody can lose his bearings for long. Directly he takes to the wrong path he stumbles, and is thus re-directed to the right path. Therefore the pursuit of Truth is true *Bhakti* (devotion). . . . There is no place in it for cowardice, no place for defeat.[28]

The path of Truth is believed to be narrow as it is straight; it is like balancing oneself on the edge of a sword. The slightest inattention brings one tumbling to the ground.

Gandhi contended that evil is good or truth misplaced.[29] This does not mean that (as Bentham might say) any motive which is evil, when under certain circumstances it leads to harmful actions, may be good in other circumstances when it inspires harmless actions. It is rather implied that every evil action is based on a mistaken belief (itself a perversion of a partial truth) or a failure to see things as they really are. The mind when swayed by desires becomes a deceiver, a distorting mirror, a tool for rationalizing selfish intentions. Satan speaks at times as the voice of God, untruth masquerades as truth. Satan is illusory in the last analysis, but we are deluded through our ignorance. This is the real difficulty, not the fact that in practice the truth we possess is only relative. As the mind works through innumerable media, argued Gandhi, and as the evolution of the mind is not the same for all, it follows that what may be truth for one may be untruth for another. It is therefore necessary that certain conditions must be observed in making experiments with truth. "Just as for conducting scientific experiments there is an indispensable scientific course of instruction, in the same way strict preliminary discipline is necessary to qualify a person to make experiments in the spiritual realm."[30] It is because we have at present everybody claiming the right of conscience without going through any discipline whatsoever that we cannot cope with the enormous untruth being delivered to a bewildered world. Truth is not to be found by anybody who has not got an abundant sense of humility. "If you would swim on the bosom of the ocean of Truth, you must reduce yourself to a zero."[31] The full apprehension of truth is available only to those who have chosen to fulfill certain ethical conditions. Truth in its totality is at once intellectual and moral in nature, involving the perfection of the knower in both thought and deed.

While a definite discipline is required if we are to go from relative truth to closer approximations to the Absolute Truth or God, we must recognize that in practice we live in a world of relative truths. When Gandhi was cross-examined by the Hunter Committee in 1919, he was asked by the counsel, Sir Chimanlal Setalvad, how the truth was to be determined in the case of conflicting standpoints held honestly by different people. Gandhi replied that the individual himself must determine in each case what he holds to be the truth, that honest striving after truth differs in regard to every individual, but there need not be any confusion.[32] A man must adhere to what he believes to be the truth until he is persuaded to acknowledge his errors. Truth is one but we see it through a glass darkly, only in part, and each according to his own light. The result is naturally a multitude of viewpoints. Where there is honest effort, what appear to be different truths will be like different leaves of the same tree. "Viewpoint is a matter of reasoning, the mind, the intellect. It may shift from time to time without touching the heart."[33]

The significance of Gandhi's distinction between absolute and relative truth lies in the acceptance of the need for a corrective process of experimentation with our own experience, and this presupposes our readiness to admit openly our errors and to learn from them. The politician and the social worker must, like the scientist, conduct experiments with utmost accuracy, forethought and minuteness, and never claim finality or make any subtle pretension to infallibility on behalf of any kind of authority. Gandhi explicitly declared that the right to err and the freedom to experiment constitute the universal and indispensable condition to all progress. Evolution is always experimental, and all progress is possible only through mistakes. This, he felt, is the law of individual moral growth as well as of social and political evolution.[34] Although we must be prepared to visualize Absolute Truth, in practice we must ever regard truth not as a cast-iron dogma, a final statement or a fixed formula, but rather as a many-sided, evolving and dynamic dialectic. Though we must aim always at knowledge which is entire and genuine, we must never suppose that we have it. He wrote to Mirabehn that the way to truth is paved with skeletons over which we have to dare to walk.[35] We must safeguard ourselves against the hypnotism induced by the repetition of an untruth or any device of self-deception.[36] While the possibility of stumbling is implicit in all experimentation, our experimentation must always be undertaken in the name, and with the ideal vision, of Absolute Truth. Similarly, he wrote to a journalist that if he resolved upon adhering to the truth at all costs and on exposing political, social or economic abuses, irrespective of consequences and no matter where they were found, he had cause for hope and encouragement in exact proportion to the depression from without.[37]

In general, Gandhi felt that a man of truth must ever be confident and diffident at the same time, confident in his devotion to truth but humble because of his consciousness of fallibility.[38] His confidence need not be affected by past errors if they are freely admitted, as the discovery of error is a risk that must equally affect all beliefs. Errors of calculation need not affect our constant appreciation of truth, and once we have come to a definite conclusion after groping through errors we need have no doubt about the truth. Where there is no desire for personal advantage the temptation to indulge in untruth is diminished.[39] The deepest truths are always unutterable, and though there is room for confidence, there is no need for missionary zeal or proselytizing fervor.[40] In our attempt to secure acceptance of the relative truths to which we hold, we are naturally drawn into camouflage and exaggeration and a measure of falsehood, but truth, like the sun, shines in the midst of the darkness of untruth. "To belittle truth is like the pranks of children who gloat over their apparent success in hiding the sun when they cover their eyes with the palms of their hands."[41] Truth embodied in the living example of an individual is far more potent than tons of propaganda based on falsehood.[42] People who *live* truth in every one of their acts, be it ever so small, need never repent. It will certainly bear fruit in its own time which, however long it may seem, is still the shortest. Those who have that living faith never fear anything or anybody. "Their truth is their defence and armour, their faith their impregnable shield."[43]

Despite his optimistic view of the triumph of truth in human life and society, Gandhi was well aware of the cynical disregard of truth by politicians and organizers of every sort. As early as 1896 he said that great men alter convictions as often and as quickly as they change clothes if it is to their advantage to do so, though they always simulate sincerity.[44] Far from regarding the practice of truth as common in politics and society Gandhi believed that there was an eternal struggle between forces of good and of evil, of truth and of falsehood, non-violence and brute force:[45]

There are two methods of attaining the desired end: Truthful and Truthless. In our scriptures they have been described respectively as divine and devilish. . . . The final triumph of Truth is always assumed for the divine method. Its votary does not abandon it, even though at times the path seems impenetrable and beset with difficulties and dangers and a departure however slight from that straight path may appear full of promise. His faith even then shines resplendent like the midday sun and he does not despond. With truth for sword, he needs neither steel nor gunpowder.[46]

But truthlessness has opposite attributes, as was illustrated, Gandhi felt, in the first Great War:

The wielder of brute force does not scruple about the means to be used. He does not question the propriety of means, if he can somehow achieve his purpose. This is not *Dharma,* it is *Adharma.* In *Dharma,* there cannot be a particle of untruth. . . . Sacrifice of Truth is the foundation of a nation's destruction.[47]

Truth is the first and heaviest casualty in war.[48] Although truth is by nature simple and self-evident, a purificatory discipline is required to remove *avidya,* or ignorance, that is the basis of evil and which obscures the truth; this ignorance is about one's own true or long-term interest as well as the working of the Moral Law that is the expression of the unity of the universe. If untruth endured and nothing were true to itself and to others, if all laws of life and nature were uncertain and undependable, the universe would turn into chaos.

Gandhi thus combined a metaphysical view of Absolute Truth, a realistic view of relative truth, a Manichean view of the struggle between truth and falsehood, a liberal optimism and a form of spiritual Whiggery. He used the word "truth" in several senses and it is not always clear which is to be taken in a particular context. He believed that there never could be any compromise with error, though there must be compromise and reconciliation between relative truths, and that error ceases to be error when corrected. "A devotee of Truth may not do anything in deference to convention."[49] He must always hold himself open to correction and whenever he discovers himself to be wrong he must confess it at all costs and atone for it. "The seeker after truth must have a heart tender as the lotus and hard as granite."[50] Difficulty of practice must not be confused with disbelief. If we have no zest for this Himalayan expedition in search of truth and if we cannot fulfill its prescribed conditions of success, it is largely owing to the weakness of our faith: "What we see with our physical eyes is more real to us than the only Reality. We know that the appearances are deceptive. And yet we treat trivialities as realities. To see the trivialities as such is half the battle won. It constitutes more than half the search after Truth or God."[51]

Gandhi was once severely criticized for his insistence on moral and metaphysical truths as fundamental in all walks of life. "Don't you think that a preconceived idea of a God, Truth, or Reality might colour the whole trend of our search and hence be a great impediment and may defeat the very purpose of our life?"[52] He replied that no search is possible without some workable assumptions. "If we grant nothing, we find nothing." Since belief in God or the Absolute is coexistent with mankind, its existence is treated as a fact more definite than that of the sun:

> This living faith has solved a large number of puzzles of life. It has alleviated our misery. It sustains us in life, it is our one solace in death. . . . We embark upon the search, because we believe that there is Truth and that it can be found by diligent search and meticulous observance of the well-known and well-tried rules of search. There is no record in history of the failure of such search. Even the atheists who have pretended to disbelieve in God have believed in Truth. The trick they have performed is that of giving God another, not a new, name. His names are Legion. Truth is the crown of them all.[53]

The trouble of course is that this line of reasoning cannot carry general conviction, as its acceptance or rejection is not a matter of factual evidence but of faith and choice. Gandhi wanted to make the willingness to die as fundamental to his political and social thought as Hobbes wished to take the fear of death as unchangeable and universal. He presupposed a Platonic archetype rather than a Hobbesian God at the apex of his image of the universe. Nothing short of the Absolute could justify the insistence on absolute values and induce the sacrifices and self-purificatory discipline that

Gandhi required of those who wished to become heroic leaders and men of conscience, determined to revolutionize the existing political and social order.

THE VOW OF TRUTH

Gandhi recognized that his highly exalted and exacting conception of truth could be comprehended and practiced by only a few. Most people cannot be expected to take the vow of truth, but in the end this is the only way in which men can reach toward the *summum bonum*, the Absolute Truth which is beyond space and time, which is unconditional and eternal. The vow of truth, which he advocated, does not consist merely in verbal truthfulness, but in the increased and constant observance of truth in thought, speech and action. There is no sense in saying that we will observe the truth as far as possible;[54] the sanctity of our pledge requires that we aim at total reliability and make no exceptions. It may not be easy to do so, but this and nothing less must be the aim. It is not abstract truth, but the concrete truthfulness of the individual which constitutes the crucial criterion of value. The vow of truth cannot be taken properly without also taking the vow of fearlessness. Gandhi thought that exact truthfulness follows real fearlessness and that when a man abandons truth in any way, he does so owing to fear in some shape or form.[55] The vow of truth means that there is no place for prejudice, evasion, deception, secretiveness or distortion. Irrelevance is always untruth and should never be uttered.[56] Silence becomes cowardice when the occasion demands speaking the whole truth and acting accordingly.[57] What does it matter if truth is widely abused and fraud commonly practiced so long as those who take the vow of truth feel that they cannot help adhering to it even in the face of hardship?[58]

He believed, like Mark Twain, that all truth is safe and nothing else is safe, and he who keeps back the truth or withholds it from motives of expediency is either a coward or a criminal or both. Gandhi, like Tolstoy, commended Lloyd Garrison's remark, "I will be as harsh as truth and as uncompromising as justice."[59] He was willing to compromise on non-essentials as he was never sure that he was wholly in the right and as life is made up of such compromises.[60] The readiness to agree with one's adversary quickly is generally praiseworthy, but there should be no self in one's action, no fear, no untruth and no compulsion. Any compromise must be natural to oneself, not imposed from without. The desire to compromise must, however, never make the pledged votary of truth cautious in his affirmation of it. "I object not to harsh truth but to spiced truth."[61] As none of us knows the absolute truth, we need to safeguard against bitterness, which blurs the vision even of limited truth. People are prone to exaggerate, to embellish or to modify the truth, wittingly or unwittingly, "a natural weakness of man."[62] And yet, if a votary of truth cannot keep his pledge, this is only because of his indulgence in rationalization. No untruth is ever pardonable in such a man, from whom many sacrifices are demanded by the "stern Goddess" of truth.[63] Gandhi felt that to think, speak and act truly is the best and easiest sacrifice, or *yajna*.[64] We must always distinguish between what is salutary and what is pleasant, between *sreyas* and *preyas*.[65] The votary of truth must achieve a harmony between thought, word and deed, and his life thus becomes a fulfilled oath, a constant vow, or *vrata*, a perpetual pilgrimage, a continual sacrifice, the means to *moksha* or salvation. The votary of truth is not a muddled idealist but a man who meditates before getting into action. He does not take refuge in theoretical speculation but remains steadfast in contemplation while constantly trying to endow his whole life of conscious activity with a pervading sanctity of *pavitra*. He has taken nothing less than "a vow of saintship." It is only by personal steadfastness, by holding on to his vow that a man may be useful to others to an exceptional degree. It is impossible to live as a saint in the midst of society if one's entire life is not a fulfilled oath.

It is obvious that the exacting vow of truth, tantamount to a vow of saintship, can be taken only by a few. Such men, Gandhi felt, can become "experts in truth and non-violence." Just as a society organized on the basis of untruth and violence needs experts, so, too, we must make it possible not only for individuals but for groups and nations to practice truth and non-violence. "That, at any rate, is my dream."[66] We must get rid of mass inertia and enable people to get out of the old ruts and rooted prejudices.[67] The process of spiritual discipline will naturally differ for different individuals. "The highest truth needs no communing; it is by its very nature self-propelling and radiates its influence silently like the rose its fragrance without the intervention of a medium."[68] In the logician's sense of truth, only propositions can be true. All knowing is assertive. For Gandhi, the knowledge of the highest truth does not involve making an assertion or judgment, and is not an act of knowing as commonly understood. It is a knowing in which the knower is self-consciously receptive, though to become capable of it he must have practiced self-discipline in the past.

The apathy of the masses is connected with their formal adherence to blind beliefs and it can be shaken only by the force of individual example, not of propaganda. A mechanical vote or a grudging assent is wholly inadequate if not injurious to a worthy cause.[69] If there is any vital truth in the message of the leaders of society, "it should be self-propagating and reach millions by the sheer force of thought."[70] No doubt, the masses cannot be expected to do more than respond to the call of truth delivered by leaders in whom they could trust as the vow of truth cannot be taken by large numbers. Gandhi, however, believed in the capacity of the masses to suffer and sacrifice for truth in certain circumstances; it may be limited, but to him it was undeniable. If all of us regulate our lives by truth, there would be no need for civil resistance, but it is required as long as only a few are governed by the sovereign principle of truth:[71]

If the evolution of forms takes aeons, why should we expect wonders in the evolution of thought and conduct? And yet the age of miracles is not gone. As with individuals, so with nations. I hold it to be perfectly possible for masses to be suddenly converted and uplifted. Suddenness is only seeming. No one can say how far the leaven has been working. The most potent forces are unseen, even unfelt, for long. But they are working none the less surely. Religion to me is a living faith in the supreme Unseen Force. That Force has confounded mankind before and it is bound to confound us again. Buddha taught us to defy appearances and trust in the final triumph of Truth and Love. This was his matchless gift to Hinduism and to the world. . . . The best propaganda is not pamphleteering but for each one of us to try to live the life we would have the world to live.[72]

There is, unfortunately, too much expediency even among some of the best of religious men, who think that standing forth in the face of prejudice will impair their usefulness for service. Such an attitude is "a concession, although totally unconscious, to Satan."[73] While it is true that we seem to see in nature and society both the benignant and the malignant forces in full activity, it is the prerogative of man to rise superior to the eternal duel and the only way this can be done is by employing "truth-force" to the fullest extent.[74]

TRUTH IN POLITICS AND SOCIETY

Gandhi pleaded for "a truthful programme and truthful parties." "Let people only work in programmes in which they believe implicitly. Loyalty to human institutions has its well-defined limits. To be loyal to an organization must not mean subordination of one's settled convictions."[75] Even a lawyer must recognize that his duty is always to help judges to arrive at the truth.[76] Parties may fall and rise again, but the deep convictions of votaries of truth must be unaffected by such passing changes. Loyalty requires the stability of truth. There is no need of a wall of protection against criticism, for then our conviction is only skin-deep. Fear of disloyalty to a party, trade union or government that does not respect the truth is, in fact, a form of disloyalty to truth. Gandhi felt that India had to choose between the modern "Western" maxim "might is right" and the "Eastern" one that "truth alone conquers" (*satyam eva jayate*). "The choice is to begin with the labouring class."[77] Western politicians are honest in that they do not take bribes, but they are open to subtler influences. People are bribed with honors. Neither real honesty nor living conscience are common. Newspapers are especially dishonest and mislead the voters, whose views swing like the pendulum of a clock and are never steadfast. Honesty is sacrificed to patriotism.[78] All this can be changed if pledged votaries of truth, revolutionaries with integrity, give a proper lead to the masses.

The constant concern to maintain a respect for truth, objectivity and dialogue in a world delivered more and more into illusion and cynicism may sometimes degenerate into a sort of dogmatic hauteur, an apology for abstention from public activity. But truth, as

Gandhi understood it, can be known only in living engagement. It is born of a community of destiny, from the cares, the problems, even the errors of those whose fate we share. "Truth binds man to man in association. Without truth there can be no social organization."[79] It emerges from the comradeship of the crowd rather than from the solitary speculations of the recluse. This might seem puzzling at first sight. It is obvious that in order to acquire at least some kinds of understanding, it is not enough to be an observer; we must involve ourselves in relations with other men. No doubt, even in such matters solitude and reflection are also needed, a standing away from oneself and one's actions as well as from other people and their actions. The trouble with politicians today is that they neither have the time to meditate nor the desire to share the life of the common people. The alienation between rulers and ruled, politicians and the people, is both the cause and the index of the extent of untruth and deception that have entered into social relationships and political affiliations. No wonder Marx and Lenin explicitly rejected the absolute validity of truth-telling and regarded men's ethical ideas merely as part of their social consciousness, which is often a false consciousness, reflecting and veiling, transfiguring and glorifying specific needs, class interests and requirements of authority. Gandhi thought that social discord and political conflict result from the incompatibility of opposed relative truths, each claiming or pretending to be absolute. Like Dr. Stockmann in Ibsen's play, he felt that all our spiritual sources of life are poisoned, our whole bourgeois society rests on a soil teeming with a pestilence of lies. The function of cant in society is to allow an individual or a people to do anything whatsoever, provided they preserve appearances and obstinately maintain that everything is going on for the best for everybody.

Although Gandhi believed that the integrity of the individual is tested by the intensity of his search for the certainty of absolute truth, his efficacy in society is determined chiefly by the extent to which he is earnest in his experiments with relative truth. "To tread the path of truth implies an active life in the world of men."[80] The measure of a man's greatness lies in his capacity for courageous and open struggle against conventional falsehoods and sanctified untruth. Like William James, Gandhi felt that truth should energize

and do battle, that it could be of the greatest practical utility in all
worldly as well as spiritual affairs. A man who has learned to respect the truth is entitled and required to uphold the truth against
the very society which has taught him to respect it. He deserves to
be respected by his fellow men owing to his own quest for the truth,
and he will secure the respect due to him from those who share his
fundamental search even if they reject most of his beliefs and opinions. This is the indispensable foundation of a free and egalitarian
society and of every liberal association in a civic community.

Gandhi quoted the Indian story of the six blind men and the
elephant and added that we too are blind. We must be content with
believing the truth as it appears to us at any given time in any particular situation.[81] Truth is what we believe in our hearts, not what
we profess.[82] A mechanical adherence to a "belief" is useless.
Hence the folly of forcible conversion, of intimidating propaganda,
of systematic proselytizing. "A man of truth must also be a man of
care."[83] Truth without humility is an arrogant caricature. There is
no remedy against hypocrisy, but the world cannot be fooled all the
time.[84]

Furthermore, if we cannot distinguish between a man and his
views or his deeds, we cannot claim to be genuinely in search of
truth. There was an element of skepticism in Gandhi's view of
truth because of his Hindu belief in the ubiquity of error. Like
Emerson, he felt that no man must be a conformist. "Truth is not
truth merely because it is ancient."[85] He recognized that all society
today is founded on intolerance and it was a point of honor with
him to privilege heresy and to respect criticism. He also thought
that we are deprived of the truth by the energy with which we im-
merse ourselves in a truth. To be wholly one-sided or dogmatic is
to evoke an equally extreme reaction and thus generate personal
bitterness and destructive conflict. The only safeguard is for men to
emulate each other in upholding the supreme sanctity of truth in relation to all other concerns. Any actual moral decision stops the infinite regression of the search for reasons, and this holds also for a
general decision in human society to set up truth as the supreme
value.

It is undeniable that Gandhi's application of his exalted notion of
truth to the explosive atmosphere of political controversy rendered

him vulnerable to the accusations of subjectivism and of unconscious bias. But he never made any special claims for himself other than that he was conducting his experiments in a scientific spirit and with a humanitarian objective, that he was groping toward the realization of "truth in action." He did not accuse his, rationalistic critics of being deaf and blind to a higher truth to which he had privileged access. He tried to show where the boundary between reason and faith is supposed to run but he was no more decisive on this than Aquinas, Pascal or Kant, who made similar attempts. In regard to the practical application to politics and society of his concept of truth, certain dilemmas and difficulties were raised by Nehru, who was Gandhi's most critical follower. Should he compromise? To compromise is to slide down a dangerous and slippery slope, and yet to refuse to do so is to lose touch, to be cut off from those one works for and works with, to become isolated. "I am not talking," said Nehru, "about the ultimate truth but rather of the right step, the right direction in which to go, the right step to take, the truth for the present, whatever it may be."[86] Ultimately we have to rely upon a process of trial and error. The politician, unlike the prophet, unlike the seeker after ultimate truth, has always to think in terms either of compromises or of a choice of evils and he has to choose what he considers the lesser evil lest the greater overwhelm. Gandhi was not unaware of these difficulties but he refused to believe that these were any greater than those faced by scientists or explorers. Like them, politicians were also being tested at each step, were facing a continual challenge to their integrity and their courage, their strength of faith.

It is reasonable to wonder whether Gandhi's view of truth obscures the intractable nature of disagreements and conflicts in society, whether it flavors too much of liberal optimism and of dangerous notions of invulnerability and inevitability in its assumption that truth will always triumph in the end. Gandhi conceded that the victory of truth was neither easy nor self-evident at any given moment, that we do not always know wherein our real interests or real good lie, and yet he took it as a matter of faith that the eternal rule is that truth quenches untruth. He could never accept any failure as final because he was bound by his presuppositions to regard it as the reflection of the extent of impurity in one's quest for truth. Un-

less the votary of truth wholly shuns all bluff and bluster and camouflage, he cannot hope for success. Even the subtlest element of
egotistic dogmatism, of mental violence or unconscious dishonesty
could be ruinous to one's cause, however just or sincerely upheld.
Truth must triumph, by definition; if it does not, it cannot really be
truth. But we cannot say conclusively at any given time whether it
has triumphed, for we cannot predict the length of time required
for it to succeed in any particular context. This looks like extreme
skepticism, for if we cannot know when truth has finally triumphed,
it could be argued that we do not ever know what truth is. The
main thing for the votary of truth to realize is that it is always better to appear untrue to the world than be untrue to himself.[87] Gandhi took it as a golden rule that we must never judge lest we be
judged; it is only we ourselves who can tell whether we are genuinely in search of the truth or not when we are involved in controversy or in dialogue with others.

If Gandhi believed that no nation or individual has ever gained
by the sacrifice of truth, he was merely expressing his conviction
that moral growth alone is real and material progress or success is
not, because the latter cannot last in the absence of the former, and
further we should never be deceived by the latter into taking the
former for granted. Also, he felt that it is physically impossible for
a man to speak or pursue untruth consistently and invariably; in
any case, if he did, he could not continue to exist as a rational being. As a man becomes more and more systematically untruthful,
his whole personality becomes distorted and he progressively loses
his hold on reality until he behaves like a lunatic, as though neither
any person or thing nor he himself really existed. It is not merely
that truth is certain of eventual victory but also that it is, in Gandhi's view, absolutely essential to survival. Untruth is founded in
fear and insecurity, and no man, according to Gandhi, can be really
happy or stable in such a state. On the other hand, a man who is
God-fearing—and Truth *is* God—cannot be afraid of any man.

Even if untruth and evil seem to prevail over truth and good,
Gandhi's concept of time and his belief in rebirth enabled him to
retain his faith in the eventual triumph of truth in a manner that is
neither open nor satisfactory for one who lives and works with a
much shorter time scale. Whiggery can make sense for a believer

in the finality of death only if he subscribes to a long view of history, and even this is open to dispute and equally capable of rival interpretations, according to what one chooses to emphasize. He was, however, frankly and fully aware of his presuppositions, unlike most worldly Whigs; he recognized that if we grant nothing, we find nothing. No empirical explanation can ever be complete, but instead of stopping at the frontier of rational inquiry beyond which reasons cannot be given (and we do not know what good reasons are), he was willing to explain even the empirical world in terms of his metaphysical presuppositions. He was more daring than any rationalist metaphysician of the seventeenth century; he stood in the tradition of the Stoics and Thomists and the ancient metaphysicians of India. If his approach to politics was metaphysical, it was no less practical or intelligible than the outlook to be found in the Indian epics or the Greek myths. Further, his metaphysical notions were never regarded as either fixed or final, as beyond argument or criticism. In the spirit of the Upanishadic philosophers, he regarded all metaphysical systems and ethical codes as partial and imperfect and extended indefinitely, for no man dare prescribe limits to human experience and the progress of the human spirit.

Gandhi's particular form of "theological utilitarianism" made him believe that honesty as a policy is not ultimately different from honesty as a creed. "A particular practice is a policy if its application is limited to space and time. Highest policy is therefore fullest practice."[88] A dishonest man does not know his real interests, but a votary of truth, knowing that truth will triumph, still pursues it for its own sake. "What a pure heart feels at a particular time is true; by remaining firm in that, undiluted truth can be attained."[89] Purity in this context implies honesty in thought, word and deed. A man who is swayed by his passions, who is not relatively free from anger, selfishness and hatred, will never find the truth.[90] Gandhi thus inflated the meaning of truth far beyond its conventional usage, but if he did not redefine the term in this way, he could clearly be open to the charge of being pre-Freudian in his view of truth. His concept of *satya* was commended by him for its therapeutic as well as its theoretical value, although he did not throw light on the dark corners out of which conventional morality and conventional truth grow. The disinterested pursuit of truth in the midst of society enables us to perceive, and get beyond, our complexes and prejudices and passions. At the same time, our measure of success in actually finding the truth, in its application to our actions in the political and social sphere, reflects the extent of our inward purity and the degree to which we have freed ourselves from the blinding influence of the passing passions.

THE SIGNIFICANCE OF *SATYA*

Gandhi's concept of truth was developed in an effort to undermine external authority and to reaffirm the moral autonomy and authority of the individual as an agent and an active performer in the arena of politics and social life. "I would reject all authority if it is in conflict with sober reason or the dictates of the heart. Authority sustains and ennobles the weak when it is the handiwork of reason but it degrades them when it supplants reason sanctified by the still small voice within."[91] When the quest for truth becomes universal, then the need for authority is distinctly lessened in society and individuals enter into their own inheritance of real freedom. Although the Gandhian notion of truth, with its exacting implications and universal reference, deprives external authority of its glamour and protects individual integrity from public encroachment, it is also meant deliberately to discourage political disengagement. The individual must turn inward not to abdicate from social and political responsibility but to equip himself in his struggle against external authority. In his battle against untruth he requires the moral courage and spiritual equilibrium that come from a capacity to withdraw into himself while working in the midst of society. "In the attitude of silence the soul finds the path in a clearer light, and what is elusive and deceptive resolves itself into crystal clearness. Our life is a long and arduous quest after Truth, and the soul requires inward restfulness to attain its full height."[92] The votary of truth must thus acquire a natural simplicity, an intellectual and spiritual humility that carries with it a certain naïve wonder that flees before the breath of dogmatism as well as a serene but unshakable courage that is willing to fight falsehood and injustice. He must pursue truth not only for its own sake but also so that he can appeal to it as the ultimate anchor of sanctity, beyond positive law and the State and the pressures of mass society.

Karl Jaspers, in his *Truth and Symbol*, shows authority to be a configuration of truth, springing from the tension between the truth that is known and the truth that is in the process of being discovered. What may be true at one time ceases to be true as new insights develop. Beyond each truth there is still another truth, a new horizon which renders it partial. Even at the point of farthest reach, the seeker must accept something lying beyond as unanalyzable, i.e., on the basis of authority. The act of acceptance is the recognition of the inherent need of authority itself, the admission by the truth-seeker of the finiteness of all found truth as contrasted with the infinity of all truth to be found. For each man, there is no alternative but to hold on to his own truth, the vital assimilation and affirmation of which is his alone. To concede the same autonomy to others is to accept the need for authority. No authority, however, can be absolute as every man's truth is relative, while at the same time we cannot wholly dispense with authority as none of us can lay claim to absolute truth.

Gandhi, like Plato and St. Augustine, believed that a man, by intuitive apprehension rather than by reason, could gain a transfiguring glimpse of cosmic order, of the Eternal Truth underlying the totality of things, a supernal realm in which all doubts disappear and all conflicts vanish. Yet he recognized that we cannot construe reality with Hegelian completeness. He did not start with a Cartesian conception of the distinctness and clarity of isolated truths; indubitability pertains to the core of reality that mystical vision may mirror and not to the propositions that reason may regard as universally valid and as the legitimate foundation of rational systems. In practice, he relied chiefly on the pragmatic approach of the *karma yogi*, the dedicated man of action. He believed in the abstract promise of the perfectibility of human awareness, not in the actual possibility of perfection on earth. We cannot hope to have a total and ideal vision of the Heavenly City or of the infinite and ultimate possibilities of human and cosmic achievement. We cannot discover the final summation of life before we come close to its complete realization.

All actions contain an element of error, of illusion and imperfection. All formulations are partly false, exaggerated and extravagant. Provided we are all sincerely and ceaselessly involved in the quest for truth, there is ample room for experimentation, disagreement, self-correction, tolerance and humility. While individual experience is the sole basis and the decisive test for affirmations of truth, any form of dogma or ideology, with its spurious claims to completeness and certainty, is both dishonest and violent. Political systems and ideologies possess a deceptive air of authority, a bogus universality, a pretended invulnerability. Formal conversion becomes more important than inward conviction, agreement becomes more attractive than genuine assent. We seek to impose our half-believed half-truths on others, and in this lie the seeds of human conflict and of political warfare. Systems become identified with individuals, conflicts become personal, irreconcilable, self-perpetuating and ruthless regarding the means employed. The common end—the discovery and the application of pure truth—becomes obscured in our attachment to partial assertions that are not backed by adequate experience. Gandhi was thus led to give a psychological explanation for the prevalence of untruth, a Hobbesian stress on the connection between fear, insecurity, force and fraud. The pursuit of truth, however, becomes a liberal, Lockean undertaking, requiring skepticism, reasonableness, open-mindedness and civility.

To keep moving is the chief Gandhian requirement; it is a conception of truth that goes far beyond a Lockean love of stability and involves a continual, spiritual restlessness. And yet, while admitting this Faustian element in the Gandhian concept of truth, we must give even greater importance to the Kantian element—the belief that truthfulness is a duty that is the basis of all duties, a sacred unconditional command that cannot be sacrificed in the interest of immediate expediency. Gandhi realized that abstract truth, when detached from veracity, does not constitute a problem of the personal life at all, let alone a social and political matter.

He also held to the Indian belief that a man who has lived in accord with the law of his true nature—which is identical with the cosmic law of causality and retribution—can cause anything to happen by the simple act of calling to witness the power of Truth or God. Such a man becomes a living channel of cosmic power, the power of Eternal Truth, the highest expression of his inmost soul. The concept of *sacchakriya*—making an "act of truth"—endows the Gandhian notion of truth with a magical quality and supernatural force that seem utterly strange to the modern man. The Moral Law is the law of our own being, as objective and dependable as any law in the physical world, and the recognition of it provides a sanction and a practical source of support to the votary of truth. Truth is within ourselves as well as in the universe of law of which we are a part. "There is an inmost centre of us all, where Truth abides in fulness. Every wrong-doer knows within himself that he is doing wrong. . . . Those men who are most depraved and who never obey the Moral Law take pride in calling themselves virtuous or moral men, since even they recognize the obligation of the Moral Law."[93] In this view Gandhi went even further than Kant, for even the most elaborate rationalist metaphysics cannot compare with the fire of spiritual conviction. "Earth and Heaven are in us. We know the earth, we are strangers to the Heaven within us."[94] The Moral Law is the Law of Truth; *satya* is identical with *dharma*, and *rta* (cosmic equilibrium) is the same as *Sat* (Absolute Truth). Even the wheel of worldly power must turn in accord with the motion of the wheel of eternal truth or cosmic justice.

Gandhi was prepared to sacrifice even national freedom for the sake of truth and non-violence. Like the Aryan heroes of the golden age of Indian mythology, Gandhi too wanted to be able to say that his lips had never uttered an untruth or compromised with injustice. The truthful man who in his every attitude and action is genuine and straightforward is the objective man in the highest sense of that word. The utmost veracity can come only from the recognition of the common basis of cosmic order and natural law, all true community life, every meaningful personal relationship, growth in self-awareness in daily life as well as the highest mystical communion. *Satya* is the active power of evolution in the universe, and it must be likewise in society. The rejection of all external authority as morally sacrosanct would be possible, Gandhi felt, only if truth were regarded as the highest value as well as the very ground of the universe. Social institutions obscure and subvert the truth insofar as they exact conformity, and political obligation that is not derived from our ultimate loyalty to truth produces compromises that are degrading to men.

8

Ahimsa

NONVIOLENCE AS A
CREED AND A POLICY

At its lowest the practice of Non-violence may express nothing more noble or more constructive than a cynical disillusionment with the fruitlessness of a Violence which has been previously practised ad nauseam without having produced the intended results. . . . Alternatively, Non-violence may express a conviction that Man's divinely allotted role in the economy of the Universe is to adopt a patiently passive attitude towards a mundane scene on which it is God's exclusive prerogative to execute His divine will through His own action—which would be hampered, and not assisted, if Man were to presume to intervene in what is wholly God's business. . . . This second philosophy of Non-violence is as pious and as scrupulous as our first is unprincipled and cynical; but at the same time it resembles the Non-violence of Disillusionment in being unconstructive. Non-violence may, however, also be practised as a means to some constructive end; and such an end, again, may be either mundane or "Otherworldly."

ARNOLD TOYNBEE

Although Gandhi regarded *satya*, or truth, as the highest value, his name is commonly identified with the concept of *ahimsa*, or nonviolence. It has been suggested that "Gandhi will be remembered as one of the very few who have set the stamp of an idea on an epoch. That idea is Non-violence."[1] While nonviolence has been preached by religious prophets as a cardinal moral virtue, political philosophers have generally concentrated on the justification of force and the exercise of power. Was Gandhi merely blind to the permanent gulf between moral ideals and social facts in believing that *ahimsa* is a political instrument and a social goal that can have immediate relevance and application? Or was Gandhi a dogmatic pacifist who could not grasp the actual nature of social and political conflicts? Neither is true, and if he has been much misunderstood, it is only because more attention has been generally paid to his partial success as a politician than to his innumerable attempts to formulate, clarify and qualify the doctrine of *ahimsa*. His statements at different times are not free from ambiguities, formal inconsistencies and other difficulties, but he did evolve a subtle and complicated doctrine that cannot be easily grasped or lightly dismissed, and the very word "nonviolence" has passed into the vocabulary of politics.

The word *ahimsa* literally means non-injury, or, more narrowly, non-killing, and, more widely, harmlessness, the renunciation of the will to kill and of the intention to hurt any living thing, the abstention from hostile thought, word and act.[2] *Ahimsa* was essential to Hinduism, Buddhism and Jainism in different ways. It was regarded as equivalent to *dharma* or the Moral Law—it was a necessary means to *moksha* or salvation and a vital part of the spiritual discipline prescribed by teachers of yoga like Patanjali. *Ahimsa* was given both a minimal and a maximal meaning and its interpretation has ranged between the extremes of formal insistence and scholastic flexibility. The Jains, the most rigorous practitioners of daily *ahimsa*, have classified *himsa* or violence under various heads, and broadly under *arambhaja* and *anarambhaja,* unavoidable and intentional violence.[3] The former includes *udyami* or *himsa* unavoidably committed in the exercise of one's profession, *graha-*

rambhi or *himsa* unavoidably committed in the performance of domestic duties, and *virodhi* or *himsa* unavoidably committed in
defense of person and property. In the Jain tradition as in the Hindu
epics, complete *ahimsa* could be practiced with success only by a
saint who has renounced all worldly pursuits. In Buddhism it is an
essential requirement for every monk. *Ahimsa* is invoked in the
Mahabharata to condemn cruel practices, to point to the futile de-
structiveness of worldly existence, to underline the sanctity of all
life and to proclaim the dignity and the redeemability even of anti-
social delinquents. On the other hand, the unavoidability and the
protective role of force in the polity has been asserted in Hindu
political thought, mildly by Manu and Bhishma, forcefully by
Kautilya.

Gandhi's refusal to accept different standards for saints and for
ordinary men, and his desire to give ancient Indian concepts a social rather than a mystical use, led him to extend the meaning of
ahimsa and to interpret and apply it in an original manner. Although he repeatedly declared that *ahimsa* was advocated in the
Gita, the Bible and the Koran and was particularly stressed by the
Buddha and the Jain teachers, Gandhi claimed that his belief in
nonviolence was independent of the sanction of scriptures.[4] As a
young man he was familiar with the principle of winning over an
enemy with love as expressed by the Gujarati poet, Shamalbhatta,
but when he read the *Gita* in 1889 he had not thought much about
ahimsa.[5] Later on, he based his concept of *ahimsa* on the *Gita* and
linked it to the idea of non-attachment and freedom from hatred,
pride and anger. His early hesitances about nonviolence were overcome by reading Tolstoy's *The Kingdom of God Is Within You* and
he became a firm believer in *ahimsa*. He thought that Tolstoy's remarkable development of the doctrine of nonviolence put to shame
the narrow and lopsided interpretations put upon it by its votaries
in India despite the great discoveries in the field of *ahimsa* made by
ancient Indian sages.[6]

As early as 1916 Gandhi distinguished between the *negative* and
the *positive* meanings of *ahimsa*.

In its *negative* form it means not injuring any living being
whether by body or mind. I may not, therefore, hurt the person

of any wrong-doer or bear any ill-will to him and so cause him mental suffering. This statement does not cover suffering caused to the wrong-doer by natural acts of mine which do not proceed from ill-will. . . . *Ahimsa* requires deliberate self-suffering, not a deliberate injuring of the supposed wrong-doer. . . . In its *positive* form, *Ahimsa* means the largest love, the greatest charity. If I am a follower of *Ahimsa,* I must love my enemy or a stranger to me as I would my wrong-doing father or son. This active *Ahimsa* necessarily includes truth and fearlessness.[7]

In *From Yeravda Mandir* Gandhi held that *ahimsa* is not the crude thing it has been made to appear to be in India, that non-injury was only the least expression of *ahimsa*. Toward the end of his life, he regretted that in Indian politics as in religious life nonviolence was mainly taken to imply non-killing. Sometimes killing, he said, is the cleanest part of violence. Harassment could be worse than killing outright a mischief-maker.[8]

Gandhi thus extended the meaning of *ahimsa* beyond mere non-killing or even non-injury. The principle of *ahimsa*, he held, is "hurt by every evil thought, by undue haste, by lying, by hatred, by wishing ill to anybody, and by our holding on to what the world needs."[9] The path of *ahimsa* is the path of non-attachment and entails continuous suffering and the cultivating of endless patience. In its relatively narrower sense, it means not to hurt any living creature by thought, word or deed, even for the supposed benefit of that creature.[10] *Ahimsa* implies not merely a certain attitude of detached sympathy toward an enemy, but also the denial of the very existence of an enemy. At times Gandhi equated *ahimsa* with innocence and declared that complete nonviolence is complete absence of ill-will, that active nonviolence is goodwill toward all life, that nonviolence in this sense is a perfect state and the goal toward which mankind moves naturally though unconsciously.[11] At other times Gandhi identified *ahimsa* with reason[12] and defended it in terms similar to the Golden Rule. "The basic principle on which the practice of non-violence rests is that what holds good in respect of oneself equally applies to the whole universe. All mankind in essence are alike. What is, therefore, possible for one is possible for everybody."[13] Total *ahimsa* is a state of soul and mind, the complete innocence of a St. Francis or a Sita, but the practice of non-violence is a deliberate exercise that could be justified rationally.

It is true that Gandhi sometimes inflated the term *ahimsa* to include all the moral virtues; he equated it with humility, forgiveness, love, charity, selflessness, fearlessness, strength, non-attachment, meekness and innocence. Similarly, he stretched *himsa* or violence far beyond its ordinary usage to include "trickery, falsehood, intrigue, chicanery and deceitfulness—in short, all unfair and foul means come under the category of *himsa*."[14] Although this extreme elasticity of the Gandhian use of *himsa* and *ahimsa*, which, like most other Indian concepts, are marked by their open texture to an indefinite degree, can be confusing, it can be clarified by reference to two important considerations.

First of all, Gandhi believed that although *ahimsa* was universally applicable, its exercise had to be exemplified by a few votaries who took vows and underwent a comprehensive moral and spiritual discipline in which they would be made to see the all-embracing and ever-elusive nature of total *ahimsa*. They would thus not fall into the ritualism of many Indian practitioners of *ahimsa* in whose hands the theory had become "a wooden, lifeless dogma," enabling hypocrisy and distortion to pass under the name of religion.[15] Secondly, Gandhi held to the Buddhist and Jain view that all sins are modifications of *himsa*, that the basic sin, the only sin in the ultimate analysis, is the sin of separateness, or *attavada*. According to a Jain maxim, he who conquers this sin conquers all others and he who does not conquer this central weakness cannot effectively exemplify any virtue. Violence, rooted in this common weakness, can assume subtle forms and is mistaken for something else when it masquerades under a moral disguise. "Wherever there is a clash of ephemeral interests, men tend to resort to violence."[16] Exclusive concern for individual interest, the desire for personal benefit at any cost, represents the *himsa* arising out of the dire heresy of separateness. When an action is not based on attachment to results, there is no temptation for *himsa*.[17] True nonviolence does not blind itself to the causes of conflict or hatred, but in spite of the knowledge of their existence, operates upon the person setting the causes in motion.[18] Even when this does not actually happen, the votary of *ahimsa*, as a result of the deliberate observance of *ahimsa*, experiences a "second birth or 'conversion.' "[19]

Although at times Gandhi made *ahimsa* an all-embracing term, he was also willing on occasion to sharpen his use of the word and to distinguish it from *daya*, or mercy, *anasakti*, or selflessness, and Pauline charity or love. "*Ahimsa* is a quality of the disembodied soul alone"[20] and in its fullness belongs only to a man of *vitaraga*, or detachment. Mercy is "*ahimsa* in the flesh."[21] *Ahimsa* implies an inability to go on witnessing another's pain and from it thus spring mercy, heroism and all other virtues associated with *ahimsa*. Gandhi challenged the prevailing Indian view of detachment: "It is bad logic to say that we must look on while *others* suffer,"[22] merely because we wish to take a detached view of our own suffering. Nonviolence had been too narrowly interpreted in India and in the West because of the extreme fear of death and the mistaken notion that the pain of death is always greater than the pain of living. *Ahimsa*, in Gandhi's view, was a broader notion than *daya* but less exalted than *anasakti*. While the root of *ahimsa* is uttermost selflessness and complete freedom from a regard for one's body,[23] *anasakti*—the central teaching of the *Gita*—transcends *ahimsa*, which is a necessary preliminary, and is included in it.

Gandhi did not like to translate *ahimsa* as "love" because the latter word has also other connotations in the English language. He preferred "charity" to "love" because it implies pity for the wrongdoer.[24] "*Ahimsa* is love in the Pauline sense and something more than the love defined by St. Paul, although I know St. Paul's beautiful definition is good enough for all practical purposes."[25] *Ahimsa* includes the whole of creation and not only human beings. Although Gandhi preferred to use a negative word like "nonviolence," he regarded it as a positive force superior to all the forces of brutality. The negative word had its advantages for Gandhi. He wanted the acceptance of *ahimsa* to imply a deliberate stand against ill-will, a method of action based upon self-restraint. *Ahimsa* may ultimately be identical with divine love, the sense of oneness with all, that belongs to the great prophets and mystics. But in its immediate and daily application it must be distinguished from the feeling of love and from benevolence as well as from the mere hatred of violence. Nonviolence is not a resignation from all real fighting against wickedness, but a more active fight against wickedness than retaliation which, by its very nature, increases wickedness. "I seek entirely to blunt the edge of the tyrant's sword, not by putting up against it a sharper-edged weapon but by disappointing his expectation that I would be offering physical resistance."[26] Nonviolence, as Gandhi saw it, actually presupposes the ability to strike. Besides, it is a conscious, deliberate restraint put upon one's desire for vengeance.[27]

A close follower and associate of Gandhi, K. G. Mashruwalla, has emphasized the distinction between "anti-violence," or benevolence, and nonviolence, or *ahimsa*. One cannot be benevolent and in the same breath enforce a claim. Gandhi taught that one could enforce it nonviolently, i.e., without violence against the usurper. There is a large field in between; on the one hand, benevolence and unselfishness (*parartha*), and violence at the other extreme. Practical nonviolence is therefore defined as a form of "just selfishness without malevolence and with a touch of benevolence."[28] This interpretation of *ahimsa* is plausible but not adequate. No doubt, Gandhi distinguished between *anasakti,* selfless action, and *ahimsa,* which in practice need not necessarily be entirely selfless or wholly benevolent. But there were two essential elements in *ahimsa*, as Gandhi saw it, and these are excluded by Mashruwalla's definition. *Ahimsa* is intended and expected to convert rather than to coerce the wrong-doer, however slightly and slowly, and it is also capable of producing in its user a "second birth or conversion." Another important ingredient in *ahimsa*, perhaps the crucial one, is the notion of "self-suffering," a refusal to submit to injustice, and the acceptance of personal discomfort and tribulations. This conception of *ahimsa* is not the same as benevolence or the withholding of just claims, but it includes the idea of helping the wrong-doer by nonviolent resistance to his wrong-doing. A benevolent man need not suffer, and it could even be argued, as Hume did, that he is benevolent only because he enjoys it. On the other hand, "suffering injury in one's own person is . . . of the essence of non-violence."[29]

The Gandhian concept of *ahimsa* is attended with ambiguity, not just because he used it in different senses, more restricted or more extended in different contexts, but mainly owing to the fact that he both commended it as a method of action superior in its moral and practical efficacy to violence, and also regarded it as an ethical injunction that is universally valid, as the supreme moral principle. *Ahimsa*, in the wider sense, means the willingness to treat all beings as one's very self (*atmavat sarvabhuteshu*), a standpoint repeatedly stressed in the *Gita*. But although such freely flowing love may be a worthy ideal, *ahimsa* (in the weaker sense of deliberate abstention from harm and from ill-will) is the minimal and mandatory demand of human morality. This is justified in terms of the Golden Rule, but also on the basis of the belief in the sanctity and oneness of all life and the identity of interests of all men by virtue of their common dignity and their moral interdependence. *Ahimsa* is important not just as a desirable virtue or merely as the means for the purification and ennobling of the soul but even more as the fundamental and perhaps the only way in which we can express our respect for the innate worth of any human being. It is an essential and universal obligation without which we would cease to be human.

Ahimsa for Gandhi is not a denial of power as influence or persuasion, pressure or moral force, but only of power in its violent and compulsive forms. Far from denying the distinction commonly made between force and power, Gandhi emphasized it but continued to talk of force when in fact he meant only non-physical force or the creative power in man, his capacity for constructive and non-aggressive action. In this sense it is called "soul-force" because it is independent of pecuniary or material assistance, usable by all men, women and children, applicable to all human relationships. It is to violence and to all tyranny and injustice what light is to darkness,[30] "one of the world's great principles which no power on earth can wipe out."[31]

AHIMSA IN POLITICS AND SOCIETY

In politics the use of *ahimsa* is based, in Gandhi's view, upon the immutable maxim that government is possible only as long as the people consent, either consciously or unconsciously, to be governed. It is natural for those in authority to want to command and to use force, but those who obey commands are in a majority and could choose to express their will either by physical force or by "soul-force." If they prefer physical force, then the rulers and ruled

alike become like so many madmen, but if they choose to employ
"soul-force" they could honorably disregard unjust commands.[32]
Further, Gandhi pointed out, peasants are never subdued by the
sword and never will be. Neither peasants nor even industrial laborers have been truly educated in the art of effective nonviolent
action.[33] In all our mutual relations an attitude of nonviolence is a
necessary condition for the removal of tension.[34] Disregard of nonviolence is the surest way to destruction, and the world is inexorably moving either to self-destruction or to a nonviolent solution of
all its ailments.[35]

We must ultimately choose between coercion, which has temporary results, and peaceful conversion, which has lasting benefits.

> True democracy or the *Swaraj* of the masses can never come
> through untruthful and violent means, for the simple reason that
> the natural corollary to their use would be to remove all opposi-
> tion through the suppression or extermination of the antagonists.
> That does not make for individual freedom. Individual freedom
> can have the fullest play only under a regime of unadulterated
> *ahimsa*.[36]

While this is the ideal, a believer in nonviolence, though pledged
not to resort to violence, is not precluded from helping men or institutions that are themselves not based on nonviolence.[37] Nonviolence must be used to influence power politics without suc-
cumbing to its corrupting influence, but the moment nonviolence
assumes political power, it contradicts itself and becomes contami-
nated.[38] Gandhi recognized that it is not possible for a modern
State, based as it is on force, to resist, with no violence whatsoever, forces of disorder, external or internal. "A man cannot serve
God and Mammon, nor be temperate and furious at the same
time."[39]

But Gandhi believed that a State could be organized largely
(though not entirely), on the basis of nonviolence, and cited
Asoka's example. In general, he argued in a manner reminiscent of
Rousseau's "general will," a nonviolent State "must be broad-based
on the will of an intelligent people, well able to know its mind and
act up to it."[40] In nonviolent *Swaraj*, there can be no encroachment

upon just rights and no one can possess unjust rights[41] because of Gandhi's assumption that "non-violence in the very nature of things is of no assistance in the defence of ill-gotten gains and immoral acts."[42]

Just as Gandhi believed that in a nonviolent State, by definition, the general will is expressed in the absence of every form of coercion (however subtle), so too he thought that in a nonviolent society, by definition, there could be no exploitation and that thus the problem of unemployment is automatically solved.[43] Unemployment in this unorthodox view is mainly a problem of distribution rather than of production. A nonviolent system of government is clearly an impossibility, according to Gandhi, so long as the wide gulf between the rich and the hungry millions persists.[44] Inequality offends against the doctrine of non-possession and arises out of an attachment to private property and to power which is a form of *himsa*. As long as the *himsa* of attachment to property in a society is not removed, the *himsa* of attachment by the State to coercive power cannot be reduced let alone eliminated. A violent and bloody revolution is a certainty some day, unless there is a voluntary abdication of riches and the power that they give, and yet the violent way of abolishing inequalities has not succeeded anywhere. Since nonviolence is a process of conversion, the process must be permanent. "A society or nation constructed non-violently must be able to withstand attack upon its structure from without or within."[45] The world is sick of armed rebellions, and heroism and sacrifice in a bad cause are so much waste of splendid energy and hurt the good cause by drawing away attention from it by "the glamour of misused heroism and sacrifice in a bad cause."[46]

Similarly, Gandhi argued that democracy and the military spirit are a contradiction in terms. A true democrat relies, not on the arms his State could flaunt in the face of the world, but on the moral force that his State could put at the disposal of the world.[47] If one depends only upon superior violence in order to destroy violence of the Hitler type, then small nations would have hardly any chance of survival. Unless they could develop the courage needed for nonviolent resistance, democracy could never survive.[48] It was this conviction that made Gandhi concern himself with the possibilities of setting up a nonviolent police force, a nonviolent army, peace brigades and the like to mobilize popular opinion behind constructive programmes. The central notion underlying all these Utopian-sounding schemes was not merely the doctrine of *ahimsa* but also the idea that people must everywhere learn to defend themselves against misbehaving individuals,[49] that self-defense must be part of individual self-respect. "My notion of democracy is that under it the weakest should have the same opportunity as the strongest. That can never happen except through non-violence. No country in the world today shows any but patronizing regard for the weak."[50]

Gandhi realized that nobody can practice perfect nonviolence, but he chose to regard the notions of a nonviolent State, a nonviolent society and a nonviolent democracy as Euclidean models that could provide standards of assessment and incentives to alter existing situations. He also recognized that governments in power cannot rule without legislation, but he believed that the coercive element in legislation could be reduced progressively in a real democracy. "Legislation imposed by people upon themselves is non-violence to the extent it is possible in society. A society organized and run on the basis of complete non-violence would be the purest anarchy."[51] The nearest approach to purest anarchy would be a democracy based on nonviolence. "Perfect non-violence whilst you are inhabiting the body is only a theory like Euclid's point or straight line. . . ."[52]

Gandhi distinguished between four fields of practical *ahimsa*.[53] First of all, there is nonviolence in its operation against constituted authority. Secondly, there is the exercise of nonviolence in internal disturbances such as riots. Thirdly, there is the use of nonviolence against external invasion. The fourth and best field for *ahimsa* is the family field, in a wider sense than the ordinary. "The alphabet of *ahimsa* is best learnt in the domestic school,"[54] such as an *ashram* or any institution the membership of which is intimate rather as in a family. Nonviolence as between the members of such families should be easy to practice and if we fail in this, we cannot succeed in applying it on the wider scale or in developing the capacity for pure nonviolence. "For, the love we have to practice towards our relatives or colleagues in our family or institution, we have to practice towards our foes, dacoits, etc."[55] To a nonviolent person the whole world will increasingly seem to be a single family, and he will thus fear none, nor will others fear him. Gandhi also believed that an army, however small, of truly nonviolent soldiers is likely some day to multiply itself. Although such dedicated votaries must be prepared to die to uphold the doctrine of *ahimsa*, they must also recognize that it is much more difficult to live for nonviolence than to die for it[56] and must, therefore, attempt to apply it to all their relationships against every form of coercion and in every conflict.

In his interesting attempt to apply game theory to human conflicts, Anatol Rapaport[57] divides conflicts into three varieties: fights, in which opponents try to destroy each other; games, in which they attempt to outwit each other; and debates, in which they strive to convert each other. The last variety is the only kind which could be productive, and our best hope of survival is to convert fights into games, and games into debates. Under Gandhi's conception of *ahimsa* its votary pits his refusal to hurt or injure his opponent—despite the inconveniences of such an attitude to himself—against those who desire to fight or outwit him; and he seeks to convert them to the use of non-coercive methods to gain their ends by finding an area of common interest, based upon common humanity, which would put the conflict of aims into a proper perspective. In the arena of power politics, power experts meet power experts and the struggle continues to be cast in power-play maneuvers if not in terms of outright or subtle coercion. The framework of assumptions which underlies the strategy of power conflicts may make it impossible for rivals or antagonists to choose the mutually advantageous course because there is nothing in their experience which allows them to make the assumption of similarity in regard to their relative positions. If they could do this, they might solve the dilemma to the advantage of both. Indulgence in *himsa* is the result of short-sightedness, lack of vision, arising out of the inability to put oneself in the position of an antagonist and to disarm or convert him so that he ceases to regard himself as an irreconcilable enemy. Far from denying the existence or reality of conflicts of interest in human society, Gandhi admitted their existence in every walk of life and sought to make *ahimsa* the basis of a method of action which could cope nonviolently with such conflicts by limiting if not wholly removing the *himsa* involved.

It is part of liberal and democratic doctrine that the method of persuasion is morally and even practically superior to that of pressure, that free discussion and rational argument are better than coercion or brute force. We commonly distinguish between force, which usually means physical constraint; power, which implies the use of reason or of other skills; and authority, which presupposes the recognition by those who accept it of the moral and political legitimacy of its exercise by its holder. T. H. Green's dictum "will, not force, is the basis of the State," the earlier attempt to invoke the notion of a social contract, Locke's "tacit consent," Hume's appeal to political prudence and the artificial virtues, Rousseau's "general will," are all traditional examples of the present-day sociologist's concern with the social consensus which provides the framework for peaceful conflicts conducted under recognized rules of the game. The notion of non-coercion is essential to the respect that we accord to the human personality, and the concern with justifying minimum coercion as a necessary evil to secure a larger good is itself a recognition of the superiority of *ahimsa* over *himsa*. There was an anarchistic and utopian element in Gandhi's doctrine of *ahimsa* in that he proclaimed the ultimate need for the State and for all institutions totally to abjure all *himsa*. This was because he recognized that, in the broader meaning of *ahimsa*, even a liberal who abstains from physical force or shrinks from slaughter could indulge in subtler forms of *himsa* or pressure.

The main thing for Gandhi is that more and more people must be prepared to accept the absolute moral value of *ahimsa*, not as an elusive ideal or a pious hope, but as a widely relevant principle of social and political action. Force thrives on fear but if more and more individuals and groups become fearless, force increasingly fails to serve its intended purpose and its exercise may be effectively opposed and even consistently frustrated. Today, we are prepared to question the retributive theory of punishment and to condemn forms of *himsa* like capital punishment, duelling, slavery, torture, collective retaliation or revenge, acts of aggression by States, preventive wars, cruelty to animals, flogging and corporal punishment, which were all quite respectable at one time. We are now stricter about the notion of minimal coercion or the use of force as a last resort and we also increasingly recognize that a progressive reduction of the content of minimal coercion is the mark of civilization, progress and enlightenment. But we still base our degrees of repugnance or condemnation of force upon our valuation of the rightness of the cause in which it is employed and upon our assessment of the amount of suffering caused in relation to existing suffering or the future suffering avoided.

There are many kinds of revolutionaries and reactionaries, desperate rebels and rulers in distress, who to this day would subscribe to the sophisticated justification of violence that we find in Georges Sorel's neglected writings. Sorel argued that people who have devoted their life to a cause which they identify with the regeneration of the world could not hesitate to make use of any weapon. Violence is justifiable when carried on in broad daylight, without hypocritical attenuation, for the purpose of ruining an irreconcilable enemy. Violence and deception are the only procedures which can be used by the proletariat and the bourgeoisie respectively to bring the actions of individuals into concert.

Gandhi's position as a social philosopher was directly opposite to that of Sorel. Nonviolence or *ahimsa* is the only admissible ethic in society. *Satya* and *ahimsa* are absolutes which could be made the basis of effective devices—the only valid, safe and fruitful devices in the long run—to bring the actions of individuals into concert. In this he went much farther than liberals; *ahimsa* is an immediate necessity and not an ultimate desideratum; *himsa* could never be a lesser good even if it sometimes seems to be a necessary evil. Gandhi recognized that so long as man continues to be a social being, he cannot but participate in the *himsa* that the very existence of society involves. He also realized that a government cannot succeed in being entirely nonviolent because it represents all the people. "I don't conceive of such a golden age. But I do believe in the possibility of a predominantly non-violent society."[58]

Gandhi insisted that force does not change its moral character according to the circumstances of its use, and denied that the use of force to prevent a greater evil could ever acquire any inherent moral or political legitimacy. His attitude toward *ahimsa* was never literalist, but it was nonetheless absolutist rather than utilitarian. He declared that a votary of *ahimsa* cannot subscribe to the utilitarian formula. He will strive for the greatest good of all and die in the attempt to realize the ideal. He will therefore be willing to die so that others may live. . . . The absolutist's sphere of destruction will always be the narrowest possible. The utilitarian's has no limit. Judged by the standard of non-violence the late war was wholly wrong. Judged by the utilitarian standard, each party has justified it according to its idea of utility. . . . Precisely on the same ground the anarchist justifies his assassinations. But none of these acts can possibly be justified on the greatest-good-of-all principle.[59]

Although Gandhi's conception of *ahimsa* was absolutist on the ethical plane, it was anything but an abstract moral attitude owing to his intense conviction that individuals and groups and even the masses could be trained in "the white art of non-violence" just as they could be in "the black art of violence."[60] The individual votary of *ahimsa* must learn that it needs far greater physical and mental courage than the delivering of blows.[61] He has to pass many a sleepless night and go through many a mental torture before he can even be within measurable distance of the goal of utter humility and goodwill even toward his most bitter opponent.[62] In any conflict between two parties, he is bound, when the occasion arises, to say which side is just but he cannot grade different species of violence according to whether it is defensive or offensive.[63] Strength does not come from physical capacity but from indomitable will.[64] The votary of *ahimsa* must cultivate the habit of unremitting toil, sleepless vigilance, ceaseless self-control.[65] Such a man will not meekly submit to the will of an evil-doer but put his whole soul against the will of a tyrant. "Working under this law of our being, it is possible for a single individual to defy the whole might of an unjust empire."[66]

Gandhi recognized that it would be difficult to get large masses of men to be nonviolent in this exalted sense, but he was convinced that if even a band of intelligent and honest men with an abiding faith in *ahimsa* could be formed and trained, it could ensure the nonviolent atmosphere required for the working of civil disobedience in accord with *ahimsa*.[67] It should be possible to train small communities in the difficult art of nonviolence and use their influence for peaceful mass action. It should be possible to get large numbers of people to learn to do without the protection of both the military and the police during communal troubles.[68] Gandhi thought it was gross self-deception to believe that men could risk death only if they had learned and practiced the art of killing but not otherwise.[69] There is no *prima facie* reason why the masses, if trained in nonviolent action, should be incapable of showing the discipline displayed usually by a fighting force. The example of a few men and women, if they have fully imbibed the spirit of nonviolence, is bound to infect the whole mass in the end.[70]

AHIMSA AS A CREED AND AS A POLICY

The preference for persuasion to coercion was not merely for Gandhi as for the Greeks a mark of the civilized by contrast with the barbarians, but also an affirmation of the innate dignity and divinity of man as against the bestial and depraved in him. He believed that physical force and moral power cannot go together, that a reliance upon the former is a sign of weakness while the latter proceeds from inward strength.

Although nonviolence has been commended by several religious and social thinkers, Gandhi alone has clearly and continually distinguished between nonviolence as a creed and as a policy, or between the nonviolence of the strong and the nonviolence of the weak. The creed of violence, propounded chiefly by Nietzsche or Sorel, has been repudiated by most social and political thinkers, and yet many have sought to sanction the use of violence as a policy. Similarly, it is possible for people to advocate nonviolence as a policy in particular circumstances, while remaining unwilling to accept it as an absolute creed. Reason could be employed to enjoin *ahimsa* in certain situations and contexts, but to believe in *ahimsa* as a creed demands an act of faith. Gandhi's own dilemma lay in the fact that he wished to propagate *ahimsa* as a creed, yet, as a politician, he also tried to justify it as a policy. He became increasingly aware during his later life that the failure of *ahimsa* as a policy could discredit the creed which he cherished despite temporary setbacks or seeming failure. While some pacifists[71] have held firmly to their faith in *ahimsa* as a creed and hardly cared about its feasibility as a policy, a few[72] have claimed so much effectiveness for nonviolence as a policy that they have failed to bring out the force of the faith of those who hold to it as a creed regardless of results.

To Gandhi *ahimsa* was definitely a creed, "the breath of my life,"[73] but he sometimes spoke of it as a policy to be adopted on prudential grounds, and he called himself "an essentially practical man dealing with practical political questions."[74] This has naturally made him open to the charge of elevating an expedient policy to an absolute creed, though intelligent critics like Philip Spratt (even in his Marxist phase) have recognized the sincerity of his faith and accused him merely of unconscious rationalization rather than outright dishonesty. Such a charge is difficult to sustain for any serious student of his writings, since he sharply distinguished between *ahimsa* as the policy of the weak and as the creed of the strong. He himself was unmoved by the suggestion that his advocacy of *ahimsa* was dictated by expediency. "I have been taunted as a *bania*.[75] I regard that as a certificate of merit. The article in my possession is an invaluable pearl. It has to be weighed in the proper scales and those who can pay the price for it can have it. It can't be bartered away even for independence."[76]

Gandhi sadly confessed in 1947 that the Congress had embraced the policy of nonviolence because they were unable, though not unwilling, to offer armed resistance, whereas with him *ahimsa* had always been a creed. He pointed out that a policy takes the shape of a creed while it lasts and no longer, but a creed cannot admit of any change.[77] As early as 1935 he had argued that a creed has to be all-pervasive and cannot pertain only to certain activities and ignore others, while a policy cannot have the strength of "a lifeforce."[78] He laid down five simple axioms of this creed.

    a. "Nonviolence implies as complete self-purification as is humanly possible."

This implies a rigorous ethical discipline and the taking of vows.

    b. "Man for man the strength of non-violence is in exact proportion to the ability, not the will, of the non-violent person to inflict violence."

This implies that a government which renounces nuclear weapons is potentially though not automatically capable of displaying *ahimsa* to an enormous extent.

   c. "Non-violence is without exception superior to violence, i.e., the power at the disposal of a non-violent person is always greater than he would have if he was violent."

This presupposes the idea that power is not merely independent of force but that the greater the power of a moral or political authority, the less the force needed for the exercise of that authority. What Gandhi assumed but did not establish was that the less force is used, the greater the power.

   d. "There is no such thing as defeat in non-violence. The end of violence is surest defeat."

This implies that nonviolence, by definition, cannot fail, and apparent failure can be explained in terms of the moral inadequacy of the user; and similarly violence seems to succeed only if we take too narrow or shortsighted a view of success.

   e. "The ultimate end of non-violence is surest victory—if such a term may be used of non-violence. In reality, where there is no sense of defeat, there is no sense of victory."

This implies that the votary of *ahimsa* never aims at defeating anyone but merely at achieving a desirable result.

In enunciating *ahimsa* as a creed, Gandhi expanded the meaning of nonviolence to such an extent that it bears little relation to the ordinary usage of the word. He felt that without self-purification, the observance of the law of *ahimsa* is an empty dream.[79] The votary of *ahimsa* must seek to reduce himself to zero and to put himself last among his fellow creatures so that the pursuit of *ahimsa* becomes nothing less than a path of salvation. *Ahimsa* must be placed before everything else if it is to become irresistible. Otherwise, it will only be "an empty husk, a thing without potency or power."[80] The creed of *ahimsa* is applicable under all circumstances and can admit of no exceptions. "Laws to be laws admit of no exceptions" and nonviolence is the law of our being.

> If love or non-violence be not the law of our being, the whole of my argument falls to pieces, and there is no escape from a periodical recrudescence of war. . . . Modern science is replete with illustrations of the seemingly impossible having become possible within living memory. But victories of physical science would be

nothing against the victory of the Science of Life, which is summed up in love, which is the law of our being. I know that it cannot be proved by argument. It shall be proved by persons living it in their lives in utter disregard of consequences to themselves. There is no real gain without sacrifice.[81]

Gandhi regarded all so-called exceptions to the creed of *ahimsa* as mere concessions to human weakness, deviations from the Moral Law. It is better to recognize our limitations than to seek to cover them by determining exceptions.[82] The final criterion of the genuineness of nonviolence is the intention underlying the act.[83] There is a causal connection between the purity of the intention and the extent of effectiveness of nonviolent action.

Ahimsa as a creed represented for Gandhi an ideal to be reached, a fact of life as well as an act of faith. As it is the law of life, there is no credit for observing it in obvious ways or for recognizing its underlying principle of the sanctity and kinship of all life.[84] Our actions are undoubtedly inconsistent with this belief, but human life is an aspiration, a continual striving after perfection and the ideal must not be lowered because of our weaknesses.[85] *Himsa* proceeds from fear and the casting out of fear is no intellectual feat but a feat of the heart, requiring faith. Gandhi pointed out that there is a philosophy behind the modern worship of brute force with a history to back it, but the microscopic non-militant minority has nothing to fear from it if only it has immovable faith behind it.[86] He thought that it was possible for the dedicated votaries of *ahimsa* to bring to bear the same single-mindedness and perseverance in evolving their *ahimsa* which Hitler showed in perfecting the weapons of *himsa*. "If intellect plays a large part in the field of violence, I hold it plays a larger part in the field of non-violence."[87]

The creed of *ahimsa* presupposes the existence of an immortal essence in the human personality and the readiness to die while unwilling to kill. It is not impossible, though it may seem irrational to some, that anyone not believing in immortality should die to vindicate his faith in the creed of *ahimsa*. *Ahimsa* is not a quality to be displayed to order, but an inward growth depending for sustenance upon intense individual effort,[88] and it can be effectively taught only by living it. It is not a mere passive quality but the

mightiest force man is endowed with.[89] "Where there is an unmistakable demonstration of its power and efficacy, the weak will shed
their weakness and the mighty will quickly realise the valuelessness
of the might and becoming meek acknowledge the sovereignty of
non-violence. It is my humble effort to show that this is no unattainable goal even in mass action."[90]

Ahimsa as a creed, as Gandhi expounded it, is an ethical absolute based upon metaphysical beliefs and issuing in a religious conviction requiring an act of faith. As such it cannot be empirically
verified in any manner which would make it acceptable to someone
who held to a different moral principle or a dissimilar metaphysical
presupposition, or to a skeptic who rules out any act of faith in
the domain of politics. Belief in the creed was regarded by Gandhi
as a precondition for testing it by reference to experience so that,
though the creed involves the notion of a universal moral law
(which is neither falsifiable nor conclusively verifiable), it is not
universifiable at any rate in an age in which the "soul" means little
or nothing to many people and in a society in which there is deep
disagreement about ends, moral principles and metaphysical beliefs.
Gandhi was aware of this and explicitly declared that he was not
advanced enough for the great task of preaching universal nonviolence although he himself believed in it as a universal panacea.[91]
He realized that most people could not be made to become absolutists in regard to *ahimsa*, and he therefore commended the relevance and reasonableness of *ahimsa* as a policy.

When *ahimsa* is adopted as a policy, how is the individual to
determine the nature and extent of *himsa* that he must commit or
excuse? Gandhi answered this by saying that society has set down
a standard and absolved the individual from troubling himself about
it to that extent, but every seeker after truth has to adjust and vary
the standard according to his need and to make a ceaseless endeavor to reduce the circle of *himsa*. Each case must be judged
individually and on its merits.[92] Gandhi recognized that it would be
difficult to expect "non-violence of the brave"—the will not to kill
even in retaliation and the courage to face death without revenge
—on a mass scale. But he could not accept that *ahimsa* must, therefore, be restricted in advance to exceptional individuals. He also
granted that the acceptance of nonviolence as a policy did not rule

out the use of force in self-defense, but he was concerned that there should be no camouflage.[93] If force was used, people should openly admit that they had adopted *ahimsa* only as a policy and that they could go no further. Even *ahimsa* as a policy, i.e., as a conditionally accepted technique, is different from a mere tactic of temporary expediency. The same action may outwardly be taken by the believer and the unbeliever in nonviolence but the motive alone decides its quality.[94]

Ahimsa as a policy was regarded by Gandhi as the next best thing to *ahimsa* as a creed rather than a mere rationalization of physical weakness or an expression of mere expediency. Although he stressed the moral necessity of *ahimsa,* he also wished to point out its political necessity in certain circumstances and it was thus that he was led to advocate *ahimsa* as a policy. He thought that as Indians had not received enough training in the use of arms and they were not capable of a violent overthrow of alien rule, they could be made to see the merits of nonviolence, which did not require any outside training or supply of arms. They could justifiably adopt nonviolence as a policy even if they did not believe in *ahimsa* as a creed, provided they did not pretend to so believe. "By experience I have also found that people rarely become virtuous for virtue's sake. They become virtuous from necessity. Nor is there anything wrong in a man becoming good under the pressure of circumstances. It would be no doubt better, if he becomes good for its own sake."[95]

It is not surprising that Gandhi should have tried to plead for *ahimsa* as a policy by using arguments to convince people of the futility of violence. Force is used when men are filled with fear and what is gained through fear is retained only for as long as fear is present.[96]

Hitler and Mussolini on the one hand and Stalin on the other are able to show the immediate effectiveness of violence. But it may be as transitory as that of Jenghis's slaughter. But the effects of Buddha's non-violence persist and are likely to grow with age. And the more it is practised, the more effective and inexhaustible it becomes, and ultimately the whole world stands agape and exclaims, "a miracle has happened."[97]

Gandhi objected to violence because when it appears to do good, the good is only temporary; the evil it does is more lasting.[98] Revolutionary violence is intended to exert pressure but it is the insane pressure of anger and ill-will, which cannot be as effective as the pressure exerted by nonviolent acts.[99] "History teaches one that those who have, no doubt with honest motives, ousted the greedy by using brute force against them, have in their turn become a prey to the disease of the conquered."[100] Violence always thrives on counter-violence.[101]

Gandhi was prepared to advocate *ahimsa* as a policy not merely to fighters for freedom and revolutionaries but also to the Czechs, the Poles, the Norwegians, the French and the English in their resistance to Hitler. He believed that Hitler could not digest as much power as he was seeking and would eventually go as empty-handed as Alexander. He could not sustain the burden of the crushing weight of a mighty empire and could not hold all the conquered nations in perpetual subjection. If European nations defended their freedom with the force of nonviolence rather than with the force of arms, "Europe would add several inches to its moral stature. And in the end I expect it is the moral worth that will count. All else is dross."[102] Here again, Gandhi's appeal to nonviolence as a policy is based upon a certain view of what is dross and of the value of moral victory which underlies *ahimsa* as a creed.

Gandhi was not very successful in maintaining the distinction between creed and policy or in producing purely empirical arguments for *ahimsa* as a policy because of his conviction that nonviolence, if it is real, cannot, by definition, fail; and that violence is always bound to fail in the long run. He believed both that nonviolence is the nobler way and also that it is the swifter way, but his ultimate reason for believing the latter was that the ignoble must also be the ineffective and its effectiveness was not merely temporary but also unreal. The method of nonviolence "is the swiftest the world has ever seen, for it is the surest."[103] Similarly, he declared that the nonviolent way to freedom will be found to be the shortest, even though it may appear to be the longest to our impatient nature.[104] He could only justify this by the view that if India gained freedom through violence more quickly, it would not be real freedom, in terms of his moral and political convictions.

The price that Gandhi paid for overstating his case for *ahimsa* as a policy, because of his inability to hold consistently to the distinction between creed and policy, was his eventual disillusionment with the results of "non-violence of the weak." In 1925 he argued that though he taught the active nonviolence of the strongest, the weakest can partake in it without becoming weaker, and could only become stronger for having been in it.[105] The rooted prejudice that to practice pure *ahimsa* is difficult is due to the inertia that becomes an incubus and a vice when it ties the mind down to old ruts.[106]

> Man often becomes what he believes himself to be. If I keep on saying to myself that I *cannot* do a certain thing, it is possible that I may end by becoming incapable of doing it. On the contrary, if I have the belief that I *can* do it, I shall surely acquire the capacity to do it even if I may not have it at the beginning.[107]

This explains Gandhi's readiness to make claims for nonviolence as a policy which were consistent only with nonviolence as a creed. But he clearly saw in the last years of his life that nonviolence as a policy could easily become a form of cowardice and that there is nothing more demoralizing than the fake nonviolence of the weak and impotent.[108]

Gandhi was always concerned to dissociate bravery from violence and to insist that cowardice was actually incompatible with nonviolence. The greater the possession of brute force, the greater coward does the possessor become,[109] and hence an authoritarian regime, inwardly insecure though apparently powerful, stops at nothing. Similarly, a political assassin, though patriotic and apparently brave, is cowardly insofar as he is willing to kill for his cause. Dhingra, the Indian anarchist, was a patriot whose love was blind and whose sacrifice was misguided because of a false view of courage.[110] On the other hand, simple but truly brave peasants cannot be cowed down by brute force.[111] It is, however, one thing to say that *nonviolent* resistance requires more courage than *violent,* but quite another to say that willingness to resort to violence is by itself evidence of cowardice. Gandhi held both these propositions, which are logically independent of each other.

Active *ahimsa,* as Gandhi saw it, necessarily springs from fearlessness. A man cannot practice *ahimsa,* "the most soldierly of a soldier's virtues,"[112] and be a coward at the same time. Where the only choice seems to be between cowardice and violence, Gandhi said he would advise violence.[113] Hatred has its origin in fear and perfect love casts out all fear. When we are unmanly, this is not because we do not know how to strike the oppressor but because we fear to die.[114] *Ahimsa* calls for the strength and courage to suffer without retaliation, to receive blows without returning any.[115]

Nonviolence for Gandhi necessarily presupposes the willingness to suffer and the readiness to die for one's convictions. The exercise of nonviolence, he said, is summed up in "die for your honour and freedom" instead of "kill if necessary and be killed in the act." A brave soldier kills only if necessary and risks his own life, but nonviolence demands even greater courage and sacrifice.[116] Gandhi was always deeply struck by the heroism and readiness to die shown by brave soldiers in battle. As early as 1902, he compared the holy stillness that pervaded a Trappist monastery he visited with the atmosphere he found in some war camps with their perfect order, perfect stillness and dedicated preparation to put forth the greatest energy and selflessness in the face of the gravest ordeal.

> Tommy was then altogether lovable. . . . There was, shall I say, a spirit of brotherhood irrespective of colour or creed. . . . As a Hindu, I do not believe in war, but if anything can even partially reconcile me to it, it was the rich experience we gained at the front. It was certainly not the thirst for blood that took thousands of men to the battlefield. If I may use a most holy name without doing any violence to our feelings, like Arjun, they went to the battlefield, because it was their duty. And how many proud, rude, savage spirits has it not broken into gentle creatures of God?[117]

These soldiers were ready to die rather than anxious to kill and, in Gandhi's view, were merely brave instruments of the cowardly will to kill of those who sent them to battle but were themselves not so ready to die.

In later life Gandhi went so far as to say that when a man is fully ready to die he will not even desire to offer violence. He even put down as "a self-evident proposition" what many people would question—that the desire to kill is in inverse proportion to the willingness to die.[118] This statement cannot be grasped or defended without reference to the Indian concept of *tanha*—the will to live, the driving force behind physical survival and bodily attachment. It is believed that the greater the *tanha,* the more ruthless and violent a man becomes in his mental outlook. For Gandhi an essential element in *himsa* is the degree of mental violence.

Gandhi regarded the use of violence in self-defense differently from its exercise in aggression, though he insisted that nonviolence becomes meaningless if violence is automatically permitted for self-defense.[119] "People must learn to defend themselves against misbehaving individuals, no matter who they are. . . . No doubt the non-violent way is always the best, but where that does not come naturally the violent way is both necessary and honourable. Inaction there is rank cowardice and unmanly."[120] Whereas the violence of the weak has never been known to prevail against the violence of the strong, the success of even the nonviolence of the weak is a daily occurrence, argued Gandhi. The use of physical force is preferable to cowardice, i.e., it is wrong not to use force when we have a mind to do so but do not use it merely because we fear to die. Gandhi preferred that India should resort to arms in order to defend her honor than that she should, in a cowardly manner, become or remain a helpless witness to her own dishonor.[121] His objection to fleeing from danger was that it is not merely cowardly but that in spite of his flight a coward commits mental *himsa.*[122] There is hope for a violent man to be some day nonviolent but there is none for a coward.[123]

The reason why Gandhi went into all these qualifications of his position in regard to *ahimsa* was that he was concerned about the misinterpretations of his teachings that had gained currency. He could not condone a hypocritical use of nonviolence and declared that hypocrisy has acted as an ode to virtue but it could never take its place.[124] "The world's history shows that you cannot be violent towards one and non-violent towards another."[125] It is not possible to use nonviolence against alien rule if violence toward compatriots is condoned. Gandhi had always pointed out that for nonviolence we must rely more upon quality than quantity,[126] and he declared explicitly at the end of his life that there is no such thing as nonviolence of the weak and it is a contradiction in terms.[127] The distinction between nonviolence of the weak and that of the strong could be made in arriving at moral appraisals, but not as a guide to moral decisions. Gandhi was far less concerned with moral judgments than with moral conduct.

When Azad had told Gandhi that "when we gain power we shall not be able to hold it non-violently," he related the moral of Tolstoy's story of *Ivan the Fool.* Ivan became nonviolent even when he became king and there were scores of such stories in the Hindu scriptures. However, Gandhi soon came to feel that the truly nonviolent man can never hold power himself, but if he did, he would derive all his power from the people he served, and for such a man or such a government a nonviolent army would be a perfect possibility. "Non-violence does not signify that man must not fight against the enemy, and by enemy is meant the evil which men do, not the human beings themselves."[128] Given the distinction between evil acts and their doers, the emphasis was again on the absence of hatred and on the subjective nature of *ahimsa,* but Gandhi also believed that even a government could desist from actual violence if it organized training in the use of *ahimsa.*

Although Gandhi was an absolutist in regard to his faith in *ahimsa* as a creed, he was clearly willing to make qualifications and to treat nonviolence in so subjective a manner that he cannot be called an orthodox pacifist. He valued *satya* even more than *ahimsa,* justice even more than abstention from violence, courage more than mere non-participation in war. He had no use for pacifism as an abstract moral attitude. "To refuse to render military service when the particular time arrives is to do the thing after all the time for combating the evil is practically gone. . . . Refusal of military service is much more superficial than non-cooperation with the whole system which supports the state."[129]

While universal conscription in military service was repugnant to Gandhi, he was prepared to advocate the conscription, during an emergency, of skilled and unskilled productive labor as the "easiest and the most effective method of organizing society on a peaceful footing."[130] He was insistent that nonviolence does not and should never mean abject surrender and that it could confound all modern tactics of war.[131] But although he believed that peace has its victories more glorious than those of war, he did not want peace at any price. "I do not want the peace that you find in the grave."[132]

Gandhi, the believer in *ahimsa,* was also scathing about the appeasement at Munich. "Europe has sold her soul for the sake of a seven days' earthly existence. The peace Europe gained at Munich is a triumph of violence; it is also its defeat. If England and France were sure of victory, they would certainly have fulfilled their duty of saving Czechoslovakia or of dying with it. But they quailed before the combined violence of Germany and Italy."[133]

Although Gandhi was against war and every form of violence, he was quite willing to take sides and to hold that one of two warring parties is in the wrong.[134] The party whose cause is just deserves every moral support. "While all violence is bad and must be condemned in the abstract, it is permissible for, it is even the duty of, a believer in *ahimsa* to distinguish between the aggressor and the defender. Having done so, he will side with the defender in a nonviolent manner, i.e., give his life in saving him."[135] Even more, Gandhi thought it quite possible to organize and train a nonviolent army in which the general and the officers are actually elected, or as if elected, in view of their moral rather than material authority.[136] He also considered the formation of a peace brigade to deal, for example, with riots and local disturbances. Such a brigade could be made up of some whole-time workers and mainly of volunteers willing to cultivate[137] friendly relations with the people living in their circle of operation. Nonviolence or its constituent element, pacifism, must not, therefore, mean an abdication of moral responsibility or merely a personal gesture of protest on conscientious grounds but rather an ardent and continual participation in social activity in an area of conflict.

Gandhi differed from many Western pacifists not merely in their exclusive emphasis on conscientious resistance to conscription and military service but also in that he did not share their sense of uniqueness in loathing war. While he consistently condemned all violence in terms of universal principle rather than personal sentiment, he also felt that "if war had no redeeming feature, no courage and heroism behind it, it would be a despicable thing, and would not need speeches to destroy it."[138]

It is not surprising that Gandhi defended his participation in the Boer War and in the First World War before his critics, especially the Belgian pacifist de Ligt and the Tolstoyan Tcherkoff. In 1925 he pointed out his reason for enlisting men for ambulance work in the First World War. "I had to advise and lead men who believed in war but who from cowardice or from base motives, or from anger against the British Government refrained from enlisting."[139] Further, he argued in 1929 that a nonviolent man will instinctively prefer direct participation to indirect participation in a system which is based on violence and to which he has to belong without any choice being left to him. If his only choice was between paying for an army and being a soldier himself, he would prefer to enlist.[140] Again, in 1936 Gandhi said that just as he had reluctantly acquiesced in his family's conduct toward untouchables when he was a boy, so too he took seriously in 1914 his deep loyalty at the time to the British Empire and felt it his duty to participate in the war despite his avowal of *ahimsa*. "Indeed, life is made of such compromises. *Ahimsa,* simply because it is purest, unselfish love, often demands such compromises. The conditions are imperative. There should be no self in one's action, no fear, no untruth, and it must be in furtherance of the cause of *ahimsa*. The compromise must be natural to oneself, not imposed from without."[141] Here again the stress is on inward rather than on outer *ahimsa,* on the spirit rather than the letter of the law of nonviolence. In general "in the ticklish question of *ahimsa* each one should be his own authority not on the law but on interpretation."[142]

UNAVOIDABLE *HIMSA*

Ahimsa was an absolute principle to Gandhi insofar as he could not morally extol, even if he might condone, *himsa* under any circumstances whatsoever. On the other hand, he so widened and deepened the content of *ahimsa* that anyone who claims to embody it adequately in his own life is necessarily indulging in self-deception or self-righteousness. If Gandhi was not an ordinary pacifist, that was because he never lost his acute and painful awareness that bodily life inevitably involves a certain amount of *himsa*. *Ahimsa* may be the law of nature and of society (in different senses of "law") but *himsa,* at least to a certain extent, is unavoidable both in nature and in society. Perfect nonviolence is impossible so long as we exist physically and is only a theoretical construct like Eu-

clid's point or straight line.[143] There is no such thing as unadulterated violence in the world[144] but neither is there unalloyed nonviolence. "We are helpless mortals caught in the conflagration of
himsa. Man cannot live for a moment without causing or unconsciously committing outward *himsa.*"[145] The votary of *ahimsa* will
be constantly growing in self-restraint and compassion, but he can
never become entirely free from outward *himsa.* So long as he continues to be a social being, he cannot but participate in the *himsa*
that the very existence of society involves. Gandhi believed that
"he who has no power of resisting war, he who is not qualified to
resist war, may take part in war, and yet wholeheartedly try to free
himself, his nation and the world from war."[146]

Gandhi's standpoint in regard to *himsa* was in accord with Hindu
scholastics. Traditionally, *himsa* has been divided into three classes.
First of all, there is the man who is guilty of acts of violence. This
is the *krita* form of *himsa.* Secondly, a man who aids, instigates or
conspires with another in acts of violence is equally guilty of *himsa.*
This is the *karita* form of *himsa.* Thirdly, there is the *anumodita*
form of *himsa,* which consists in passively watching, and passing
over without protest or interference, the acts of *himsa* committed
by others. If a man sees a wrong done, and does not move himself
to put it down, he is again equally guilty of committing *himsa.*
Ahimsa, therefore, consists not only in checking one's own
thoughts, feelings and acts, but also in becoming concerned with
the commission of acts of *himsa* of anyone or of all collectively in
human society. "The yoga of *ahimsa* consists in the devising of
means and the doing of acts, calculated to check the evil tendency
of this *HIMSA,* and to eliminate to the best of one's power, the
effects of the commission of such acts from human society."[147]
The forms of *himsa* are innumerable. *Ahimsa* connotes all that
leads to the highest development of a human being, all that tends
to the unification of human interests, even the grouping together
of men for various purposes. Patanjali saw *ahimsa* as a branch of
kriya yoga, the yoga of action. It is in the doing of the work of the
world that this virtue can be practiced. *Ahimsa* is the supreme
moral restraint that must be applied to every branch of human action in the midst of society.

Although some *himsa* is unavoidable, Gandhi thought that it is

possible for the votary of *ahimsa* to be honest, strenuous and un-
ceasing in his attempt to live up to his creed. His success will always be relative but his faith in *ahimsa* must be absolute. "Possession of a body like any other possession necessitates some violence,
be it ever so little. The fact is that the path of duty is not always
easy to discern amidst claims seeming to conflict one with the
other."[148] As long as there is any attachment to the body or to
bodily life or physical comforts, or even to basic needs or any form
of self-interest, a certain amount of at least mental *himsa* is inescapable, and to fail to see this is only to deceive oneself. All life in
the flesh exists by some *himsa* and none, while in the flesh, can be
entirely free from *himsa* because no one ever completely renounces
the will to live. "Of what use is it to force the flesh if the spirit
refused to cooperate?"[149] It is precisely because *himsa* cannot be
wholly avoided that Gandhi felt it necessary to use a negative word
like *ahimsa,* or nonviolence.[150] "The world is not entirely governed
by logic. Life itself involves some kind of violence and we have to
choose the path of least violence."[151] Hence Gandhi's stress on the
need for tolerance in our judgments regarding the *ahimsa* of others
and the recognition that "in the garden of non-violence there are
many plants. They are all from the same parent. They may not be
used simultaneously. Some are less powerful than others. . . . All
are harmless. But they have to be handled skilfully."[152]

In his recognition that some *himsa* is inescapable, Gandhi once
came close to contradicting his basic position by his statement that
what is inevitable is not regarded as a sin and may even be thought
meritorious. This was because Gandhi came under fire from Indian
critics when he advocated the extermination of pests and the killing
of a rabid dog instead of allowing it to die a slow death, and especially by his killing of an ailing calf.

> If I wish to be an agriculturist. . . . I will have to use the mini-
> mum unavoidable violence in order to protect my fields. . . . If
> I do not wish to do so myself I will have to engage someone to do
> it for me. There is not much difference between the two. To allow
> crops to be eaten up by animals in the name of *ahimsa* while
> there is a famine in the land is certainly a sin. Evil and good are
> relative terms. What is good under certain conditions can become
> an evil or a sin under a different set of conditions.[153]

There is more *himsa*, he said, in the slow torture of men and animals, the starvation and exploitation to which they are subjected out of selfish greed, the wanton humiliation and oppression of the weak and the killing of their self-respect, than in the mere benevolent taking of life. To use force to prevent a child from rushing at a fire is an unselfish act of *ahimsa*.[154] Even more,

> taking life may be a duty. We do destroy as much life as we think necessary for sustaining our body. . . . Even manslaughter may be necessary in certain cases. Suppose a man runs amuck and goes furiously about sword in hand, and killing anyone that comes in his way, and no one dares to capture him alive. Anyone who despatches this lunatic, will earn the gratitude of the community and be regarded as a benevolent man.[155]

Although *ahimsa* was a comprehensive concept for Gandhi, he felt that in view of the unavoidability of some *himsa,* it was necessary to put first things first and not to reduce *ahimsa* merely to a doctrine of *jivadaya* or kindness to animals or to an emotional loathing of every form of violence.

It would be wrong to think that Gandhi's insistence on *ahimsa* as a general principle, qualified by his recognition of the unavoidability of some *himsa,* comes to the same thing, in practice, as the standpoint of those who start off by showing the unavoidability of force and then proceed to accept the desirability of maximum consent and minimum coercion. In Gandhi's view, the man who starts justifying the use of force will become addicted to it, while the man who renounces it from the start may find that he has to come to terms with the practical limitations of nonviolence, but he ceaselessly tries to reduce *himsa* and replace it by *ahimsa*. The difference between a belief in *ahimsa* and a belief in *himsa* is the difference between north and south, life and death.

CRITICS OF *AHIMSA*

Gandhi has been criticized repeatedly both for his theory of nonviolence and for his actual applications of it, and he in turn has often criticized what he regarded as misinterpretations or misapplications of his theory. It would be worthwhile to give a few examples here of the actual criticisms made to Gandhi and then to

consider inherent difficulties in his theory. In 1924 Motilal Nehru
was perturbed by Gandhi's opposition to entry into the Legislative
Councils. Motilal Nehru thought that his acceptance of *ahimsa*
merely committed him to the refraining from inflicting or contemplating violence of any kind. He could not accept Gandhi's view
that entry into the Councils was tantamount to participation in
violence.

> I understand this to refer to the fact that the Councils are estab-
> lished by a Government which is based on violence. I maintain
> that no one living under such a Government can help participate
> in violence in that sense. . . . The very act of living and adopt-
> ing the most essential means of sustaining life under such a Gov-
> ernment would be tantamount to participation in violence. . . .
> There may be some who take the extreme view of non-violence
> that Mahatma Gandhi does in theory but I do not know a single
> follower of Mahatma Gandhi who acts upon it. It is true that
> non-violence even in the limited sense that I give to it must relate
> both to word and deed and cannot be confined to abstention from
> physical hurt only. But non-violence in thought must be ruled out
> entirely as impractical.[156]

The difficulty here was that Motilal Nehru could not take Gandhi's
view that alien rule was satanic, though seemingly benevolent,
despotism, while Gandhi could not but regard as *himsa* any active
participation in an inherently undemocratic system when there was
an alternative organized program of nonviolent resistance.

Again, the Reverend B. de Ligt felt that by concentrating on a
nonviolent struggle for national independence, Gandhi was limiting his horizon and causing his tactics to swerve from the universal application of *ahimsa*. Gandhi, however, stressed the need for
nonviolent action in the immediate setting in which one found oneself and also argued that the peace we seem to prize is a mere
makeshift bought with the blood of starving millions, that it was a
sin against *ahimsa* for a man to sit passively until "the existing rule
of spoliation has ended."[157] He also told de Ligt that all activity
for stopping war must prove fruitless so long as the causes of war
are not understood and radically dealt with, and the prime cause
of modern wars, in his view, is the inhuman race for exploitation
of the so-called weaker peoples of the earth.[158]

It has also been said that Gandhi's insistence that *ahimsa* is a universally effective social institution made of it a coercive instrument[159] and that he could not as a politician carry permanent conviction in his very personal expression of his principle of nonviolence. Although Gandhi used the misleading phrase "moral coercion," he explicitly stated on several occasions that there is no virtue in nonviolence as such so long as the nonviolence is a threat. It may well be that as a politician Gandhi sometimes tended to use his magnetic power to secure consent and response to his creed of *ahimsa* and to his acts of *ahimsa* under conditions in which others did not feel free to do otherwise, but there can be no doubt that in his theoretical exposition of *ahimsa* Gandhi always emphasized that it excluded any form of violation of free and fully voluntary consent. He never denied that *ahimsa,* in its application to individual and social problems, involves a subtle form of pressure but it must be based on love and the result secured must be morally defensible and worthy in itself. *Ahimsa* is intended to replace coercion by persuasion and to result in the conversion of a violent opponent. It is, of course, very difficult to draw the line between persuasion and intimidation when no physical means are employed, between entirely peaceful and forceful conversion when no physical force or material inducement is used.

A more serious criticism against Gandhi's notion of *ahimsa* is that it is merely a guide to individual conduct and cannot be taken as a practicable technique of universal application in the social and political spheres, and that to preach *ahimsa* to the masses is merely a means of precipitating violence and chaos. The only concession Gandhi made to this criticism was that it was difficult to discover techniques for the universal application of *ahimsa* in that experiments can be made only when an occasion for them arises, and such occasions are naturally rare. "Success calls for a clear concept of the full ideal of *ahimsa* on the part of the researcher or the pioneer."[160] This admission was made by Gandhi in a letter to his colleague Mashruwalla, in which he declared that he could never concede the criticism that nonviolence is for the individual only—and that, too, essentially for the enlightened or for the recluse.

If Gandhi conceded the criticism that it is either dangerous or delusive to think that nonviolence can be taken as a universally applicable injunction, then clearly his entire doctrine of *ahimsa,* even with all the many qualifications and reservations he made, would break down. He has been criticized for his qualifications and called a conditional pacifist, and he has also been criticized for being an absolutist and a dogmatist. If it can be shown that it is logically (and not merely empirically) impossible to follow the injunction to practice *ahimsa* in all situations or if it can be shown that it is strictly impossible to do so according to the laws of nature, then clearly the doctrine of *ahimsa* is devoid of any significance. But it can be argued that it is logically impossible only if we so define man that he cannot be expected or obliged to practice *ahimsa* in all walks of life. Similarly, it can be shown to be strictly impossible only if we believe that there is no such thing as a natural law of *ahimsa* or if we think there is a contrary law of nature. In either case, a rejection of the doctrine of *ahimsa* would merely amount to a rejection rather than a refutation of the presuppositions underlying it. But otherwise, it would be difficult to hold categorically that *ahimsa* is an impossible ideal.

When a citizen or a politician is told to perform what he regards as a saintly or heroic act, he could no doubt reply that he is neither a saint nor a hero and that if Gandhi and his co-votaries of *ahimsa* were saintly and heroic, their conduct could have no practical moral implication for him. But his objection does not suggest that there is any logical or physical impossibility in regard to the practice of *ahimsa.* Anyone can imagine himself as a saint or a hero even if he is convinced that he is not. Moral ideals depend upon the force of men's imagination. Gandhi urged men to be nonviolent but he was tolerant of human weaknesses and imperfections. He urged others to rise to a saintly or a heroic level without requiring it of them—unless they were votaries who had taken the vow of *ahimsa.* It is precisely because ordinary men and women cannot be expected to behave like saints and heroes that we set these rare exceptions apart from the rest of mankind. It is enough, and not unreasonable to hope, that more people should try to be a little like them. Saints and heroes differ from ordinary people to an enormous degree, but it is important to notice that the difference is still one of degree, not of kind.

Gandhi's moral exhortation and political idealism were based firmly upon his view that most men, however prone to violence, were not incurably addicted, like permanent alcoholics, to violence. "*Himsa* does not need to be taught. Man as animal is violent but as spirit is non-violent. The moment he awakens to the spirit within he cannot remain violent."[161] The doctrine of *ahimsa* is nothing less and nothing more than a call to human beings to regard themselves not as superior animals and to remind themselves of their moral and spiritual status, their dignity as human beings. However imperfect or however infrequent this realization, it could still act as a brake against *himsa* and arouse the power of *ahimsa* or love latent in every human soul. Even if men were not able to practice *ahimsa* while regarding it as desirable and as preferable to *himsa,* it would be better for them to be concerned with *ahimsa* rather than to come wholly to terms with *himsa*. This line of argument was essential to Gandhi's advocacy of *ahimsa* because of his belief that human nature is such that it must either sink or soar. Either a man progresses toward *ahimsa* or he rushes to his doom. If all or most men became convinced that *ahimsa* was a wholly impossible ideal in society and in personal life, then it would be inevitable that men destroy themselves or be destroyed.

As Gandhi believed that mankind has steadily progressed toward *ahimsa,* he thought it right to infer from his view of past history that mankind has to and will progress still further in the practice of nonviolence. "Nothing in the world remains static, everything is kinetic. If there is no progression, then there is inevitable retrogression. No one can remain without the eternal cycle."[162] Gandhi also felt that the present era marks the saturation point in the pursuit of violence and also spells doom, and yet *ahimsa* has never before been appreciated by mankind as it is today. "It may be long before the law of love will be recognised in international affairs. The machineries of Governments stand between and hide the hearts of one people from those of another. Yet . . . we could see how the world is moving steadily to realise that between nation and nation as between man and man, force has failed to solve problems."[163] This was in 1919. Gandhi was less optimistic but more categorical in 1946: "Unless now the world adopts non-violence, it will spell certain suicide for mankind."[164] He was equally firm to his compatriots: "If *ahimsa* disappears, Hindu *Dharma* disappears."[165]

ASSESSMENT

Gandhi's extreme advocacy of *ahimsa* is clearly bound up with his presuppositions about nature, man and history. At times he did not seem to show adequate awareness of the difficulty experienced by people who did not share his presuppositions in accepting his attitude to *ahimsa*. He was both an exponent of *ahimsa* and a propagandist for it. He felt that it was his mission and India's destiny to deliver the message of *ahimsa* to mankind. "It may take ages to come to fruition. But so far as I can judge, no other country will precede her in the fulfilment of that mission."[166] In an appeal to the Indian princes in 1942 he pointed out the lesson which he thought Europe had to learn from the French Revolution, that if a revolution is brought about by violence, the position will be reversed but not altered for the better. It is only with nonviolence that a new era could be brought into being. The French motto— "Liberty, Equality, Fraternity"—is a heritage for all mankind, but the missing factor is nonviolence. "What the French never realised, it is open for us to do."[167]

Gandhi was clearly a propagandist for nonviolence and directed his message especially to India but also the rest of the world. He said to Dr. Thurman that "It may be through the Negroes that the unadulterated message of non-violence will be delivered to the world."[168] He was more concerned that the message should be given to mankind than that India should give it. He even said that "should India take to the sword, she would cease to be the India of my dreams and I should like to betake me to the Himalayas to seek rest for my anguished soul."[169] When the hour of disillusionment came, he did not retire into the seclusion of an anchorite as Ramana Maharshi thought he should, but risked his life among the frenzied rioters in an experiment which he thought might be his last act of *ahimsa*. When his countrymen betrayed the faith he placed in their nonviolent mission, he held fast, content to be alone, in his total devotion to *ahimsa*. He was not unprepared for this, although he did not expect the enormity of violence that broke out in the last phase of his life. As early as 1924, he had written that if the Indian masses did not respond to his call for *ahimsa*, "I should be content to be alone and rely upon its ultimate invincibility to convert the masses."[170] Again in 1939 he wrote that the progress of nonviolence is seemingly a terribly slow process though violence, even for the vindication of justice, is played out; but "I am content to plough a lonely furrow, if it is to be my lot that I have no co-sharer in the out-and-out belief in non-violence."[171] If Gandhi was a propagandist for his creed of *ahimsa,* no propagandist could have shown greater courage and greater faith than he did, or been as lonely in his crowning endeavor for his cause as he was.

No doubt, Gandhi's exposition of *ahimsa* suffered to some extent from the fact that he was so ardent a propagandist for his ideas, so devout a missionary for his creed. It was also this which led him to overestimate the capacity for nonviolence of his own countrymen and to wish that India should teach *ahimsa* to mankind. But he was led to his faith in India as the land of nonviolence not through any narrow nationalism or blind patriotism but rather because of his continual awareness that the presuppositions underlying his doctrine of *ahimsa* are taken seriously there and were proclaimed in ancient India. Less than a year before his death he said that the lesson of nonviolence was present in every religion but "perhaps it was here in India that its practice had been reduced to a science" in view of the *tapascharya* (the meditations and austerities) of many saints.[172] Gandhi thought that the burden of the *Ramayana* and the *Mahabharata* was to teach *ahimsa,* that Rama and Krishna could not be taken merely as historical characters, that Ravana and Kamsa represented *himsa* or the evil force in man.[173] Patanjali's *Yoga Sutra* stated that when *ahimsa* had been fully established, it would completely liquidate the forces of enmity and evil in the neighborhood.[174] Gandhi also drew from the story of Nachiketas the moral that love could melt mountains.[175] *Ahimsa* was for him an integral part of *yajna,* the traditional Indian concept of sacrifice, and thus *ahimsa* became an act of self-examination and self-purification, whether by the individual, group or a nation.[176] It was in terms of his metaphysical presuppositions derived from Indian thought that Gandhi believed that the moral force generated by nonviolence was infinitely greater than the force of all the arms invented by man's ingenuity.[177]

Gandhi could be questioned even in terms of his own presuppositions. Was he in danger of expecting of men in *Kali Yuga,* the Age of Darkness, what heroes were said to have displayed in *Satya Yuga,* the Golden Age? By transcendentalizing the concept of *ahimsa,* did not Gandhi recognize that a utopian element had entered into his doctrine and that he could not, therefore, expect to secure assent to his extreme formulation of *ahimsa* from those who did not believe in rebirth, natural law or spiritual forces at work in the cosmos? Even a believer in rebirth who did not also accept the Moral Law of *ahimsa,* might be less against violence than a nonbeliever on the ground that sending a creature to another life is less dreadful than ending its life for ever. Is it surprising that those who reject Gandhi's presuppositions should argue that *ahimsa* succeeded against the British with their moral doubts and qualms but it would not have succeeded against Hitler, Stalin, or the Chinese in Tibet? It would be quite impossible to concede this last criticism without demolishing the entire doctrine of *ahimsa,* which is, in principle, capable of universal application even if it is difficult to lay down the specific conditions for particular experiments in *ahimsa,* conducted by fallible men of faith. But it could be asked whether, even if *ahimsa* were practiced against a ruthless invader like the Chinese in Tibet, its votaries were prepared to face the fact that while a few may be ready to lay down their lives bravely, others would merely be committing suicide. *Ahimsa,* Gandhi would perhaps reply, may involve martyrdom, but would be incompatible with suicide. The difficulty here is that a votary of *ahimsa* might, when driven to desperation, rationalize his desire to commit suicide as a readiness for martyrdom. If this happened, would we be entitled to condemn his cowardice and declare him to have been a practitioner of *ahimsa* of the weak? Gandhi's profound tolerance and compassion may have prevented him from judging harshly a weak-minded votary of *ahimsa,* but he perhaps did not realize how easily *ahimsa* could be abused.

Although the transcendental and the utopian elements in Gandhi's conception of *ahimsa* may not be acceptable to those who do not share his presuppositions or his aims, it would be insensitive and unimaginative to refuse to see the basic relevance and far-reaching significance of the doctrine of *ahimsa* today. We might prefer to regard *ahimsa* merely as an inflated version of the liberal faith in consent and intellectual conversion. Or we might consider liberal optimism and its trust in peaceful methods as merely a watered-down, a more attractive but less compelling, version of *ahimsa*. In either case we cannot fail to see the connection between the doctrine of *ahimsa* and the cardinal tenets of liberal, democratic faith. Gandhi was convinced that present-day society is essentially based upon force and the toleration of violence, and "my endeavour," he said, "is no less than to get rid of this worship of force."[178] No one else in the modern age has so consistently and so forcefully pointed out that all violence carries with it some amount of demoralization.[179]

> The truth requires constant and extensive demonstration. This I am endeavouring to do to the best of my ability. What if the best of my ability is very little? May I not be living in a fool's paradise? Why should I ask people to follow me in the fruitless search? These are pertinent questions. My answer is quite simple. I ask nobody to follow me. Everyone should follow his or her own inner voice. If he or she has no ears to listen to it, he or she should do the best he or she can.[180]

Thus Gandhi's appeal to *ahimsa* was ultimately an appeal to the conscience and the reason of the individual, an affirmation of the dignity and divinity of the human soul, the apotheosis of purity of means in the pursuit of any social or political goal. "I have often said that if one takes care of the means, the end will take care of itself. Non-violence is the means."[181]

But Gandhi achieved far more than this by his doctrine of *ahimsa*. He converted a passive principle of meek submission to evil and injustice into a dynamic doctrine of nonviolent activity in the cause of truth and justice, a universal commandment to exercise the power of love and compassion on the basis of inner strength, not outer weakness. As Albert Schweitzer has said, "Gandhi continues what the Buddha began. In the Buddha the spirit of love set itself the task of creating different spiritual conditions in the world; in Gandhi it undertakes to transform *all* worldly conditions."[182] Gandhi may well have been mistaken in being more optimistic and more impatient than the Buddha, but he could hardly be blamed for his crusading zeal and his enthusiasm as a social reformer. His belief that all society is held together by non-violence, even as the earth is held in her position by gravitation, was also held by the Buddha. His faith was that when a society is deliberately constructed in accordance with the law of nonviolence, its structure will be different in material particulars from what it is today, and that there would be far-reaching consequences comparable to those yielded by the discovery of the law of gravitation and of which "our ancestors had no knowledge." And yet Gandhi felt that he could not say in advance what the government based wholly on nonviolence would be like.[183] Gandhi wrote as a political moralist without any prospectus for the future, but was convinced that *ahimsa* would come to be accepted as a universal criterion and an effective method in social and political life. In this he may well have been far ahead of his time.

We could, however, value the message of *ahimsa* without entertaining any hope, like Gandhi, that human nature or human society would be fundamentally altered in the future in its attitude to the exercise of *himsa*. A prophet and visionary cannot, by definition, be proved or disproved in his own time.

It is undeniable that the doctrine of *ahimsa* has challenged a common presupposition, the belief that the use of force becomes morally permissible because it has an ethical end, and it has also pointed out that there is a nonviolent and a violent manner of exercising force. A Muslim apologist for force has pointed out that its obnoxious feature is only that the wrong side may win, and regards it as a divine gift, a sacred trust to be used only for the sake of justice.[184] To Gandhi *ahimsa* could never enable the unjust to prevail because they would be less capable of embodying it than the just. A schoolmaster at Harrow, Mr. Rae, deplored the fact that even children have been indoctrinated with the idea of inevitable killing and have no vision of a world, no desire for a world, in which killing is as out of date and as uncivilized as cannibalism. He further referred to three myths dangerous to the young—first, that violence is not only justified but laudable; second, that war is fun, a great game; and third, that physical courage is the finest virtue and that moral courage, as shown by the conscientious objector, is contemptible. "The myths were not, of course, created and spread by those who were doing the fighting; no one who has looked war in the face could describe it as a game. The myths were an essential part of the home front, offspring of official propaganda and human blindness."[185] Mr. Rae may well be right in thinking that it is inevitable for a generation which grew up in a world that glorified violence to become violent; that we cannot separate the different forms of killing—state-owned and private enterprise; that where one breeds, so will the other, for "when it comes to reproducing itself, violence can compete with an amoeba."[186] He believes that wars are made possible not by megalomaniac dictators or religious fanatics or foolish politicians or blind patriots, but because the majority of people in the world have been brought up to accept war and violence as a normal part of life. Above all, he thinks that it is possible to bring up children to think of killing not just as something abhorrent but also as something of which they themselves are incapable, to be taught that the existing state of affairs need not be permanent and that man is as capable of outgrowing killing as he has outgrown cannibalism. "This vision—naïve, subversive, fantastic—whatever you choose to call it, can nevertheless be expressed in practical terms."[187]

Gandhi did not identify *ahimsa* with mere non-killing. He blamed the leaders of society and the policy-makers even more than the general climate of public opinion. He pinned his hopes not merely on children but even more on women, whom he regarded as "the incarnation of *ahimsa*," because of their infinite capacity for suffering.[188] It was Gandhi's dream that in an age of *ahimsa* every man and every woman would be the custodian of his or her own honor. Gandhi would have agreed, with a few qualifications, with Mr. Rae's courageous and moving article. He knew always that his vision of the general adoption of *ahimsa* as a social gospel was naïve, fantastic and subversive in the eyes of those who prided themselves on their realism and sophistication and patriotism. But he also firmly believed that his vision could be expressed in practical terms, and could be ignored by our world only at its peril.

APPENDIX: ATTITUDES TOWARD
NONVIOLENCE BEFORE GANDHI

In order to appreciate the originality of Gandhi's doctrine of *ahimsa,* it would be useful to set it in the context of earlier attitudes toward non-violence especially in the West. Zeno taught that *homonoia,* harmony or sympathy, binds the universe and *homonoia* became in Latin *concordia,* to which Tiberius dedicated a temple. The Stoics believed that it is a man's duty to endure the consequences of violence without resentment or anger. Epictetus said "Chain me? My leg you will chain —yes, but my will—no, not even Zeus can conquer that." These Stoic notions as well as the Jewish conception of the suffering Servant passed into early Christianity. Jesus stands at the end of a long line of Hebrew religious seers who dissociated themselves from military aspirations and looked forward to a Kingdom of Universal Peace.

Until about A.D. 170 the entire Church was consistently and abso-lutely pacifist, and Christians rejected the obligation of military service in the Roman armies but held to the ideal of martyrdom. From about A.D. 170 to A.D. 313 there is evidence of Christians serving in the army, but Irenaeus and Clement of Alexandria both imply that Christians are necessarily pacifist. How could the peaceable teaching, which does not allow men to take vengeance on their enemies, ever win the day, argued Origen, as long as compulsory military service was generally accepted? However, from Constantine's edict of toleration for Christianity in 313 and with the identification of State and Church in the Roman empire, the conception of a just war gradually began to take shape. St. Augus-tine of Hippo in the fifth century defended the doctrine of just war and defined it as "one that avenges wrongs." St. Thomas Aquinas went even further and laid down three requisites for a just war, but included among them not merely the worldly duty to the sovereign and the jus-tice of a national cause but also the presence of a rightful intention, defined as the advancement of good or the avoidance of evil. He allows clerics to urge other men to engage in just wars as a moral duty, but they must not in any circumstances fight themselves. Despite the de-parture from the pacifism of the early Church, there was clearly an ele-ment of *ahimsa* in the doctrines of St. Augustine and St. Thomas. St. Augustine distinguished between the positive and negative forms of the doctrine of non-resistance—"It is a small matter merely to abstain from injuring, unless you also confer a benefit as far as you can." But he thought that the principle of love does not preclude infliction of such requital as is needed for correction and as compassion itself dictates. Gandhi gave a stricter interpretation of the Sermon on the Mount than St. Augustine but he would have endorsed his statement in his *Reply to Faustus* that "what is here required is not a bodily action but an inward disposition." Again, Gandhi would have agreed with Aquinas's stress on rightful intention but he could not go so far as he did in thinking that just laws must necessarily command a strong force.

It is interesting to see that the extreme position of the early Church Fathers and the more moderate and flexible position of St. Augustine and Aquinas in regard to the use of force are mirrored after the Middle Ages in the attitudes of Erasmus and Grotius. In *The Complaint of Peace,* Erasmus held that peace is the order of nature, that the celestial bodies move in perfect harmony, that even in trees and plants there are signs of amity and love, that even wild animals and savages do not harm each other, and that man, instead of being at war with himself and with his fellow men, could, if he sincerely chose, fulfill the supreme obligation of mutual concord and cordial love. Grotius, on the other hand, regarded this attitude of his fellow countryman as a necessary but exaggerated protest against violence and considered the right of defence and the place of punishment in human society. But even he recognized man's impelling desire for peaceful social life and declared in his *De Jure Belli ac Pacis* that whatever is clearly at variance with the wish for order is contrary to the law of nature and the nature of man.

Up to the nineteenth century, violence was regarded as strictly instrumental, a means that needed an end to justify it. Whereas most political thinkers since Hobbes have accepted the need for self-preservation and have sought for a principle of political legitimacy that would justify the use of force to secure this end, a few like Kant have said that to maintain one's own life is a conditional duty but it is an unconditional duty not to take the life of another who does not injure one. In the nineteenth century we find the extreme positions in regard to violence adopted by authoritarians and by anarchists, and both extremes are to be found among the advocates of stability as well as among the apostles of progress. De Maistre argued that there is nothing but violence in the universe and challenged the assumptions of the Enlightenment, while Saint-Simon postulated a dogma of the future which will inculcate into everyone love for all, unite all wills into one will, and direct all efforts toward a single social goal. Comte asserted that without love no society can exist and that men should perform acts of love or sacrifice for the sake of others, regardless of personal reward. Love is the principle, order the basis, and progress is the end of human society.

The anarchists differed in their attitudes to nonviolence. To Godwin every form of coercion is evil, for it constitutes in essence a systematic interference with the activity of reason. Coercion, he said in *Political Justice,* has nothing in common with reason and cannot generate virtue. Proudhon propounded the theory of mutuality and invoked the Golden Rule to support his notion of Reciprocity. Max Stirner believed that the individual is above the State and that his violence (*gewalt*) is justified and essential. Bakunin, on the other hand, thought that even if bloody revolutions are often necessary because of human stupidity, they are always a monstrous evil and a great disaster, not only for the victims but also for the sake of purity of purpose. Kropotkin, however, felt that though the first act of the social revolution will be a work of destruction and that naturally the fight will demand victims, the social revolution will not continue as a reign of terror and that the public prosecutor, the guillotine and the corpse-cart will speedily become repulsive.

Most thinkers have shown a tendency to condemn or to justify particular, and usually the more obvious, forms of violence and coercion in terms of reason or revelation, by an appeal to nature or to society, by pointing to the past or the future. It is only Tolstoy in the West who thought deeply about nonviolence as the only permissible ethic in society, and he defended his position with the same extremism that is found in Sorel's elaborate justification of the ethic of violence. Tolstoy strongly reacted to the very idea of a struggle for existence and to its pseudo-scientific as well as its pseudo-religious justification; how could human existence be essentially a struggle if its whole point was universal love and if we accept as we must the principle that every human life is sacrosanct? In his essay "The Law of Violence and the Law of Love," written in 1908 and in his essay "The Only Commandment" written in 1909, he dealt with the reasons why educated men, and even people who call themselves religious, ignore this eternal, all-embracing Law of Love. This law can admit of no exception condoning violence, but people cannot put up with the denial of violence because that would destroy the basis of their life—the entire set of assumptions upon which their social institutions are founded.

Tolstoy foretold a spiritual awakening that would liberate men from the rule of force, but so long as not all people have abjured force and coercion, the individual who recognizes the Law of Love must follow the Golden Rule and recognize that the defense of violence is only the justification of our worst vices. The general belief in violence is super-stition and a perpetual obstacle to true progress—acting on one another, people are drawn from perfecting themselves inwardly. It is necessary and possible for at least a few to awaken from the hypnotism which hides from man the real consciousness of humanity derived from a common divinity. In his *The Kingdom of God Is Within You,* which Gandhi treasured, Tolstoy asserted that it is incomparably safer to act justly than to act unjustly, to bear an insult than to resist it by violence, that even if there were a considerable minority who believed this they would have such a corrective moral effect upon society that every cruel punishment would be abolished, and if these men formed a majority they would establish the reign of love and goodwill on earth. The circle of violence was defined by Tolstoy as consisting of four expedients: intimidation, bribery, hypnotism and organized militarism. The circle is complete and there is no escape except through nonviolence.

Tolstoy's apotheosis of nonviolence has been dismissed by a Western writer as escapist and un-Christian, as "a Buddhistic flight from him-self," as a compensation for what Turgenev thought was his failure to show real love to any human being. He has also been called anti-Christian for his acceptance of the law of *Karma,* i.e., "of automatic moral retribution, independent of the existence or non-existence of God."[189] Whether Tolstoy was right or not in his view of what is true and what is pseudo-Christianity, there is no doubt that his extreme formulation of the gospel of nonviolence has many parallels in Indian, especially Buddhist and Jain, thought. It is also remarkably similar to the doctrines of Mencius, who denied that there are any just or right. eous wars in the annals of States, and of Mo-Tze, who asserted that the Will of Heaven could be served only if the leaders of society showed that it is possible to love all men everywhere alike.

Mo-Tze, like Tolstoy, felt that the leaders of society simply do not know what is to their ultimate profit, that no ruler has embodied the doctrine of mutual all-embracing love in his government and no knight has embodied it in his conduct, though what is inherently good cannot really be unusable. Gandhi tried to account for this universal disparity between the doctrine of love and the practice of coercion. In an essay "The Bond of Sympathy," written as early as 1906, he remarked that most of the evil wrought by man against man is the result of lack of imagination and that the sentiment of cooperation and brotherhood is widely disregarded because rulers and ruled everywhere are not bound together by the consolidating bond of sympathy but separated and alienated by mutual distrust, fear and resentment.

If violence is natural to man and it seems reasonable to accept it and to define its limits or to moralize its use, it is equally natural for men to be repelled by violence and sometimes to wonder why people usually pay only lip service to the ideals of brotherhood and universal benevolence. If men like Mo-Tze, Tolstoy and Gandhi went to the extreme in extolling nonviolence, it was because they were concerned to protest against the popular complacency and moral flabbiness in regard to the acceptance of violence. "The main reason," Freud wrote to Einstein in his famous letter "Why War?" in 1932, "why we rebel against war is that we cannot help doing so." The truly civilized, like Tolstoy and Gandhi, develop a "constitutional intolerance" of violence and war. They could not, however, have agreed with Freud in thinking that their civilized attitude to brutality and death meant that they were living psychologically beyond their means. Marx identified action with violence and thought that violence is the midwife of history and that only in periods of violence does history show its true face and dispel the fog of hypocritical dialogue and moral pretensions. Gandhi identified the will to act with the force of *ahimsa* and regarded *himsa* as an unnatural reversion to animality, and further believed that nonviolence is the midwife of history, and that violence thrives on the hypocrisy of extolling nonviolence as a religious creed, while pursuing violence as a political technique and as a practical policy.

Gandhi clearly could not regard force, as Burke did, as "the dreadful exigence in which morality submits to the suspension of its own rules in favour of its own principles," and he went much further than Pascal's view that opinion is the queen of the world and force is its tyrant. Moral power could affect public opinion. The word "power," like the Latin *potentia,* indicates its potential character—its elusive, unpredictable quality. Just as a small, well-organized group can rule for a long time over a large and populous empire, so too, popular revolt, led by a few, can prevail against materially strong rulers even if it foregoes the use of violence. Tyranny, as Montesquieu saw, generates impotence and represents the abortive attempt to substitute violence for power. If a revolutionary movement, on the other hand, asserts its power by exercising violence and justifies it in the name of the subsequent establishment of nonviolence, it betrays a failure to grasp the interaction between violence and power.

9

Satya and *Ahimsa*

THE RELATION BETWEEN
TRUTH AND NONVIOLENCE

"Truth in the inward parts" at once breaks down the barriers which separate us from our fellow-men, and the claims of truthfulness and charity, which sometimes seem to conflict with each other, are thus reconciled.

DEAN INGE

He whose faith is most assured, has the best reason for relying on persuasion, and the strongest motive to thrust from him all temptations to use angry force. The substitution of force for persuasion, among its other disadvantages, has this further drawback . . . that it lessens the conscience of a society and breeds hypocrisy. . . . a man who is so silly as to think himself incapable of going wrong, is very likely to be too silly to perceive that coercion may be one way of going wrong.

LORD MORLEY

No political thinker, with the possible exception of Plato, has insisted as Gandhi did on truth as an absolute value, the sovereign in the kingdom of ends, the common concern of human society. No one, certainly, compares with him in his continual stress on the primacy of nonviolence as a political and social instrument, on the purity of means required for the pursuit of any worthy end. His originality, however, lay chiefly in his commendation of both *satya* and *ahimsa* and in his insight into the interdependence of truth and nonviolence, integrity and sensitivity, fidelity to oneself and respect for the rights of one's fellow men. Whereas most thinkers have concentrated on a single value to the exclusion of all others, and even thought that the pursuit of justice or equality or liberty or fraternity would automatically bring the others in its train, Gandhi pinned his political faith entirely on these two moral absolutes of truth and nonviolence and stressed their close connection with each other. He stretched the meanings of both *satya* and *ahimsa* far beyond the everyday connotations of "truth" and "nonviolence," but he also sharpened their use by distinguishing between their absolute and relative, positive and negative, genuine and spurious, forms.

He regarded both *satya* and *ahimsa* as inherent in nature and in man, underlying the constant working of a cosmic law and constituting the only common basis of human aspiration and action in the midst of society. No society can survive without a measure of *satya* and *ahimsa*, but these were both minimal and maximal concepts for Gandhi. The minimal formulation has been put forward by Herbert Hart:

> . . . In all moral codes there will be found some forms of prohibition of the use of violence to persons and things, and requirements of truthfulness, fair dealings and respect of promises . . . such universally recognized principles of conduct which have a basis in elementary truth concerning human beings, their natural environment, and aims, may be considered the *minimum content* of Natural Law . . . without such a content laws and morals could not forward the minimum purpose of survival.[1]

Gandhi used the argument from survival, but he also asserted his faith in the moral evolution of human society i.1 accordance with Natural Law, signified for him by the comprehensive concepts of *satya* and *ahimsa*. The closest approach in the West to Gandhi's view was perhaps that of Vico, for whom the essence of Natural Law was contained in truth and nonviolence—*veritas dicti, veriloquim, veritas facti* and *gestio rei sine dolo*.

It has often been said that attachment to absolute values is a flight from reality, that absolutists soon pass from refusal to condemnation, systematize their evasions in a myth of total purity, and thus disguise their desertion by idealization. Gandhi, however, was always concerned that the pursuit of purity should lead to a new political morality that men could feasibly adopt, and not to an apolitical perfectionism or an impasse of helpless good intentions. His chief concern was not for a certain abstract honesty of concept or an ideal historical perfection, but for a consistent probity of attitude toward politics and action in the midst of society. He saw a vital connection between force and fraud, violence and deception in everyday life. This connection was sensed by Hobbes and seen more clearly by Sorel. Gandhi drew conclusions opposite to theirs from his similar observations, in part because of his metaphysical presuppositions regarding *Sat* or Absolute Truth and *Dharma* or the Moral Law, and in part because of his psychological and ethical belief that fear is the common root of force and fraud and that the dignity of man as a truth-seeker enables him to be fearless enough to be nonviolent.

Gandhi derived his metaphysical presuppositions from Hindu and Buddhist thought, but his psychological and ethical standpoint was peculiarly his own, though it has affinities with elements in Jain teaching. The Vedic word *ṛta* refers to the principle of moral interdependence and cosmic equilibrium. This word was later replaced by *dharma,* derived from the root *dhṛ,* "to sustain or uphold," referring to the Moral Law which maintains the whole world, human society and the individual. This cosmic law was identified with truth and regarded as the ultimate authority to which earthly rulers had to yield. The *Brihadaranyaka Upanishad* depicts *dharma* as the sovereign power ruling over *kshatra* or temporal power and we are told that even the weak can overcome the strong with the help of *satya,* which is *dharma,* as with the help of a king. The *Mahabharata* states that for the sake of the promotion of strength and efficacy among beings the declaration of *dharma* is made. Further, whatever is attended with nonviolence (*ahimsa*), that is *dharma.* Bhishma declared that *dharma* involves abstention from injury to creatures as well as what upholds them. In the *Taittiriyaranyaka* it is said that upon *dharma* everything is founded, that it is the highest good by means of which one drives away evil. Thus *satya* and *ahimsa* are both traditionally identified with *dharma,* the cosmic law which governs and determines human conduct.

In the Buddhist tradition *himsa* and *asatya* alike proceed from *attavada,* the dire heresy of separateness. They equally constitute violence against the omnipresent truth, the subjection of the whole to a part or the pretence of the part to be the whole. In Jain texts it is said that falsehood (*asat*) inevitably leads to subtle or open violence (*himsa*). Further, the individual life-monad, when cleansed of beclouding passions and of *himsa,* is capable of mirroring the highest truth and reflecting reality (*Sat*) as it essentially is and not as it seems to the senses and the deluded mind.

Gandhi invoked the *Mahabharata* in support of his view that *dharma* signifies the way of truth and nonviolence and not the mere observance of externals. The scriptures, he said, have given us two immortal maxims—(1) *ahimsa* is the supreme law or *dharma* and (2) there is no other law or *dharma* than *satya* or truth. These two maxims provide us the key to all lawful *artha* and *kama,* "the royal road of *dharma* that leads both to earthly and spiritual bliss."[2] Although in 1940 Gandhi justified his appeal to *satya* and *ahimsa* as inseparable values in terms of scripture, he wrote as early as 1919 to a Burmese friend that he came to nonviolence because of his unadulterated love of truth. "I made the early discovery that if I was to reach God as Truth and Truth alone, I could not do so except through nonviolence. And, when in 1890 or 1891, I became acquainted with the teaching of the Buddha, my eyes were opened to the limitless possibilities of nonviolence."[3] In 1931 he said that "Violence hides Truth and if you try to find Truth by Violence you will betray the horrible ignorance in the search of Truth, and, therefore, Non-Violence without any exception whatsoever, I have come to realize, is the essence of life."[4]

In his own moral and political quest Gandhi found that *satya* led him to *ahimsa,* but he also came to believe that they are like two sides of the same coin as the universe is governed by the Law of Truth or Love. "If we have truth in us, it is bound to have its effect, and truth is Love, but without love there can be no truth."[5] We can remain true to our principles and yet also remain free from ill-will toward one another.[6] Toward the end of his life Gandhi said that the root of all his activity lay in truth, "otherwise known to me as non-violence."[7]

But though he sometimes equated *satya* with *ahimsa,* he was concerned at other times to distinguish clearly between them. *Satya,* he once said, is positive, whereas *ahimsa* is negative, and yet "non-violence is the highest religion."[8] He distinguished between the positive and the negative meanings of both *satya* and *ahimsa,* but he regarded *ahimsa* as negative in relation to *satya* because of his identification of truth with reality, the derivation of *satya* from *Sat.* In order to grasp reality and find the truth about nature and man, we must recognize violence as unreal, based upon a false view of life, a failure to appreciate the cohesive force binding all beings. Gandhi also held to the ancient Indian belief that Absolute Truth (*Sat*) or God is unmanifest as well as manifested in nature. He regarded *ahimsa* as the manifest part of Truth. Men cannot reach up to the unmanifest and transcendental ground of Absolute Truth, but they can perceive its manifestation through love. "Even the *darshan* (vision) of Truth in her non-violent manifestation can only be attained by the man of pure detachment. Anger, greed, pride, fear, all these things draw a veil across the seeker's eyes."[9] He was here speaking from a mystical standpoint to Mirabehn.

Gandhi's basic position in regard to *satya* and *ahimsa* was stated in *Yeravda Mandir,* his letters from prison to the inmates of Satyagrahashram. He thought that *ahimsa* and *satya* are so intertwined that it is practically impossible to disentangle and separate them.

They are like the two sides of a coin, or rather of a smooth unstamped metallic disc. Who can say, which is the obverse, and which is the reverse? Nevertheless *ahimsa* is the means; Truth is the end. Means to be means must always be within our reach, and so *ahimsa* is our supreme duty. If we take care of the means, we are bound to reach the end sooner or later. When once we have grasped this point, final victory is beyond question.[10]

There was thus a significant shift of emphasis in Gandhi's view of the relation between *satya* and *ahimsa*. The pursuit of *satya* leads to the recognition of the need for *ahimsa* to a point where we hold to *ahimsa* as the immediately relevant, tangible part of the ultimate Truth. Both Absolute Truth and perfect nonviolence are unattainable on earth, but the seeker after truth must accept the overriding obligation of nonviolence in all his relationships. The means to the goal becomes also the test of progress and is essentially inseparable from the goal, partaking of its very nature. It is more important to travel on the proper path than to arrive at the goal, especially as earthly attainment of the *summum bonum* is impossible for any man. Indian mystics have repeatedly pronounced the paradox that one cannot travel on the path unless one has become that path itself, and then one's attachment to the attainment of the ultimate goal becomes irrelevant and even disappears.

The problem for the seeker is to put himself in advance in that very position in which alone he can properly receive the fruit of his search, and which is the position he aspires to attain. The practical implication of the paradox is that our concern must continually be with the next step rather than the summit, and the exhilaration of climbing becomes an end in itself, rendering irrelevant the attainment of the peak. Gandhi's favorite Christian hymn was that of Newman and he often repeated the phrase "one step enough for me." The searcher for truth advances step by step; he aims at increasing his understanding and cannot, of course, foresee what he will know when he has increased it. There is an obvious sense in which one who seeks knowledge does not know exactly what he is seeking. This gives him a genuine humility which prevents him from coercing others into compliance with his immediate, imperfect formulations of the truth.

Although in practice Gandhi emphasized *ahimsa* rather than *satya,* he consistently maintained that *satya* is superior to *ahimsa* if a comparison must be instituted between inseparable concepts.[11] The lover of truth, he felt, is bound to make a discovery of nonviolence sooner or later whereas the believer in nonviolence may fail to see that untruth is tantamount to violence. For although *satya* and *ahimsa* were "convertible terms,"[12] if circumstances arose in which we have to choose between the two, Gandhi felt that he would not hesitate to throw nonviolence to the winds and to abide by the truth, which is supreme.[13] It is better to hold even to one's truth, though relative, than to make a fetish of "non-violence of the weak." We must never lose sight of justice and become sentimental about passive nonviolence, though it is impossible to proceed on the quest for truth without accepting the need for active nonviolence. Gandhi tried to make his position clear to Bajaj in 1922.

> As I proceed in my search for truth it grows upon me that Truth comprehends everything. It is not in *ahimsa* but *ahimsa* is in it. What is perceived by a pure heart and intellect is truth for that moment. Cling to it, and it enables me to reach pure Truth. There is no question there of divided duty. But often enough it is difficult to decide what is *ahimsa*. For instance, the use of disinfectants is *himsa,* and yet we cannot do without it. We have to live a life of *ahimsa* in the midst of a world of *himsa,* and that is possible only if we cling to truth. That is how I deduce *ahimsa* from truth. Out of truth emanate love, tenderness, humility. A votary of truth has to be humble as the dust. His humility increases with his observance of truth.[14]

The relative priorities of truth and nonviolence was the subject of an important disagreement between Benjamin Constant and Kant. Constant held that the moral principle that it is one's duty to speak the truth, if it were taken singly and unconditionally, would make all society impossible. It is a duty to tell the truth only to him who has a right to the truth. No man who injures others has a right to the truth. Therefore, to tell a falsehood to a murderer to protect a friend is a duty. To Kant this was a crime. "By a lie I do wrong to men in general." A lie is defined as an intentionally false declaration toward another man—"it always injures another; if not another individual, yet mankind generally, since it vitiates the course of justice."[15] To be truthful in all declarations is, therefore, a sacred, unconditional command of reason and not to be limited by any expediency.

Gandhi would have agreed with Kant that one should never tell a lie but not that one must *always* tell the truth, and he could not agree with Constant that one may tell a lie if it will avert a great and immediate evil. One must never lie, but one may refuse to tell people what they want to know when they are likely to put the information to evil purpose. To hold to *satya* means far more than truth-telling. "Truth must be told at any cost. But one is not always bound to disclose facts."[16] A votary of *satya* is entitled to keep silent when morally required to do so even if he incurs injury to himself. To lie to the murderer and violate the canon of *satya* would be worse than to be partly responsible for the murderer's *himsa* to another (whether friend or stranger), but this moral quandary could arise only because of one's own unwillingness to die, i.e., one's inability to adopt *ahimsa* at the cost of death in order to conform to *satya*. To tell a lie is a breach of *satya* but a brave silence is not. *Satya* is even more important than *ahimsa,* but in this case the only way of preserving *satya* and of preventing *himsa* (itself a violation of *satya*) is by offering *ahimsa* even at the risk of injury to oneself.

Gandhi's view of the relationship between *satya* and *ahimsa* may be put in the form of three propositions clarifying his puzzling belief that *satya* and *ahimsa* are tantamount to the same thing though *satya* is higher than *ahimsa*. First of all, the pursuit of *satya* gives us the humility to accept the need for *ahimsa* in our relationship with our fellow men, who are also truth-seekers in their own way. *Satya* implies *ahimsa*. Secondly, the pursuit of *ahimsa* shows that *himsa* is rooted in fear which can be removed only by the strength that comes from *satya*. *Ahimsa* presupposes *satya*. Thirdly, *ahimsa* is the means to *satya,* but as the end ever eludes us, the means becomes supremely important. Thus, although *satya* is higher than *ahimsa, ahimsa* is in practice more important than *satya*. More generally, we can take it as a working rule that the degree of *ahimsa* we display is a measure of the degree of *satya* we possess.

The first proposition shows us why ideologists, unlike truth-seekers, condone, and even demand, violence as a means to the imposition on others of what they regard as the total truth. They mistake relative truth for absolute truth, the search for truth ceases, and they come to rely on violence rather than to recognize the need for nonviolence. The second proposition shows us why visionaries and moralists who preach, rather than pursue, nonviolence are ineffective and fail to come to terms with the irrational element in human nature—the fear instinct. Similarly, the fanatical pacifist cannot help men in their struggle against injustice and tyranny as long as he cannot see these men as truth-seekers who can cooperate confidently only if they are helped to reach a point where they can pursue *satya* by their own independent efforts. The third proposition invokes the belief that neither tolerance nor civility can exist without the other in a liberal society, and is used to formulate a peaceful method to resolve political and social conflicts in a manner that promotes coexistence and the common good. These three propositions point to a contingent connection between *satya* and *ahimsa* but their necessary connection is a metaphysical rather than a logical truth.

Gandhi supported the first proposition in the following manner:

> It appears that the impossibility of full realization of truth in this mortal body led some ancient seeker after Truth to the appreciation of *ahimsa*. The question which confronted him was: "Shall I bear with those who create difficulties for me, or shall I destroy them?" The seeker realized that he who went on destroying others did not make headway but simply stayed where he was, while the man who suffered those who created difficulties marched ahead, and at times even took the others with him. . . . The more he took to violence, the more he receded from Truth. For in fighting the imagined enemy without, he neglected the enemy within.[17]

In his autobiography Gandhi similarly argued that the search for truth is in vain unless it is founded on *ahimsa*. It is proper to resist or attack a system in the name of truth but to slight even a single human being is to offend against the truth of the oneness of mankind and to harm the whole, not merely a part. It is not possible to pursue the truth without respecting the right of others to do the same—if it is the truth, and not our own personal advantage, that concerns us. This implies abstention from violence or any infringement of the moral freedom of another which is the precondition of man's recognition of the truth. "I can say with assurance, as a result of all my experiments, that a perfect vision of Truth can follow a complete realization of *ahimsa*. To see the universal and all-pervading Spirit of Truth face to face one must be able to love the meanest of creation as oneself."[18] Gandhi thought that truth can be realized and love can be expressed only when a man is ready to efface himself and even reduce himself to a cipher.[19] He wrote to a friend: "It is quite true that what we want at the present moment is a living faith in the ultimate victory of truth in spite of all appearances to the contrary. And this faith is impossible unless one is prepared to regard suffering as the richest treasure of life."[20] *Ahimsa* is the willingness to suffer, and the furthest limit of humility. It is because the honest striving after truth differs in every case that nonviolence becomes a necessary ethical corollary of the pursuit of truth.[21]

Gandhi defended the second proposition by his statement in *Hind Swaraj* that what is gained through fear is retained only while the fear lasts, that no worthy or lasting end can be secured through violence, that *himsa* will finally fail because it is a violation of the reality of the oneness of nature and of mankind.[22] Nonviolence is impossible without deep humility and the strictest regard for truth.[23] Pride or deception is itself a form of *himsa*. Nonviolence demands fearlessness, and fearlessness is identical with truth. "A truly fearless man will defend himself against others by truth force or soul force."[24] It is not possible to employ genuine nonviolence in a cause that one knows to be unjust. Nonviolence requires the will not to kill even in retaliation and the courage to face death without revenge,[25] and this is possible only to those who are eager to uphold what they regard as the truth, as just and right. Active nonviolence enables the individual to appreciate the truth within him and in nature, immanent, if not transcendental, truth. The real offence of an act of *himsa*, Vinoba Bhave has pointed out, resides in the fundamental untruth, the lie which gave rise to the act of violence.[26] In the really nonviolent man, there is no hiatus between thought, word and deed and such a man cannot but embody truth. On the other hand, those who merely profess nonviolence but practice violence in some form cannot really respect the truth and would be prepared to use cunning and fraud where force and brutality seem to be ineffective or inadvisable.

Sorel argued that the replacement of ferocity by cunning, force by fraud, does not constitute any real progress. Gandhi would have agreed with him here and also with his view that duplicity, treachery, chicanery, deceit and fraud were far worse than physical violence. This could not, however, be a justification of violence for Gandhi as it was for Sorel. Violence may be less objectionable than untruth, but *ahimsa,* as Gandhi saw, is closely bound up with *satya.* "Non-violent conviction requires tolerance of and even generosity towards those opposite views. . . . Most of our difficulties arise from our ignorance. Unregulated sentiment is wasted like unharnessed steam."[27] Violence proceeds from ignorance which is the cause of fear, and nonviolence or love presupposes knowledge.

> Without truth there is no love, without truth it may be affection, as for one's country to the injury of others; or infatuation, as of a young man for a girl or love may be unreasoning and blind, as of ignorant parents for their children. Love transcends all animality and is never partial. True love is boundless like the ocean and swelling within one, spreads itself out and crossing all boundaries and frontiers, envelops the whole world.[28]

Real love and nonviolent virtue exemplify knowledge of the truth of cosmic and human unity.

Gandhi defended the third proposition by the argument that it is more difficult to attain truth than it is to practice nonviolence. In order to proceed toward the goal of Truth, we must concentrate on finding a means of testing relative truths as they appear to different people. This is possible only by a strict adherence to *ahimsa.* We cannot be genuine in our pursuit of truth if we are prepared to harm our fellow men. On the other hand, if we practice nonviolence in all our relationships, we promote the common pursuit of truth. The emphasis on *ahimsa* is needed to prevent our concern with *satya* from becoming too selfish or too arrogant. It is in dealing with our opponents that we discover a gap in our own awareness of the truth. Our object must not be to overreach the opponent if we are really concerned about the truth, but to regard or make him a fellow seeker in the quest for truth. Political and social tensions arise because men are more concerned with themselves and their self-interest than with the truth, and one cannot love the truth more than oneself if one is not prepared to love those who disagree or with whom one's interests conflict.

The pursuit of *satya* in the midst of society demands the development of a method of action which can be used for the constructive resolution of social and political conflicts. Men disagree about their ends because they hold to different relative truths, but if they realize that this is equally true of all of them, they recognize that their common concern for truth requires the practice of *ahimsa* toward each other. The credentials of a seeker after *satya* lie in his practice of *ahimsa*.

While accepting all this as good liberal doctrine, some may feel that Gandhi went too far in regarding as the sole, or even the chief, test of truth, action based on the refusal to do harm. He was led to this position by his belief that truth is to be secured only through action rather than by ratiocination, and by his identification of truth with reality, as well as his metaphysical doctrine of the oneness of nature and mankind. The votary of *ahimsa* must be ever willing to admit error and to regard all his acts as experiments in relative truth. The man who disdains *ahimsa* and wishes to coerce his fellow men is not in possession of *satya,* however much he may be convinced that he is.

MOKSHA AND TAPAS

In order to understand Gandhi's view of the connection between *satya* and *ahimsa,* it would be useful to inflate these notions to *moksha* and *tapas,* which are basic to Hindu thought, just as we could deflate *satya* and *ahimsa* to the familiar notions of tolerance and civility, the connection between which was first clearly perceived in seventeenth-century Europe. The foundations of modern liberal doctrine were laid in the seventeenth century when some thinkers became skeptical regarding the older notions of revealed truth and just wars, and were concerned with finding a secular basis for peaceful coexistence in society.

The problem in India, as Gandhi saw it, was to adapt the older notions of *moksha* and *tapas*—the pursuit of individual salvation through specific austerities and prolonged contemplation—to the practical needs of a society in which men were more concerned to escape than to alter the conditions of worldly life. Whereas European thinkers came to stress tolerance and civility as the result of challenging traditional notions of authority, Gandhi came to a similar position in the Indian context as a result of challenging inherited notions of individualism and saintliness. The conflict between Church and State was a crucial factor in European development and resulted eventually in the secularization of Christian values especially in Protestant countries. In India there was no conflict between Church and State, but the shift in emphasis from *moksha* to *dharma,* which came with Buddhism, was reversed during the long centuries of foreign rule that followed the effectual disappearance of Buddhist influence. The impact of Buddhism on the corrupt social order of Hindu India was comparable in its intensity and significance to the impact of the Renaissance and the Reformation on Europe. Gandhi's profound reinterpretation of Hindu values in the light of the message of the Buddha may be regarded as a constructive, if belated, response to the ethical impact of the early Buddhist Renaissance and Reformation on decadent India.

In traditional Indian thought a distinction was made between two phases of cosmic and human evolution, the phase of *pravritti,* or involvement, and of *nivritti,* or withdrawal. The ultimate aim, the final human good, is *moksha,* spiritual freedom and redemption. The word *moksha* is derived from the root *muc,* to set free, let go, release, deliver. *Nivritti* means disappearance, completion, repose, discontinuance of worldly acts or emotions. *Tapas* means that which burns up impurities, purificatory action, austerities, penance. The original meaning of the word denotes warmth or heat. Man becomes enslaved by his contact with the sensory world, falls into ignorance and involuntary suffering, is bound down by external forces and conditions. In the end he comes to seek salvation, spiritual autonomy, absolute freedom, transcendental bliss. In the attainment of *moksha* he requires *tapas,* ceaseless self-restraint, an acceptance of suffering, the dispelling of his delusions by a clear vision of his real nature and his essential identity with all other beings. The more he suffers in a conscious and creative manner, the greater is his solidarity with the cosmos, his attunement to the world's misery, and the more intensely he seeks final emancipation and full freedom.

In the course of time *moksha* became in India a largely negative notion of escape, a rejection of this irredeemable world, an intoxicating flight from reality. *Tapas* in time became identified with fixed forms of self-mortification, prescribed penances, a rigid *ascesis.* In Europe, unlike India, it was only since the sixteenth century, when society became highly individualistic (i.e., the needs and rights of the individual were stressed), that man also came to be much concerned to reform rather than to reject the conditions of worldly life. Whereas in medieval Europe *nivritti* was exalted as a means to *moksha,* Rousseau, Hegel and Marx preached *pravritti* as a means to it at a time when European society had become much more individualistic. In India, on the other hand, the Gandhian emphasis on *karma yoga,* on *pravritti,* as the necessary (and not merely a legitimate) means to *moksha,* was a blow to traditional individualism.

The doctrines of *moksha* and *tapas,* in their purer formulations, referred to a profound connection between the standpoint of the ascetic and the position of the liberated soul. All is suffering for the sage, wrote Patanjali. The revelation of pain as the law of existence can be regarded as the *conditio sine qua non* for redemption. Suffering can have a positive, constructive function and value. The man of *tapas,* by exchanging the involuntary pain of sensory life for the inward suffering of his contemplative soul, progressively emancipates himself by his increasing identification with all beings. A man can annul the *karma* that binds him, the causes that enchain him to an unending train of effects, by a deliberate attitude of detachment from the fruits of actions. *Tapas* gives him a new power over his senses, the possibility of passing beyond their limits or of suppressing them at will and thus he gains the self-knowledge and freedom of which *moksha* is the final form. Proper *tapas* gives a foretaste of *moksha* and the earnest ascetic is absorbed in his *tapas* rather than in the prospect of reaching *moksha. Tapas* meant immediate, and *moksha* meant total, absorption into the oneness of all reality. Similarly in Buddhism, *sunyata* and *karuna,* selflessness and compassion, form an indivisible whole and are inseparable.

Thinking of ourselves as unique and separate, we create unbridgeable gulfs between ourselves and others. A genuinely compassionate man (*karunika*) suffers with the sorrows of other beings and thus his ego-centered mind expands, acquiring a wider field of action. In the words of a Buddhist text, "action which is without wisdom is a fetter. Wisdom which cannot be expressed in action is a barren abstraction. Action combined with wisdom is freedom, wisdom combined with action is freedom."[29] Discrimination and compassion reinforce each other.

Moksha for Gandhi signified the vision of Absolute Truth, to be attained by means of *tapas* or "self-suffering," and the relation between *moksha* and *tapas* was mirrored in the relation between *satya* and *ahimsa*. In the preface to his autobiography Gandhi declared that the aim of all his strivings was *moksha* or self-realization. "I live, move, and have my being, in pursuit of this goal. All that I do by way of speaking and writing, and all my ventures in the political field, are directed to this same end."[30] At the close of this book he concluded: "My uniform experience has convinced me that there is no other God than Truth. And if every page of these chapters does not proclaim to the reader that the only means for the realization of Truth is *ahimsa*, I shall deem all my labour in writing these chapters to have been in vain."[31] He regarded his political and social work as part of his training for freeing his soul from the bondage of flesh. "I have no desire for the perishable kingdom of earth. I am striving for the Kingdom of Heaven which is *moksha*. To attain my end it is not necessary for me to seek the shelter of a cave. I carry one about me, if I would but know it."[32]

Gandhi regarded the aim of human life as *moksha*,[33] liberation from impure thought, and the total elimination of impure thought is possible only as a result of much *tapasya*.[34] The utter extinction of egoism is *moksha* and he who has achieved this will be the very image of Truth or God.[35] Government over self is the truest *swaraj* (freedom); it is synonymous with *moksha* or salvation."[36] He also said that "*ahimsa* means *moksha* and *moksha* is the realization of Truth."[37] The test of love is *tapasya* and *tapasya* means self-suffering.[38] Self-realization is impossible without service of, and identification with, the poorest.[39] The quest of Truth involves *tapas*—self-suffering, sometimes even unto death.[40] *Satya* then requires the *tapas* of *ahimsa* and this means self-suffering and self-sacrifice in the midst of society.

> I cannot practise *ahimsa* without the religion of service and I cannot find the Truth without practising the religion of *ahimsa*. . . . I am striving for the Kingdom of Heaven, which is spiritual deliverance. For me the road to salvation lies through incessant toil in the service of my country and of my Humanity. I want to identify myself with everything that lives. In the language of the *Gita*, I want to live at peace with both friend and foe. My patriotism is for me a stage on my journey to the land of Eternal Freedom and Peace. Thus it will be seen that for me there is no politics devoid of religion. They subserve religion. Politics bereft of religion is a death-trap because they kill the soul.[41]

Gandhi's interpretation of *moksha* as the full realization of Truth and his justification of *ahimsa* as an exercise in *tapas*, the self-suffering and service needed for the attainment of *satya*, gave traditional values a new meaning and a fresh relevance to politics and to society. In deriving *satya* and *ahimsa* from what were essentially religious notions he not only gave spiritual values a social significance but also infused into his political vocabulary an other-worldly flavor. His emphasis on suffering as an intrinsic good needed to secure the *summum bonum* is somewhat reminiscent of Kierkegaard's assertion of the concreteness of suffering men against the concept of man as an *animal rationale*. Kierkegaard held that as gold is purified in fire, so is the soul in suffering. Unlike passive and impotent suffering, active and meaningful anguish takes away the impure elements in human nature. It is always man himself that stands in his own way, who is too closely attached to the world, to the environment, to circumstances, to external relationships, so that he is not able to come to himself, come to rest, to have hope, "he is constantly too much turned outward, instead of being turned inward, hence everything he says is true only as an illusion of the senses."[42] If a man has love beyond all measure, he has thereby been laboring for all. All the time he was laboring for his own sake to acquire love, he has been laboring for all others. "It is required of the sufferer that he call a halt to his erring thought, that he reflect what the goal is, that is to say, it is required of him to turn himself about. . . . The difference between man and man is whether they succeed or not in attaining it."[43]

TOLERANCE AND CIVILITY

Although Gandhi used religious language similar at times to that of Kierkegaard, his main concern was to draw lessons for social and political morality. Just as the attainment of salvation in the Kingdom of Heaven that lies beyond death requires suffering and penance, so too the securing of salvation in the earthly kingdom requires that men should love and suffer each other as equally errant truth-seekers. Just as the pursuit of transcendental truth demands the willingness to suffer the ordeals of the quest, so too the collective pursuit of truth in the midst of society and politics calls for the readiness to suffer for their convictions of those who are most anxious to propagate their relative truths against the errors of their dogmatic opponents and the apathy of those indifferent to the truth. The earnest seeker of truth in the social and political sphere comes soon to a recognition of the need for tolerance and civility in the midst of those who wish to coerce others into assent to their half-truths and exaggerated claims. The doctrine of *satya* means far more than mere tolerance and presupposes faith rather than skepticism, the belief that it is possible for all men to progress through their experiments with relative truths toward the transcendental goal of Absolute Truth. Similarly, the doctrine of *ahimsa* is concerned with far more than civility and presupposes not merely the conviction that coercion is futile but also the positive faith that active nonviolence could convert opponents into co-seekers, effectively resist injustice and remove untruth, protect the weak against the strong. Further, *ahimsa* is the means and *satya* is the common end, whereas it would be strange to regard civility as the means and tolerance as the common end. And yet, it would be worthwhile to see the relation between *satya* and *ahimsa* by deflating these terms to tolerance and civility and we could then grasp more clearly Gandhi's rejection of the ends-means dichotomy that is built into our political and social vocabulary.

The ideals of tolerance and civility emerged in Europe out of the bitter struggles of the sixteenth and seventeenth centuries, but it would be a mistake to think that they were entirely new. In the ancient world tolerance presented no problem within a polytheistic society or syncretistic civilization. Quintus Symmachus gave expression to the tolerance that sprang from an awareness of the multitude of cults and religions: "The heart of so great a mystery (as that of the Divine) cannot ever be reached by following one road only." The problem of tolerance clearly arises where an individual or group claims to have a vision of absolute truth or to be in possession of a unique revelation embodied in a single scripture or system. It is natural for such fanatics to feel that they have the solemn duty of making the truth prevail by persuasion, if possible, by force, if necessary. The intolerance in the Old Testament is that of men who thought themselves to be executing the will of Jehovah. For the early Jewish people and the prophet Elijah, there was no midway between God and Baal. History was a unique and universal drama moving inexorably toward its predetermined climax, and faith in religious truth meant trust in the ultimate victory of God as the Lord of history. Archbishop Soderblom has suggested that it was the tragedy of India that it never possessed an Elijah who was zealous for the Lord and said No to morally inferior cults, who denounced what was evil and contrary to God's purposes in history. Man belongs either to God or Satan and those fortunate to be on God's side must fight those who have thrown in their lot with the Enemy. Callous intolerance was the besetting sin of most apocalyptic theology, Jewish or Christian, and writers from Anselm to Calvin depicted the bliss of the righteous as the greater because of the spectacle of the tortures of the damned. The revengeful eschatology in apocalyptic literature since the Book of Enoch, the sharp division of men into good and evil and the harsh judgment of the wicked and the unbeliever, is repellent to us today. But it was natural for the medieval Church to persecute because it believed itself to be in exclusive possession of the only truth.

Even in Judaism and Christianity there was a clear, continuous alternative to intolerance and revengefulness. While there was no place for tolerance within the theocracy of the Jewish people as conceived by the Torah, the Mosaic religion showed remarkable consideration toward those who were regarded as heathens, a point repeatedly stressed in the tracts of Christians pleading for religious toleration during the sixteenth and seventeenth centuries. In the Bible itself, Elijah is rebuked for his excessive zeal and Abraham pleads for God's mercy and forgiveness. Later, Rabbi Joshua's doctrine of tolerance was powerfully reinforced from the notion of natural law which Judaism, along with Islam and Christianity, inherited from Greek philosophy, notably Stoicism. Christianity continued the earlier tradition of Hellenic Judaism, particularly of Philo, and made its peace with the pagan world. However, the modern doctrine of toleration arose only with the emergence of religious individualism, the idea that every man has his own separate "wire to eternity," the claim to freedom of conscience.

The Reformation by itself did not result in religious liberty, but proclaimed the principle *cujus regio ejus religio* so that in each nation or regional unit the effective government determined which of the rival systems of Catholicism and Protestantism was to prevail. The confrontation between two exclusive forms of Christianity, each claiming to be the custodian of *satya* and denigrating the other as a diabolical perversion, led to some of the most bitter *himsa* in modern history. It was analogous in some ways to the ideological conflict of today, the apparent absolute logical impasse between competing doctrines that can never meet—mutually exclusive systems neither of which seems secure until the other is undermined. In the post-Reformation period it was practical considerations that induced *politiques* in France to launch their direct assault on religious intolerance and plead that the bloodshed must be brought to an end. Toleration was at first only a *pis aller*, the only feasible policy that remained when it proved impossible to go on fighting any longer. The Socinians were willing to tolerate any differences of opinion because of their indifference to matters of doctrine. But there were also those who pressed the case for freedom of conscience precisely on religious grounds. Religion was seen to be too important for one man to thrust it upon another and even an entire society could not impose it upon an individual. The decisive moment came when the man who thought his religion to be absolute realized that he must equally grant this right to another's claim to his religion as absolute.

Although the notions of tolerance and civility found political expression only in the modern era of individualism and nationalism, the connection between *satya* and *ahimsa*, truth and goodness, was affirmed by early Christian as well as Renaissance thinkers. St. Augustine had distinguished between *ratio scientiae* and *ratio sapientiae*, human reason and the grace of God, truth and faith. St. Thomas sought in the *Summa* to identify goodness, the object of will, with truth the object of reason. "Truth and good include one another; for truth is something good, or otherwise it would not be desirable; and good is something true, or otherwise it would not be intelligible."[44] The intellectual and moral virtues are subsumed by the indispensable virtue of prudence, equated with *recta ratio agibilium*, "right reason about things to be done." This *recta ratio*, derived partly from Stoic sources, is that immutable coalescence of truth and goodness whose source is God and whose formative cosmic role is manifested in all the workings of nature. The truth about the good life is available only to those who attempt to live that life. The Stoic concept of right reason is based upon the assumption, associated with Socrates, that knowledge and virtue are in their ideal state one and the same. For Epictetus, good and evil lie entirely within the control of man's will. The power of judgment which belongs to the soul implies by its very nature the will to right action as long as there is the desire to know the truth. "Just as it is the nature of every soul to assent to what is true and dissent from what is false, and withhold judgment in what is uncertain, so it is its nature to be moved with the will to get good and the will to avoid what is evil."[45] This conception lay at the heart of Renaissance optimism and recurs in Milton, who tried to ground truth in morality, to show that to think right is to do right, both truth and goodness being intelligible to the faculties that belong to man *qua* man. Erasmus too and Christian humanists in general believed that ideally all man's faculties may be fused in the pursuit of that goodness which constitutes the highest truth.

With the breakdown of traditional religious authority, the vacuum was filled by the postulation of a law of nature which represented those moral absolutes that are binding on human conduct. In Hooker's theocratic universe all forms of knowledge are modes of goodness in that they derive from the wisdom of God. For Hooker as for Socrates knowledge is virtue, for in doing evil "we prefer a less good before a greater, the greatness whereof is by reason investigable and may be known."[46] With neo-Stoicism and the growth of deism we find the increasing secularization of this religious conception of the correspondence of reason and piety. Both movements represent the search for those absolutes—metaphysical, epistemological, moral—which the accretions of time and error had obscured. Jeremy Taylor declared that "all violence is an enemy to reason and counsel."[47] The Cambridge Platonists asserted the validity of the human quest for religious truth and sought to subordinate the doctrinal struggles of their age to a simple morality of charity and toleration. The dignity of man consists in the fusion of truth and goodness, the manifestation of the latter being the first fruit of the successful pursuit of the former. "He knows most, who does best."[48]

The belief in the connection between truth and goodness was based upon a metaphysical certainty and a secure optimism that could lead men to cherish the virtues of tolerance and civility. They could also, however, be derived from skepticism and an awareness of the limits rather than the potentialities of development of human faculties. We find this typically expressed in Montaigne's *"Que sais-je?"* and Cromwell's "I beseech you, in the bowels of Christ, think it possible you may be mistaken." The skeptic is aware of the human propensity for the static and his emphasis is more upon the means to arrive at a decision rather than upon the decision itself. It is better to begin in doubts than in certainties, to care for processes rather than for results. The seeker after truth is involved in a ceaseless struggle with himself and is more likely to tolerate rather than to coerce others. He is both humble and open-minded, and willing to question features of society that others regard as sacrosanct. His confidence in the power of truth is matched by his conviction that he has not yet apprehended it. Pyrrho and the Epechists were regarded by Montaigne as the worthiest of philosophers because of their belief that they were still seeking after truth.

Renaissance skepticism found its fruition in the seventeenth century, marked by a burning passion for the pursuit of truth and an ever-deepening movement toward tolerance. If truth is one and equally available but also equally elusive to all men, it seems unreasonable to make a serious issue of creedal differences and to go to war over them. A theory of progressive revelation was evolved and there was a positive confidence, as in *Areopagitica*, that truth is armed with sufficient power to overthrow all error. There was a shift in emphasis from speculation to conduct, from contemplation to action. What men do is vastly more important than what they think they know. The road to truth can be traversed only by a soul which through right action has been rendered pure. Richard Baxter said:

> Truth is absolute, knowledge relative. Truth, in itself one and entire, is reflected diversely in a myriad of facets in the reasons of men. . . . Pride then stops the process of search and discovery, of distinguishing the true from the false, by which knowledge grows, while we go about extirpating not error, which is always with us, but our opponents, who may be wiser than we.[49]

Falkland similarly recommended a skeptical humility, a search for truth which would absorb every man and leave him disposed to permit to every other man the same freedom. There was an increasing reluctance to accept blindly any traditional authority. Truth must be sought, not prescribed.

The essence of tolerance is the belief that differences can and should be settled by reason, not by force, and this belief may often be founded on faith in the eventual vindication of truth. Civility, the virtue of the citizen, refers to the sense of affinity felt by individuals with the society to which they belong. Tolerance makes possible the coexistence of competing forms of partisanship, while civility requires an attempt to transcend partisanship in the pursuit of the common good. Tolerance and civility both point to the limitations of human powers, the folly of dogmatism and the futility of violence, the common search for truth by equal citizens in the service of the common good. They provide the basis of a respect for the inalienable freedom and the fundamental equality of all citizens united in their concern for truth and peace. To hold an opinion deeply is no doubt to throw our feelings into it, but our awareness of our fallibility must be sufficiently strong to prevent our feelings from overriding our sense of human solidarity. Tolerance could be an act of faith in the ultimate victory of truth or it could be a mere expedient to avoid the inconveniences of intolerance. Civility could arise out of a profound sense of social obligation or it could merely proceed from a prudent awareness of the costs of violence and discord. Tolerance could degenerate into indifference and passivity could masquerade as civility.

The more deeply founded tolerance is, the more meaningful and profound civility becomes. The stronger the roots of civility, the richer the fruits of tolerance. Thus tolerance and civility constitute the minimal foundations of a liberal society as well as the mature graces of the good society.

There is no doubt that by deflating *satya* and *ahimsa* to tolerance and civility something significant is lost, just as by inflating *satya* and *ahimsa* to *moksha* and *tapas* there is also an important change of meaning. The advantage of this procedure is merely to reveal the metaphysical roots as well as the immediate social relevance of Gandhi's concepts of *satya* and *ahimsa*. In the West the powerful impact for centuries of messianic and missionary religions made it inevitable that minimal notions of tolerance and civility should acquire a peculiar importance at a time of religious doubt and skepticism when men were sick of civil wars in the name of religion.

In India, on the other hand, a lazy, latitudinarian and fatalistic attitude had prevailed for centuries. The first ruler to exalt the virtues of tolerance and civility was Asoka. As Lord Acton recognized, Asoka in 250 B.C. was the first sovereign in history to enact religious toleration. Hinduism, which was sometimes messianic but never missionary until recent times, had been confronted by Buddhism, which was a missionary but not a messianic religion. Asoka's 12th edict was a positive and powerful plea for toleration among the various sects of the day. Toleration was not passive sufferance but an active search for dialogue and concord, based upon the notion that in the honoring of other sects lies the welfare and honor of one's own. An individual or a group is enhanced by the display of active tolerance and genuine fellow-feeling. Concord was regarded as meritorious and it was required that all sects should listen to and profit from each other. The 12th Major Rock Edict says:

> On each occasion one should honour another man's sect, for by doing so one increases the influence of one's own sect and benefits that of the other man. . . . Again, whosoever honours his own sect or disparages that of another man, wholly out of devotion to

his own, with a view to showing it in a favourable light, harms his own sect even more seriously. Therefore, concord is to be commended, so that men may hear one another's principles and obey them.[50]

In the long course of Indian history since the time of Asoka, during centuries of alien rule, tolerance had become a misnomer for complacency and indifference, and a fatalistic passivity was passed off for nonviolence. Hypocrisy and cowardice coexisted with contempt and cruelty, often latent but sometimes open. The genuine seekers after truth loved their fellow men in the abstract and retreated to the solitude of the cave. Gandhi gave a new meaning to *satya* and *ahimsa*, salvation and suffering, tolerance and civility in the context of political and social activity.

The pursuit of truth was clearly a social activity for Gandhi; it could only emerge out of our daily struggle with the concrete problems of living. A man's devotion to truth, his veracity and integrity, are most sharply tested in his relations with opponents and opposing views. The obstacles to veracity are indifference to truth, resentment of criticism or failure to face it, a barren negativism, obsession and want of balance and listless *acidia*. Truth is what we believe in our hearts, not what we profess.[51] A mechanical adherence to certain beliefs is useless. Hence the folly of forcible conversion, of intimidating propaganda, of systematic proselytizing. An opponent is entitled to the same regard for his principles as we would expect others to have for ours.[52]

> The golden rule of conduct . . . is mutual toleration, seeing that we will never all think alike and we shall always see Truth in fragment and from different angles of vision. Conscience is not the same thing for all. . . . Even amongst the most conscientious persons, there will be room enough for honest differences of opinion. The only possible rule of conduct in any civilized society is, therefore, mutual toleration.[53]

Gandhi saw a causal connection between political and religious intolerance, between religious dogma and political ideology. He did not like the word "tolerance" because of its implication of condescension.

Everybody is right from his own standpoint, but it is not impossible that everybody is wrong. Hence the necessity for tolerance, which does not mean indifference to one's own faith, but a more intelligent and purer love for it. Tolerance gives us spiritual insight, which is as far from fanaticism as the north pole from the south.[54]

The religion of our conception, unlike ideal religion, and similarly the political truth of our conception, unlike ideal truth, are always subject to a process of evolution and reinterpretation. There must be no barbarity, no impatience, no insolence, no undue pressure in politics or in religion. Intolerance betrays want of faith in one's cause.[55] We shall retard our cause if we suppress opinion by intolerance. The indispensable condition of success in the common pursuit of truth is that we encourage the greatest freedom of opinion.[56] Tolerance is not indifference and it is real only if it brings true understanding and purer love.[57] Bitterness means bias, and intolerance based on insecurity breeds violence.

Gandhi's conception of tolerance and amity was influenced by his acceptance of the Jain doctrines of *anekantavada* and *syadvada*. He was committed to the view that many apparently conflicting judgments are possible about any subject and that each gives only a partial truth, but everything has multiple facets or aspects.

It has been my experience that I am always true from my point of view and often wrong from the point of view of my honest critics. I know that we are both right from our respective points of view. And this knowledge saves me from attributing motives to my opponents or critics. . . . I very much like the doctrine of the manyness of reality. It is this doctrine that has taught me to judge a Mussulman from his own standpoint and a Christian from his. . . . My *anekantavada* is the result of the two doctrines of *satya* and *ahimsa*.[58]

Anekant logic both guarantees man's capacity to know the truth and provides him with criteria by which to test the relativity and the extent of error in his knowledge. Everything may be seen differently by different people, in different spatio-temporal contexts. On the other hand, the doctrine of *syadvada* is based upon the belief that everything in the universe is related to everything else and hence we ought not to narrow our vision by taking account of only one set of facts or relations. To do this is to generate not merely a variety of conflicting dogmas but also personal bitterness and destructive conflict. The greater our sympathy with others and our imaginative identification with their particular situations, the less constricted is our vision and the less incomplete and partial our perception of truth. Therefore, Gandhi said, "My appeal to you is to cleanse your hearts and to have charity. Make your hearts as broad as the ocean. . . . Do not judge others lest you be judged."[59]

The extent of *satya* that we possess thus depends upon the amount of *ahimsa* that we display toward others with whom we deal. Bitterness could be the cause and not merely the consequence of intolerance. It has been observed that the distrust which men everywhere display toward their adversaries, at all stages of historical development, may be regarded as the immediate precursor of the notion of ideology. When this distrust of man toward man becomes explicit, conflicting groups detect an ideological taint in the utterances of each other. The notion of ideology, according to Karl Mannheim, "refers to a sphere of errors, psychological in nature which, unlike deliberate deception, are not intentional, but follow inevitably and unwittingly from certain causal determinants."[60] It is worth noting that in the past when vital beliefs were passionately held by some and meant nothing to others, the charge was often made by the former against the latter that their dissent or apathy was willful. Heretics have been persecuted not only for holding views which were not orthodox but also for their obstinacy in refusing to abandon them. This intrusion of the will into matters of belief was called by Pico della Mirandola in the fifteenth century *actus tyrannicus voluntatis*, a tyrannical act of the will. These tyrannical acts of the will need not, however, be confined to external pressures, as internally, too, our will sometimes interferes with our recognition of the truth. A man who is full of *himsa* is indeed sometimes unwilling to give up a theory or an intellectual position to which he has become attached or which seems to be in his interest. But if a man holds to *satya* without any *himsa* or any selfish attachment, then no external *himsa* or pressure on his will can affect his inward conviction.

Truth for Gandhi was a matter of experienced knowledge, not of borrowed belief, and hence his distrust of ideologies and *isms*. We are dogmatic to the extent of the inadequacy of our experience, and we become more truly tolerant as we have made more experiments and acquired greater experience of "truth in action." A political judgment is made true only when it works satisfactorily in experience. Values without action are barren and action without values is blind. A society is tolerant and open insofar as free choice is maximized and the use of pressure to enforce social norms is minimized. The habit of philosophical doubt does not justify lack of commitment in fundamental matters of social action. Every sovereign principle, other than that of truth, every ideology that pretends that it must not be put in doubt in the interests of society or civilization or something else, becomes the natural basis for dogmatism or fanaticism. In Socratic terms, all *logos* must be submitted by its author or follower to critical examination, with the same sincere will to understand the criticism of others and, if necessary, to proceed to the requested corrections and adjustments of views which the other participants in the dialogue are expected to show. Such a common pursuit of *satya* is impossible except in a community which accepts the need for *ahimsa*. Tolerance cannot thrive except in an atmosphere of civility. The fact that a truth-seeker sees no error in his relative truth obliges him to pursue it actively in the midst of society. The possibility that he may be in error obliges him not to inflict harm upon others. "My knowledge of psychology tells me that if our actions or words produce upon others an effect contrary to what was intended, the cause for it must be searched for within ourselves."[61]

In the pursuit of truth, if we are constant and consistent in our quest, we come closer to others, but unless we are initially prepared to treat our fellow men with respect and some sympathy, the common pursuit of truth in society cannot even be commenced. Gandhi's view of the connection between *satya* and *ahimsa* was based upon the belief that truth and nonviolence are both unifying forces, while error and violence are divisive factors, in human society. Truth needs no violence for its diffusion and is, in fact, obscured by violence. Violence is not only a sign of insecurity and incomplete conviction but it also makes victory more important than truth, distorts the truth and renders its free acceptance more difficult. No one can be forced to become free to see the truth.

Partial truth, blindly held and imposed on others against their will, thrives temporarily on violence and pins its faith on immediate results, formal assent and illusory triumphs. Where reason fails, love could, but violence cannot, succeed. The truth-seeker suffers for his convictions and wins over others by example, not by precept. To the votary of *satya* the first truth to get hold of is that all men are equally entitled to their beliefs and that violence is a failure to recognize the equality and similarity of all men as truth-seekers. Thus *ahimsa* becomes the precondition for the collective pursuit of *satya* in society. Tolerance presupposes a measure of civility. Civility, thought Gandhi, was not incompatible with fearlessness. "Civility does not here mean the mere outward gentleness of speech cultivated for the occasion, but an inborn gentleness and desire to do the opponent good."[62] The attainment of truth is the ultimate end of all men, but the practice of nonviolence is the immediate test, the universally available means to the pursuit of truth. Men may legitimately disagree about the truth while they are still engaged in this endless quest, but they must agree at all times about the need for nonviolence.

10

Satyagraha

ACTIVE AND PASSIVE RESISTANCE

No doubt the rebel demands a certain freedom for himself; but in no circumstances does he demand, if he is consistent, the right to destroy the person and freedom of someone else. He degrades no one. The freedom which he demands he claims for everybody; that which he rejects he forbids all others to exercise. He is not simply a slave opposing his master but a man opposing the world of master and slave.

ALBERT CAMUS

Gandhi's concepts of *satya* and *ahimsa* lie at the heart of his entire social and political philosophy. He nurtured his own vision of the radical transformation of the existing social order and political system, but he was even more concerned to evolve a revolutionary approach to political action and social change within the limits of the prevailing conditions of politics and society. Immediate resistance to injustice and coercion as well as a long-term program of social and political reconstruction must alike be legitimated in terms of the twin absolutes of truth and nonviolence. His concept of *satya*, with *ahimsa* as the means, determined his doctrine of *satyagraha* or active resistance to authority, while the concept of *ahimsa*, with *satya* as the common end, enabled him to formulate his doctrine of *sarvodaya* or nonviolent socialism.

The doctrine of *satyagraha* was meant to show how the man of conscience could engage in heroic action in the vindication of truth and freedom against all tyranny, in his appeal to justice against every social abuse and sectional interest. Gandhi challenged the conventional notions of authority, law and obligation by appealing to his conceptions of natural law or *dharma* and self-suffering or *tapas*. *Satya* and *ahimsa* alone can secure an enduring basis for social consensus and political loyalty. There is no external authority that can claim a higher status than *satya* either in the religious or in the political sphere. There is also no political or social sanction that can be assigned a legitimacy superior to *ahimsa*.

Like Proudhon, Gandhi visualized the establishment of a new system of moral sanctions in society, based on the idea of a universal harmony in nature. Nature and society are both subject to a single law of justice and unity. Every social order, no doubt, requires a minimum of cohesive force, a measure of tolerance and civility, but this, thought Gandhi, could be provided only by the collective pursuit of truth and the general acceptance of nonviolence. Any challenge of the orthodox legitimation of political action and the rule of law may indeed be interpreted as a subversive attack on the community itself. However, as Gandhi condemned the values and the very structure of modern civilization as a system of untruth and coercion, injustice and mutual exploitation, he was

obliged and entitled to seek a new method and legitimating principle of political action.

Proudhon too had argued that the moment moral certainty disappears and inner truth disintegrates, the traditional system of
sanctions loses its authenticity and its authority. Just as Bentham
asserted the primacy of the physical sanction and saw in it an effective means of securing utilitarian ends, Proudhon asserted the
supremacy of universal conscience, whose standard of judgment is
the idea of justice. "The exultation of the universal conscience is
the signature and seal by which the authenticity of the moral law
is recognized, the joy and remorse of the soul are its penal sanctions. Everything in this world takes place within it."[1] The problem that Proudhon neglected and Gandhi tried to face was how the
law of inner sanction could be concretely realized in a specific situation. The doctrine of *satyagraha* was really an attempt to raise the
deliberate suffering of a man of outraged conscience to a moral
sanction that compels respect and secures results.

The State, in Gandhi's view, cannot claim inalienable, unchallengeable authority for itself or its laws as long as it is an essentially coercive agency, even if it secures the tacit assent and acquiescence of its citizens or the active consent of a majority of their
chosen or nominated representatives. His adherence to *satya* and
ahimsa led him to an unorthodox, though not entirely anarchist,
conception of the relation between the State and the citizen. Just as
men appealed to the *jus naturale* and *lex naturalis* when they felt
oppressed by the power of positive laws and the moral pretensions
of coercive States, Gandhi felt that the citizen was entitled to appeal to the law of *dharma*, with which both *satya* and *ahimsa* were
identified, in the face of the overwhelming might of the centralized
State of today. He challenged the maxim that might is right which
has been reinforced in practice, if not always in theory, by varying forms of legal positivism and historical relativism. The modern
doctrine of sovereignty, originally invoked against religious authority and transcendental claims, has strengthened the emphasis on
the formal regulation of human conduct by legalized force without
continual reference to its moral justification. Similarly historicism,
which arose as a reaction against the abstract doctrine of rational
right in the eighteenth century, has resulted in a refusal to separate

norm from fact in the realm of social reality, a disinclination to appraise social institutions and State action in terms of abstract and universal moral values.

Gandhi regarded the State as a "soulless machine."[2] "The State represents violence in a concentrated and organized form. The individual has a soul, but as the State is a soulless machine, it can never be weaned from violence to which it owes its very existence."[3] This would appear at first sight to be a false antithesis. When the State acts, it is always individuals who act, and as they are souls, they too could, in principle, be weaned from violence. Gandhi's view was, however, that people, in their official capacities, are inclined to take legalized coercion for granted. He conceded that the State is justified if it uses the minimum of violence, but the fear is always that the State may use too much violence against those who differ from it.[4] His concern with the consequences of the excessive centralization of power made him concede merely a minimal role to the State. He did admit that State ownership is preferable to private ownership involving exploitation of the masses, but in general he thought that the violence of private ownership is less injurious than the violence of the State. "However, if it is unavoidable, I would support a minimum of State-ownership."[5]

Gandhi held to an anarchist view of the State as the ultimate ideal but in practice his conception of the State amounts to a doctrine of minimum State intervention. In a State of enlightened anarchy, "everyone is his own ruler. He rules himself in such a manner that he is never a hindrance to his neighbour. In the ideal state therefore there is no political power because there is no State. But the ideal is never fully realized in life. Hence the classical statement of Thoreau that the government is best which governs the least."[6] Gandhi believed that men were capable of developing their moral capacities to such an extent that exploitation could be reduced to the minimum. "I look upon an increase in the power of the State with the greatest fear, because, although while apparently doing good by minimizing exploitation, it does the greatest harm to mankind by destroying individuality, which lies at the root of all progress."[7]

His view of the relation between the State and the citizen followed from his exaltation of *satya* and *ahimsa* as the ultimate values on which individual and social morality must be based. The moral authority of the citizen derives from his consistent pursuit of *satya*. The State should not be a positive instrument in the collective pursuit of *satya* though it may ensure the conditions for such endeavor. Insofar as it relies upon *himsa*, there is always a danger that its laws and acts would violate *satya*. Under such conditions, the citizen can appeal to his conception of *satya* against the authority of the State as long as the means he employs to enforce the claims of *satya* are based upon *ahimsa*. It is the citizen's capacity to pursue *satya* and employ *ahimsa* that puts him in a moral position superior to that of the State. This is what is meant by the contrast between the citizen's soul and the soulless machine of the State. The degree of coercion shown by the State toward its citizens is an index of the extent to which *satya* and *ahimsa* are prevalent in any society. As the path of social progress must lie in furthering the pursuit of *satya* and *ahimsa*, it would be accompanied by a weakening of the coercive role of the State. But the reverse is also true for Gandhi. The greater the decentralization of power in any society, the greater the chances for the collective pursuit of *satya* and the reliance upon the nonviolent sanction of *ahimsa*.

The citizen's obligation to accept the authority of the State at any given time is dependent upon the extent to which the laws of the State are just and its acts non-repressive. A government, said Gandhi, that is loyal to the governed commands their loyalty as a matter of course. "A Government is an instrument of service only in so far as it is based upon the will and consent of the people. It is an instrument of oppression where it enforces submission at the point of the bayonet. Oppression therefore ceases when people cease to fear the bayonet."[8] Thus although Gandhi regarded the State as a soulless machine, he was perfectly prepared to distinguish between a democratic and an authoritarian State and to see that this distinction has a bearing upon the citizen's obligation to submit to the laws of the State. "Submission to the State law is the price a citizen pays for his personal liberty. Submission, therefore, to a State wholly or largely unjust is an immoral barter for liberty."[9]

The mere fact that an authoritarian State or an unjust political system does not become totalitarian and violate all the essential liberties of the citizen is not an adequate ground for acquiescence and compliance. "When . . . there is only a caricature of responsible government, things can be much worse than under a frankly and purely autocratic government. The latter, not depending upon the votes of any class, can afford to be impartial to all. The former dare not."[10] It is thus not enough to distinguish between a democratic and an autocratic government to establish the extent of the citizen's obligation to submit to the laws and the will of the State. His responsibility is even greater under a democratic regime, which is in danger of being subverted by vested interests or of becoming corrupt and farcical. The citizen ever retains his moral authority which is logically prior to the authority of any State. The misuse of power is an endemic danger under any State so that the citizen can never afford to let his conscience go to sleep or to lose his distrust of State authority, which is founded upon suspicion rather than trust of the citizen. Justice is like a debt which has to be discharged by the State to the citizen. "I am no believer in the doctrine that the same power can at the same time trust and distrust, grant liberty and repress it," he said.[11] Even when the State confines its sway over the life of the citizen to the minimum, Gandhi believed that "every citizen renders himself responsible for every act of his government."[12] Here we find the most extreme statement ever given of the doctrine of the collective responsibility of all citizens for the acts of the government and the very nature of the State.

This view is merely a political application of Gandhi's belief in the Law of *Karma*, which is based on the idea of the moral interdependence of all men. The corollary for Gandhi is that it is quite proper to support a government so long as its actions are bearable, but when they harm the citizen and the nation, it becomes his duty to withdraw his support. "It is the inherent right of a subject to refuse to assist a government that will not listen to him."[13] When a government does not represent the will of the people, when it supports dishonesty and terrorism, the judges and the executive officials, by retaining office, become instruments of dishonesty and terrorism, *asat* and *himsa*. The least that they can do is to cease to be agents of a dishonest and terrorizing government. When a whole country has been denied justice, it is no longer a question of party politics, "it is a matter of life and death." It then becomes the duty of every citizen to refuse to serve a government which misbehaves and flouts the national will. This duty can be properly performed only if the citizens "generally appreciate the laws of the State and obey them voluntarily without the fear of punishment. . . . We must tolerate many laws of the State, even when they are inconvenient."[14]

Clearly, in Gandhi's view of the relation between the State and the citizen, "There is no half-way house between active loyalty and active disloyalty."[15] He came closest to expounding his doctrine of political obligation in a strongly worded article, "The Duty of Disloyalty."[16]

> There is much truth in the late Justice Stephen's remark that a man to prove himself not guilty of disaffection must prove himself to be actively affectionate. In these days of democracy there is no such thing as active loyalty to a person. You are therefore loyal or disloyal to institutions. When therefore you are disloyal you seek not to destroy persons but institutions.

If a State is corrupt and many of its laws governing the conduct of a person are positively inhuman, if its administrators are capricious and regulated by nothing but their own whims and fancies and form an almost secret but extremely powerful corporation, if the system of government is based upon a merciless exploitation of millions of people, then "loyalty to a State so corrupt is a sin, disloyalty a virtue."[17]

It would be cowardly to seek to destroy the administrators of an unjust system, who are but creatures of circumstance. The purest men entering the system will be affected by it, and will be instrumental in propagating the evil. "You assist an administration most effectively by obeying its orders and decrees. An evil administration never deserves such allegiance. Allegiance to it means partaking of the evil. A good man will, therefore, resist an evil system of administration with his whole soul. Disobedience of the laws of an evil State is therefore a duty."[18] Violent disobedience may remove or replace men but it leaves the evil itself untouched and often accentuates it, unlike nonviolent disobedience. Thus a just and truly democratic State deserves active loyalty, while the citizen retains the right to disobey particular laws which are unjust or repressive, and a corrupt, undemocratic, tyrannical State is one in which (in Gandhi's phrase)[19] sedition itself becomes a religion.

Gandhi rejected the extreme views of the State of the collectivist and the anarchist. He was not satisfied with the half-way house of the liberal view of State sovereignty in a free society, derived from theories of the social contract or of constitutional legitimacy. He was also not willing to take the Marxist view that a State is wholly evil under a capitalist system in a bourgeois society and that it would automatically wither away when State socialism emerges through a violent revolution. If we make the individual morally and totally dependent on the State, as Hobbes or de Maistre or even Burke did, then there can be no room for the Gandhian insistence on the right of the citizen to challenge the authority or the acts of the State. The extreme view of the absolutist, that the State is endowed with innate value and even a divine dignity, is matched by the equally extremist view of the anarchist that the State is intrinsically or even wholly evil. In the latter case there could be no room for what Gandhi called the citizen's "active loyalty" to the State.

Gandhi wanted to find place in his conception of the State both for active loyalty and for the sacred right of disobedience. He no doubt came closer to the anarchist than to the absolutist view of the State, insofar as he thought a stateless society was conceivable, but he wished to leave it open to the citizen to decide in any given State, inevitably imperfect and unavoidably coercive, whether he felt obliged to show active loyalty or total opposition to that particular State, to resist none or all or a few of its laws. The onus of responsibility lies upon the conscience of the citizen, who is required to uphold *satya* and display *ahimsa*. The citizen cannot relinquish a portion of this responsibility in the name of a social contract or legal sovereignty or tacit consent or the rule of law or similar notions implicit in democratic constitutionalism. For Gandhi there can be no unconditional consent for the sake of peace, even if secured under majority rule, nor can the limits of State action be laid down in advance in a manner that will automatically secure the citizen his natural rights. Gandhi showed a Marxist distrust of even a democratic state under conditions of class conflict, and he also had a Rousseauite suspicion of mere institutional safeguards, especially when factions are strong. He felt that the majority could easily be wrong, regardless of the nature of the political system.

It is true that the theory of consent moralizes political authority and obligation by admitting their legitimacy only when certain moral criteria are satisfied, but it cannot let the individual, as Gandhi wanted to, retain the power of veto over State action at all times.

For Gandhi, as for Kant, the individual alone is a moral personality, and this no institution and no State could ever be or become. He could never agree with Durkheim's view that the State is an entity, the principal function of which is to think for the sake of guiding collective conduct. He was deeply attracted to the Socratic standpoint in regard to the State. The citizen can always, like Antigone, appeal to the eternal unwritten laws against the laws of men and of States and the commandments of religion, but he must, like Socrates, willingly accept the consequences of his challenge to the laws of States. Gandhi felt that such an attitude was even more, not less, necessary in the States of today, with their increasing centralization of power and greater impersonality, their augmented power of material *himsa*, their cynical disregard of *satya*, even in representative democracies in mass societies.

The State, as an institution, has gradually acquired an immense prestige in the long period since the doctrine of *jure divino* gave way. The religious aura of authority around the State in modern society is not unconnected with the monarchic and monistic conception of God in the cosmogony of early theological systems. If the State is viewed as a monadic whole superimposed on the body politic or absorbing it into itself, it comes to be credited with a quasi-mystical sovereignty, a supreme power which is absolute and may be exercised without accountability even when there are institutional safeguards and political fictions meant to prescribe limits to State authority. The rapid increase of State activity and the diminution of social power is more and more seen as one of the greatest dangers facing the mass societies of today. The whole of life becomes bureaucratized and the individual citizen feels helpless before the governmental machine. Since the late nineteenth century there has been a strong tendency to set off civil laws from all rules which, like the principles of morality, are enforced by an indeterminate authority, and the idea has even grown up that social morality consists solely or mainly in respect for the laws of the State.

It is in the context of present-day attitudes to the State and the seeming impotence of the individual citizen that Gandhi's view of the State and the citizen must be seen. The Nuremberg trials have raised the question whether men are to be held responsible for heinous acts which they were required to perform by the laws of tyrannical States. No doubt, a legal system cannot exist without a widely diffused sense of moral obligation to obey the law, but morality itself becomes meaningless if this cannot be overridden by a stronger obligation not to obey particular iniquitous laws, or to oppose wholeheartedly a wholly unjust or corrupt or tyrannical State. No authority can be absolute because no set of individuals can lay claim to absolute truth. The derivative authority of any institution, as apart from its force or power, presupposes the moral authority of its members, their right to recognize its commands as reasonable or unreasonable, as worthy or unworthy of acceptance, as morally and legally valid or invalid. The final court of appeal must be truth and right, *satya* and *ahimsa*, not as disembodied archetypes but as embodied, however partially, in individual citizens, and the right to resist an oppressive measure or system must belong equally to all in a just and free society.

THE DOCTRINE OF PASSIVE RESISTANCE

Neither the doctrine nor the practice of passive resistance originated with Gandhi, for they are to be found in the political thought and tradition of both Asia and Europe. He himself pointed out in 1908 that the idea of passive resistance was as old as the human race, that the doctrine was understood and commonly practiced in India[20] long before it came into vogue in Europe. At the same time he stressed that the doctrine of *satyagraha* was different from earlier notions of passive resistance. Before expounding the Gandhian conception of *satyagraha* it would be useful to take note of its antecedents in Asia and in Europe.

In the political thought of ancient India the failure of the ruler to fulfill his regal obligations (*rajadharma*) made him not merely morally culpable but also liable to removal by the people, in whom rested the right of resistance to injustice. There were extreme champions of this right like Bamadeva and Bhishma in the *Ma-*

habharata who enunciated a doctrine of tyrannicide. We also find this elsewhere as in the sixty-first chapter of the *Anusasana*. On the other hand, we have Sukra's enunciation of the principle of the passive obedience of subjects to rulers, qualified by the view that an unrighteous king forfeits his title to obedience. In making this the utmost limit of the right of resistance against an evil ruler, Sukra does not go so far as the advocates of tyrannicide.

Apart from resistance to State authority, the doctrine of passive resistance has been widely practiced in more limited spheres. The weapon of *dhurna* (from *dhr,* "to hold"), holding out by sitting in a hunger strike, was employed by creditors at the door of debtors who ignored legitimate claims on them. This has been described in Bishop Heber's Indian journal: "To sit in *dhurna* or mourning is to remain motionless in that position, without food, and exposed to the weather, till the person against whom it is employed consents to the request offered, and the Hindus believe that whosoever dies under this process becomes a tormenting spirit to haunt and afflict his inflexible antagonist." This method was sometimes used by a whole community to secure their just demands from a ruler. It was also known for people to resort to *hartal* (strike or stoppage of work, closing of shops) when there was intense public dissatisfaction. When all else failed against a recalcitrant and oppressive ruler, it was regarded as reasonable to abandon a kingdom (*deshatyaga*). A widely respected sage who thus quitted a kingdom as a protest against a ruler could undermine his position in ancient India. But, on the whole, *dhurna, hartal* and *deshatyaga* were silent expressions of protest against recognized injustice, intended to arouse the oppressor's sense of shame rather than to evoke his sense of guilt.[21] The response to the methods, if any, may be determined merely by considerations of prudence and prestige rather than those of atonement or conscience. On the other hand, the practice of fasting was widely employed in families and small groups as a means of arousing the conscience of a loved one.

In modern India the doctrine of passive resistance was expounded chiefly by Aurobindo Ghose as a political tactic rather than a spiritual therapeutic. In a series of articles published in 1907, Aurobindo defended the policy of militant non-physical resistance advocated by a new party in Bengal. "Organized resistance to an existing form of government may be undertaken either for the vindication of national liberty, or in order to substitute one form of government for another, or to remove particular objectionable features in the existing system without any entire or radical altera- tion of the whole, or simply for the redress of particular griev- ances."[22] Under such conditions the only alternatives, in his view, are armed revolt, aggressive resistance involving assassinations, ri- ots and insurrections, and, lastly, passive resistance. He regarded the first method of armed revolt as the readiest and swiftest, and most thorough in its results, demanding the least suffering and the smallest sacrifices. Against the anarchy created through the second method even the best organized and most repressive government would feel helpless, though the cost of human life would be colos- sal. As an example of the third method, Aurobindo cited Par- nell's obstructionist tactics in Parliament and his campaign of non- payment of rents in Ireland.

While Aurobindo did not wish to rule out in advance armed re- volt or aggressive resistance as criminal and unjustifiable in all cir- cumstances, he pointed to passive resistance as the most natural and suitable weapon for India at the time he wrote. The brutality of a regime justifies aggressive resistance, and when issues of life and death for an entire nation are at stake, armed revolt is needed as an urgent and desperate remedy. But where the oppression is le- gal and subtle in its methods, and respects life, liberty and prop- erty, and there is still breathing space, the method of resolute but peaceful resistance is needed. "Passive resistance, while less bold and aggressive than other methods, calls for perhaps as much heroism of a kind and certainly more universal endurance and suffering."[23]

While the method of the aggressive resister is to do something to cause positive harm to the government, the method of the passive resister is to abstain from doing something by which he would be helping the government. For Aurobindo the essence of passive re- sistance lay in a general policy of boycott, a successfully organized refusal of assistance which would render administration impossi- ble. The boycott of courts of law, the civil service, alien schools and colleges could be reinforced by the refusal to pay rents and taxes. The example of the English Dissenters and of the American colonists was cited. A policy of lawful abstention from any kind of cooperation with the government—a progressive extension of the method of boycott—would leave to the bureaucracy the onus of forcing a more direct, sudden and dangerous struggle. This passive resistance was a preparatory device, a political expedient to be followed by the use of organized violence. Legality is not an essential condition of passive resistance and its continuance must not be counted upon. The passive resister is entitled to break an unjust and oppressive law and take the legal consequences, as the Nonconformists did in England in refusing to pay the education rates, or as Hampden did when he refused to pay ship-money. The passive resister is certain to suffer for his creed, but he must regard the violation of an unjust law as not only permissible but, in certain circumstances, a solemn moral duty.

Aurobindo's doctrine of passive resistance was justified in terms of English rather than Indian precedents; it was a wholly borrowed creed. Similarly, C. R. Das pointed out that both the doctrine of passive obedience and the right of resistance were part of English tradition. He challenged the political philosophy of the bureaucracy —the maintenance of law and order at any cost and the obligation of passive obedience on the part of the subject.

> But was not that the political philosophy of every English king from William the Conqueror to James II? And was not that the political philosophy of the Romanoffs, the Hohenzollerns and of the Bourbons? And yet freedom has come, where it has come, by disobedience of the very laws which were proclaimed in the name of law and order. Where the government is arbitrary and despotic and the fundamental rights of the people are not recognized, it is idle to talk of law and order.[24]

Das referred to the long and bitter struggle between the Stuarts and Parliament, the vindication of the principle for which the revolution of 1688 stood in the celebrated case of the impeachment of Dr. Sacheverell. His enunciation of the doctrine of unconditional passive obedience was challenged by Walpole who argued that it was first invented to support arbitrary and despotic power. Major-General Stanhope denounced the doctrine as inconsistent with the law of reason, the law of nature and the practice of all ages and countries. The conclusions that Das drew from his reading of English history were that no regulation is law unless it is based upon the consent of the people, that where such consent is wanting the people are under no obligation to obey, that where laws not only are not founded on popular consent but also violate fundamental rights the subjects are entitled to compel their withdrawal by force or insurrections and, finally, that the rule of law under democracy must not be confused with the plea for law and order made by absolutism.

Neither the doctrine of passive obedience nor the right of resistance were peculiar features of English absolutism or of the English struggle for freedom. In his classic monograph published in 1914, Fritz Kern showed the significance of both doctrines in Europe in the Middle Ages. Both the doctrine of passive obedience and the right of resistance were deeply rooted in primitive Christianity as well as among the early Germanic peoples and the Pharisees of the Jewish nation under Roman rule. The conflict between the doctrines of passive obedience and the right of resistance was inevitable when a religious minority found itself subject to a regime of non-believers. Tertullian asserted that even if Christians had the power of active resistance, they would not do otherwise than passively suffer the wrongs inflicted by earthly rulers. But when the State itself became Christian this policy was considered to be no longer applicable. The Christian martyrs set an example of the way in which the duty of resistance should limit obedience to the State, while the resistance itself should be limited by the duty of obedience. The right of passive resistance on behalf of religion was always regarded without qualification as an immutable law of nature, but gradually the right was extended to other spheres.

The right of resistance was an integral part of medieval Germanic constitutional ideas and we find it in its purest form in early Scandinavia. In Nordic royal sagas a twofold appeal to customary law was recognized. There was the appeal to the royal tradition of deciding questions after hearing the opinions of the people. There was also the appeal to the equally venerable tradition of the people, of abandoning and slaying the king when he acted lawlessly. Resistance to a king did not necessarily aim at his dethronement. The general idea that the community's duty of obedience to a ruler was not unconditional was deep-rooted. The subject, according to the theories of the early Middle Ages, owed his ruler not so much obedience as fealty, both being equally bound by their allegiance to the law. The coercive powers of the State were thought to be insufficient or unreliable and were repudiated or evaded so that redress by self-help was accorded some legal sanction. The Germanic conceptions of the forfeiture of the right to govern implied that the prince passed judgment upon himself by his own actions. Unjust government is in itself void and the verdict of men justifying resistance has only a declaratory, not a constitutive character. Unconditional respect for lawful authority was combined with resistance to tyranny through the idea that a tyrannical ruler automatically lost his own authority. In England the sixty-first article of the Magna Carta incorporated the right of resistance in the written public law of a nation, and we have here the beginnings of rules for constitutional resistance.

Before the rise of the modern nation-state and its legal sovereignty it was widely recognized that there would never be a political power whose authority could be absolute. Political power is always bound to the laws of justice. Both theologians and Roman lawyers interpreted the maxim, *Princeps legibus solutus*, in the sense that the prince is free from legal coercion, but the power and authority of the natural law remains unbroken. There was no serious challenge to the dictum, *Rex nihil potest nise quod jure potest*. Sedition is forbidden by the divine law, but to resist an unjust authority or to disobey a tyrant does not have the character of revolt or sedition. In the sixteenth century, however, there was again a greater stress upon the doctrine of unconditional obligation, upon the need for order and the evils of rebellion. Even the potential rebels among the Elizabethan Puritans held that if the ruler commanded anything contrary to the word of God, it would not be lawful for subjects to rebel or resist and they would be required to bear with patience and humility the punishment laid upon them. On the other hand, the divine right of rebellion was recognized, though carefully restricted and qualified, in the *Vindiciae contra Tyrannos* in 1579. Whereas the right to make a judgment belongs to the individual, the right to act on the judgment and to engage in active resistance belongs to the community and its accredited representatives. The Huguenot thinkers based government upon a double pact—a pact with God and with their ruler. Resistance against a tyrant is a duty, not just a right. Government itself is sanctioned by the law of nature, but the form of government has no such sanction: *in radice* government is prescribed, *in modo* it is voluntary.

Although the right of resistance was recognized in Indian as well as in Western political thought from the earliest times, it was bound up with religious and political notions that have since lost their original force. The sovereignty of the modern nation-state, buttressed by legal positivism and unprecedented concentration of coercive power, cannot readily be challenged in terms of traditional ideas of resistance. For a clear antecedent to the Gandhian doctrine of *satyagraha* we must look to the writer who most influenced him in this matter. Thoreau's essay "Civil Disobedience" came out just a year after the *Communist Manifesto*, in 1849, but its approach cannot appeal to Marxists any more than to conservatives today. To Thoreau government is at best but an expedient, but most governments are usually, and all are sometimes, inexpedient. Even a government based on majority rule—indeed such a government especially—cannot conform to justice.

> Must the citizen ever for a moment, or in the least degree, resign his conscience to the legislator? Why has every man a conscience, then? I think that we should be men first, and subjects afterward. It is not desirable to cultivate a respect for the law, so much as for the right. The only obligation which I have a right to assume is to do at any time what I think right. . . . Law never made men a whit more just; and, by means of their respect for it, even the well-disposed are daily made the agents of injustice. . . . The mass of men serve the State thus, not as men mainly, but as machines, with their bodies. . . . All men recognize the right of revolution; that is, the right to refuse allegiance to, and to resist, the government when its tyranny or its inefficiency are great and unendurable. But almost all say that such is not the case now.[25]

Thoreau rejected Paley's attempt in his essay "Duty of Submission to Civil Government" to resolve all civil obligation into expediency. In Paley's view the justice of every particular case of resistance is reduced to a calculation of the gravity of the grievance and the probability (and expense) of redressing it. Thoreau was more concerned with the cases to which the rule of expediency does not apply, in which an individual or a people is led by conscience to feel that justice must be done whatever the cost.

Whereas the right of resistance had been invoked earlier as a justification for rebellion in extreme circumstances, Thoreau wanted to assert its continual relevance to the citizen's responsibility in any State. He recognized that the individual cannot assume an Atlas-like burden of cosmic responsibility, that it is not his duty to devote himself, as a matter of course, to the eradication of any, even the most enormous, wrong. But it is his duty, at least, to wash his hands of it and to give it no support, for all practical purposes. This would still be a more significant act than voting for the right, which is doing nothing for it but merely expressing feebly a desire that it should prevail. Action from principle is essentially revolutionary, dividing States, churches, families, even the individual, "separating the diabolical in him from the divine." A man cannot do everything but at least he can abstain from *something* wrong. Under an unjust government the true place for a just man is prison. When a subject refuses his allegiance and an officer resigns his office, then "a peaceable revolution" is accomplished. Such a man cannot be forced by a State, armed with superior physical strength and the support of the multitude. "They only can force me who obey a higher law than I. They force me to become like themselves."[26] It is open to the individual to refuse allegiance to the State, to withdraw and stand aloof from it effectually, quietly to declare war on the State. He is not unwilling to conform to the laws of the land when they do not conflict with reason or conscience. The world is not governed by policy and expediency alone.

> Is a democracy, such as we know it, the last improvement possible in government? Is it not possible to take a step further toward recognizing and reorganizing the rights of man? There will never be a really free and enlightened State until the State comes to recognize the individual as a higher and independent power, from which all its own power and authority are derived, and treats him accordingly.[27]

As we shall see, Gandhi's doctrine of *satyagraha* is much closer to the views of Thoreau than of T. H. Green, with whom he has sometimes been compared. Thoreau based his conception of civil disobedience upon the idea that the individual's status as a human being is morally and logically prior to, and always more meaningful than, his role as a member of society or a citizen of any State. Green, on the other hand, argued that an individual can have no rights against society as such. He has also no rights against the State insofar as it is the sustainer and harmonizer of social relations. However, as actual States at best fulfill only partially this ideal function, the citizen is not obliged under all conditions to conform to the law of his State. He is entitled to disobey only when he is able to point to some public interest, generally recognized as such, which is involved in the exercise of power claimed by him as right. He must be able to elicit from the conscience of his fellow citizens social recognition for the legitimacy of his exercise of his right of resistance.

> As a general rule, no doubt, even bad laws, laws representing the interests of classes or individuals as opposed to those of the community, should be obeyed. There can be no right to disobey them, even while their repeal is urged on the ground that they violate rights, because the public interest, on which all rights are founded, is more concerned in the general obedience to law than in the exercise of those powers by individuals or classes which the objectionable laws unfairly withhold.[28]

Green did consider the case in which the public interest is best served by a violation of some actual law, e.g., sanctioning slavery. But even here the right to resist a law on behalf of a slave would lose its force if the violation of law were to result in general anarchy. Gandhi's position was not wholly like Thoreau's and he would concede the importance, stressed by Green, of invoking the public interest (*sarvodaya*). He would also agree that the dictates of individual conscience, if genuine, would culminate in conduct that would arouse and appeal to the conscience of others. But Gandhi could not make the individual's duty to follow his conscience dependent upon social recognition. Gandhi's concern was always with duties rather than with rights; in fact, there is no concept of "rights" in Indian political thought. Further, his emphasis on *ahimsa* as the means to be used in the vindication of *satya* required him to believe that the resistance to injustice, properly conducted, could not lead to general anarchy. Thus Gandhi differed from Thoreau only in that his language and his emphasis were less anarchistic, but he fundamentally differed from Green (whom he never read) in his conception and justification of the right of resistance to the State.

The primacy of public peace and the danger of anarchy have been stressed from the earliest times as an argument against resistance to the laws of the State and not merely against open rebellion and revolutions. Democritus held that the peacebreaker, every enemy of public order, may be put to death. Thucydides pointed out that the welfare of the State depends on the maintenance of the authority of laws, even though they may not be the best possible. Is there a form of resistance which is compatible with respect for law and order? In showing that there could be, Socrates stands alone and it is his example that most appealed to Gandhi, who wrote a Gujarati paraphrase of the *Apology* called *The Story of a Satyagrahi*. Socrates in prison praises to Crito the laws of Athens, and prefers the unjust hemlock to an escape which would flout these laws. His respect for law is sincere but not idolatrous. When he vindicates the City, it is for his own reasons, not for reasons of state. His way of obeying is itself a way of resisting.

THE DOCTRINE OF *SATYAGRAHA*

The term *satyagraha* was coined by Gandhi in 1906 in the early phase of his South African campaign to secure the elementary human rights of Indian immigrants, most of whom were brought in as indentured labor. He felt that the phrase "passive resistance" gave rise to confusion. It was both misleading and shameful to use a foreign expression for the movement to be launched. A small prize was announced in *Indian Opinion* for the best designation for the Indian struggle. Maganlal Gandhi suggested the word *sadagraha*, meaning "firmness in a good cause."

> I liked the word, but it did not fully represent the whole idea I wished it to connote. I therefore corrected it to "*satyagraha*." Truth (*satya*) implies love, and firmness (*agraha*) engenders and

therefore serves as a synonym for force. I thus began to call the Indian movement *"satyagraha"* that is to say, the force which is born to Truth and Love or non-violence, and gave up the use of the phrase "passive resistance." . . .[29]

By 1909, when Gandhi wrote *Hind Swaraj,* his ideas about *satyagraha* had matured and he felt he had realized its universality as well as its excellence.[30]

The term *satyagraha* is new, but the concept has its affinities with similar expressions in Sanskrit literature. Classical heroes like Rama, Bhishma and Harischandra were commended by appellations such as *satyavarta*—"one whose life is pledged to truth"—*satyadhriti*—"adhering firmly to truth"—*satyanishta*—"constant in absolute loyalty to truth"—*satyasandha*—"wedded to truth."[31] The word *"agraha"* in *sadagraha,* which Gandhi changed to *satyagraha,* is derived from the root *grah*—"to seize or to grasp, to get hold of, to grapple with." *Satyagraha* is, therefore, "a relentless search for truth and a determination to reach truth,"[32] an ideal which deeply stirred Gandhi even in early youth. The story of Prahlad and the drama of Harischandra had a lifelong influence upon him, and he cherished their exemplary devotion to truth, combined with the spirit of non-retaliation. When, as a young man, he read the New Testament and especially the Sermon on the Mount, he was "simply overjoyed" and found his own opinion confirmed where he least expected it.[33] The doctrine of *satyagraha* was derived from many sources, from the Sermon on the Mount and the *Bhagavad Gita,* from Tolstoy and Thoreau. Gandhi's campaign of *satyagraha* was actually well under way in South Africa before he saw Thoreau's writings. (He may have partly inherited the spirit of resistance from his father who, as Dewan, stood up to the British agent in Porbandar as well as to the Maharaja.)

In March 1921 Gandhi declared that *satyagraha* is literally holding on to Truth and it means, therefore, "truth-force or soul-force." It excludes the use of violence because man is not capable of knowing the absolute Truth and is, therefore, not competent to punish.[34] The word was coined to distinguish the nonviolent resistance of the Indians in South Africa from the contemporary passive resistance of the Suffragettes in England. It is not conceived as a weapon of the weak, and it includes all courageous but nonviolent resistance in order to uphold the truth. Toward the end of his life, Gandhi reiterated his conviction that *satyagraha* is a law of universal significance as well as "a process of educating public opinion such that it covers all the elements in the society and, in the end, makes itself irresistible. Violence interrupts the process and prolongs the real revolution of the whole social structure."[35]

Gandhi came to prefer the term *satyagraha* to "passive resistance." "I do not like the term 'passive resistance,' it fails to convey all I mean. It describes a method, but gives no hint of the system of which it is only a part. Real beauty, and that is my aim, is in doing good against evil."[36] And yet he sometimes used the phrase "passive resistance" because it is well known and easily understood. "Soul-force" is superior to "physical force" since it is not intended to cause suffering to others, as its misuse injures the users and not those against whom it is used. "Like virtue, it is its own reward. There is no such thing as failure in the use of this kind of force."[37] It also calls for greater courage than violent resistance. Those who recognize the immeasurable power of soul-force would be willing deliberately to accept physical suffering as their lot and, when this is done, their very suffering becomes a source of joy to the sufferers. Christ, Daniel and Socrates represent the purest form of passive resistance or soul-force, as all these teachers counted their bodies as nothing in comparison with their souls.

In *Hind Swaraj* Gandhi defined passive resistance as a method of securing rights by personal suffering.

> When I refuse to do a thing that is repugnant to my conscience, I use soul-force. For instance, the government of the day has passed a law which is applicable to me. I do not like it. . . . If I do not obey the law and accept the penalty for its breach, I use soul-force. It involves the sacrifice of self. . . . Everybody admits that sacrifice of self is infinitely superior to sacrifice of others. Moreover, if this kind of force is used in a cause that is unjust, only the person using it suffers. He does not make others suffer for his mistakes. . . . No man can claim to be absolutely in the right or that a particular thing is wrong because he thinks so; but it is wrong for him so long as that is his deliberate judgment. It is, therefore, meet that he should not do that which he knows to be wrong, and suffer the consequence whatever it may be. This is the key to the use of soul-force.[38]

If a man would only realize that it is unmanly to obey laws that are unjust, no tyranny could enslave him. Gandhi felt that it is a superstition and an ungodly thing to believe that an act of a majority binds a minority. Many examples can be given in which acts of majorities will be found to have been wrong, and those of minorities to have been right. All reforms, in his view, owe their origin to the initiative of minorities in opposition to majorities. So long as the superstition exists that men should obey unjust laws merely because they have majority approval, so long will they remain slaves. Passive resistance requires courage but it could be offered even by those who are weak in body, by women as well as men, by the masses as well as by solitary individuals. It does not require the training of an army, but control over the mind is alone necessary. Those who want to become effective passive resisters must discipline themselves by vows, observe perfect chastity, adopt poverty, follow Truth and cultivate fearlessness. In this way they come to acquire the moral and spiritual strength necessary to exemplify the virtues of passive resistance.

Gandhi summed up his panegyric of passive resistance in *Hind Swaraj* in the following words: "Passive Resistance is an all-sided sword, it can be used anyhow; it blesses him who uses it and him against whom it is used. Without drawing a drop of blood it produces far-reaching results. It never rusts and cannot be stolen. Competition between passive resisters does not exhaust. The sword of Passive Resistance does not require a scabbard."[39]

A year after *Hind Swaraj* was written, Gandhi pointed out in an article in an Indian journal that passive resistance is an infallible panacea for Indian ills. It is the only weapon suited to the genius of a land that is the nursery of the most ancient religions and has little to learn from modern civilization "based on violence of the blackest type, largely a negation of the Divine in man, and which is rushing headlong to its own ruin."[40]

Although Gandhi sometimes used *satyagraha* and passive resistance as synonyms in *Hind Swaraj* and elsewhere, he sharpened the distinction between them in *Satyagraha in South Africa*. He regarded the difference between the two as great and fundamental and pointed to five differences between passive resistance and *satyagraha*.

First of all, if we continue to believe ourselves, and let others believe, that we are weak and helpless and, therefore, offer passive resistance, our resistance would never make us strong, and at the earliest opportunity we would give it up. On the other hand, if we offer *satyagraha* believing ourselves to be strong, two clear consequences follow. Fostering the idea of strength, we grow stronger and stronger every day. With the increase in our strength, our *satyagraha* too becomes more effective and we would never be casting about for an opportunity to give it up.

Secondly, while there is no scope for love in passive resistance there is not only no place for hatred in *satyagraha*, but it is a positive breach of its ruling principle.

Thirdly, while in passive resistance there is no scope for the use of arms, the two may be offered side by side or the former may be looked upon as a preparation for the latter; in *satyagraha* physical force is forbidden even in the most favorable circumstances. Brute force is a negation of *satyagraha*, but not necessarily of passive resistance.

Fourthly, *satyagraha* may be offered to one's nearest and dearest, whereas passive resistance cannot unless they have ceased to be dear to us.

Fifthly, in passive resistance, there is always present an idea of harassing the other party, while in *satyagraha* there is not the remotest idea of injuring the opponent.[41]

In short, *satyagraha*, unlike passive resistance, "postulates the conquest of the adversary by suffering in one's own person." Gandhi did not wish to suggest that these differences are to be seen in every movement which passes by the name of passive resistance. He regarded Jesus Christ, "the Prince of Passive Resisters," as a true *satyagrahi*. He also commended as a fine example of *satyagraha* the patient suffering in the face of oppression endured by thousands of devout Christians in the early days of Christianity. Another example of *satyagraha* was, in his view, the resolute resistance offered by the Doukhobors of Russia. On the other hand, the resistance offered by nonconformists to the Education Act was a case of passive resistance by the weak, some of whom were not averse to the use of arms. Similarly with the Suffragettes in their militant tactics to secure the vote. Gandhi conceded that not all who call themselves *satyagrahis* are capable of exemplifying real *satyagraha*. His main purpose in making a sharp distinction between *satyagraha* and passive resistance, connected with the distinction between *ahimsa* as a creed and as a policy, or nonviolence of the strong and of the weak, was to show that *satyagraha*, in all its implications, is essentially different from what people generally (and often pejoratively) mean by the English phrase "passive resistance." The concept of *ahimsa* is so fundamental to the doctrine of *satyagraha* that he once went so far as to say that "*satyagraha* differs from passive resistance as the North Pole from the South."[42] A *satyagrahi* must be, whereas a passive resister need not be, a model citizen like Daniel, who defied the laws of the Medes and Persians and meekly suffered punishment, or Socrates, who upheld the truth and bravely suffered the punishment of death.

Gandhi's chief purpose in distinguishing between passive resistance and *satyagraha* was to protect the latter from the taint of weakness implicit in the adjective "passive." The real contrast for him was between violent and nonviolent, not between active and passive, resistance. In 1926 he wrote to Wilhelm Wattenberg: "My non-violent resistance is activized resistance on a different plane. Non-violent resistance to evil does not mean absence of any resistance whatsoever but it means not to resist evil with evil but with good. Resistance, therefore, is transferred to a higher and absolutely effective plane."[43] Again in 1928 he wrote to a persistent critic, the Reverend Boyd Tucker: " 'Resist not evil,' with me has never meant passive resistance. The word 'passive resistance' I have described as a misnomer for 'resistance' which I have known and offered. The paraphrase of 'resist not evil' means 'resist not evil with evil' and therefore necessarily means 'resist evil with good.' "[44] A month before his assassination he wrote to Madame Privat:

> I see that you have grasped the fundamental difference between Passive Resistance and Non-Violent Resistance. Resistance both forms are, but you have to pay a very heavy price when your resistance is passive, in the sense of the weakness of the resister. Europe mistook the bold and brave resistance, full of wisdom, by Jesus of Nazareth for passive resistance as if it were of the weak. As I read the New Testament for the first time I detected no pas-

sivity, no weakness about Jesus as depicted in the four gospels and the meaning became clearer to me when I read Tolstoy's *Harmony of the Gospels* and his other kindred writings. Has not the West paid too heavily in regarding Jesus as a Passive Resister?[45]

Gandhi not merely distinguished firmly between passive resistance and *satyagraha*, but also brought out the difference between the closely connected notions of non-cooperation, civil disobedience and *satyagraha*. *Satyagraha* is a much broader concept than civil disobedience or non-cooperation. Civil disobedience, he said, is "civil breach of unmoral statutory enactments."[46]

> The expression was, as far as I am aware, coined by Thoreau to signify his own resistance to the laws of a slave State. He has left a masterly treatise on the duty of Civil Disobedience. But Thoreau was not perhaps an out and out champion of non-violence. Probably, also, Thoreau limited his breach of statutory laws to the revenue law, i.e., payment of taxes. Whereas the term Civil Disobedience as practised in 1919 covered a breach of any statutory and unmoral law. It signified the resister's outlawry in a civil, i.e., non-violent manner. He invoked the sanctions of the law and cheerfully suffered imprisonment. It is a branch of *satyagraha*.[47]

Non-cooperation, according to Gandhi, chiefly implies the withdrawal of cooperation from a State that, in the non-cooperator's view, has become corrupt.[48] Non-cooperation too is a branch of *satyagraha* but it excludes civil disobedience of the "fierce type" described above. Whereas non-cooperation can be safely practiced by the masses, civil disobedience can be practiced only as a last resort and by a select few—at any rate in the beginning. Civil disobedience is more difficult than non-cooperation because it presupposes the habit of willing obedience to laws without fear of their sanctions.

Gandhi's terminology was not always consistent. He sometimes used the phrase "civil resistance" to differentiate his conception from that of "civil disobedience" in Thoreau's essay. On one occasion, however, Gandhi restricted the meaning of civil resistance to contrast it with his own conception of civil disobedience. "Civil resistance does not mean even civil disobedience of the laws and rules promulgated by constituted authority. It simply means non-payment of a portion of a tax which . . . has been improperly and unjustly imposed."[49] When Gandhi used the phrase "civil resistance" in a commendatory sense, he wanted to stress the difference between his own position and that of the typical anarchist.

> Civil disobedience must not be carried beyond the point of breaking the unmoral laws of the country. Breach of the laws to be civil assumes the strictest and willing obedience to gaol discipline, because disobedience of a particular rule assumes a willing acceptance of the sanction provided for its breach. And immediately a person quarrels both with the rule and the sanction for its breach, he lends himself to the precipitation of chaos and anarchy. A civil resister is, if one may be permitted such a claim for him, a philanthropist and friend of the State. An anarchist is an enemy of the State and is, therefore, a misanthrope. . . . But I hold the opinion firmly that Civil Disobedience is the purest type of constitutional agitation. Of course, it becomes degrading and despicable if its civil, i.e., non-violent character is a mere camouflage.[50]

The reason why Gandhi was anxious to stress this point was his insistence that if the reliance on nonviolence and the meaning of true civility are accepted, there is no warrant for condemning even the "fiercest disobedience" because of the likelihood of its leading to violence and disruption.

The civil resister of Gandhi's conception cannot protest at being put into prison for the violation of laws that he regards as immoral and unjust. He meekly and willingly submits to the penalty of disobedience and cheerfully accepts jail discipline and its attendant hardships. His imprisonment gives him a chance to demonstrate to his jailer that he is not like a thief or a dacoit, that he wishes them no ill and wants to convert rather than destroy his opponents.[51] The civil resister earns the right to break the laws of the State only if he can show that he respects the rules that he accepts.

> Rules voluntarily passed by us, and rules which carry no sanction save the dissapproval of our own conscience, must be like debts of honour held far more binding than rules superimposed upon us or rules whose breach we can purge by paying the penalty thereof. It follows that, if we have not learnt the discipline of obeying our own rules, in other words, carrying out our own

promises, we are ill-adapted for disobedience that can be at all described as civil.[52]

In order to make his position clearer, Gandhi distinguished explicitly between civil and criminal disobedience.[53] First of all, civil disobedience must never be followed by anarchy, while criminal disobedience can lead to it. Secondly, every State must put down criminal disobedience by force if it is to survive, but to put down civil disobedience is to attempt to imprison conscience. Thirdly, as the civil resister never uses arms, he is harmless to a State that is at all responsive to the voice of public opinion. He is dangerous for an autocratic State. If a State becomes autocratic or corrupt, he is entitled to regard it as lawless. "A citizen that barters with such a State shares its corruption or lawlessness."[54]

Civil disobedience presupposes a scrupulous and willing observance of all laws which do not hurt the moral sense or violate individual conscience. It is not a state of lawlessness, but does demand a law-abiding spirit combined with self-restraint.

> When a man wilfully breaks his own laws, the disobedience becomes criminal. For, he commits the breach not against himself but against some one else, and not only escapes punishment for the breach, for there is none provided against himself by the makers of laws, but he avoids also the inconvenience caused by their observance. What is true of the individual is true of the corporation.[55]

In a well-ordered State it is rare that the occasion for civil resistance arises, but when it does it becomes a duty that cannot be shirked by one who holds his honor (i.e., conscience) above everything.[56] Gandhi felt that we must give greater value to the adjective "civil" than to "disobedience." "Disobedience without civility, discipline, discrimination, non-violence, is certain destruction."[57] He also distinguished between aggressive and defensive civil disobedience.[58] Aggressive or offensive civil disobedience may be outwardly nonviolent but it is willful if obedience to the law does not really involve any moral turpitude and its breach is undertaken merely as a symbol of revolt against the State. Defensive civil disobedience, on the other hand, is involuntary or reluctant nonviolent disobedience of such laws as are in themselves bad and obedience to which would be inconsistent with one's self-respect or human dignity. When law fosters untruth, it becomes a duty to disobey it.

Gandhi thought that there are no rules which can tell us how, when, where and by whom civil disobedience may be carried out. There are also no rules to tell us which laws foster untruth. "It is only experience that can guide us, and it requires time and knowledge of facts."[59] It is possible to question the wisdom of applying civil disobedience in respect of a particular act or law; it is possible to advise delay and caution. But the right itself cannot be questioned as Gandhi regarded it "a birthright that cannot be surrendered without surrender of one's self-respect."[60] The citizen cannot give up his inherent right to civil disobedience without ceasing to be a man, but this right cannot be extended to include violent revolt. In civil disobedience the resister suffers the consequences of disobedience. As a man he owes it to himself to suffer, if necessary, for his conscience. As a citizen it is his duty to suffer the consequences of his conscientious disobedience to the laws of the State. Further, civil disobedience, if it is really civil, must appear so even to the opponent. He must feel that the resistance is not intended to do him any harm. Gandhi assumed that even a tyrant or an authoritarian regime will come to accept the integrity, and respect the intention, of the conscientious objector or civil resister, though no mercy may be shown to him. The resister, if a real *satyagrahi,* invites suffering upon himself and requires no mercy.

Gandhi's analysis of civil disobedience conflated two separate notions—the natural right, the universal obligation, of every human being to act according to his conscience in opposition, if necessary, to any external authority or restraint, and secondly, the duty of the citizen to qualify himself by obedience to the laws of the State to exercise on rare occasions his obligation to violate an unjust law or challenge an unjust system, and to accept willingly the consequences of his disobedience as determined by the legal sanctions of the State.

> Civil disobedience is a terrifying synonym for suffering. But it is better often to understand the terrible nature of a thing if people will truly appreciate its benignant counter-part. Disobedience is a right that belongs to every human being, and it becomes a sacred duty when it springs from civility, or, which is the same thing,

love. . . . The condition of this terrible resistance . . . is possible of fulfilment only by a long course of self-purification and
suffering.[61]

Such a concept of civil disobedience can only apply infrequently
and can apply only to the individual. Gandhi did, however, envisage the need for "complete civil disobedience" or a state of
peaceful rebellion, a refusal to obey every single State-made law.[62]
When violence is corroding the entire body politic, such civil disobedience will be "but a purifying process and may bring to the
surface what is burrowing under and into the whole body."[63] Civil
disobedience can be made "a sovereign remedy for all our ills" if
we can produce the necessary atmosphere for it. For individuals,
there always is that atmosphere, except when their civil disobedience is certain to lead to bloodshed. Even then, when neglect of the
call means a denial of truth, civil disobedience becomes a peremp-
tory duty.[64]

Mass civil disobedience stands on a different footing. First of
all, said Gandhi, it must be tried in a calm atmosphere. It must be
the calmness of strength not weakness, of knowledge not ignorance.
Secondly, individual civil disobedience may be, and often is, "vicarious." Mass civil disobedience may be, and is usually, selfish in
the sense that individuals expect personal gain from their disobedience. In South Africa, Kallenbach and Polak offered civil disobedience though they had nothing to gain from it, while thousands
offered it because they expected personal gain in the shape of the
removal of the annual poll-tax levied upon indentured laborers.
Gandhi realized that it is not possible to expect large numbers of
people to offer nonviolent resistance from entirely altruistic motives, although these may move individuals of an exceptional order.
In mass civil disobedience he thought it sufficient if the resisters
understood the working of the doctrine. Civil disobedience is exercised by the masses as an inherent and legitimate right to secure
the recognition of claims that they regard as due to them as citizens. In the case of individual resisters, their civil disobedience is
simply the performance of a duty that they owe themselves under
the dictates of their conscience. As Gandhi rejected the notion of a
mass conscience, he would not apply the same arguments in justification of mass civil disobedience as he felt he could in regard to

individual civil disobedience. What is common to both is the willingness to suffer the penalties of disobedience and the determination to abstain from violence in the campaign of resistance.

The difference between individual and mass civil disobedience does not mean that the latter could be manufactured by a group of leaders with troubled consciences, seeking wider support. Gandhi asserted that mass civil disobedience cannot be made; it must be spontaneous if it is to deserve the name and if it is to be successful. He argued that there will be no mass response where the ground has not been previously tilled, nurtured and watered, i.e., where *ahimsa* has not taken root among the people. The greatest precaution has to be taken everywhere against an outbreak of violence. "Two opposite forces can never work concurrently so as to help each other. The plan of civil disobedience has been conceived to neutralize and ultimately entirely to displace violence and enthrone non-violence in its stead, to replace hatred by love, to replace strife by concord."[65] Where the ground is adequately prepared, mass civil disobedience would spontaneously occur. Gandhi even went so far as to say that mass civil disobedience "means spontaneous action." He thought that the disciplined and dedicated leaders would merely guide the masses in the beginning, and that later on the masses would regulate the movement themselves.

Gandhi recognized that there were dangers in mass civil disobedience, but he thought that nothing could be achieved without direct action. He argued that it was direct action in South Africa which converted General Smuts—a determined opponent of Indian aspiration in 1906—to the extent that in 1914 he took pride in doing tardy justice by removing from the Statute Book a disgraceful measure which in 1909 he had told Lord Morley would never be removed. Again, it was direct action in Champaran which removed an age-long grievance of the peasants.

A meek submission, when one is chafing under a disability or a grievance which one would gladly see removed, not only does not make for unity, but makes the weak party acid, angry and prepares him for an opportunity to explode. By allying myself with the weak party, by teaching him direct, firm but harmless action, I make him feel strong and capable of defying the physical might. He feels braced for the struggle, regains confidence in himself and knowing that the remedy lies with himself, ceases to harbour the spirit of revenge and learns to be satisfied with a redress of the wrong he is seeking to remedy.[66]

Any danger that there might be in civil disobedience exists because it is still only partially tried and has always to be tried in an atmosphere surcharged with violence. When tyranny is rampant much rage is generated among the victims, and, although the rage remains latent because of the weakness of the victims, it bursts out in all its fury on the slightest pretext.

> Civil disobedience is a sovereign method of transmuting this undisciplined life-destroying latent energy into disciplined life-saving energy whose use ensures absolute success. The attendant risk is nothing compared to the result promised. When the world has become familiar with its use and when it has had a series of demonstrations of its successful working, there will be less risk in civil disobedience than there is in aviation, in spite of that science having reached a high stage of development.[67]

Although in 1921 Gandhi had sharply distinguished between civil disobedience and non-cooperation, he had stretched the meaning of civil disobedience to such an extent by 1930 that he regarded it as a necessary part of non-cooperation. But his terminological shifts should not prevent us from seeing why he distinguished between the two concepts in 1921. He was then concerned to stress the difference between the individual's right to resist unjust laws and the duty of entire groups to withhold cooperation from the State or to boycott social institutions that maintain an iniquitous system. Civil disobedience was regarded by him as a narrower concept with important political implications. Non-cooperation was conceived in a much wider context as an instrument of social action. Civil disobedience was regarded as a universal human right, which in practice only a few were capable of exemplifying in a spirit of *tapas* or self-suffering. Non-cooperation was considered to be a readily universifiable method of social change, which made fewer spiritual demands on its users. In 1921 Gandhi did not rule out the possibility of mass civil disobedience, but by 1930 he was much exercised over the practical implications of widespread resistance to the laws of the State as a means of withholding cooperation from a system he considered to be inherently wrong. He still saw that civil disobedience and non-cooperation were conceptually different but, as they were both aspects of the political campaign of a growingly mass movement, he began to use the terms interchangeably and to merge their meanings into each other.

In 1921 his emphasis was on *tapas* in civil disobedience and on *ahimsa* in non-cooperation, although both concepts contained the elements of self-suffering and nonviolence.

> In Civil Disobedience, the resister suffers the consequences of disobedience. This was what Daniel did when he disobeyed the laws of the Medes and Persians. This is what John Bunyan did, and this is what the *ryots* have done in India from time immemorial. It is the Law of our Being. Violence is the Law of the Beast in us. Self-suffering, i.e., Civil Resistance, is the Law of the Man in us.[68]

In the same year he defined non-cooperation in his controversy with Tagore as "a protest against an unwitting and unwilling participation in evil."[69] He argued that non-cooperation is intended to pave the way to honorable and voluntary cooperation based on mutual respect and trust. It is a struggle "against compulsory cooperation, against one-sided combination, against the armed imposition of modern methods of exploitation masquerading under the name of civilization."[70] When non-cooperation is nonviolent, it is neither punitive nor vindictive nor based on malice or hatred. Gandhi insisted that non-cooperation is not unconstitutional if it is undertaken only in conditions in which it is not followed by anarchy or disorder. And yet the purpose of non-cooperation is to put pressure upon a government by making it difficult for it to govern. "I believe, and everybody must grant, that no government can exist for a single moment without the cooperation of the people, willing or forced, and if people suddenly withdraw their cooperation in every detail, the government will come to a stand-still. . . . Cooperation with a just government is a duty; non-cooperation with an unjust government is equally a duty."[71]

Gandhi tended here as elsewhere to confuse intentions with consequences. It is not impossible to imagine a condition in which people totally withhold their cooperation from a government without intending or producing an anarchic and lawless state of general confusion. In practice this would be very unlikely, as no actual society could even begin to advance to the goal of *Rama Rajya,* based upon a general adherence to *satya* and *ahimsa,* if it is governed by a wholly unjust regime. In classical Hindu political thought the quality of government and the degree of coercion were taken as an index of the moral level of a society. Gandhi's extreme suspicion of government as a coercive, soulless machine led him to place too heavy a burden of responsibility upon it for the moral enslavement of a people. And yet, paradoxically, he was inclined to do this precisely because of his concern to induce the populace to assume considerable moral and political responsibilities. But it would be wrong to dismiss his creed of non-cooperation, which a few critics have done, as a doctrine of negation and despair. For him non-cooperation with evil is as much a duty as cooperation with good. This needed stressing in a country in which it had become, as he said, disloyal and almost sacrilegious to say No to the government.

> This deliberate refusal to cooperate is like the necessary weeding process that a cultivator has to resort to before he sows. Weeding is as necessary to agriculture as sowing. Indeed, even whilst the crops are growing, the weeding fork, as every husbandman knows, is an instrument almost of daily use. The nation's Non-Cooperation is an invitation to the government to cooperate with it on its own terms as is every nation's right and every good government's duty.[72]

Gandhi's excessive claims for the harmlessness of nonviolent non-cooperation (a "natural and religious doctrine") were the result of regarding it as the sole superior alternative to "the unnatural and irreligious doctrine of violence." This kind of disjunctive reasoning is not, of course, uncommon among political thinkers. Hobbes provides the clearest example in his insistence that an intolerable state of nature is the only alternative to the unconditional acceptance of an unchallengeable sovereign. In fairness to Gandhi, however, it must be said that he did recognize that non-cooperation would entail suffering. But he held that non-cooperation is not violence when the refusal of the restraint is a right and a duty even though by reason of its performance some people may have to suffer. It will be an act of love when non-cooperation is resorted to solely for the good of the wrong-doer. Indian non-cooperation is a right and a duty, but cannot be regarded as an act of love because it has been undertaken by a weak people in self-defence.[73]

Gandhi regarded non-cooperation as "a movement of purification" which brings to the surface all our weaknesses as also the excesses of even our strong points.[74] The quality of non-cooperation, even more than of government, is indeed a reflection of the level of moral development and political maturity of a people. Non-cooperation derives its significance from the fact that it is

a programme of propaganda by reducing profession to practice, not one of compelling others to yield obedience by violence, direct or indirect. We must try patiently to convert our opponents. If we wish to evolve the spirit of democracy out of slavery, we must be scrupulously exact in our dealings with opponents. . . . We must concede to our opponents the freedom we claim for ourselves and for which we are fighting. The stoutest cooperationist will bend to the stern realities of practice if there is real response from the people.[75]

Thus Gandhi was prepared to recognize that non-cooperation was no painless panacea or authoritarian dogma. It is still easier to grasp his notion of civil disobedience as exemplified by individuals because there are clear and valuable historical precedents. It is far more difficult to think of similar instances of successful non-cooperation on a mass scale. He rightly regarded himself as a pioneer in the field of nonviolent non-cooperation. It is perhaps pardonable for a pioneer to indulge occasionally in the tendency to idealize his conception and to endow it with the transcendental aura of a religious vision.

I consider non-cooperation to be such a powerful and pure instrument, that, if it is enforced in an earnest spirit, it will be like seeking first the Kingdom of God and everything else following as a matter of course. People will have then realized their true power. They would have learnt the value of discipline, self-control, joint action, non-violence, organization and everything else that goes to make a nation great and good, and not merely great.[76]

Gandhi envisaged both civil disobedience and non-cooperation as nonviolent methods of resolving conflicts as well as peaceful devices for producing positive changes in social and political life. In either case, he was more concerned to affect prevailing attitudes and values than with obstructing particular policies. A failure to grasp this fact would force us to regard the doctrine of *satyagraha,* as some Marxists have done, merely as an extravagant rationalization of political expediency in the attainment of immediate ends. He clearly felt that his life was dedicated to the spread of the religious teaching of non-retaliation[77] by showing its relevance to the handling of political and social conflicts and to the constructive transformation of the political and social order. As early as 1919 he put the emphasis upon the basic values underlying his doctrine of *satyagraha.*

> *Satyagraha* is like a banyan tree with innumerable branches. Civil disobedience is one such branch. *Satya* [truth] and *ahimsa* [non-violence] together make the parent trunk from which all the innumerable branches shoot out. We have found by bitter experience that whilst in an atmosphere of lawlessness civil disobedience found ready acceptance, *satya* [truth] and *ahimsa* [non-violence], from which alone civil disobedience can worthily spring, have commanded little or no respect. Ours, then, is a Herculean task, but we may not shirk it. We must fearlessly spread the doctrine of *satya* and *ahimsa* and then, and not till then, shall we be able to undertake mass *satyagraha.*[78]

Gandhi recognized that if all of us regulated our lives by this "eternal law of *satya* and *ahimsa,*" there would be no occasion for civil or other resistance. Civil resistance, he said, comes into play when only a small body of men endeavor to follow *satya* in the face of opposition. He conceded that "it is difficult to know what is Truth, when to defend it to the point of civil resistance, and how to avoid error in the shape of violence in one's pursuit after Truth."[79] These difficulties are inherent in the application of the doctrine of *satyagraha,* but they did not undermine Gandhi's faith in the validity and applicability of the doctrine. Although he approached politics from the standpoint of the rebel rather than the ruler, he was prepared to look at *satyagraha,* though inadequately, from the governmental angle. When cross-examined by the Hunter Committee, he was asked what he would say, if he were a governor, to a movement started with the object of breaking laws. He answered:

> If I were in charge of the government and brought face to face with a body of men who, entirely in search of truth, were determined to seek redress from unjust laws without inflicting violence, I would welcome it and would consider that they were the best constitutionalists, and, as a Governor, I would take them on my side as advisers who would keep me on the right path.[80]

This is easier said than done, but no other answer is possible for a *satyagrahi* whose aim, by the very definition of *satyagraha,* is to convert rather than to coerce his opponents.

Although Gandhi sometimes formulated the doctrine of *satyagraha* in a typically individualistic fashion, he was fully aware that it was dependent in practice upon the sanction, not only of individual conscience (*satya*) and *ahimsa* but also of public opinion. "An awakened and intelligent public opinion is the most potent weapon of a *satyagrahi.*"[81] He must first mobilize public opinion against the evil which he is out to eradicate, by means of a wide and intensive agitation. When public opinion is sufficiently roused against a social abuse, "even the tallest will not dare to practise or openly lend support to it."[82] Gandhi refused to set up the *demos* as a demi-god and he could recognize no higher court of appeal than "the Court of conscience." And yet he was willing to see that the success of the *satyagrahi*'s efforts must necessarily depend not merely on the appeal to his own conscience but even more on the awakening of the slumbering conscience of a large number of people, and ultimately, the stifled conscience of those responsible for enacting or administering unjust laws and social abuses.

In its appeal to public opinion, to the prevailing or potential respect in society for *satya* and *ahimsa,* and to the moral sensitivity of those whose acts are being challenged, *satyagraha* differs from the methods of rational persuasion and violent action chiefly in its unique reliance upon *tapas* or self-suffering. Gandhi argued that experience has shown that mere appeal to the reason produces no effect upon those who have settled convictions. "The eyes of their understanding are opened not by argument, but by the suffering of the *satyagrahi*. The *satyagrahi* strives to reach the reason through the heart. The method of reaching the heart is to awaken public opinion. Public opinion, for which one cares, is a mightier force than gunpowder."[83] In his early years in South Africa, he began by relying heavily upon petitions and memoranda, legalistic arguments and appeals to expediency, using to the utmost his training as a lawyer and the example of Gokhale in the patient study of the facts. The conviction rapidly grew within him that things of fundamental importance to the people are not secured by reason alone, but have to be purchased with voluntary suffering.

> Suffering is the law of human beings; war is the law of the jungle. But suffering is infinitely more powerful than the law of the jungle for converting the opponent and opening his ears, which are otherwise shut, to the voice of reason. Nobody has probably drawn up more petitions or espoused more forlorn causes than I, and I have come to this fundamental conclusion that if you want something really important to be done, you must not merely satisfy the reason, you must move the heart also. The appeal of reason is more to the head, but the penetration of the heart comes from suffering. It opens up the inner understanding of man. Suffering is the badge of the human race, not the sword.[84]

In stressing the value of suffering and in distrusting mere reason, Gandhi was challenging, like Marx and Kierkegaard, the deeply cherished philosophy of political change that is based upon the central assumption of the eighteenth-century French Encyclopædists—the adequacy of appeals to reason—and the dominant belief of the nineteenth-century English utilitarians—the universal quest for happiness as the ultimate political criterion. It is hardly surprising, therefore, if Gandhi's faith in the religious and temporal value of suffering should seem to a few Westerners as an atavistic retrogression to so-called "Oriental" pessimism and masochism. In our own century appalling tortures and massive crimes have occurred which human reason could not comprehend, let alone combat. It could be contended that the utilitarian creed has done much to alleviate human misery but it has not resulted in greater freedom or fulfillment for most people, while it has made many too soft to endure the mental and physical suffering that nothing can wholly eliminate. This is not an argument for the total abdication of reason or the abandonment of all concern for human happiness. Gandhi wished for neither in advocating the doctrine of *satyagraha*. He elevated truth above happiness as the supreme end and criterion of political and social action and he valued nonviolence or love more than reason. But he also recognized that "the end to be sought is human happiness combined with full mental and moral growth. I use the adjective moral as synonymous with spiritual."[85]

Further, Gandhi wanted to employ reason before turning to *satyagraha* and even if it became necessary to resort to suffering, the purpose must remain to convert as well as convince his opponent.

> Since *satyagraha* is one of the most powerful methods of direct action, a *satyagrahi* exhausts all other means before he resorts to *satyagraha*. He will, therefore, constantly and continually approach the constituted authority, he will appeal to public opinion, educate public opinion, state his case calmly and coolly before everybody who wants to listen to him; and only after he has exhausted all these avenues will he resort to *satyagraha*.[86]

Also, in *satyagraha*, the cause as well as the means has to be just and clear.[87] If the doctrine requires suffering, this is for two reasons connected with the chief aim and an essential assumption of *satyagraha*. First of all, the *satyagrahi* seeks to convert his opponent by sheer force of character, by resigning himself to being excommunicated, debarred from privileges and deprived of his property, by attempting to bear his hardships cheerfully and to show active love toward his persecutors.[88] In trying to carry out his reform he does not wish to sacrifice others but he is eager to discipline and purify himself. Secondly, Gandhi assumed that three-fourths of the miseries and misunderstandings in the world would disappear if we were to step into the shoes of our adversaries or to think of them charitably. If we believe they are wrong, we can best show them this by our own voluntary suffering rather than by making them suffer.

> I have found that mere appeal to reason does not answer where
> prejudices are age-long and based on supposed religious author-
> ity. Reason has to be strengthened by suffering. . . . Therefore,
> there must be no trace of compulsion in our acts. We must not be
> impatient, and we must have an undying faith in the means we
> are adopting.[89]

Satyagraha may seem to ask too much of human nature in the eyes
of those who reject its metaphysical presuppositions and unprovable assumptions. But if it is to be used only where reason and
persuasion fail, what alternative to *satyagraha* is left besides the
path of violence which cannot succeed against greater violence and,
if successful, leaves a trail of bitterness behind; or besides the in-
activity of despair or the shame of acquiescence in an acknowledged evil? The only alternative to voluntary self-suffering under
such conditions is to inflict suffering upon one's opponent or to do
nothing about the sufferings of those who are weaker than ourselves. One may rule out *satyagraha* as beyond one's own capacities or no better than the admittedly unpleasant alternatives, but
who can say in advance that *satyagraha,* by those capable of it,
would be wholly useless when it has been so little tried? The doctrine of *satyagraha* may savor of religious dogmatism but to dismiss it would also be an expression of spiritual or political dogmatism.

The concept of *tapas,* upon which the doctrine of *satyagraha* is
based, is religious rather than political, and those who object to
satyagraha as unworthy of consideration are often merely expressing their distaste for introducing religious notions into politics.
For Gandhi this was a religious as well as a political necessity.
He believed that the best and most lasting self-defence is self-purification.

> When our ancestors saw affliction surrounding them, they went in
> for *tapasya*—purification. . . . It will be time to fight, when we
> have done enough *tapasya.* . . . Have we even done willing pen-
> ance for the sin of untouchability, let alone the personal purity of
> individuals? Are our religious preceptors all that they should be?
> We are beating the air whilst we simply concentrate our attention
> upon picking holes in . . . the conduct [of others].[90]

The suffering and self-criticism of the *satyagrahi* must not be mistaken for abject surrender. "The surrender advised by me is not of honour but of earthly goods."[91] Gandhi also believed that no country has ever risen without being purified through the fire of suffering.[92] The purer the suffering, the greater is the progress. "Hence did the sacrifice of Jesus suffice to free a sorrowing world. . . . Thus did the sufferings of a Harischandra suffice to re-establish the kingdom of truth."[93]

Satyagraha is thus ultimately "the argument of suffering." It assumes that "the hardest heart and grossest ignorance must disappear before the rising sun of suffering without anger and without malice."[94] Gandhi went so far as to believe that suffering will melt the stoniest heart of the coldest fanatic;[95] if it did not, he felt we must take it that the suffering was not sufficiently pure or intense. Even if *tapas* or self-suffering does not make a direct appeal to the soul of the oppressor, it could arouse public opinion, but if it does not do even that, it could at least purify the sufferer. Further, true suffering "brings its own joy which surpasses all other joys."[96] It is, of course, possible to deny that suffering necessarily purifies instead of embittering the *satyagrahi,* or that it could be genuine and still induce a surpassing joy. The fact of the matter is that this notion of *tapas* is tied up with metaphysical assumptions—the theory of *Karma* which holds that present suffering would result in future gain in another life in a just universe, and the idea that self-inflicted suffering or *tapas* has a magical efficacy. But even those who do not share these assumptions could agree with Hartmann that if with his suffering a man purchases the highest values, the thought of a will to suffer has nothing absurd in it, and whoever assumes great burdens must have it. It is nothing unusual for a man to want to suffer for the sake of a high goal or an ennobling idea or for the sake of communal life. As Gandhi put it, "Whilst we must try always to avoid occasions for needless suffering, we must ever be ready for them. Somehow or other, those who will walk along the right path cannot avoid suffering notwithstanding the attempt to avoid it. It is the privilege of the patriot, the reformer and, still greater, of the *satyagrahi.*"[97]

It would be both dishonest and unfair to Gandhi to ignore the fact that in the last analysis, the doctrine of *satyagraha* rests upon a religious and metaphysical belief. As early as 1909 Gandhi pointed out that the one condition of a successful use of *satyagraha* was a recognition of the soul, as apart from the body, and its permanent and superior nature, and this recognition must amount to a living faith and not a mere intellectual grasp.[98] Again, in 1931 Gandhi declared:

> It is a fundamental principle of *satyagraha* that the tyrant, whom the *satyagrahi* seeks to resist, has power over his body and material possessions, but he can have no power over the soul. The soul can remain unconquered and unconquerable even when the body is imprisoned. The whole science of *satyagraha* was born from a knowledge of this fundamental truth.[99]

Further, according to the "science of *satyagraha*," the greater the repression and lawlessness on the part of authority, the greater should be the suffering courted by the victims. "Success is the certain result of suffering of the extremest character voluntarily undergone."[100] But although Gandhi tried to translate the religious faith underlying the doctrine of *satyagraha* into the verifiable laws of a "science," he conceded as late as 1939, "I have no set theory to go by. I have not worked out the science of *satyagraha* in its entirety. I am still groping."[101] Six months earlier, he had similarly confessed:

> I am myself daily growing in the knowledge of *satyagraha*. I have no text-book to consult in time of need, not even the *Gita* which I have called my dictionary. *Satyagraha*, as conceived by me, is a science in the making. It may be that what I claim to be a science may prove to be no science at all, and may well prove to be the musings and doings of a fool, if not a mad man. It may be that what is true in *satyagraha* is as ancient as the hills.[102]

Having, as Gandhi did, inflated *satyagraha* to the status of a religion and of a science, which it assumed for Gandhi, can we now deflate it to its minimal political assumption? In its least demanding formulation, the doctrine merely asserts the inherent right to civil resistance of citizens against unjust laws, or the universal possibility of nonviolent non-cooperation by small or large groups in relation to a corrupt or tyrannical regime or system. But even as a purely political doctrine, it does more than this. It holds that more can be gained—more quickly and more certainly—by a resort to *satyagraha* than by the pursuit of political power, by social pressure and political education than by mere legislation.

Legislation in advance of public opinion has often been demonstrated to be futile. We have everywhere emphasized the necessity of carrying on the constructive activities as being the means of attaining *swaraj* (real self-rule). . . . Public opinion . . . is only now becoming a vital force and developing the real sanction which is *satyagraha*.[103]

11

THE SCOPE AND SIGNIFICANCE OF *SATYAGRAHA*

There is quite another order of means, of which our Western civilization is hardly aware, and which offers the human mind an infinite field of discovery—the spiritual means systematically applied to the temporal realm, a striking example of which has been Gandhi's satyagraha. *I should like to call them "means of spiritual warfare." . . . There are two different orders of means of warfare (taken in the widest sense of the word), as there are two kinds of fortitude and courage, the courage that attacks and the courage that endures, the force of coercion or aggression and the force of patience, the force that inflicts suffering on others and the force that endures suffering inflicted on oneself. There you have two different keyboards that stretch along the two sides of our human nature, though the sounds they give are constantly intermingled: opposing evil through attack and coercion—a way which, at the last extremity, leads to the shedding, if need be, of the blood of others; and opposing evil through suffering and enduring—a way which, at the last extremity, leads to the sacrifice of one's own life. To the second keyboard the means of spiritual warfare belong . . . while being the most difficult, they are also by nature the most powerful means. . . . Whether they follow the method of Gandhi or some method yet to be invented, men who attach importance to spiritual values are likely to be led willy-nilly to a solution along these lines.*

JACQUES MARITAIN

The doctrine of *satyagraha* was conceived by Gandhi as an extension of the rule of domestic life into the political. He held that family disputes and differences are generally settled according to the "Law of Love." The injured member has so much regard for the others that he suffers injury for the sake of his principles without retaliating and without anger against those who differ from him. As repression of anger and self-suffering are difficult processes, he does not dignify trifles into principles, but in all non-essentials readily agrees with the rest of the family and thus contrives to gain the maximum of peace for himself without disturbing that of others. Thus, his action, whether he resists or resigns, is always calculated to promote the common welfare of his family:

> It is this Law of Love which, silently but surely, governs the family for the most part throughout the civilized world. I feel that nations cannot be one in reality, nor can their activities be conducive to the common good of the whole humanity, unless there is this definition and acceptance of the law of the family in national and international affairs, in other words, on the political platform. Nations can be called civilized only to the extent that they obey this law.[1]

This rule of domestic life or the Law of Love may require self-suffering or some form of non-cooperation. If the father does an injustice it is the duty of his children to leave the parental roof. Similarly, argued Gandhi, if the headmaster of a school conducts his institution on an immoral basis, the pupils must leave the school. If the chairman of a corporation is corrupt, the members must wash their hands clean of his corruption by withdrawing from it. Even so, if a government does grave injustice, the subjects must withdraw cooperation wholly or partially, but sufficiently to wean the ruler from his wickedness.

As early as 1919 Gandhi regarded "the Law of *Satyagraha*"[2]—the Law of Love—as an eternal principle, although the principles of *satyagraha* constitute a gradual evolution.[3] Once its simple basic principles—adherence to truth and insistence upon it by self-suffering—are understood, anybody can practice it. "It is as difficult or as easy to practice as any other virtue,"[4] and it is not necessary for its practice that everyone should understand the entire philosophy of *satyagraha*. In 1914 he described it as a "force" that may be used by individuals as well as by communities, in political as in domestic affairs. "Its universal applicability is a demonstration of its permanence and invincibility. It can be used alike by men, women and children."[5] The reason why it is universally applicable is that it is independent of pecuniary or other material assistance.[6] Gandhi stressed the universal scope of *satyagraha* until he died. In 1946 he still described it as a law of universal application. "Beginning with the family, its use can be extended to every other circle."[7]

When Gandhi spoke about the universality of the scope of *satyagraha,* he combined two completely separate notions. He believed that *satyagraha* is a law which all men must accept—acceptance involving no more than a moral preference for nonviolence—and also that it is a force which is universally present in nature and in society. It would be difficult to challenge the latter notion as he claimed that this force is non-physical and "works silently and apparently slowly."[8] A similar confusion or combination of two quite different senses of "law"—as a moral precept and as an operative force or process in nature—may be detected in some thinkers in the West who employed the concept of Natural Law. What Gandhi meant by calling this divine force in nature (expressed in man as soul-force) universal is merely that it "necessarily makes no distinction between kinsmen and strangers, young and old, man and woman, friend and foe."[9] There is also a third sense closely connected with the second, in which Gandhi regarded *satyagraha* as universal, and this is the easiest to grasp as well as the most useful way of regarding it. In this sense, he meant simply that it is an effective method of action, an instrument which he regarded as universally applicable in society. When he called *satyagraha* a universal law, he meant that "it is a universal principle of universal application."[10] The former two senses are important to him insofar as he wanted to show that this instrument is based upon an ethical principle or precept which all men must accept, and that it is invariably bound to be effective if soul-force is properly employed. It is easier to make the notion of the universal scope of *satyagraha* in society intelligible when we remember Gandhi's stress on the educative role of *satyagraha*. "*Satyagraha* is a process of educating public opinion, such that it covers all the elements of society and, in the end, makes itself irresistible. Violence interrupts the process and prolongs the real revolution of the whole structure."[11]

Although Gandhi talked about the universal scope of *satyagraha,* he also laid down at different times stringent conditions and prerequisites for the application of *satyagraha*. "Every measure carries with it conditions for its adoption. *Satyagraha* is no exception."[12] The prerequisites, conditions and rules may be listed as follows.

First of all, there can be no *satyagraha* in an unjust cause, as it is, by definition, a commitment to upholding truth. Also, Gandhi held the belief that it is only if the cause is really seen to be just that *satyagraha* would be legitimate, and further, those espousing the cause will be determined, and capable of fighting and suffering to the end.[13]

Secondly, *satyagraha,* by definition, excludes the use of violence in any shape or form, whether in thought, speech or deed.[14] "*Satyagraha* demands absolute non-violence."[15] Gandhi said that his experience had taught him that civility is the most difficult part of *satyagraha*[16]—not merely outward gentleness and courtesy of speech, but an inward gentleness and genuine desire to do the opponent good and wish him well. There must be no vilification of an opponent, but this does not mean there should not be a truthful characterization of his acts. There should be no hostility to persons, but only to acts when they are subversive of morals or the good of society.[17] There should be no intention to embarrass the wrongdoer.[18]

Thirdly, *satyagraha* presupposes a reasoned and willing obedience to the laws of the State, i.e., a compliance which is free and voluntary and fearless (not motivated by the fear of punishment). It is only in circumstances in which people are by nature fearless and are lovers of liberty that *satyagraha* is applicable. (This condition can be generalized so as to refer to compliance not merely with State laws but also with the restraints imposed by any association in which *satyagraha* is offered.) A precondition of *satyagraha* is tolerance—the toleration of many laws even where they are inconvenient. It is only when people have proved their active loyalty by obeying or tolerating the many laws of the State which are not actually immoral that they have earned the right to offer *satyagraha* against intolerable, immoral laws.[19]

Fourthly, *satyagraha* presupposes the capacity and willingness to suffer. He who has not the capacity of suffering, of sacrificing his property, of undergoing the "fiery ordeal," should not attempt *satyagraha*. A whole people cannot be regarded as ready for *satyagraha* until not only a few individuals, but a large number, have put in initial preparation.[20]

Fifthly, "discipline is obligatory." Individuals must engage in constructive social work in order to develop the required qualities.[21] No *satyagraha* by the masses is possible unless the crowd can behave as disciplined soldiers. In order to offer *satyagraha* individuals must be able to remain calm and unperturbed under fierce fire of provocation.[22] *Satyagraha* requires the cool courage that comes from discipline and training in voluntary obedience.[23]

Sixthly, *satyagraha* requires the unobtrusive humility of those whose solid actions are allowed to speak for their creed and whose strength lies in their reliance upon the correctness of their position.[24]

Seventhly, *satyagraha* cannot be resorted to for personal gain but only for the good of others. It can be resorted to only under wise guidance or after prolonged discipline.[25]

In short, "a *satyagraha* struggle is impossible without capital in the shape of character."[26] It is not a movement of "brag, bluster or bluff."

> It is a test of our sincerity. It requires solid and silent self-sacrifice. It challenges our honesty and our capacity for national work. It is a movement that aims at translating ideas into action. And the more we do, the more we find that much more must be done than we had expected. And this thought of our imperfection must make us humble.[27]

It is obvious from all this that most movements today that employ methods of passive resistance and non-cooperation cannot be commended in terms of the doctrine of *satyagraha,* though it is often invoked together with the halo around the name of Gandhi. The causes espoused by such movements may be worthy in their way and the sincere good intentions of their leaders and followers may also be unquestionable, but good causes and good intentions are hardly enough to exemplify the spirit of *satyagraha.* Gandhi certainly had no monopoly over the methods of *satyagraha,* nor can it be claimed that all the movements he launched fulfilled the strict conditions he laid down. He himself made neither claim. He was experimenting all the time with himself and in different spheres of activity, but he did have a clear and exalted vision of the moral implications and practical difficulties of the application of the doctrine of *satyagraha.*

Gandhi not merely indicated the prerequisites and conditions for the application of *satyagraha,* but also set down rules for the behavior of *satyagrahi*s during the campaign and inside prison. All these rules need not be repeated here, especially as some of them were devised in the context of particular campaigns he launched in Indian conditions. It would be useful, however, to summarize these rules.[28] A *satyagrahi* will harbor no anger but will suffer the anger of the opponent, put up with assaults but never retaliate nor submit out of fear to orders given in anger. He will voluntarily submit to arrest and not resist the removal of his property by the authorities, but he will refuse to surrender property in his possession as a trustee even at the risk of injury or death. He will never swear or curse, or insult his opponent and he will seek to protect officials from the insult or attack of his companions. He will behave courteously toward prison officials but refuse to submit to humiliating and unconventional orders. He will not make distinctions between an ordinary prisoner and himself, or regard himself as superior in any way to the rest, or ask for special favors, or fast to obtain conveniences. He will act with the most scrupulous honesty, cooperate with prison officials, set an example to co-prisoners, and perform his allotted tasks. During the campaign he will joyfully obey the orders issued by the chosen leader of the corps and, if they appear insulting or foolish, he will comply while also appealing to higher authority. He must determine the fitness of the corps before joining, then submit to its discipline however irksome, and if the sum total of the energy of the corps seems to be improper or immoral he has a right to sever his connection but not to commit a breach of discipline.

Gandhi gave much thought to these rules for *satyagrahi*s, using

his wartime as well as his *ashram* experiences, because of his concern with mass *satyagraha*. He was cautious in advising mass *satyagraha* anywhere because training and discipline were inadequate.[29]
But he did exercise himself over the course of discipline, including
physical training, needed for the formation of a non-violent army
or a *satyagraha sangha*.[30] The basis of the training must be a mass
constructive program of social work—"maximum of work and minimum of speech must be your motto."[31] It is true that he regarded
mass civil disobedience as something that must be spontaneous
and not manufactured, but he believed that there will be no mass
response where the ground has not been previously tilled, manured
and watered. The greatest precaution has to be taken everywhere
against an outbreak of violence.[32] The plan of mass civil disobedience must be so conceived as to "neutralize and ultimately entirely to displace violence and enthrone non-violence in its stead, to
replace hatred by love, to replace strife by concord."[33] It is not
meetings and demonstrations that would give victory but "quiet
suffering."[34] Gandhi believed that there is no *prima facie* reason
why the masses, if trained, should be incapable of showing the
discipline which in organized warfare a fighting force normally
does.[35]

Even in mass *satyagraha* "it is never the numbers that count; it
is always the quality, more so when the forces of violence are uppermost."[36] Not only is mere protestation by the leaders of their
opinion not enough, but in matters of vital importance they must
act contrary to the popular consensus if it does not commend
itself to their reason. The *satyagraha* leader is useless when he acts
against the prompting of his own conscience, surrounded as he
must be by people holding all kinds of views.[37] Gandhi thought that
the quickest and the largest response in mass *satyagraha* would be
in the matter of suspension of payment of taxes, but this should not
be advised until the masses (especially the peasantry) were trained
to understand the reason for civil non-payment and were prepared
for the confiscation of their holdings.[38]

In the last analysis, complete mass *satyagraha* is recognized by
Gandhi to be tantamount to "rebellion without the element of violence in it."[39] He went so far as to say that when a body of men
disown the State under which they have hitherto lived, they have

nearly established their own government—nearly, for they do not go to the point of using force when they are resisted by the State. "Their business, as of the individual, is to be locked up or shot by the State, unless it recognizes their separate existence, in other words, bows to their will."[40] This kind of extreme measure is only justified, said Gandhi, "as the most powerful expression of . . . anguish and an eloquent protest against the continuance of an evil State."[41] But even under such conditions there is grave risk in mass *satyagraha*, the risk that the remedy may prove worse than the disease. Gandhi was aware of this danger in his doctrine—if not always in his conduct as a politician—and hence his preference for *satyagraha* by the individual, or by a highly trained few, to mass *satyagraha*.

> A body of civil resisters is, therefore, like an army subject to all the discipline of a soldier, only harder because of want of excitement of an ordinary soldier's life. And as a civil resistance army is or ought to be free from passion because free from the spirit of retaliation, it requires the fewest number of soldiers. Indeed one PERFECT civil resister is enough to win the battle of Right against Wrong.[42]

Gandhi regarded the doctrine of *satyagraha* as universal in scope, yet made the conditions for its application so stringent, and showed such caution in envisaging mass *satyagraha*, that serious doubts may be raised about the practical applicability, despite the theoretical universifiability, of his doctrine. As a thinker he was tempted to idealize his concept of *satyagraha* to such an extent that it seems to become empty of practical content and relevance. As a politician he was inclined to emphasize the ease of application of his demanding doctrine to a degree that made him vulnerable to the charge of *naïveté* in the eyes of constitutionalists and rulers, as well as to the charge of self-deception and dishonesty in the eyes of terrorists and communists who pinned their faith on violent revolution. He was aware of this dilemma in practice if not in theory, but the best defense that could be offered on behalf of the relevance of his doctrine is that he both considered and employed a wide variety of methods. The greater the range of devices that may be employed in *satyagraha* (individual or collective) the easier it is to protect the purity of the doctrine, ensure its practical relevance and recognize its difficulties as well as its possibilities. The onus is thus put, as he intended and stressed, on those who wish to advocate or employ a specific technique of *satyagraha* in a particular context in time and space.

The methods of *satyagraha* may be broadly classified into four categories: purificatory, penitential devices; forms of non-cooperation; methods of civil disobedience; the Constructive Programme. All of these may be employed by individuals, groups or mass movements in the political arena and in different spheres of social life. The division is mainly for conceptual clarity and convenience of presentation. There is an inevitable overlap, especially in practice but even in theory, between these four categories. It is also not possible, given the assumptions underlying Gandhi's doctrine of *satyagraha,* to order these categories or the devices grouped under them, in terms of their importance or intensity or purity or effectiveness. What is common to all of them is that they are intended, in Gandhi's doctrine, to uphold *satya* (only in the sense of relative truth), the dictates of individual conscience concerning justice and morality in the relations between men and between groups, to exemplify *ahimsa* (adopted as a creed or a policy, aiming at the conversion and excluding the coercion of others) and to involve *tapas* (in the narrower sense of penance or in the broader sense of "self-suffering").

The different methods available are legitimized by the concept of *satya*, moralized by the application of *ahimsa* and spiritualized by the performance of *tapas*. The purity of a particular method in a specific context will be determined by the extent of rightness of the purpose to which it is put, the degree and genuineness of non-violence and non-retaliation displayed and the intensity of inconvenience and suffering resulting to the user as well as the amount of penance undergone (determined by the unselfishness of his motive). I see no way of measuring any of these factors, in view of the strong subjective elements in the concepts of *satya, ahimsa* and *tapas*. In order to come to rough-and-ready judgments regarding the use of any method in a given situation, we must clearly consider the character and position of the *satyagrahi* and his opponent or tormentor, the facts of the case and the practical results achieved. In many ways, the best judge of the use of a particular device in a concrete situation is the *satyagrahi* himself, much depending upon his intelligence, honesty and self-examination. It would certainly be wrong to judge entirely on utilitarian grounds, on the practical results achieved. The doctrine of *satyagraha* is essentially dependent on non-utilitarian assumptions, and yet it will be tempting (even for the *satyagrahi*) to adopt a *post hoc* utilitarian criterion of judgment.

Under the first head of purificatory, penitential devices, we may include pledges, prayers and fasts. The pledge is a solemn public declaration of one or more *satyagrahis* that he or they will abstain from, or perform, certain acts to combat untruth (in themselves or in others) or recognized injustices. The religious notion of prayer is involved in the invocation of "soul-force" or of external spiritual agencies as an act of purification and self-surrender. This notion may be secularized so as to mean merely the avowed determination to discover the general will or the common good in a concrete context as a result of quiet contemplation or solitary reflection and patient self-examination. A pledge could take the form of a prayer, and prayer could precede the taking of a pledge. A third device could be a purificatory fast of short duration for the purpose of atonement or introspective meditation over a specific issue. These three devices could be used by those in authority to secure social compliance for a worthy end or to reverse an undesirable social trend. They could also be used against the acts of authority by prominent leaders or ordinary citizens whose consciences are outraged.

In the second category of modes of non-cooperation, we could include *hartal*, boycott, strikes, fasting unto death, and *hijrat*. *Hartal* is a traditional form of protest in India, a temporary strike with advance notice as to its duration, the closing down of shops and businesses and sometimes the halting of the work of administration. This usually lasts for a single day in India, but it is prolonged if the cause is regarded as sufficiently serious or if there is a strong public grievance. Although *hartal* is a minor measure, it makes sense only if all other forms of protest are unavailable, ineffective or too heavy-handed in relation to the issue causing concern. *Hartal* was once described by Gandhi as designed to strike the imagination of the people and the government; it means "a general cessation throughout the country."[43] It has to be entirely voluntary, employing persuasion and propaganda, conducting peaceful marches and processions, excluding physical force. The police may intervene to keep order but they must act with proper restraint and forbearance.

The boycott of public institutions (government schools and colleges and law courts) is intended to protest against or even paralyze an unjust or iniquitous political system. It may also be employed against a particular institution indulging in corrupt or unfairly discriminatory practices. In the former case, "suspension does not mean stagnation"[44]—for example, lawyers who suspend practice must improvise arbitration boards to settle disputes quickly and cheaply. In both cases, alternatives must be devised where they do not already exist. Boycott may be economic, intended to keep out foreign goods where their importation (without popular consent) results in unemployment or retards internal industries, or causes some moral principle to be violated. Gandhi held that a nonviolent boycott is legitimate when we are required to compromise with what we believe to be an untruth, but he felt that it would be a dangerous thing if we were to adopt *social* boycott when there are differences of opinion.

Social boycott is an age-old institution. . . . It is the one terrible sanction exercised with great effect. . . . It answered when every village was a self-contained unit, and the occasions of recalcitrancy were rare. But when opinion is divided, as it is today, on the merits of non-cooperation, when its new application is having a trial, a summary use of social boycott in order to bend a minority to the will of the majority is a species of unpardonable violence. . . . Moreover, social boycott to be admissible in a campaign of non-violence must never savour of inhumanity. It must be civilized. It must cause pain to the party using it, if it causes inconvenience to its object. . . . Impatience and intolerance will surely kill this great religious movement. We may not make people pure by compulsion. Much less may we compel them by violence to respect our opinion. It is utterly against the spirit of democracy we want to cultivate. . . . But the alternative to social boycott is certainly not social intercourse. . . . But we dare not deny social service . . . it would be wisdom to err on the right side and to exercise the weapon even in the limited sense . . . on rare and well-defined occasions.[45]

Gandhi pointed out that to declare a strike to redress a wrong is to cease to take part in the wrong and thus leave the wrong-doer to his own resources, i.e., enable him to see the folly of continuing the wrong. He laid down three maxims for the guidance of all strike leaders. There should be no strike without a real grievance; there should be no strike if the persons concerned are unable to support themselves out of their own savings or by engaging in some temporary occupation such as spinning and weaving; strikers must fix an unalterable minimum demand and declare it before embarking upon their strike. There is no room in a civil strike for violence in the shape of intimidation, incendiarism or otherwise. During the strike of the Ahmedabad mill-workers in 1918 Gandhi stressed that there should be no breach of the peace and no pressure of any sort upon those who returned to work, and that the convinced strikers should remain firm however long the strike might continue. He also fasted to bring pressure on the mill-owners but then went on in penance when he felt that such pressure was a form of violence on his part, while the strike was not. In later years Gandhi became worried that in strikes, as in boycotts, the danger of creating bitterness is real, and turned to the more positive notion of trusteeship.[46]

Gandhi regarded fasting as a great institution in Hinduism, provided it is undertaken entirely voluntarily and also does not have a trace of coercion over others. Fasting unto death is, however, more a Gandhian than a traditional device. "Sacrifice of self even unto death is the final weapon in the hands of a non-violent person. It is not given to man to do more."[47] Gandhi embarked upon a fast unto death as a method of self-purification and also of vicarious atonement for the sin of untouchability (and its entrenchment in separate electorates), and for the crimes of communal bloodshed on the eve of his assassination. Although he regarded fasting as a potent weapon in the armory of *satyagraha,* "a fiery weapon," a device of last resort, it may be seriously questioned as a method that seems peculiarly coercive to those who are required to act in order to save a human life. Whatever be the view we take of Gandhi's own fasts with their strong religious overtones, it could be ruled out as a method that can hardly be repeated by others without violating the spirit of *satyagraha*, at least in the context of everyday politics and existing societies.

Hijrat, voluntary migration or temporary withdrawal out of the boundaries of a State, was advocated by Gandhi to the Bardoli peasants in 1928 but by 1931 he came to think that this traditional device of despairing protest is not a necessary part of the purest form of *satyagraha*. It has been adopted usefully by some of the Doukhobors, by Hungarian and Tibetan refugees, but it is misleading to call it a method of *satyagraha* except in the most literal sense and even then only if it is completely voluntary (as in the case of the Dalai Lama).

In the third category of methods of civil disobedience we have picketing, marches, non-payment of taxes and deliberate defiance of a specific law. The first two need no elaboration and the last has been already considered in the account of Gandhi's view of civil disobedience. Only one further point need be mentioned here—his puzzling remark in 1939 that when civil disobedience results in an accentuation of repression of the people, its suspension would itself become *satyagraha* in its ideal form.[48] This is presumably because the admission of error and the reduction of violence are at the core of the doctrine of *satyagraha*. The non-payment of fines, rents and taxes is one of the best known devices employed by passive resisters and it was commended by Thoreau. Gandhi himself urged in 1922 the "greatest caution before embarking upon the dangerous adventure."[49] He thought that this device, though one of the quickest methods of overthrowing a government, would be an act of unpardonable madness without the necessary discipline which is extremely difficult to achieve among the masses. "Instead of leading to *swaraj* (freedom) it will lead to no-*raj* (anarchy)."[50] The readiness to resort to it is a "fatal temptation."

In regard to the second and third categories of methods, Gandhi entered into so many qualifications and reservations that we are entitled to assume his awareness of the negative, unreliable and limiting nature of all these familiar modes of *satyagraha*. It was especially in regard to the simplest, readily comprehensible and applicable device—such as strikes and boycott, picketing and non-payment of taxes—that he entertained the greatest caution and laid down the strictest conditions. His difficulty lay in that he was advocating *satyagraha* in conditions in which not only was *tapas* not involved, but in which *satya* and *ahimsa* had not become the prime movers even among a few, let alone a large number of, citizens. He was convinced that in a radically reformed society, founded upon the general acceptance and observance of *satya* and *ahimsa*, the philosophy and varieties of *satyagraha* would become as integrated into social and political activity as those of constitutional liberalism are in a mature democratic society. At the same time he continued to experiment, to correct and to improve his applications and his formulations of the philosophy of *satyagraha*, even amid the grave limitations of a poor, illiterate, fatalistic and enslaved society.

By the late twenties, however, Gandhi came to stress in the Constructive Programme the positive role, and the most novel mode, of *satyagraha*. As early as 1925, soon after a spate of essays on different aspects of *satyagraha* appeared in *Young India*, he stressed the need for *satyagrahi*s to engage in silent, active, constructive work of reform and social service.[51] In 1928 he pointed out that votaries of *satyagraha* must store up the necessary non-violent energy that could set free an irresistible force in society, that "they will not become a non-violent organization unless they undergo a process of what may be called continuous corporate cleansing. This they can only do by engaging in carrying out a well thought out constructive programme requiring combined effort and promoting the common good."[52] He later pointed out that all this constructive work should be "for its own sake. And yet be sure that it will develop the quality required for non-violent responsible government."[53] He felt that the energy spent in gaining political power means so much loss of energy required for urgent social reforms. In fact, the capacity to take political power will increase in "exact proportion" to the ability to achieve success in the constructive effort. "That is to me the substance of political power. Actual taking over of the government machinery is but a shadow, an emblem."[54] It is only through such a Constructive Programme that a system of nonviolent self-rule could emerge, that a new social order could be built.

In 1941 Gandhi wrote a pamphlet on the Constructive Programme, stressing in the Indian context the need for working toward communal unity, the removal of untouchability, a program of adult education and village improvement, peasant uplift and the development of nonviolent labor unions, economic and social equality, decentralized economic production and distribution through the promotion of cottage and small-scale industries, and the abolition of various social evils. He pointed out that, whereas civil disobedience could be most effective in the redress of local wrongs or in the arousing of local consciousness or conscience, it could never be directed for a general cause such as is possible with the Constructive Programme. Also, the "handling of civil disobedience without the Constructive Programme will be like a paralyzed hand attempting to lift a spoon."[55] This would imply that civil disobedience would be ineffective in a communist society unless it were employed by those very cadres which engage in constructive, social work. Civil disobedience is itself an aid to constructive effort, and a full substitute for armed revolt, but at the same time the best training for proper civil disobedience is through the Constructive Programme. Finally, three days before his assassination Gandhi declared that political freedom would not be meaningful to the individual citizen without the attainment of economic, social and moral freedom. "These freedoms are harder than the political, if only because they are constructive, less exciting and not spectacular. All-embracing constructive work evokes the energy of all the units of the millions."[56]

Altogether, Gandhi elaborated and employed a wide range of methods, from the most negative and limited to the most positive and comprehensive, in his various campaigns of *satyagraha*. It is not possible or necessary here to consider the different occasions on which he employed diverse devices of *satyagraha*. He gave much thought to the tactics as well as the modes of *satyagraha*.

In a *satyagraha* campaign the mode of fight and the choice of tactics, e.g., whether to advance or retreat, offer civil resistance or organize non-violent strength through constructive work and purely selfless humanitarian service are determined according to the exigencies of the situation. A *satyagrahi* must carry out whatever plan is laid out for him with a cool determination giving way to neither excitement nor depression.[57]

He also concluded from his early experience that every good movement passes through five stages: indifference, ridicule, abuse, repression and respect. He thought that every movement that survives repression, mild or severe, invariably commands respect "which is another name for success."[58]

Gandhi referred to a basic and distinctive feature of the application of *satyagraha*, what he called the Law of Progression.

> My experience has taught me that a Law of Progression applies to every righteous struggle. But, in the case of *satyagraha* the law amounts to an axiom. As the Ganga advances, other streams flow into it, and hence at the mouth it grows so wide that neither bank is to be seen and a person sailing upon the river cannot make out where the river ends and the sea begins. So also as a *satyagraha* struggle progresses onward, many another element helps to swell its current, and there is a constant growth in the results to which it leads. This is really inevitable, and is bound up with the first principles of *satyagraha*. For, in *satyagraha,* the minimum is also the maximum, and as it is the irreducible minimum, there is no question of retreat, and the only movement possible is an advance. In other struggles, even when they are righteous, the demand is first pitched a little higher so as to admit of future reduction, and hence the Law of Progression does not apply to all of them without exception. . . . The Ganga does not leave its course in search of tributaries. Even so does the *satyagrahi* not leave his path which is sharp as the sword's edge. But as the tributaries spontaneously join the Ganga as it advances, so it is with the river that is *satyagraha*.[59]

Clearly, *satyagraha* radically differs from the process of compromise and negotiation, as normally understood. Gandhi's antagonists found this to their cost and to his amazement—Smuts in South Africa over the Indian question,[60] Lord Pethick-Lawrence in India over the Cabinet Mission proposals,[61] Lord Mountbatten and Nehru over the issue of partition.[62] While bargaining is regarded as the very stuff of politics, in which expediency may combine with a strong sense of duty, the *satyagrahi*, considering politics to be a matter of principle and of conscience, is willing to compromise in regard to details and self-interest but is adamant and increasingly insistent when he feels that "eternal principles" and his individual conscience are at stake. The difficulty between the *satyagrahi* and the conventional politician is that on the former's, but not on the latter's, premises, it is both logical and inevitable that a battle for strictly limited objectives should grow into a battle for wider objectives. Like Lord Pethick-Lawrence, we could also desist from concluding that this difficulty is due to the fault of either party or of either conception of politics. The uncompromising radical can be tiresome especially if he elevates what generally seems to be a concrete dispute to the level of abstract principles, or if his preoccupation with his own conscience makes him insensitive to the sense of duty of other people and their own anxiety to come to a settlement. On the other hand, the pragmatist and gradualist can be intolerable when they reduce a grave matter of moral import, involving basic human needs and concerns, to the level of purely expedient or formal solutions.

It is, however, clear that the application of *satyagraha*, despite the universality of scope claimed for it, is no simple matter. Individual instances of *satyagraha* could be accommodated within a stable political system and a settled social order founded chiefly upon a liberal, democratic faith in compromise, bargaining and negotiation. Some techniques will be more awkward than others, some *satyagrahi*s and negotiators more tiresome than others, some occasions for *satyagraha* or its repression more dubious than others. It is not possible to pronounce generally on the legitimacy or efficacy of *satyagraha* in existing political systems; legitimacy may seem to be stronger under authoritarian regimes or in undemocratic systems and efficacy may seem to be greater under governments more or less sensitive to public opinion and to individual freedom or in societies which are tolerant in regard to all nonviolent methods of political action. But one can judge the merits of a method of *satyagraha* in a concrete context only. It is not impossible, but it is difficult, to envisage a political system and a society in which the doctrine of *satyagraha* is generally adopted and carefully applied. As long as human nature remains as unreliable as we now think it to be, such a polity and society may seem to us to be peculiarly unstable, anarchic and explosive. If, on the other hand, we are prepared to think that *satya* and *ahimsa* could be deeply instilled into the members of small communities, *satya-*

graha may be safe to employ, but the occasions for its use few and far between.

THE LIMITS AND ABUSE OF *SATYAGRAHA*

In expounding the doctrine of *satyagraha* Gandhi pointed to the dangers inherent in its different branches. In explaining its scope and application he also laid down stringent conditions and rules. In describing its various devices he stressed the need for caution, vigilance and self-criticism in their use. As a result of his enormous experience of the working of *satyagraha* in many campaigns he launched, and in his minor uses of it in his personal relations and in his ashrams, Gandhi came to see the abuses of the doctrine, his own mistakes in its application and the limits to its use. It is necessary to indicate the limits and some of the abuses of *satyagraha* and then to consider the place of *satyagraha* in a democracy. Owing to the frequent use and abuse of the doctrine and of some of its methods in India since Gandhi's death, there has been much controversy both among Gandhians and others as to the legitimacy of *satyagraha* in a free, democratic country. Similarly in the West, doubts have been expressed, and strong criticisms voiced, regarding the rightness of using the methods of *satyagraha* in a society in which other avenues of protest are available.

In his *Satyagraha in South Africa*, published in 1928, Gandhi introduced the notion of *duragraha* or the persistence in wrong-doing. He argued that the Indian community in South Africa was not bound as to when and regarding what matters they should offer *satyagraha*. In deciding this question "they must only not transgress the limits prescribed by wisdom and appreciation of their own capacity. *Satyagraha* offered on every occasion seasonable or otherwise would be corrupted into *duragraha*. And if any one takes to *satyagraha* without having measured his own strength and afterwards sustains a defeat, he not only disgraces himself but he also brings the matchless weapon of *satyagraha* into disrepute by his folly."[63]

There are several difficulties in this passage. The word "seasonable" is imprecise and question-begging. How exactly does one measure one's strength before actually undertaking *satyagraha*?

When can we be certain that defeat is not temporary but final, not seeming but real? If we can judge such matters only after the event, the notion of *duragraha* could become a merely pejorative term applied on the basis of a purely utilitarian criterion. Also, it might help to appraise but not to avoid the abuse of *satyagraha*.

These difficulties are theoretically important, but not insurmountable in practice. The distinction between *duragraha* and *satyagraha* is a matter of moral and political judgment. All such judgments are not easy to make, still less to reduce to some simple naturalistic criterion. In a concrete situation, we can come to some view generally regarded as reasonable by unbiased outsiders but we cannot be certain about the grounds on which we decide that an act is wrong and inappropriate, since it could be right and timely in other situations. We cannot avoid such subjective judgments in morals or even in politics. If a person develops through self-criticism and self-examination a high degree of honesty and self-awareness, he may often be in the best position to judge himself by standards he accepts and by comparison with his acts on earlier occasions. The *satyagrahi* is required by his doctrine to develop these qualities, and he must also be open to criticism from others. Even if he refuses to admit to *duragraha*, it is possible for others to regard his conduct as such and this must be relevant to a *satyagrahi*. Although ultimately he alone can chide himself acceptably as a performer of *duragraha*, he also knows that he cannot convince his opponent that he has offered *satyagraha* if a significant number of outsiders or an experienced *satyagrahi* cannot in all honesty describe his conduct as *satyagraha*. The pair of opposites, *satyagraha* and *duragraha*, like the notions of good and evil, are strongly subjective as they have moral connotations, but the distinction is not useless or unintelligible. If Gandhi took consequences into account, this was not because he was a utilitarian but rather because in politics we cannot—even an idealist cannot, especially if he is a reformer—entirely ignore results.

In distinguishing between true and false *satyagraha*, Gandhi took the motive into account, more so than the consequences.

> What one regards as true *satyagraha* may very likely be otherwise. *Satyagraha* . . . cannot be resorted to for personal gain, but only for the good of others. A *satyagrahi* should always be

ready to undergo suffering and pecuniary loss. . . . The triumph of *satyagraha* consists in meeting death in the insistence on truth. A *satyagrahi* is always unattached to the attainment of the object of *satyagraha* . . . fasting for the sake of personal gain is nothing short of intimidation and the result of ignorance.[64]

Also, *satyagraha*, unlike *duragraha*, is never adopted abruptly and never till all other and milder methods have been tried.[65] "Thoughtless disobedience means disruption of society."[66] Civil disobedience is, in Gandhi's view, like a knife, to be used sparingly, if at all. The man who cuts away without ceasing, cuts at the very root, and finds himself without the substance he was trying to reach by cutting off the superficial hard crust. Applying this analogy to an organism, Gandhi held that the use of civil disobedience will be healthy, necessary and effective only if we otherwise conform to the laws of all growth. "Disobedience combined with love is the living water of life. Civil disobedience is a beautiful variant to signify growth, it is not discordance which spells death."[67] In other words, *satyagraha* is a healthy and natural device for purifying and strengthening society, while *duragraha* is an unhealthy and unnatural interference.

Gandhi was concerned that the word "*satyagraha*" is often most loosely used and is made to cover veiled violence. He felt that often the evil thought or the evil word may, in terms of *satyagraha*, be more dangerous than physical violence used in the heat of the moment and perhaps repented and forgotten the next moment. Unlike *duragraha*,

> *Satyagraha* is gentle, it never wounds. It must not be the result of anger or malice. It is never fussy, never impatient, never vociferous. It is the direct opposite of compulsion. It was conceived as a complete substitute for violence. The reformer must have consciousness of the truth of his cause. He will not then be impatient with the opponent, he will be impatient with himself. . . . Even fasts may take the form of coercion. But there is nothing in the world that in human hands does not lend itself to abuse. The human being is a mixture of good and evil, Jekyll and Hyde. But there is least likelihood of abuse when it is a matter of self-suffering.[68]

Satyagraha does not admit of any suppression of any body or organization. In 1940 Gandhi felt that, as an experienced *satyagrahi*, he must sound the warning that whoever launches civil resistance without the proper training and a full appreciation of the conditions of *satyagraha* is likely to bring disaster to the cause he espouses. In general, he assumed that if the votary of *satyagraha* is wrong, he can harm only himself, not his opponent. Hence he felt that despite the possibility of its abuse, *satyagraha* is the most harmless as also the most potent remedy against wrongs.[69] But it is important that no man should mock at *satyagraha* or parody it.[70]

Gandhi gave several further tests of true *satyagraha* in order to safeguard against abuses. In *satyagraha* there is no place for fraud or falsehood or any kind of untruth.[71] There is nothing in *satyagraha* whereby we may under certain circumstances tell untruths or practice other deception.[72] Further, secrecy does no good to the cause of *satyagraha*. "*Satyagraha* is more than cleverness. Secrecy takes away from its dignity."[73] *Satyagrahis* have no reason to have secret books or secret funds. It is contrary to the spirit of *satyagraha* to do anything secretly or impatiently, and a *satyagrahi* has no secrets to keep from his opponent or so-called enemy.[74] A *satyagrahi* bids goodbye to fear and is, therefore, never afraid of trusting the opponent.

> Even if the opponent plays him false twenty times, the *satyagrahi* is ready to trust him the twenty-first time; for, an implicit trust in human nature is the very essence of his creed. No matter how often a *satyagrahi* is betrayed, he will repose his trust in the adversary so long as there are not cogent reasons for distrust. . . . He will not . . . be misled by the mere fear of suffering into groundless distrust. . . . Distrust is a sign of weakness and *satyagraha* implies the banishment of all weakness and, therefore, of distrust, which is clearly out of place when the adversary is not to be destroyed but to be won over.[75]

The *satyagrahi* may not regard anybody as irreclaimable, and should try to understand the psychology of the evil-doer, who is very often the victim of circumstances.[76] He must believe in truth and nonviolence as his creed and therefore have faith in the inherent goodness of human nature which he expects to evoke by his truth and love expressed through his suffering.[77]

Further, a *satyagrahi* must always allow his cards to be examined and re-examined at all times and make reparation if an error is discovered.[78] Also, "a *satyagrahi* never misses, can never miss, a chance of compromise on honourable terms, it being always assumed that in the event of failure he is ever ready to offer battle . . . his cards are always on the table."[79] The campaign of *satyagraha* must be boldly carried on "in the light of the blazing sun of openness."[80]

Again, a *satyagrahi* fights only for essentials,[81] has a single objective from which he cannot recede and beyond which he cannot advance, which can in fact be "neither augmented nor abridged."[82] In every step he takes, he is bound to consider the position of his adversary.[83] When *satyagraha* is aimed at a wicked government, its concern must not be so much with paralyzing government as with being proof against wickedness. In general, it must aim not at destruction but at construction and deal with causes rather than with symptoms.[84] "A *satyagrahi*'s first concern is not the effect of his action. It must always be its propriety. He must have faith enough in his cause and his means, and know that success will be achieved in the end."[85] Even where the cause is just, *satyagraha* must be kept within its proper limits.[86] The reformers should realize their responsibility to the full and not swerve by a hair's breadth from their self-imposed discipline.[87] *Satyagrahi*s like Caesar's wife must be above suspicion."[88]

The greatest danger to a *satyagraha* movement comes, according to Gandhi, from the arrogant assumption of superiority on the part of its leaders and votaries.

Intolerance is itself a form of violence and an obstacle to the growth of a true democratic spirit. . . . When self-satisfaction creeps over a man, he has ceased to grow. He who offers a little sacrifice from a lowly and religious spirit quickly realizes the miserable littleness of it. Once on the path of sacrifice, we find out the measure of our selfishness, and must continually wish to give more and not be satisfied till there is a complete self-surrender. And this knowledge of so little attempted and still less done must keep us humble and tolerant. . . . Our motto must ever be conversion by gentle persuasion and a constant appeal to the head and the heart. We must therefore be ever courteous and patient with those who do not see eye to eye with us. We must resolutely refuse to consider our opponents as enemies of the country.[89]

From all these observations of Gandhi, it is easy to see the many abuses that could vitiate a *satyagraha* movement or campaign. The criteria suggested above are so exacting that *satyagraha* could easily become *duragraha*. However, Gandhi pointed out that every powerful thing is liable to misuse. Opium and arsenic are most potent and useful drugs, and lend themselves to great abuse, but this is no reason for stopping their good use. "A thing has to be judged by its effect."[90] Risk of misuse has undoubtedly to be run, but with the increase in the knowledge of its right use, the risk can be minimized.[91] Gandhi thought that one safe thing about *satyagraha* is that in the end its abuse recoils more upon the users than upon those against whom it is used.

Having considered the abuses of *satyagraha* and the means by which we can identify *duragraha*, we must now see what Gandhi had to say about the limits of even proper *satyagraha*.

First of all, a particular device like fasting has its own well-defined limits. Fasts are coercive when they are intended to attain a selfish object. No doubt the dividing line between a selfish and an unselfish end is often very thin, but a person who regards the aim of another's fast to be selfish should resolutely refuse to yield to it.[92] *Satyagraha* of certain types is limited by the nature of its object.

Secondly, *satyagraha* involving non-cooperation is limited by the pledge of nonviolence, by the possibility of indiscipline or anarchy. "Non-cooperation, when its limitations are not recognized, becomes a licence instead of being a duty and therefore becomes a crime. The dividing line between right and wrong is often so thin as to become indistinguishable. But it is a line that is unbreakable and unmistakable."[93]

Thirdly, *satyagraha* involving civil disobedience is limited by the fact that it is only when a person has intelligently and freely obeyed the laws of society that he is in a position to judge as to what particular rules are good and just and which unjust and iniquitous.[94]

Fourthly, the limit for *satyagraha* in general is prescribed by the capacity of its votaries as a whole for self-sacrifice and self-suffering.[95] This is particularly true in regard to mass *satyagraha*. "Suffering has its well-defined limits. Suffering can be both wise and unwise, and when the limit is reached, to prolong it would be not unwise, but the height of folly."[96] However, in the case of the individual *satyagrahi* "there is no time limit . . . nor is there a limit to his capacity for suffering" as he may be willing to invite martyrdom.[97]

Apart from these obvious limits to the application of *satyagraha*, and their corollaries, is there any place for *satyagraha* against the State, or any special limit to its use in a free, democratic society? Since the death of Gandhi there has been a controversy on this matter between the advocates of the rule of law and some orthodox disciples of Gandhi.

In an essay "Law and Liberty"[98] Mr. N. V. Gadgil, former Governor of East Punjab, has deplored the tendency in India today to start *satyagraha* in the form of civil disobedience on the slightest pretext. In certain circumstances, as when the majority is so marginal that it cannot be taken to represent the real will of the majority of citizens, or in any situation in which a citizen's conscience is violated, there is room for *satyagraha*. The individual is also entitled to awaken the conscience of the community by civil disobedience, but his disobedience to law must not run counter to the basic moral foundations of society. On the other hand, the enforcement of a bad law may itself undermine the moral stature of a community. There is, however, no room for mass civil disobedience, violent or even nonviolent, in a constitutional democracy. Once the precedent is established that a government freely elected by a majority can be thrown out by recourse to unconstitutional and illegal means, the very foundations on which parliamentary democracy and constitutional government rest are seriously weakened. Anarchy is bound to result.

Mr. K. Santhanam has similarly argued that general *satyagraha* against a democratic government cannot be justified, but he also allows for some marginal cases. If a government pushes through controversial measures touching matters of fundamental importance at the fag-end of its term of office, or refuses to submit them to an electoral verdict, it is legitimate to use *satyagraha*. On the other hand, a government cannot be challenged merely because it passes unpopular measures not included in the party's election manifesto. He also considers exceptional cases justifying *satyagraha* on the ground that a majority has no right to coerce a minority.

This cannot affect measures which do not discriminate against any individual or group, or measures like taxation, which can be reversed and therefore resisted through constitutional means. If a government seeks to confiscate property without paying reasonable compensation, or if it tries to spread its net widely and interfere with property rights on a large scale, *satyagraha* is justified. Again, the reform of religious institutions through legislation is an issue which may provoke legitimate *satyagraha*.

On the whole, Mr. Santhanam concludes that individual *satyagraha* has a definite place in a democracy as a corrective against the misuse of political power and as a safeguard for the preservation of the democratic spirit. This argument that a democratic regime may be resisted in the name of democracy is similar to the controversial claim that a citizen's liberty could be restricted in the name of liberty. In both cases the terms "democracy" and "liberty" undergo a hidden change of meaning. Mr. Santhanam also suggests how *satyagraha* may be countered.

> The common foundation of both *satyagraha* and democracy is persuasion. In democracy, rational democracy is backed by physical force. In *satyagraha* moral persuasion is supported by self-suffering. As the probabilities of persuasion are inversely proportional to the use of physical force and directly proportional to the intensity of self-suffering, refusal to resort to physical force or inflict suffering on the opponent is the best method of countering *satyagrahic* resistance. Where either cannot be completely avoided, social and conscious effort to reduce to the minimum the use of physical force and the suffering of the opponent is necessary to give the maximum opportunity for public opinion to make itself felt.[99]

Mr. Santhanam concludes that *satyagraha* can serve as a supplement and in some cases as a substitute to law in a modern society, based upon the rule of law. If the laws are unjust or oppressive and constitutional remedies are not available owing to the attitudes of the rulers or majorities, *satyagraha* is a legitimate weapon of the injured individuals or groups. However, in the preface to Mr. Santhanam's book, the Chief Justice of the Supreme Court of India, B. P. Sinha, points out that the rule of law, as usually understood, does not permit individuals or groups to indulge in law-breaking.

"Either the concept of the rule of law has to undergo a radical change in order to admit of such breaking of the law, or the breaking of the law has got to be stopped by all legal and legitimate means."[100]

While some constitutionalists in India are prepared to allow a restricted, marginal role for *satyagraha* even in a democratic system, some Gandhians[101] too have been eager to stress the minimal rather than the maximal role of legitimate *satyagraha* under an elected, popular regime. At the same time, just as Justice Sinha and other champions of the rule of law cannot concede even a minimal role to *satyagraha* which would not conflict with the basic premises of a liberal democracy, so too there are Gandhians at the other extreme who have held that full-fledged *satyagraha*, even mass civil disobedience, cannot be ruled out in a democracy.

Mr. S. G. Bharve, a staunch social and political worker, has argued this case in an article "*Satyagraha* and Democracy."[102] As *satyagraha* is not a mere political weapon, it is not restricted to any individual group or to any one system. If the aim of *satyagraha* is to seek and uphold the truth and to establish the rule of truth, there is no reason why it should abdicate its role in a democratic system. Majority rule makes no difference to the individual quest for truth, and in any case the so-called majority view may really be that of only a chosen few who are able to secure the compliance of the majority. It is no doubt an essential feature of democracy that it is government by discussion and persuasion, but *satyagraha* too is a peaceful means of persuasion and conversion. The *satyagrahi* does not consider truth to be his monopoly and by its very nature, *satyagraha* rules out every form of coercion. The *satyagrahi* will take recourse to *satyagraha* when all else fails solely for the redress of public wrongs affecting large sections of people—not for any personal grievance. Even in a democracy a nonviolent conflict on a mass scale cannot be avoided when there is no other alternative. Whereas even democratic governments rely on force and serve sectional interests, *satyagraha* relies on nonviolence and serves the common good. Democracy is not a religious dogma or a divine, infallible instrument, but an imperfect means to an end which needs to be supplemented by other means. To allow only individual *satyagraha* and to rule out mass action in a democracy is simply to preserve the *status quo*, but *satyagraha* is concerned with the raising of a ferment in society to achieve radical changes in human conditions.

In this kind of controversy it is very difficult for the orthodox democrat to avoid idealizing democracy and emphasizing the stringent conditions, impossibly exacting, required by *satyagraha*. If we start by treating political democracy and constitutional procedures as sacred, it will be very tempting to regard any threat to them from the application of *satyagraha* as a form of *duragraha*. It is equally difficult for the champion of *satyagraha* to abstain from belittling the working of political democracy or the notion of the rule of law and also from idealizing *satyagraha* or overestimating the ease and effectiveness of its application. At the extremes there is an element of truth on both sides, which could be put equally in the language of democracy and of *satyagraha*.

The democrat is right to be concerned about the danger of anarchy and irresponsible disobedience engendered by the resort to *satyagraha* especially in a community in which law-abiding habits have not taken deep root and constitutional procedures are unfamiliar to the majority. The *satyagrahi* is also justified in insisting on the right to *satyagraha* even in a democracy, for it is all too easy to denounce all appeals to natural law in the name of *raison d'état*, legal sovereignty or paternalistic State action. It is between these two extreme positions—the prerequisites of effective government and the claims of conscience—that it becomes peculiarly difficult to give a general criterion for the legitimacy and the limits of *satyagraha* in a democratic system.

Gandhi himself said little explicitly on this vexed question, but even this gives some idea of his own position, which is neither simple nor dogmatic. In 1919 he told the Hunter Committee that he could conceive the necessity of *satyagraha* in opposition to a regime of "full, responsible self-government." He pointed out that in England it can happen that ministers could continue to stay in office even though they lose public confidence and that the same thing may happen in India too after independence. "I can imagine a state of things in this country which would need *satyagraha* even under Home Rule."[103] Again, in 1930 he said: "My non-violence would not prevent me from fighting my countrymen on the many questions which must arise when India has become free."[104] On the other hand, he firmly declared in 1946 that "total non-violent non-cooperation has no place in popular *Raj*, whatever its level may be."[105]

In general, the doctrine of *satyagraha* asserts the right of resistance to every form of injustice but it also lays down the need for active loyalty and the acceptance of collective responsibility in a well-ordered system. Its application as a method of resistance requires, even in the face of flagrant injustice, the fulfillment of strict conditions and the observance of several rules, and especially presupposes the habit of willing and fearless compliance with laws that do not conflict with conscience. The indiscriminate use of *satyagraha* in any society is tantamount to misuse of the notion of conscience. Further, Gandhi shrewdly saw that a genuine response to a higher law is itself connected with the exemplary compliance with civil laws. "A *satyagrahi* is nothing if not instinctively law-abiding, and it is his law-abiding nature which exacts from him implicit obedience to the highest law, that is the voice of conscience which overrides all other laws."[106] Before resorting to civil disobedience in the name of his conscience or the higher law, he must take recourse to other methods that are constitutionally guaranteed and politically open.

From all this it would be reasonable to interpret Gandhi on the side of caution. In the statements quoted above in favor of *satyagraha* Gandhi was mainly asserting that *satyagraha* was conceivable even under democratic self-government, thus denying that there was any theoretical limit (other than those implicit in the doctrine) to the exercise of *satyagraha* that is determined merely by the democratic nature of the system. But to say that a doctrine held to be universal in scope could be *conceivably* applied even in a proper democracy is to say nothing about the likelihood of its application. If anything, the doctrine presupposes conditions which reduce the likelihood of legitimate *satyagraha* in a democracy, though they do not rule it out.

This interpretation of Gandhi's position may be supported by two further passages from his writings. In 1920 he said:

Most people do not understand the complicated machinery of the government. They do not realize that every citizen silently but none the less certainly sustains the government of the day in ways of which he has no knowledge. Every citizen therefore renders himself responsible for every act of his government. And it is quite proper to support it so long as the actions of the government are bearable. But when they hurt him and his nation, it becomes his duty to withdraw his support.[107]

The second passage is from an article written in 1939.

A born democrat is a born disciplinarian. Democracy comes naturally to him who is habituated normally to yield willing obedience to all laws, human or divine. I claim to be a democrat both by instinct and training. Let those who are ambitious to serve democracy qualify themselves by satisfying first this acid test of democracy. Moreover, a democrat must be utterly selfless. He must think and dream not in terms of self or party but only of democracy. Only then does he acquire the right of civil disobedience. . . . If you must dissent, you should take care that your opinions voice your innermost convictions and are not intended merely as a convenient party cry.[108]

From these passages it is easy to see why Gandhi in 1946 ruled out total non-cooperation in a democracy, although he was prepared at different times to conceive of the possibility of individual civil disobedience. It is plausible to suggest that, in practice, there would be very few and rare occasions in a democracy when such individual *satyagraha* would become the only means available to vindicate one's conscience and the truth (*satya*). Other means are usually available in a democracy and they could be reasonably effective.

However, it would be wrong to interpret Gandhi's position solely on the side of caution and to rule out *satyagraha* in a democracy, for all practical purposes. Mr. Dhebar, former President of the Congress, goes too far in saying that there is very little occasion for *satyagraha* in a democracy, that its use can be justified only against the perpetration of an act or undertaking which destroys the very foundations of the State, that the election finally settles for an organization as between who is right and who is wrong.[109]

Gandhi, on the other hand, was aware that considerations of *raison d'état* could conflict with truth and that they could be far too easily invoked, thus minimizing the role even of individual *satya-*

*grahi*s in a democracy. His position is very different from that of
Dhebar.

> Authority takes the place of law in the last resort. There is a
> maxim in English Law that the king can do no wrong. The con-
> venience of the powers that be is the law in the final analysis.
> This objection is applicable to all governments alike. . . . Some-
> times adherence to ordinary laws is itself open to objection.
> When the authority charged with and pledged to the public good
> is threatened with destruction by the restraints imposed upon it,
> it is entitled in its discretion to disregard such restraints. But oc-
> casions of such a nature must always be rare. If the authority is
> in the habit of frequently exceeding the limits set upon it, it can-
> not be beneficial to the commonweal.[110]

The upshot of this passage is that if the resort to *satyagraha* must
be rare in a democratic system, the appeal to *raison d'état* against
the *satyagrahi* must also be made on rare occasions.

Even if the use of *satyagraha* (in the narrower sense of civil resistance) must be restricted in a democracy, its application (in
the broader sense of constructive action) is even more relevant in
a democratic than in an authoritarian system. In the last year of his
life, Gandhi felt that looseness in the use of the word *satyagrahi*
harms the community and degrades the doctrine, but at the same
time he reaffirmed his conviction that *satyagraha*, transcending
parties and the divisions of class and creed, should "permeate the
whole of our being and society."

> This I do say, fearlessly and firmly, that every worthy object can
> be achieved by the use of *satyagraha*. It is the highest and infalli-
> ble means, the greatest force. Socialism will not be reached by
> any other means. *Satyagrahis* can rid society of all evils, political,
> economic and social.[111]

It is precisely here that the democrat and the *satyagrahi* differ. A
democratic system works reasonably when citizens come to terms
with the imperfections of society at least to some extent, when they
accept that its political procedures cannot be easily maintained if
governments and ruling parties are daily determined to bring about
a radical transformation of society. Democracy is founded upon an
awareness of the limits as well as the possibilities of political action.

Satyagraha, on the other hand, is not merely a doctrine of resistance to injustice, but also a far-reaching concept of a nonviolent revolution through social and political action.

The *satyagrahi* may display patience and humility in his campaign over any particular issue, but in a deeper sense he is a man in a hurry, a restless idealist who wishes to remove every social abuse and every form of injustice even if he is required by his doctrine to concentrate on one thing at a time. As long as society is imperfect and the desire is deep-rooted in men to exploit their fellows, there can be no limit to the legitimate application of *satyagraha.* But even so, the *satyagrahi* would be wise to recognize not merely his own limitations but also those of others at any given time. The limit to the scope of *satyagraha* in any particular society, authoritarian or democratic, must be determined by the level of moral development of its members as well as by the adequacy and flexibility of available instruments of social change and political action.

The *satyagrahi* is a radical insofar as he wants far-reaching changes to be brought about in society, a revolutionary in that he is prepared to challenge an entire system, but he is also a reluctant gradualist (unlike most radicals and revolutionaries) insofar as he relies entirely on peaceful, non-violent means to achieve his long-term ends, even if he can at times secure his immediate objectives with dramatic suddenness. It is not easy to find a middle position between inertia and impatience, between our limitations and our aspirations. If *satyagraha* is interpreted too strictly and applied too cautiously, there is little to distinguish it from the peaceful methods of democracy. If the *satyagrahi* is too adventurous, he may become ruthless or connive at violence.

CRITICISMS AND ASSESSMENT

Satyagraha has been criticized at different times, in part owing to the results of particular cases of its application by Gandhi or his followers, in part in terms of its assumptions, claims and demands. It is difficult to keep the doctrine apart from the use made of it, especially as the doctrine itself is completely new in the form in which it was formulated and as its systematic use on a mass scale is unprecedented in history. Gandhi himself was continually aware of the novel and tentative nature of his experiments with *satyagraha,* "a science in the making."

Although he never claimed to be the original *satyagrahi,* he felt he was the first to have applied the doctrine of *satyagraha* on an almost universal scale, "and it yet remains to be seen and demonstrated that it is a doctrine which is capable of assimilation by thousands upon thousands of peoples in all ages and climes."[112] The only book he wrote on the subject was undertaken to give an idea of the development in South Africa, "the first attempt to apply the principle of *satyagraha* to politics on a large scale."[113]

> In actual practice the secret of *satyagraha* is not understood by all and the many are apt unintelligently to follow the few. Again as Tolstoy observed, the Transvaal struggle was the first attempt at applying the principle of *satyagraha* to masses or bodies of men. I do not know of any historical example of pure mass *satyagraha.* I cannot however formulate any definite opinion on the point, as my knowledge of history is limited. But as a matter of fact we have nothing to do with historical precedents. Granted the fundamental principles of *satyagraha,* it will be seen that the consequences I have described are bound to follow as night the day. It will not do to dismiss such a valuable force with the remark that it is difficult or impossible of application. Brute force has been the ruling factor in the world for thousands of years, and mankind has been reaping its bitter harvest all along, as he who runs may read. There is little hope of anything good coming out of it in the future.[114]

Gandhi felt it was his mission to teach by example and precept the use of the "matchless weapon of *satyagraha,* which is a direct corollary of non-violence and truth."[115] He wanted to show that it was not an impossible ideal and ordeal but "man's prerogative and birthright."[116]

Whereas Gandhi saw *satyagraha* as the only alternative to violence and armed rebellion, his critics generally tended to judge it in terms of the gap between its application and the claims made for it. In 1920 a critic pointed out that "direct action however potent does not work for unity."[117] It may be a powerful political weapon for uniting the educated and the uneducated, but it introduces new division—"group unities"—into politics. Gandhi replied that nothing was ever achieved without direct action and that submission to injustice merely resulted in an undercurrent of resentment instead of producing unity. Another critic of Gandhi, Mr. Weatherly, held in 1924 that non-cooperation is a way of violence and not of love, that it is an appeal in the end to violence rather than reason.[118] Gandhi denied that this was a universal proposition, that non-cooperation was necessarily violent merely because love, which is an active quality, cannot always be inferred from the act itself. *Satyagraha* need not be violent though some people have to suffer as a consequence of non-cooperation.

Though *satyagraha* is not necessarily a way of violence, it could lead to it when it is introduced prematurely. Gandhi conceded this on several occasions. He admitted to a critic in 1919 that he had underestimated the power of hatred and ill-will which entered into his campaign in India, but reiterated his conviction that India's salvation lay in adopting soul-force or *satyagraha* as the sole weapon to fight wrongs.[119] His critics were unconvinced. In the same year Annie Besant also expressed her doubts about mass *satyagraha*. "I have always been ready to break a bad law and suffer the penalty; I have never been ready to break all laws (without moral sanction), leaving my conscience to be ruled by a committee. The first is the act of a reformer; the second of an anarchist."[120]

In 1931 Jamshed Mehta, Mayor of Karachi, criticized the consequences of the *satyagraha* movement, the indiscipline and hatred engendered among the people and the habit of indiscriminate lawbreaking. He felt that Gandhi must take the responsibility for the misuse of "this pointed bayonet of *satyagraha*."[121] Gandhi responded by agreeing with his criticisms, by insisting that *ahimsa* meant far more than abstention from physical violence, and by condemning indiscriminate resistance to authority which "must lead to lawlessness, unbridled licence and consequent self-destruction."[122] He urged these misguided lawbreakers to retrace their steps and repent of their wrongs, while pointing out that it was the villagers who had instinctively observed nonviolence and that their nonviolence had been conducive to the growth of political consciousness in the country.

Most of the criticisms of *satyagraha* are of this nature, pointing to the undesirable results of its application on a mass scale, but not denying its value or legitimacy when adopted by exceptional individuals as a conscientious protest against an unjust law. Gandhi himself soon came to recognize the dangers of *"limited and mechanical"* adherence to *ahimsa* in mass *satyagraha*. He had to learn these lessons from bitter experience in India, where the true spirit of *satyagraha* did not readily take root as it had among the Indian community in South Africa. Philip Spratt has rightly pointed out that the struggle in South Africa was a model of what *satyagraha* ought to be, an impression confirmed by reading Gandhi's own moving account of it. In Spratt's words,

> It was conducted against very heavy odds by poor and ignorant people—the majority indeed were illiterate—but there was hardly an instance of breach of the principles. It dragged on in all for eight years: the longest fight he has ever conducted. People became disheartened. At one time he could count upon only sixteen followers. But in the end the "law of growth" prevailed. Almost the whole community again entered the fight, and satisfactory terms were obtained. He was left with an apparently immovable faith in the capacity of ordinary poor people to undergo these trials and to observe the principles; and a no less indestructible faith in the efficacy of the method.[123]

The pages of *Indian Opinion* reveal Gandhi's continued gratitude for the response of the Indians in South Africa, whereas the pages of *Young India* and of *Harijan* are full of admonitions and regrets.

It would be interesting to speculate about the reasons why the *satyagraha* campaign in South Africa was "purer" than the prolonged movement in India, but this is not the place for such an enquiry. It is enough to say that the Indian political atmosphere had been demoralized by the militant nationalism and terrorist tactics launched by the extremists in Bengal and Bombay even before Gandhi entered the scene. On the other hand, the moderates in the older tradition of liberalism had become increasingly out of touch with the new political climate and the emerging political consciousness of the masses. Gandhi secured a band of exemplary *satyagrahis*, notably Vinoba Bhave, and also stirred the peasants as well as the women into action, but he could not impart the spirit of *satyagraha* to most of his young followers in the cities. The enormity of his undertaking in the Indian context as well as the difficulties in the application of so exacting a doctrine as *satyagraha* became clear to him within a decade after his arrival in India. In 1925 he wrote: "Much corruption has crept into our religion. We have become lazy as a nation, we have lost the time sense. Selfishness dominates our action. There is mutual jealousy amongst the tallest of us. We are uncharitable to one another. . . . I can only hope you will realize the import of what you are doing (in adopting *satyagraha*)."[124] In India, unlike South Africa, Gandhi had to contend also with the hypocrisy of his followers, engendered by false religiosity, and of his opponents, who had become the victims of their moral and political pretensions. Far from being applicable only in India, *satyagraha* as Gandhi conceived it—requiring capital in the shape of character—was peculiarly difficult to apply to the demoralized conditions in India. It is not surprising that he himself thought in his latter years that the English people and the American Negroes were more likely than Indians to carry on the tradition of *satyagraha* after his death, at least in the short run.

While criticisms of the working of *satyagraha* may be readily met in terms of its theoretical requirements, more serious objections have been raised to the doctrine itself. In 1910 Mr. Wybergh of the Transvaal legislature, wrote at length to Gandhi on reading *Hind Swaraj*. He thought that soul-force and passive resistance in themselves have nothing to do with love or spirituality.

> In advocating these things instead of physical force you are only transferring the battle and the violence from the physical to the mental plane. Your weapons are mental and psychic, not physical, but also not spiritual. You are still fighting to win, and fighting harder than ever, and, in my opinion, all fighting in modern times is tending to become more and more a matter of intellectual and psychic force and less of physical force. It is not thereby becoming more moral or less cruel, rather the reverse, but it is becoming more effective.[125]

He went even further and held that the use of soul-force for concrete ends is dangerous in the extreme. He did not deny the unselfish sacrifices made by Gandhi and his followers in South Africa. His quarrel was with their methods rather than their motives. The truest heroism consists in suffering as private individuals and saying nothing about it. Further, the physical sufferings of soldiers vastly exceed those of passive resisters with their creed of "self-suffering." Finally, non-resistance is a legitimate goal for the individual saint, but it is pernicious as a political principle for adoption by ordinary men and also utterly disastrous for public welfare. Preaching as Tolstoy did against laws and governments, police and physical force, is far more injurious than mere disloyalty to a regime. When all humanity has reached sainthood, government will become unnecessary, but not till then.

In replying to Wybergh, Gandhi pointed out:

> I admit that the term "passive resistance" is a misnomer. I have used it because, generally speaking, we know what it means. . . . The underlying principle is totally opposed to that of violence. It cannot, therefore, be that the "battle is transferred from the physical to the mental plane." The function of violence is to obtain reform by external means; the function of passive resistance, i.e., soul-force, is to obtain it by growth from within, which, in its turn, is obtained by self-suffering, self-purification. Violence ever fails; passive resistance is ever successful. The fight of a passive resister is none the less spiritual because he fights to win. Indeed, he is obliged to fight to win, i.e., to obtain the mastery of self. Passive resistance is always moral, never cruel, and any activity, mental or otherwise, which fails in this test is undoubtedly not passive resistance.[126]

Gandhi also could not agree that there must be complete divorce between the saint and the ordinary man, between politics and spirituality. He held that the passive resistance of his conception (*satyagraha*) seeks to rejoin politics and religion and to test every one of our actions in the light of ethical principles. "That Jesus refused to use soul-force to turn stones into bread only supports my argument. Modern civilization is at present engaged in attempting that impossible feat."[127]

Gandhi further contended that the passive resister, far from being content with his good intentions, knows that in spite of the purity of his motives his actions may be utterly wrong and, therefore, in attempting to resist what he holds to be wrong, suffers only in his own person. Also,

I agree with you entirely that a pure passive resister cannot allow himself to be regarded as a martyr, nor can he complain of the hardships of prison or any other hardships, nor may he make political capital out of what may appear to be injustice or ill-treatment, much less may he allow any matter of passive resistance to be advertised. But all action unfortunately is mixed. Purest passive resistance can exist only in theory . . . the Indian passive resisters of the Transvaal are, after all, very fallible human beings and yet very weak, but I can assure you that their object is to make their practice correspond with pure passive resistance as nearly as possible, and, as the struggle progresses, pure spirits are certainly rising in our midst. . . . Some of us are undoubtedly not free from vindictiveness and the spirit of hatred; but the desire in us all is to cure ourselves of hatred and enmity. I have noticed, too, that those who simply became passive resisters under the glamour of the newness of the movement or for selfish reasons have fallen away. Pretended self-suffering cannot last long. Such men never were passive resisters.[128]

Mr. Wybergh's criticism is fundamental and has been echoed by others. It is significant that Gandhi's doctrine of *satyagraha* has been attacked more powerfully from a religious than from a secularist standpoint. Secularists tend to be both skeptical and utilitarian. Insofar as they cannot understand or take seriously the religious assumptions underlying *satyagraha,* they are inclined to dismiss it with rationalist self-assurance rather than to attack. At the same time, their utilitarian respect for results leads them to think that *satyagraha* has achieved concrete gains—awakening of political consciousness, education of public opinion, unifying different social groups behind a broad front—only because it was a shrewd rationalization in conditions of political and physical weakness. The religious language in which *satyagraha* is couched may well seem to the non-believer to be the strictly superfluous coating mainly employed to make a novel tactic respectable in a certain social context.

Religious believers, on the other hand, unlike secularists, have been often deeply disturbed by Gandhi's doctrine of *satyagraha* and have sometimes tended to argue that it is based upon a cardinal theological error. If the application of the doctrine fails, this is seen as a confirmation of the danger of materializing spiritual truths. If it succeeds, this is regarded as an improper, though temporarily effective, misuse of religious language. The doctrine of *satyagraha* has been attacked particularly from a Hindu as well as a Christian standpoint. Sir Narayan Chandavarkar, a liberal Hindu, joined with others in 1920 in issuing a manifesto pleading that "non-cooperation is deprecated by the religious tenets and traditions of our motherland, nay, of all the religions that have saved and elevated the human race."[129] A Protestant missionary, W. H. G. Holmes, held that *satyagraha* was based upon a failure to understand the New Testament and a fanciful interpretation of the *Bhagavad Gita.*[130] An English admirer of Gandhi as well as of the Indian religious tradition, Arthur Moore, felt that "it is not a distinctly spiritual weapon any more than is armed rebellion or war."[131] A Catholic anarchist, Robert Ludlow, regretted that Gandhi retained faith in the State as an instrument of justice and in political action. In his view, "political methods are bound to fail because they carry with them the elements of *himsa* (hate) and in personal action alone and action by the people themselves will society be transformed. He understood well these things—it is only that he did not realize that political and personalist action must inevitably clash."[132]

The doctrine (though not the practice) of *satyagraha* has been sympathetically criticized by Reinhold Niebuhr. We cannot draw any absolute line of demarcation between violent and nonviolent coercion. To regard violence as intrinsically evil is an "uncritical identification of traditionalized instrumental values with intrinsic moral values" such as goodwill. He conceded that the difference between violent and nonviolent coercion lay not merely in the degree of destruction they cause but even more in the fact that destruction is intentional in the former owing to its aggressive character and not intended in the latter owing to its negative character. And yet, non-cooperation results in social consequences not totally dissimilar from those of violence. Niebuhr also felt, like Wybergh, that Gandhi had confused the non-resistance of the saints with nonviolent resistance, but unlike Wybergh, he thought Gandhi was right never to commit himself to pure non-resistance.

> A negative form of resistance does not achieve spirituality simply because it is negative. As long as it enters the field of social and physical relations and places physical restraints upon the desires

and activities of others, it is a form of physical coercion. The
confusion in Mr. Gandhi's mind . . . seems to arise from his
unwillingness or perhaps his inability, to recognize the qualifying
influences of his political responsibilities upon the purity of his
original ethical and religious ideals of non-resistance. . . . All
this is a pardonable confusion in the soul of a man who is trying
to harmonize the insights of a saint with the necessities of state-
craft, a very difficult achievement.[133]

While Niebuhr stressed the coerciveness of non-cooperation, he admitted that *satyagraha,* in its pure form, means an appeal to the
reason and goodwill of an opponent in a social struggle, that it may
be regarded as a type of resistance but it is not physical coercion.
"It may avail itself of a very vivid and dramatic method of education."[134] He felt that *satyagraha* is less confusing when Gandhi's
emphasis upon nonviolence of the spirit is considered. It really became for him a way by which he expressed the ideal of love, the
spirit of moral goodwill, involving freedom from personal resent-
ments, and a moral purpose free of selfish ambition. "It is the temper and spirit in which a political policy is conducted, which he is
really designating, rather than a particular political technique."[135]
But then Niebuhr goes on to say approvingly, but wrongly, that
Gandhi believed that even violence is justified if it proceeds from
perfect moral goodwill though nonviolence is usually the better
method of expressing goodwill. What Gandhi said was that violence
is sometimes unavoidable as long as we are in a human body and
that it is always preferable to cowardice and inaction, and also that
physical violence accompanied by mental goodwill (which is conceivable but very rare) is better than physical nonviolence accompanied by mental violence.[136]

All these criticisms from a religious or moral standpoint rest
upon two main planks: the assumption that religious criteria applicable to saints cannot and should not be imported into the political arena of mass action; and secondly, the assertion that *satyagraha*
is necessarily coercive and therefore not morally very different from
(even if somewhat superior to) methods involving physical coercion. In the first case, the critics are challenging the fundamental
starting point of Gandhi's thought, the very thing that he thought
possible, desirable and even necessary. He identified the term "re-

ligious" entirely and exclusively with the word "moral" and then pleaded that moral criteria are always applicable, that the difficulties in applying them are considerable in politics but no more so than in personal life; he also believed that the difference between the religious prophets and ordinary men was merely one of degree (however enormous) and not of kind. There is no way of settling the disagreement between Gandhi and his critics on this fundamental issue. This disagreement is rooted in radically different religious beliefs and metaphysical presuppositions, and is also confused by the different senses in which religious and moral terms are used. Gandhi may be legitimately criticized for talking at times as though the task he set himself was easier or simpler than he himself recognized at other times. This is a criticism of his conduct as a politician or of his intellectual inconsistencies (which he thought arose out of the need for differences of emphasis in different situations), but not of the value of his political concepts and doctrines.

The second main criticism arises out of the inherent ambiguity of the term "coercion" as well as out of a natural tendency to fasten upon particular formulations of the complex and evolving doctrine of *satyagraha*. Gandhi himself thought that in the absence of violence (mental and physical), it is misleading to talk of coercion. The difficulty here is that the term "coercion" is sometimes defined by reference to the aggressive intentions of the user and more often by reference to the victim—the fact that he is constrained to behave in a manner not chosen by him (whether by way of abstention or of commission). There is a further difficulty in the latter and more common use of the term "coercion." Should we adopt a subjective or a purely objective criterion? If we decide to say that a man is coerced whenever he feels that he has not chosen freely or that he no longer holds the initiative, the term "coercion" could be very much abused. In a sense, coercion of some sort enters into all human relationships insofar as men influence each other in conscious or unconscious, open or covert, ways. On the other hand, if we decide to adopt a purely objective criterion it is difficult to distinguish, as indeed we should, between force, power and authority. No doubt, we cannot ignore the intentions of the user but neither can we go solely by them in identifying instances of coercion. But there are so many degrees and varieties of coercion that we must distinguish between the types of constraining influences that are exercised. An important and relatively unambiguous way of making a distinction is to consider whether physical force has been used. It is, however, also customary to contrast coercion with rational persuasion, but there are many cases where a person may think he has complied purely on rational grounds, but may be browbeaten by a more powerful mind or brainwashed, or may even be rationalizing his submission on non-rational grounds. This difficulty arises even in intellectual life but it is crucial in politics. Niebuhr himself thinks that there is a legitimate, coercive element in all educational processes, and that this element is wholly unavoidable in politics.

The distinctiveness of *satyagraha* lies in the notions of *ahimsa* and *tapas,* while its legitimacy lies in the notion of *satya. Ahimsa* rules out any intention to inflict mental or physical injury upon the opponent, and this element in *satyagraha* determines its aim of converting rather than coercing the opponent. The conversion is not meant to take place purely by an appeal to reason but rather through *tapas* or self-suffering. When Gandhi was told that "moral pressure" was involved in his Rajkot fast, he replied: "If my fast . . . is to be interpreted as pressure, I can only say that such moral pressure should be welcomed by all concerned."[137] He thought that moral pressure was justified insofar as it evoked a moral response, i.e., if the conversion was genuine. There are, however, two inherent difficulties—both practical rather than theoretical—in the notions of *ahimsa* and of *tapas.*

First of all, even if the intention of the user of *ahimsa* is sincerely to abstain from mental or physical injury, it would be impossible to expect of any man (except a saint) that his intention be wholly pure, i.e., free from any element of ill-will or desire for victory. Secondly, even if his intention were pure, the victim might still feel that mental injury was done to him—that he was coerced even if he chose not to say so. Similarly, in regard to *tapas* there are two difficulties. First of all, it would be unreasonable to expect of any man (short of a saint) that he should perform pure *tapas,* that his self-suffering should be free from any taint of selfishness or masochism. Secondly, even if he does offer pure *tapas,* it would be difficult to expect his opponent to see it as such, or not to respond as much out of pity as admiration. Gandhi himself did not claim that his *ahimsa* and *tapas* were entirely pure, and in any case his opponents in South Africa and in India could not believe it though they came to admire and respect him.

As long as *satyagraha* is impure because of inadequacies in the *ahimsa* and *tapas* displayed, it would seem to contain an element of coercion, and at least its opponents could feel coerced even by pure *satyagraha*. Coercion has been defined by Theodore Paullin as "the use of either physical or intangible force to compel action contrary to the will or reasoned judgment of the individual or group subjected to such force."[138] In this sense of coercion, there is a coercive element in *satyagraha,* a point emphasized by C. M. Case. He regards acts of *satyagraha* as

> instances of coercion because in them suffering, though self-inflicted, aims at producing a dilemma in the mind of the opponent. Neither of the alternatives appeals to his desires or his judgment, yet he is compelled by the situation to choose between them. No violence or threat of violence is used against him, on the one hand, nor is he persuaded of the excellence of either alternative, on the other. Whichever he accept of the alternatives, he remains unconvinced, either by the assent of his judgment to facts and reasons given in argument, or by a reversal of his moral outlook through the contemplation of suffering passively endured. He is coerced, non-violently coerced it is true, but coerced nevertheless.[139]

If we insist on calling the compulsive element, the moral pressure in *satyagraha* a form of coercion, we must still distinguish it from coercion as usually understood. *Satyagraha* may cause inconvenience and suffering to the opponent though neither is intended, but its identifying property is the suffering it causes the user. Only if the intentional self-suffering of the user is less than the unintentional suffering caused to the opponent or to third parties can the use of *satyagraha* be legitimately criticized. Further, to place the opponent in an impossible situation and an unpleasant dilemma is to cause him moral discomfort but it is not to be regarded as an injury to him. It is this point which is meant by Gandhi's statement that moral pressure is to be welcomed when it secures a moral response. To the extent that there is a coercive element in *satyagraha* which is wholly unintended, it could be regarded simply as the consequence of the act or system of injustice which aroused the conscience of the *satyagrahi* in the first place. The opponent cannot legitimately talk about moral discomfort if his unjust acts have resulted in a situation in which any measure of change or opposition would cause him displeasure. In such a situation, *satyagraha* is morally superior and even different in kind from violent measures insofar as its user deliberately abstains from inflicting any injury on the opponent and enables him to compromise or give way with credit to himself. The minimal coercive element in *satyagraha* arises only in the sense that there is some interference with the freedom of the opponent, in the interests of the freedom of the people affected by his unjust acts.

Thus the coercion implicit in *satyagraha* is much less and of a different kind from the coercion that we associate with methods of violence. Admittedly, it is greater or could be greater than the coercion implicit in other peaceful, democratic methods of bringing about social and political changes. But then we must remember that *satyagraha* is only to be employed where these other methods have been used and have failed. The failure may be only temporary, but the *satyagrahi* is entitled to come to a reasonable view of the likelihood of these methods succeeding in the long run against extreme cases of injustice—such as tyranny, *apartheid* or untouchability. It is necessary to appraise *satyagraha* as an alternative to armed rebellion or violent action, where other peaceful methods have failed or have no foreseeable chance of success in an iniquitous or a very inefficient system. If we assess *satyagraha* in the abstract, we will always be confronted with the irrefutable argument that our criticisms apply only to *duragraha* and not to *satyagraha*. What is undeniable is that the calculations involved in the decision to launch *satyagraha* are so difficult that there is no room for dogmatism as to the legitimacy of *satyagraha* in any specific context. Gandhi himself stressed the need for tolerance on the part of the *satyagrahi* and he also recognized that even *satyagrahi*s may differ on a particular issue.[140] Further, he pointed out that a *satyagrahi* "gives his opponent the same right of independence and feelings of liberty that he reserves to himself, and he will fight by inflicting injuries on his own person."[141] In view of all this, it is unfair to make too much of the coercive element in *satyagraha,* though reasonable to emphasize this in the context of any particular application of *satya-graha*.

It is not only the notions of *ahimsa* and *tapas* in *satyagraha* that give rise to difficulties but also the notion of *satya*, its legitimating principle and its main object. The *satyagrahi* is only upholding relative, not absolute, truth in insisting that a particular law or system or policy is unjust. Others may see good where he sees evil, and even the evil he sees may not be unalloyed. Many who criticized *satyagraha* disagreed with Gandhi's own assessment of the laws or system he was attacking or, like those who criticized Lloyd Garrison, felt that injustice in the political or social sphere (imperialism or untouchability) could be tackled by different methods, or by relying more than he did upon the common sense and realism of the persons whose system or acts he opposed. Here again, this is merely an argument against the infallibility of the *satyagrahi* (which he is not allowed to claim by his doctrine) and not against his right to invoke his conscience. Our judgments as to the *satya* sought or the *asat* attacked pertain to the legitimacy of *satyagraha* in a specific context but not to the doctrine itself. Gandhi made his own position clear.

> I said to myself, there is no State run by Nero or Mussolini which has not good points about it, but we have to reject the whole, once we decide to non-cooperate with the system. "There are in our country grand public roads, and palatial educational institutions," I said to myself, "but they are part of a system which crushes the nation. I should not have anything to do with them. They are like the fabled snake with a brilliant jewel on its head, but which has fangs full of poison!" So I came to the conclusion that British rule in India had crushed the spirit of the nation and stunted its growth, and so I decided to deny myself all the privileges, services, courts, titles. The policy would vary with different countries but sacrifice and self-denial are the essential points.[142]

Tagore had the same feelings to a lesser extent but he took refuge in an abstract cosmopolitanism of the mind and abdicated from political action. He criticized *satyagraha* as a doctrine of negation and despair, a doctrine of exclusiveness, narrowness and separation.[143] Gandhi could not concede this criticism and he also felt that cosmopolitanism must grow out of and not preclude patriotism (*swadeshi*), but he was willing to recognize that Tagore and he had different notions of patriotism. He was genuinely prepared to respect Tagore's position while holding to his own. Tagore too came to modify his views and to respect Gandhi's standpoint without endorsing it fully.

More generally, we may recognize that a particular form of *satyagraha* like non-cooperation may become a negative doctrine, with the wrong emphasis in a given situation. This is not an argument against the doctrine of *satyagraha* as such. Gilbert Murray, who was a great admirer of Gandhi and also respected the doctrine of *satyagraha* as early as 1914, felt it necessary in 1928 to attack the Tolstoyan doctrine of non-resistance to evil as anarchic and subversive.

> It is all very well . . . to ridicule the law and peace and conventional morality when you are not in danger of being left with no law and no peace and the standards of behaviour broken. But we of the present generation have walked too deep in the valley of the shadow. . . . Our ship has got to be saved; saved with all its faults of construction and all its injustices, because only while it is safe shall we be able to correct the things that are wrong, reform the structure, improve the conditions of the cabin-boy, and bring ease to the starved and broken-legged cattle who are moaning in the hold. . . . Let us think first of the great society of which we are members and to which we owe our loyalty.[144]

This noble and wise exhortation is specially applicable to the Ship of State in India today, in which it may be more necessary to stress the Gandhian doctrines of *swadeshi* and *sarvodaya* than of *satyagraha*. At the same time we can think of situations in India and elsewhere in which, even today, the doctrine of *satyagraha* has its peculiar relevance.

The doctrine of loyalty could also be pushed too far, ruling out any role for *satyagraha* or for passive resistance in any society. This has been done not merely in the name of the political notion of *raison d'état* but also by reference to the religious duty of obedience. A Cambridge divine, W. Cunningham, attacked passive resistance in this vein in 1908. His grievance was not that it is ineffective but that it is only too effective.

It may be admitted that passive resistance is more likely to prove an effective weapon than any other that is available. No plea seems to have greater influence on the public mind than that of the conscientious objector. To compel any citizen to do what is against his conscience, . . . is generally regarded as tyrannous. . . . Further there are politicians who are much impressed by agitation of any kind; they are prepared to try and meet the views of those who clamour sufficiently loudly, but will take little pains to redress an injustice to which men submit; they are inclined to doubt whether it is a grievance at all. . . . But for all that, we are bound to consider whether it is not an unworthy course for us to pursue; there is a real danger lest the religious and conscientious objection should after all be a mere pretext, and not a genuine scruple. . . . Further, resistance, even passive resistance, is very difficult to reconcile with any observance of the duty of obedience to the civil magistrate who is ordained by God for the punishment of evil doers. . . . It surely may be a duty to submit to some injustice, rather than to set an example of defying constituted authority. Those who submit to injustice, to unjust exaction or unmerited punishment, are at least refraining from any action that weakens the hands of the government, or loosens the bonds of society. . . .[145]

This passage has been quoted at length because it embodies sentiments that contain an element of truth, a very popular and respectable line of reasoning but also an extreme conservative doctrine that could act as an effective brake against social and political change and not merely as an argument against *satyagraha*. This argument has, even more than Socratic resistance, the sanction of antiquity; it has had a long-standing prestige in Europe and a deadening influence in India. It is a useful corrective at all times to the impatience and *hubris* of the *satyagrahi* and revolutionary, but it could be abused just as much as the doctrine of *satyagraha*. It implies a view of religion as well as of politics, and of the relation between them, which Gandhi firmly rejected. He himself came to see the dangers of stressing the negative component of *satyagraha* and increasingly emphasized the positive element in the doctrine—the Constructive Programme. But he never abandoned his conviction that the religious spirit is needed in politics, that it is necessary to uphold *satya* and *ahimsa* by resisting injustice and violence through self-suffering, even at the cost of martyrdom.

As early as 1919, Gandhi said in a letter that *"satyagraha* was an attempt to introduce the religious element in politics."[146] Unless this point is firmly grasped, the doctrine of *satyagraha* cannot be appraised properly. The entire doctrine rests upon religious premises and the belief in their relevance to political and social action. There is a strong religious element in the notions of *satya, ahimsa* and *tapas*—the zeal of the prophets, the passionate quest of the mystics, the unshakable faith of the saints. Gandhi's belief in the inevitability of the triumph of truth, the invincibility of nonviolence, and the absolute efficacy of *tapas*, led him to invest *satyagraha* with the power of a magical panacea. He recognized that the doctrine could not be fully understood or accepted by those who did not share his conviction regarding the immortality of the human soul, the transcendental potency of soul-force or the universal sway of the Moral Law (*Karma*), and the moral order of the cosmos (*ṛta*). And yet Gandhi did not show enough awareness of the difficulties in his doctrine of *satyagraha* even for a believer, let alone for those who could not share all his presuppositions.

At the center of Gandhi's conception of *satyagraha* lay his image of the ideal *satyagrahi,* a religious as well as a political model, the archetype of the Good Citizen as well as of the perfect devotee of Truth. At different times he attempted a portrait of this ideal type of man and citizen, a Platonic piece of idealization and far more than a Plutarchian Hero, a figure out of the Golden Age of *Satya Yuga.* He was both Christ and Socrates, Buddha and Prahlad rolled into one; this impossible ideal fired Gandhi's imagination and shaped his daily life, but it also led him to expect too much from mortals. He was not so naïve as to think that *satyagraha* could be offered only by perfect men nor did he fail to see that growth toward the ideal must be painfully slow. He pointed out that

> the exercise of the purest soul-force, in its perfect form, brings about instantaneous relief. For this exercise, prolonged training of the individual soul is an absolute necessity, so that a perfect *satyagrahi* has to be almost, if not entirely, a perfect man. We cannot all suddenly become such men, but if my proposition is correct—as I know it to be correct—the greater the spirit of

satyagraha in us, the better men will we become . . . *satyagraha* is the noblest and best education.[147]

The *satyagrahi* must avoid artificiality in all his doings so that all his acts spring from inward conviction,[148] he must embrace poverty, engage in the ceaseless process of self-purification, develop an unshakable faith in Truth or some Supreme Power,[149] prepare himself by deliberate training for the eventuality of martyrdom, perfect his grasp and exemplification of *satya, ahimsa* and *tapas*. The ideal was depicted in the grandest of terms, but its meaningfulness was shown to Gandhi by his experience of the heroism and dedication of a few remarkable followers he had in South Africa.

> The men and women in Charlestown held to their difficult post of duty in such a stoical spirit. . . . If anyone wanted peace, he had to search for it within . . . it is in the midst of such a storm that a devotee like Mirabai takes the cup of poison to her lips with cheerful equanimity, that Socrates quietly embraces death in his dark and solitary cell and initiates his friends and us into the mysterious doctrine that he who seeks peace must look for it within himself.[150]

On his return to India Gandhi stressed the role of the *satyagrahi* as a good citizen, an exemplary servant of society.

> The solitary *satyagrahi* has to examine himself. If he has universal love and if he fulfils the conditions implied in such a state, it must find expression in his daily conduct. He would be bound with the poorest in the village by the ties of service. He would constitute himself the scavenger, the nurse, the arbitrator of disputes, and the teacher of the children of the village. Every one, young and old, would know him; though a householder, he would be leading a life of restraint; he would make no distinction between his and his neighbour's children; he would owe nothing, but would hold what wealth he has in trust for others, and would, therefore, spend out of it just sufficient for his barest needs. His needs would, as far as possible, approximate to those of the poor; he would harbour no untouchability, and would, therefore, inspire people of all castes and creeds to approach him with confidence. Such is the ideal *satyagrahi*. . . . Such a *satyagrahi* will not find himself single-handed for long.[151]

Gandhi also pointed out that in *satyagraha* it is never the numbers that count; it is always the quality, more so when the forces of violence are uppermost.[152] He not merely idealized the *satyagrahi* but he did the same in regard to a movement of pure *satyagraha*. He declared that in such a movement there is no room for hatred, that self-reliance is the order of the day, that no one has to look expectantly at another, and that there are no leaders and hence no followers or all are leaders and all are followers, so that the death of a fighter intensifies rather than slackens the struggle. Thus Gandhi could at times transcendentalize the *satyagrahi* and *satyagraha* to such an extent that they become poetic romanticism and cease to be political concepts. The visionary overshadowed the reformer, the saint obscured the revolutionary on such occasions. The heroic ideal, the monastic life, the anarchist vision were all fused into a grand conception that seems too remote from reality even for Indians today.

The religious component in *satyagraha* may be seen not merely in the ideal constructions that Gandhi offered but also in his attempt, following the *Gita,* to regard the earthly battlefield (*Kurukshetra*) as a righteous struggle (*Dharmakshetra*) between truth and falsehood, love and hate, justice and injustice, greed and altruism. He regarded the movement of non-cooperation not as a struggle between peoples but between tyranny and freedom, irreligion and religion.[153] He also held that the duty of non-cooperation with unjust men and rulers is as strictly enjoined by all the religions as is the duty of cooperation with just men and rulers.[154] He further claimed that a righteous struggle, "a *dharmayuddha,* in which there are no secrets to be guarded, no scope for cunning, and no place for untruth, comes unsought, and a man of religion is ever ready for it."[155] The struggle in South Africa was, in his view, such a spontaneous and righteous battle.

It is true that the doctrine of *satyagraha* was couched at times in religious language, thus making it unacceptable to many people and even repellent to some. It is, however, possible to regard *satyagraha* simply as the weapon of moral power which men have employed at different times in unspectacular ways but with singular effectiveness in certain situations. There are many examples in history of men who have stood firmly by their principles, upheld conscience in the face of injustice, willingly faced persecution and martyrdom, courageously refused to compromise with the dictates of State or Church. It is the presence of this spirit of stubborn adherence to basic human values and stout resistance to injustice and oppression, the heroism of the martyrs and the courage of the reformers, that Gandhi had in mind when he said that *satyagraha* was as ancient as the hills.

He himself spoke mostly about soul-force but also about the "moral power" displayed in the willing acceptance of suffering in defiance of authority and for the vindication of truth.[156] His disciple, K. G. Mashruwalla, has pointed out that this moral power is independent of a man's intellectual development or personal cultivation.

> The limits may have been prescribed by him or by those who have influenced his life. They may be very low in a first-class statesman, scientist or litterateur and very high in an illiterate or a naked aboriginal. In times of stress like famine, war, pestilence and extreme poverty, this force may have an ebb. But there is none who has not some sense or understanding of it and its nucleus. Though often associated with religion and philosophy, it has no necessary relation with either . . . we find it based on an innate desire to be good or right in our own person and conduct, and towards the world we come in contact with. . . . Besides this moral force, there is also another force in man, which, though not always active, is potentially present in every human being, and when aroused, releases tremendous energy in him. It enables him to sacrifice or resignedly suffer loss of all worldly gifts and comforts, loss of dear ones, and if necessary, bear tortures even unto death. When in full operation the force destroys the natural instinct of fear and imparts to him a new purpose in life and a missionary zeal to fulfil it. The awakening of this force —its conversion from potential state into dynamic—is the precursor of every revolution—religious, political or any other. . . . It is a force which generates indomitable will in the awakened individual and society, and may be called the "vital force." This force, however, does not always act in unison with the moral force. . . . Vital force that is not in adjustment with man's moral force is Satan or the force of Might. The same in unison with and having its ultimate stay in his moral force is *satyagraha*.[157]

Whether we believe or not in these two forces—noetic (from *nous*) and psychic (from *psyche*), derived from *Buddhi* and *Prana* (moral perception and vital energy)—and the possibility of the former using the latter, we can still attach a minimal, everyday sense to the notion of moral power, acting on the will of man. Gandhi's whole purpose was to show that this moral power and energy in man can be consciously cultivated by individuals and by groups and applied courageously to the quest for justice in politics and society. This is the rationale of *satyagraha,* reduced to its essentials. The doctrine was supported by the empirical observation that "the world learns to apply to a man the standards which he applies to himself."[158] The *satyagrahi* knows the power of opinion as a factor in politics and society, and he seeks to arouse it by his moral example in support of a just cause and in defiance of persons entrenched in positions of public or private authority. It is arguable that untouchability in India, the elementary rights of indentured labor in South Africa, the creation of a mass movement to compel the attention of the British *raj* in its most recalcitrant phase, are instances of objectives which could not be secured more worthily than by the adoption of *satyagraha.*

Broadly, we might say that there are two familiar types of infuriating people. One is the moralist; the other is the legalist. The moralist is infuriating when he wants to raise every single issue, however local and specific, to the status of an eternal principle; the legalist is infuriating when he wants to evade a crucial matter of moral principle concerning essential human rights and human dignity by invoking rule stringency or the inertia of custom and precedent. The strength of Gandhi's theory lies in its avoidance of crude moralism by showing how important and how difficult are the conditions under which men may successfully and consistently uphold eternal principles, and also in its rejection of the extremely shaky assumption of naïve legalism that there is no moral justification called for, and that the entire *onus probandi* rests always upon the citizen who dares to challenge *raison d'état* or upset public tranquillity. Even if we retain our doubts about the applicability of *satyagraha* to most social and political problems, we can hardly deny that it contains an important political truth and could fulfill an educative function.

The truth that the doctrine of *satyagraha* emphasizes is that social and political conflicts can best be resolved in an atmosphere in which the contestants respect each other's moral worth, distinguish between measures and persons, conduct their battles in a spirit of self-criticism and abstain from the cruder forms of coercion. When the coercive element is strong in conducting a conflict, it demoralizes the winner and humiliates the loser, leaves behind it a trail of continuing bitterness or suppressed resentment. Fear is always a bad counsellor, and solutions that rest on the appeal to fear are less lasting or satisfying than agreement achieved in the context of a consensus of goodwill. Further, when a conflict takes place between unequal parties, it is tempting for the stronger to regard itself as invulnerable, to identify its interests with the general good or to think it can ignore with impunity the just claims of others. In such situations, the appeal to force is useless for the weaker party and merely increases the complacency of the stronger. The weaker can compel the attention of the materially stronger by showing their reserves of moral and spiritual strength and by casting doubt on the self-assurance and moral conceit of their opponents. Even if those who resort to *satyagraha* fail to secure their ends, they retain their self-respect and are morally enhanced, although they have sometimes to pay the price of political or physical martyrdom.

Satyagraha can be easily abused, especially by those who, without preparation, expect too much from it. But at its best it is a vindication of the heroic possibilities of men in the face of evil. It is Gandhi's declaration of the dignity of suffering in a just cause.

> If our country, even in its present fallen state, can exhibit this type of bravery, what a beacon light will it be for Europe with all its discipline, science and organization! If Europe but realized that, heroic as it undoubtedly is for a handful of people to offer armed resistance in the face of superior numbers, it is far more heroic to stand up against overwhelming numbers without any arms at all, it would save itself and blaze a trail for the world.[159]

12

Swaraj and *Swadeshi*

SELF-RULE AND
SELF-RELIANCE

*As an heir, even though he were heir to the treasure of all the world,
nevertheless does not possess his property before he has come of age,
so even the richest personality is nothing before he has chosen himself,
and on the other hand even what one might call the poorest personality
is everything when he has chosen himself; for the great thing is not to
be this or that but to be oneself, and this everyone can be if he wills it.*

*He who regards life ethically sees the universal, and he who lives ethi-
cally expresses the universal in his life, he makes himself the universal
man, not by divesting himself of his concretion, for then he becomes
nothing, but by clothing himself with it and permeating it with the universal. For the universal man is not a phantom, but every man as such
is the universal man, that is to say, to every man the way is assigned by
which he becomes the universal man. . . . He who lives ethically la-
bours to become the universal man.*

KIERKEGAARD

Traditional political theory has been chiefly concerned with the relationship between individual freedom and external authority in human society. The major problem in any political community is to ensure freedom or to justify its restriction, from the standpoint of the individual as a moral agent. The same problem, when seen from the standpoint of the community or the State, is to get the individual subject to identify himself and his long-term interest with the wider community to which he belongs as well as with the acceptance of the legitimacy of State authority. Different concepts of liberty as well as different theories of society and the State may be viewed as alternative ways of asserting a peculiar connection between the moral status of a person as a free agent and his enhanced status and enlarged role as a willing member of a community and a State which have certain undefined or specific claims upon him. In early Greek thought, as well as in ancient Indian thought, the notion of self-government as applied to the collectivity of members of a polity was closely related to the conception of self-rule as applied to the moral growth of every human being. The maturity and development of a polity were regarded as a reflection as well as an index of the degree of moral maturity and self-cultivation of an élite or a generality of individuals.

In modern political thought there has been a growing gap between the abstract language of moral philosophy and the seemingly more concrete vocabulary of politics. With the emergence of large nation-states, the disappearance of even the quest for direct democracy and the radical shift of emphasis from the notion of "participation" to that of "representation," the concept of self-government has become bound up with the demand for national independence and the institutional superstructure of liberal democratic theory. Furthermore, the very idea of the autonomy of the individual, let alone the Platonic and Stoic ideal of self-rule, have been severely undermined especially by utilitarian or naturalistic ethics and by the confusing impact of the methods of the natural sciences upon social studies. In political theory, we seem to be compelled to choose between a rarefied yet defensive notion of "negative" liberty and a variety of muddled conceptions of "positive" liberty. The illegitimate heir of the ancient concept of self-rule is the romantic or revolutionary anarchist who denies not merely the legitimacy but also the need for State authority, and who seeks to escape from the oppressive claims of organized society into the cosmic empyrean or the solitude of his soul. On the other hand, the doctrine of *raison d'état* as well as the gospel of collective freedom, which are invoked by rulers in distress and by the nationalist leaders of dependent peoples, possess a deceptive if not authoritarian flavor in the eyes of those who do not or cannot share the emotions conveyed by such appeals.

At the center of Indian political thought lay the concept of *swaraj* or self-rule, connected with the notion of *swarajya* which referred to a particular mode of securing self-determination in a polity comprised of several distinct sectors. In modern India the term *swaraj* was exclusively identified by Naoroji and Tilak with the goal of national independence, and the emphasis was wholly shifted from the positive to the negative connotation of the term and its application entirely transferred from its individual to its collective scope. Toward the end of the nineteenth century—even before the term *swaraj,* in its new sense, acquired common currency in the nationalist movement—the Bengali militants sought to justify their doctrine of boycott of British goods in the name of *swadeshi* or patriotism.

When Gandhi entered the Indian scene, he was able to restore to the term *swaraj* its older meaning while retaining its newer sense, to reinterpret the term *swadeshi* and considerably extend its application and, above all, to point to the close connection between *swaraj* and *swadeshi,* between individual self-rule and individual self-reliance, between national self-government and national self-dependence. Instead of assimilating the concept of freedom to that of community by merging the individual into an organic conception of society, he derived the very notion of communal self-reliance from his doctrine of individual self-rule, and showed how the pursuit of *swaraj* must necessarily involve the acceptance of *swadeshi,* and yet the former must be taken as logically and morally prior to the latter. He achieved this result by basing *swaraj* upon *satya,* i.e., linking the notions of freedom and of truth, secondly, by deriving the doctrine of *swadeshi* from his concept of *ahimsa* (emphasizing its positive rather than its negative connotation) and thirdly, by basing the connection between *swaraj* and *swadeshi* upon the relationship between *satya* and *ahimsa.* The first two steps were taken consciously, while the third was intuitively perceived as a result of his continual preoccupation with the connection between *satya* and *ahimsa*.

In principle, *satya* is prior to *ahimsa;* though conceptually they are almost interchangeably intertwined, the former may be regarded as the end and the latter as the only legitimate means. In practice, the test and the immediate requirement of the pursuit of *satya* is the practice of *ahimsa* so that the means becomes even more important than the end at the level of conduct. Analogously, *swaraj* is theoretically of a higher order of importance than *swadeshi,* though the two are inextricably bound up even conceptually, and yet in practice, *swadeshi* has a greater immediacy and significance than *swaraj.* If *swaraj* is the end, *swadeshi* is the only legitimate means. As a validating principle, freedom or self-rule has priority over patriotism or self-dependence; as a practical test, the extent of the latter reveals the measure of the former already realized. Just as Gandhi sometimes tended in practice to make *ahimsa* almost an end in itself, so too he was inclined at times to treat *swadeshi* (and its derivatives—boycott and the spinning wheel) with a deference that annoyed those who were impatient to achieve *swaraj* in the formal sense of national independence. But in order to appreciate the significance of the way in which Gandhi connected the notions of *swaraj* and *swadeshi,* it is necessary to consider the former in some detail so as to indicate the important connection between individual and national freedom, and between individual and collective self-reliance. *Swaraj* and *swadeshi* are essential to Gandhi's political ethic, and they also have institutional implications for him in his picture of a nonviolent socialist society and a decentralized polity comprised of village republics.

In his analysis of the term *swaraj* or self-rule, Gandhi was concerned to distinguish between the fuller moral connotation of freedom and the narrower, negative meaning of individual or national independence. In 1931 he was asked to explain the significance of the phrase *purna swaraj* or complete independence, which had become the declared goal of the Congress. He replied:

> I do not know any word or phrase to answer it in the English language—I can, therefore, only give an explanation. The root meaning of *swaraj* is self-rule. *Swaraj* may, therefore, be rendered as

disciplined rule from within and *purna* means "complete." "Independence" has no such limitation. Independence may mean license to do as you like. *Swaraj* is positive. Independence is negative. *Purna Swaraj* does not exclude association with any nation, much less with England. But it can only mean association for mutual benefit and at will. Thus there are countries which are said to be independent but which have no *Purna Swaraj* e.g. Nepal. The word *Swaraj* is a sacred word, a Vedic word, meaning self-rule and self-restraint, and not freedom from all restraint which "independence" often means.[1]

At first sight, it would seem that in his desire to distinguish between freedom and license, or between national freedom and total independence from all ties with other nations, Gandhi is expressing a preference for the concept of "positive" freedom over that of negative liberty. His concern, however, is really to stress that freedom for an individual or a nation does not mean total isolation from others or an abdication of the very sense of a moral obligation toward other agents who are equally entitled to claim freedom for themselves. The free man can choose to enter into any association with other agents, but he cannot isolate himself entirely or live entirely unto himself. The same is true of nations. Gandhi equated freedom with self-rule because he wished to build into the concept of freedom the notion of obligation to others as well as to oneself, while retaining the element of voluntariness as the very basis of freedom. The notion of self-rule implies the voluntary internalization of our obligation to others which will be obstructed by our placing ourselves at the mercy of our selfish desires. A free man or nation, in Gandhi's concept of *swaraj*, cannot be selfish and need not be an isolationist (if it were ever possible to do this totally), but he has the right to choose to be selfish or not, to be isolationist or not.

Elsewhere, Gandhi pointed out that the "rule of all without rule of oneself would prove to be as deceptive and disappointing as a painted toy mango, charming to look at outwardly but hollow and empty from within."[2] A person or nation which regards its freedom as dependent upon ruling over others has exchanged the enduring substance of freedom for its evanescent shadow. To imagine oneself as free is not the same thing as to be effectively free. This elementary truth has been perhaps dangerously overstated by those who insistently distinguish between real and illusory freedom, as Marxists have done in their attacks on bourgeois freedom or utilitarians in their distinction between the hedonistic notion of pleasurable sensations and the rational recognition of real, concrete, solid interests. The danger lies, however, not so much in making this elementary distinction as in using it to deny the voluntariness even in imaginary freedom and then to justify the interference by the party or the State in the name of real freedom.

Gandhi's recognition of this point is apparent from several statements. He stressed the sanctity of the notion of freedom, whether real or imaginary. "Freedom is never dear at any price. It is the breath of life. What would a man not pay for living."[3] More explicitly, he asserted that freedom received through the effort of others, however benevolent, cannot be retained when such effort is withdrawn. In other words, such freedom is not real freedom.[4] The concept of *swaraj* implies that if a man is capable of self-rule, by definition, he also can judge whether and when he is really free, and may test this by the extent of his dependence upon others or of his desire to dominate over others. The distinction between real and imaginary freedom can never be used, in Gandhi's use of the phrase "real freedom," to justify external interference in the name of freedom or the vicarious pursuit by an individual or nation of another's freedom. Gandhi argued that "freedom is not worth having if it does not connote the freedom to err and even to sin."[5] He regarded this right as innate and could not comprehend, he said, "how human beings, be they ever so experienced and able, can delight in depriving other human beings of that precious right." The implication of this statement is that those who talk of real freedom for the purpose of denying the right to err to others, or of depriving them of their freedom (which is real to them, however imaginary it be to others) are, in fact, casting doubt on the sincerity of their belief in the value of freedom or their earnestness in pursuing their own freedom as a value in itself. Gandhi saw this clearly when freedom is understood in the setting of national politics, but he quite independently appreciated this truth in regard to individual freedom. He argued that we must grant the right to negative liberty to all men, particularly if we wish to get others to choose to accept restrictions or to make sacrifices for the sake of the wider goals of larger units.

> Individual freedom alone can make a man voluntarily surrender himself completely to the service of society. If it is wrested from him, he becomes an automaton and society is ruined. No society can possibly be built on a denial of individual freedom. It is contrary to the very nature of man. Just as man will not grow horns or a tail so he will not exist as man if he has no mind of his own. In reality even those who do not believe in the liberty of the individual believe in their own.[6]

This important passage has several implications.

Gandhi grounded the concept of freedom in the very nature of man as an autonomous moral agent and at the same time argued that the survival of society, the continuance of a community, was contingent upon the effective freedom of the individual. Proponents of negative liberty, from Mill downwards, have justified it as man's natural right which is seen as sacred and inviolable against the claims of society. On the other hand, the upholders of the concept of positive liberty have, like Hegel, made man's rationality dependent upon the fact of community and the role of the State. Gandhi, however, conflated the notions of the moral and social necessity of individual freedom. He incorporated freedom into the definition of man and his very conception of society. He saw the authoritarian's position as springing from his inability to universalize the notion of freedom, his inconsistency in denying it to others while requiring it for himself.

A more important element in the concept of *swaraj* is the corollary that if it is grounded in the very nature of man, it cannot be conferred as a gift, but must be claimed on the basis of self-awareness and earned through self-effort. Gandhi put forward the proposition that "the outward freedom that we shall attain will only be in exact proportion to the inward freedom to which we may have grown at a given moment. And if this is the correct view of freedom, our chief energy must be concentrated upon achieving reform from within."[7] The concept of *swaraj*, founded as it is on the moral autonomy of the individual, places the entire burden of responsibility entirely upon him. Any external threat to our freedom is to be explained, not so much by blaming circumstances outside our own control, as by recognizing our own weakness in the first place. Gandhi expressed this idea in the following way:

> The Devil succeeds only by receiving help from his fellows. He always takes advantage of the weakest spots in our natures in order to gain mastery over us. Even so does the Government retain control over us through our weaknesses or vices. And if we could render ourselves proof against its machinations, we must remove our weaknesses. It is for this reason that I have called non-cooperation a process of self-purification. As soon as that process is completed, this government must fall to pieces for want of the necessary environment, just as mosquitoes cease to haunt a place whose cesspools are filled up and dried.[8]

Thus an integral part of the concept of *swaraj* or self-rule is the notion of self-purification which gives the strength and capacity to make our abstract claim to freedom on moral grounds effective in the practical context of politics and society. To assert the right of an individual or nation to freedom is also to accept their willing recognition of the need to take practical steps to secure or maintain effective freedom. Gandhi declared that "a man who is mad as I now am after freedom, a man who is hungry after freedom—and a real hunger for freedom is infinitely more painful than hunger for mere bread—has got to take tremendous risks, to stake everything that he has in order to gain that precious freedom."[9]

It is obvious that in his analysis of the concept of *swaraj* Gandhi made many statements that he believed to be primarily true of individual liberty but which he was concerned to emphasize because of his concern with national freedom. All his statements about *swaraj* or self-rule and freedom are equally applicable to individuals and to groups. He repeatedly asserted the connection between the notions of individual and collective self-rule, and especially between individual and national freedom. "The first step to *swaraj* lies in the individual. The great truth: 'As with the individual so with the universe' is applicable here as elsewhere."[10] This statement expresses the ancient Indian belief that man is the microcosm of the macrocosm, that self-discovery could lead to an understanding of the nature of reality and the structure of cosmic order. As

Gandhi ascribed ontological priority to the individual as a self-conscious agent and refused to regard groups as entities (except as a manner of speaking), he declared that the "*swaraj* of a people means the sum total of the *swaraj* [self-rule] of individuals."[11] Further, "government over self is the truest *swaraj*, it is synonymous with *moksha* or salvation."[12]

Gandhi became explicit about the meaning of *swaraj* as applied to the individual when he was called upon to elaborate his view of national *swaraj*, but although he started often with the latter concept and went on to talk of the former, he saw that the notion of individual *swaraj* is logically and conceptually prior to the notion of collective or national *swaraj*. His intention is clear from the following passage:

> Self-expression and self-government are not things which may be either taken from us by anybody or which can be given us by anybody. It is quite true that if those who happen to hold our destinies, or seem to hold our destinies in their hands, are favourably disposed, are sympathetic, understand our aspirations, no doubt it is easier for us to expand. But after all self-government depends entirely on our own internal strength, upon our ability to fight against the heaviest odds. Indeed, self-government which does not require that continuous striving to attain it and to sustain it is not worth the name. I have therefore endeavoured to show both in word and in deed, that political self-government— that is self-government for a large number of men and women— is no better than individual self-government, and therefore it is to be attained by precisely the same means that are required for individual self-government or self-rule, and so as you know also, I have striven in India to place this ideal before the people in season and out of season, very often much to the disgust of those who are politically minded merely.[13]

Gandhi's reason for stressing the connection between individual and national *swaraj* was really to show that the means required for both were similar and were equally exacting. But he also recognized that both concepts involved assertions of what amounts to a natural right, even if the process of making this claim effective in practice is an arduous one. He grounded this right in the capacity for self-choice and the freedom to experiment, and argued that this referred to the law of individual and cosmic evolution, which was also embedded in the process of history. He said:

> Evolution is always experimental. All progress is gained through mistakes and their rectification. No good comes fully fashioned . . . but has to be carved out through repeated experiments and repeated failures by ourselves. This is the law of individual growth. The same law controls social and political evolution also. The right to err, which means the freedom to try experiments, is the universal condition of all progress.[14]

It is important to see that the notion of *swaraj* has both a minimal and a maximal meaning. When we talk of self-rule, we may be chiefly concerned in certain contexts to declare a natural right of self-determination against those who wish to rule over us and restrict our own freedom. At the same time, when we are interpreting the concept of self-rule to ourselves, we are concerned with its maximal and perfectionist character in order to remind ourselves that we can lose our freedom only through our own weakness, that even when we possess it we cannot make it effective without a demanding and continuous process of self-cultivation, and that without a freely chosen discipline or code of self-restraint we ourselves may abuse our freedom and not come any nearer to the exalted end of the genuinely and completely free individual. Similarly, when we are claiming the right to national freedom, we are arguing for our right to make mistakes and to rule ourselves badly against those foreigners who justify alien rule by appealing to their superior capacity for good government. In such a context we are asserting that self-government is better than good government. On the other hand, when we are contemplating our own national predicament, we must accept full responsibility when we have lost our freedom and are seeking to recover it or when we have it and are in danger of losing it. In Gandhi's words, we come to see that "freedom's battles are not fought without paying heavy prices."[15]

The advantage of inflating the notion of *swaraj* is that we see that freedom from external intervention is a necessary but not a sufficient condition for the effective and full realization of our liberty, which is the product of self-rule. Similarly, national independence by itself is merely a necessary but not a sufficient condition of national self-rule. As a moral leader of a political movement, Gandhi was concerned that his followers should set their sights high, and especially after independence he insisted that real *swaraj* had not been attained. During the struggle for independence he urged that while Indians should assert their moral claim to freedom from foreign rule, they must not blame their dependence upon their rulers rather than upon their own weakness. Both before and after the attainment of independence, he was determined to base the justification of seeking national freedom upon a concern to secure the conditions in which every individual could pursue the prolonged quest for self-rule. Thus, although he drew a close correspondence between individual and national *swaraj* he recognized from the first that the former does not automatically lead to the latter even if there is a necessary relationship between them.

Gandhi was perhaps the only leader of a nationalist movement who saw the possible force of the claim that individual liberty might be safer under foreign rule than under self-government, though he was concerned to deny that this could provide any justification for alien rule. He wrote as early as 1921:

> We seek arrest because the so-called freedom is slavery. We are challenging the might of this government because we consider its activity to be wholly evil. . . . We want to compel its submission to the people's will. We desire to show that the government exists to serve the people, not the people the government. Free life under the government has become intolerable, for the price exacted for the retention of freedom is unconscionably great. Whether we are one or many, we must refuse to purchase freedom at the cost of our self-respect or our cherished convictions. I have known even little children become unbending when an attempt has been made to cross their declared purposes be it ever so flimsy in the estimation of their parents.[16]

In this passage Gandhi was really asserting as a contingent truth that self-rule would be meaningless to most people when they had lost their self-respect under foreign rule. This does not mean that individual self-rule is totally dependent upon national self-government. In fact, Gandhi went so far as to say that "self-government means continuous effort to be independent of government control whether it is foreign government or whether it is national. *Swaraj* government will be a sorry affair if people look up to it for the regulation of every detail of life."[17] Further, "real *swaraj* will come not by the acquisition of authority by a few but by the acquisition of the capacity by all to resist authority when it is abused."[18] In other words, *swaraj* is to be attained by educating the masses to a sense of their capacity to regulate and control authority. "*Swaraj* for me means freedom for the meanest of my countrymen. I am not interested in freeing India merely from the English yoke. I am bent upon freeing India from any yoke whatsoever. I have no desire to exchange 'king log' for 'king stork.' "[19] Gandhi went even further when he asserted that "there is no freedom for India so long as one man, no matter how highly placed he may be, holds in the hollow of his hands the life, property and honour of millions of human beings. It is an artificial, unnatural and uncivilized institution. The end of it is an essential preliminary to *swaraj*."[20]

Gandhi could not regard good government as better than self-government because he believed there was a connection between individual and national self-rule. As he said, "self-evolution is wholly consistent with a nation's evolution."[21] A nation cannot advance without the units of which it is composed advancing, and conversely no individual can advance without the nation of which he is a part also advancing. "On the principle that the greater includes the less, national independence or national freedom is included in the spiritual."[22] That is to say, national self-government is less important than individual self-rule but is included in it. Although Gandhi considerably stretched the meaning of national *swaraj*, he even more widened the connotation of individual self-rule. "My conception of freedom is no narrow conception. It is coextensive with the freedom of man in all his majesty."[23]

An important and odd consequence of the idea that our freedom or self-rule depends entirely upon our self-awareness, our self-respect and our self-discipline, is the notion that when the masses of a nation are awakened to a sense of their collective and individual claims to freedom, they have already attained to *swaraj*, in a sense. This looks odd, but it has an important corollary. *Swaraj* cannot be attained by a nation even in the formal sense unless it is gained as the result of a mass movement involving the willing and conscious participation by most of the individuals who make up a nation. "*Purna swaraj* denotes a condition of things when the dumb and lame millions will speak and walk. That *swaraj* cannot be achieved by force, but by organization and unity."[24] In its full sense, *swaraj* cannot be identified with majority rule. "There could not be a greater mistake than that," said Gandhi. "If it were true, I for one would refuse to call it *swaraj* and would fight it with all the strength at my command, for to me *Hind Swaraj* is the rule of all people, is the rule of Justice."[25] Clearly, in this exalted sense no community or nation today has attained to *swaraj* just as no individual could attain to complete self-rule. Gandhi inflated the notion of *swaraj,* almost transcendentalized it out of existence, as he did with his concepts of *satya* and *ahimsa* and *satyagraha,* but this did not mean that differences of degree were not important to him. He made it possible to stress such differences by also giving a minimal, formal meaning to *swaraj.* He said on one occasion that "there is no substitute for *swaraj,* and the only universal definition to give it is that status of India which her people desire at a given moment."[26] Thus *swaraj* contains a penumbra of meanings, ranging from the most literal and formal to the most transcendental and elusive, including both minimal and maximal connotations. This can be understood when we see that the concept of individual *swaraj,* rooted in self-awareness and self-choice, is connected with the notions of self-dependence, self-criticism, self-purification, self-restraint and self-realization.

Clearly, there is a continual danger that all such abstract concepts which require authentic self-reference are especially prone to perversions and inversions when they are made to subserve collectivist goals in mass politics. The specific symbols of integrity stressed by Gandhi became sacrosanct in the political movement for formal *swaraj* and lent to *swadeshi* as a shibboleth a harsh and hypocritical fervor. As long as *swaraj* and *swadeshi* are psychologically bound up in practice with self-respect, the truth at the core of *swaraj* could be submerged in the welter of violent emotion released by those who use *swadeshi* as an instrument of moral blackmail and thus pander effectively to xenophobia and cultural narrow-mindedness. That these tendencies were deeply repugnant to the Indian tradition of expansive eclecticism was known to Gandhi as much as to critics like Tagore or to heretical followers like Nehru. Fortunately, in Gandhi's lifetime the concepts of *swaraj* and of *swadeshi* did not become the focus of inquisitorial controversies, of counter-claims and accusations in the name of "left-wing adventurism" or "right-wing chauvinism" that have been part of the ideological careers of Marxist-Leninism and of militant Mao-ism.

Since Gandhi's own martyrdom, the vital and morally significant connection between the desire for freedom and the need to belong, between *swaraj* and *swadeshi*, is much clearer today when rootless individuals in contemporary societies are unresponsive to the elevation of global homogenization in external trappings to the status of a genuinely universal culture. It may well be that the mature man of tomorrow will exemplify a dialectical skill in honoring multiple allegiances, without sacrificing either breadth or depth, by combining a much broader conception of *swadeshi* and an even deeper perception of *swaraj* than Gandhi was in a position to elaborate. Perhaps, here as elsewhere, the insights of Gandhi are more meaningful in their individual than in their collective applications, even though the logical extension of the concepts of *satya* and *ahimsa* to ever-widening groups of individuals must necessarily yield the macropolitical consequences that were crucial to Gandhi's vision of communities of free men.

13

MEANS AND ENDS
IN POLITICS

Before it move, hold it,
Before it go wrong, mould it,
Drain off water in winter before it freeze,
Before weeds grow, sow them to the breeze.
You can deal with what has not happened, can foresee
Harmful events and not allow them to be.
Though—as naturally as a seed becomes a tree of armwide girth—
There can rise a nine-tiered tower from a man's handful of earth
Or here at your feet a thousand-mile journey have birth,
Quick action bruises,
Quick grasping loses.
Therefore a sane man's care is not to exert
One move that can miss, one move that can hurt.
Most people who miss, after almost winning,
Should have "known the end from the beginning."

LAO TZU

Most political and social thinkers have been concerned with the desirable (and even necessary) goals of a political system or with the common and competing ends that men actually desire, and then pragmatically considered the means that are available to rulers and citizens. Even those who have sought a single, general and decisive criterion of decision-making have stated the ends and then been more concerned with the consequences of social and political acts than with consistently applying standards of intrinsic value. It has become almost a sacred dogma in our age of apathy that politics, centered on power and conflict and the quest for legitimacy and consensus, is essentially a study in expediency, a tortuous discovery of practical expedients that could reconcile contrary claims and secure a common if minimal goal or, at least, create the conditions in which different ends could be freely or collectively pursued. Liberal thinkers have sought to show that it is possible for each individual to be used as a means for another to achieve his ends without undue coercion and to his own distinct advantage. This occurs not by conscious cooperation or deliberately pursuing a common end but by each man pursuing diverse ends in accordance with the "law" of the natural identity of interests, a "law" that is justified if not guaranteed in terms of metaphysical, economic or biological "truths." Authoritarian thinkers, on the other hand, justified coercion in the name of a predetermined common end, the attainment of which cannot be left to the chaotic interplay of innumerable wills. The end may simply be the preservation of a traditional order, the recovery of a bygone age of glory, or the ruthless reconstruction of society from the top to secure some spectacular consummation in the future.

It appears to be common to most schools of thought to accept a sharp dichotomy between ends and means, a distinction that is deeply embedded in our ethical, political and psychological vocabulary, rooted in rigid European presuppositions regarding the very nature of human action. Distinctions have been repeatedly made between immediate and ultimate, short-term and long-term, diverse and common, individual and social, essential and desirable ends, as also between attainable and utopian goals. Discussion about means has not ignored questions about their moral implications and propriety, or about the extent of their theoretical and contingent compatibility with desired ends or widely shared values. But despite all these reservations, the dangerous dogma that the end entirely justifies the means is merely an extreme version of the commonly uncriticized belief that moral considerations cannot apply to the means except in relation to ends, or that the latter have a moral priority.

Gandhi seems to stand almost alone among social and political thinkers in his firm rejection of the rigid dichotomy between ends and means and in his extreme moral preoccupation with the means to the extent that they, rather than the ends, provide the standard of reference. He was led to this position by his early acceptance of *satya* and *ahimsa,* truth and nonviolence, as twin moral absolutes and his consistent view of their relationship. In *Hind Swaraj* he wrote that even great men who have been considered religious have committed grievous crimes through the mistaken belief that there is no moral connection or interdependence between the means and the end. We cannot get a rose by planting a noxious weed. "The means may be likened to a seed, the end to a tree; and there is just the same inviolable connection between the means and the end as there is between the seed and the tree."[1]

It is not as though violence and nonviolence are merely different means to secure the same end. As they are morally different in quality and essence, they must necessarily achieve different results. The customary dichotomy between means and ends originates in, and reinforces, the view that they are two entirely different categories of action and that their relationship is mainly a technical matter to be settled by considering what will be effective and what is possible in a given situation, that the ethical problem of choice requires an initial decision regarding the desired end and the obligatory acceptance of whatever steps seem necessary to secure it or are most likely to do so. Gandhi, however, was led by his metaphysical belief in the law of *Karma*—the law of ethical causation or moral retribution that links all the acts of interdependent individuals—to the view that the relationship between means and ends is organic, the moral quality of the latter being causally dependent upon that of the former. The psychology of human action in a morally indivisible community of apparently isolated units demands that the means-end relationship must be seen in terms of the consistent growth in moral awareness of individuals and communities and not in relation to the mechanical division of time into arbitrary and discrete intervals. If for Gandhi there was no "wall of separation" between means and end, this was because of his basic belief that in politics as in all spheres of human action we reap exactly what we sow.

Gandhi's view of the means-end relationship may be put in the form of the following statements, which overlap and yet express several distinct ideas: "For me it is enough to know the means. Means and end are convertible terms in my philosophy of life."[2] "We have always control over the means but not over the end."[3] "I feel that our progress towards the goal will be in exact proportion to the purity of our means."[4] "They say 'means are after all means.' I would say 'means are after all everything.' As the means so the end."[5]

The first statement rejects the notion that in our actual conduct we can make a firm and decisive distinction between means and ends. Gandhi's conception of the psychology of human action requires this rejection of a conventional conceptual habit which makes us ascribe to ourselves greater knowledge, and greater assurance, than we actually possess. The second statement asserts a contingent truth about the extent and the limit of our free will, that the individual's capacity to determine what he can do in any specific situation at any given time is much greater than his power of anticipation, prediction and control over the consequences of his actions. The third statement expresses the metaphysical belief in the moral law of *Karma,* under which there is an exact causal connection between the extent of the moral "purity" (detachment and disinterestedness or the degree of moral awareness) of an act and the measure of individual effectiveness in promoting or pursuing and securing a morally worthy end over a period of time. Clearly, this metaphysical belief cannot be conclusively verified or falsified by evidence. The fourth statement is a practical recommendation that we must be primarily or even wholly concerned with the immediate adoption of what we regard as a morally worthy (i.e., intrinsically justifiable) means. This recommendation may be accepted by those who subscribe to the second statement and it is mandatory for those who share the metaphysical belief implicit in the third statement.

The closest approximation to Gandhi's view of the means-end relationship is that of Jacques Maritain, who regards the problem of End and Means as *the* basic problem in political philosophy. There are two opposite ways of understanding the "rationalization of political life." There is the easier way of "technical rationalization" through means external to man *versus* the more exacting way of "moral rationalization" through means which are man himself, his freedom and virtue. It is a universal and inviolable axiom for Maritain, an obvious primary principle, that "means must be proportioned and appropriate to the end, since they are ways to the end and, so to speak, the end itself in its very process of coming into existence. So that applying intrinsically evil means to attain an intrinsically good end is simply nonsense and a blunder."[6]

If Maritain and Gandhi have no use for the "easier way of technical rationalization" or for piecemeal "social engineering," this is not merely because of their rejection of a utilitarian in favor of an absolutist (or non-naturalistic) ethic but also because of their daringly unorthodox repudiation of the so-called pragmatist view of politics and the dominant doctrine of double standards which requires sharp separation between the moral considerations applicable to individual conduct and those (if any) regarded as relevant to political action.

Gandhi's view of the morally legitimate means to be exclusively employed in furthering political ends was deeply affected by the doctrine of dispassionate action in the *Gita*.[7] He was convinced that an intense concentration upon the task at hand can and must be combined with a degree of detachment, a freedom from anxiety about the future consequences. If we are sure of the "purity" of the means we employ, we shall be led on by faith, before which "all fear and trembling melt away."[8] Unconcern with results does not mean that we need not have a clear conception of the end in view. But while the cause has to be just and clear as well as the means,[9] it is even more important to recognize that impure means must result in an impure end,[10] that we cannot attain to any truth through untruthful means, that we cannot secure justice through unjust means, or freedom through tyrannical acts, or socialism through enmity and coercion, or enduring peace through war. The man who wields force does not scruple about the means and yet foolishly imagines that this will make no difference to the end he seeks. Gandhi explicitly rejected the doctrine that the end justifies the means,[11] and went so far as to assert that a moral means is almost an end in itself because virtue is its own reward.[12]

The doctrine that the end justifies the means goes back to Kautilya in India and to Machiavelli in the West, and is connected with the notions of self-preservation at all costs and of *raison d'état* and in more recent times with the attainment of a secular millennium through revolutionary action. The doctrine was implicit in *Killing No Murder,* Colonel Sexby's incitement to political assassination published in 1657. This once-famous pamphlet argued that tyrants accomplish their ends much more by fraud than by force and that if they are not eliminated by force the citizens would be degraded into deceitful, perfidious flatterers. It is not only "lawful" and even glorious to kill a tryant, but indeed "everything is lawful against him that is lawful against an open enemy, whom every private man hath a right to kill." It is no doubt possible to justify tyrannicide without going so far as to say that a worthy end legitimizes any and every means. The difficulty, however, is that few practitioners would admit to holding to this maxim in an unqualified and unconditional form.

It has been argued repeatedly that any means is legitimate that is indispensable at least for internal security or to defend society against its external enemies. The sole reason for restricting the choice of means is expediency rather than principle, prudence rather than (non-utilitarian) morality. It is taken for granted that cunning and force must unite in the exercise of power. Power may be justified as a means to a higher end but in the attempt to employ any and every means to secure and maintain power it becomes an end in itself. The idea that one is serving some higher entity which rises far above individual life and that one is no longer serving oneself makes one no less indifferent to the morality of the means employed than the open pursuit of naked self-interest. Alternatively, we have the straightforward Machiavellian notion that the individual agent cannot escape the nature he is born with, that as *fortuna* is malicious so *virtu* must also be malicious when there is no other way open. If *virtu* is the vital power in men which creates and maintains States, *necessita* is the causal pressure required to bring the sluggish masses into line with *virtu*. If there is a moral law, it must be flouted in the practice of politics and this infringement can be justified by the plea of unavoidable necessity. This line of reasoning is commoner than we like to think and is sometimes couched in such specious or emotive language that in moments of crisis many people are hardly aware of the wider implications of a doctrine that they invoke for their special pleading in what seem to be exceptional situations. Hume thought that this doctrine was so widely practiced that it is safer in politics to assume that men are scoundrels even if we do not believe that all men are knaves.

It is true that thinkers like Machiavelli and Bentham have been rather unfairly accused of actually holding that there is an end justifying *all* means to it. Bentham said only that happiness is the end justifying all means, which is more an empty than a pernicious doctrine. Again, Machiavelli never said that power justifies all means to it, but merely that the gaining of power often involves committing some very nasty crimes. A similar defence could also be made on behalf of Kautilya. The important point, however, is not the precise standpoints of Bentham, Machiavelli or Kautilya, but the dangerous uses to which their doctrines could be put. Just as Benthamites, Machiavellians and followers of Kautilya could be charged with ruthlessness (even more than their teachers), so too Gandhians also could be accused of coercive tactics (nonviolent only in a very restricted sense) in the pursuit of worthy ends. But it would be much easier to challenge such Gandhians in terms of Gandhi's fundamental tenets than to appeal to the writings of Machiavelli or Bentham against diehard Machiavellians or Benthamite planners.

The doctrine that the end justifies the means does not even require any special justification for the Marxist who accepts no supra-historic morality, no categorical imperative, religious or secular. Engels declared in his letter to Herson Trier in 1889 that "any means that leads to the aim suits me as a revolutionary, whether it is the most violent or that which appears to be most peaceable." In his pamphlet on *Socialism and War* Lenin said that Marxists differed both from pacifists and anarchists in their belief that the justification of each war must be seen individually in relation to its historical role and its consequences. "There have been many wars in history which, notwithstanding all the horrors, cruelties, miseries and tortures, inevitably connected with every war, had a progressive character, i.e. they served in the development of mankind, aiding in the destruction of extremely pernicious and reactionary institutions . . . or helping to remove the most barbarous despotism in Europe." Whether an action is justifiable or not simply depends on what historical end it serves.

Unlike Engels and Lenin, Trotsky stressed what he called the dialectical interdependence of means and ends. He argued that the means chosen must be shown to be really likely to lead to the liberation of mankind. "Precisely from this it follows that not all means are permissible. When we say that the end justifies the means then for us the conclusion follows that the great revolutionary end spurns those base means and ways which set one part of the working class against other parts, or attempt to make the masses happy without their participation; or lower the faith of the masses in themselves and their organization, replacing it by worship of the leaders" (*Their Morals and Ours*). This is clearly an improvement on Lenin, for it at least provides a criterion by which a collectivist regime or revolutionary leaders could be criticized for pushing an exclusively utilitarian creed to extremes of practical ruthlessness in perpetuating a monopoly of power and privilege.

Although Trotsky denied that the end justifies any and every means, he still insisted that a means can be justified only by its end, which for him is the increase of the power of man over nature and the abolition of the power of man over man. For Gandhi, on the other hand, the end is *satya* or truth, which requires no justification, and the means (*ahimsa* or non-coercion) must be justified not merely with reference to the end but also in itself; every act must be independently justified in terms of the twin absolutes, *satya* and *ahimsa*. It is, therefore, not permissible or possible to *justify* a single act of untruth or violence by appealing to the past or future possession of *satya* and *ahimsa,* though no man can wholly avoid a measure of *himsa* or *asatya* or claim to possess in their fullness absolute truth and absolute, universal love. Weakness and error are ubiquitous and inescapable, but their justification and rationalization make all the difference to our personal and political integrity. We cannot condone our untruthfulness in the present on the ground that we shall be truthful tomorrow when we are stronger or conditions are more favorable. A violent revolution cannot lead (and, in any case, cannot be justified on the ground that it is expected to lead) to a nonviolent society in the fullness of time. Further, in Gandhi's view it is not sometimes, as Trotsky suggested, but always (under the moral law of *Karma*) that the end changes in character as a result of the means adopted in its attainment.

If the doctrine that the end justifies the means is invoked in the attainment of the good society through a single, violent revolution, it could also be made to justify repression in the aftermath of revolution.

In Abram Tertz's *The Trial Begins* we have the following dialogue between Rabinovich and Globov. Rabinovich holds that "every decent End consumes itself. You kill yourself trying to reach it and by the time you get there, it's been turned inside out. These Jesuits of yours made a miscalculation, they slipped up." Globov answers: "They were right. Every educated person knows that the end justifies the means. You can either believe it openly or secretly but you can't get anywhere without it. If the enemy does not surrender, he must be destroyed. Isn't that so? And since all means are good, you must choose the most effective. Don't spare God himself in the name of God. . . . And as soon as one End is done with, another bobs up on the stage of history."

Similarly, when Rubashov in *Darkness at Noon* points out that violence starts a chain of cumulative consequences, Ivanov replies that no battalion commander can stick to the principle that the individual is sacrosanct; the world has permanently been in an abnormal state since the invention of the steam engine, and the principle that the end justifies the means remains the only rule of political ethics. It is ironical that while this doctrine is increasingly taken for granted by some Benthamite planners and Kautilyan diplomats in Gandhi's India, it has been openly questioned even in the most powerful society that has adopted Marxism as a State religion. The Russian poet, Yevgeny Yevtushenko, has stated that Stalin was forgiven much in his lifetime because Soviet citizens were led to think that his acts were necessary for some higher purpose.

They steadily impressed upon us that the end justified the means. A great pain gives birth to a great "flow of energy" as Stalin once declared. But even as we lamented him, many of us recalled our kin and our friends who had perished in the prisons. Naturally, to lock up such an enormous number of people required a truly prodigious amount of "energy." But people did not ponder on the fact that the aim itself may cease to be great, if one strives after it only with great energy and without paying much attention to the means. We realized that the means must be worthy of the end. This is an axiom, but an axiom that has been proved through much suffering.

Similarly, in the most affluent society that had almost elevated Pragmatism to a State religion, the American President drew a major moral lesson in a national broadcast on the Watergate scandal (April 30, 1973):

> I have been in public life for more than a quarter of a century. . . . I know that it can be very easy, under the intensive pressures of a campaign, for even well-intentioned people to fall into shady tactics—to rationalize this on the grounds that what is at stake is of such importance to the nation that the end justifies the means. . . . In recent years, however, the campaign excesses that have occurred on all sides have provided a sobering demonstration of how far this false doctrine can take us. The lesson is clear: America, in its political campaigns, must not again fall into the trap of letting the end, however great that end is, justify the means.

Gandhi's way of countering the doctrine that the end justifies the means was by asserting not merely that unworthy means could belittle a great end but also that evil means can never, as a matter of fact, lead to good ends. Like the majority of Russian Populists, Gandhi was horrified by the advocacy of Machiavellian tactics and he thought that no end, however good, could fail to be destroyed by the adoption of monstrous means. His reason for believing this to be wholly and always true was his metaphysical conviction that the whole world is governed by the law of *Karma,* that there is a moral order (*ṛta*) at the heart of the cosmos. Those who do not share this conviction, which is common to all the great religions and is especially prevalent in peasant societies, may well think that a lesser evil could lead to a greater good. This latter belief, which is no less non-empirical than the former, is taken for granted by many contemporary intellectuals, power-holders, leaders of organizations and evangelists (whether theological teleologists or secular historicists). It is hardly surprising that Gandhi, who even earlier than Benda recognized the betrayal of and alienation from the masses of narrowly based classes of intellectuals and power-seekers, appealed over their heads to the toiling masses to find recruits willing to dedicate themselves to the Constructive Programme and the development of a new social and political ethic.

Gandhi did more than base his view of ends and means on a metaphysical faith in the moral law or his account of the necessary as well as contingent connection between *satya* and *ahimsa,* truth and nonviolence, tolerance and civility. He also rejected the moral model underlying the sharp dichotomy between ends and means. Moral life was not for Gandhi mainly a matter of achieving specific objectives, nor was politics like a field game in which a concrete objective is given in advance and known to all. No doubt, he regarded *satya* as the supreme common end for all men but its content cannot be known in advance. For Gandhi, as for the ancient Greeks, *satya* refers to the highest human activity rather than an imposed and predetermined target. He evolved his political and social ethic in terms of a theory of action under which all our thinking and activity can be corrected and justified only by reference to *satya* and *ahimsa,* which are good in themselves and not merely the means to a higher good. It is only for the sake of these goods—in order that as much of them as possible may at some time exist—that anyone can be justified in undertaking any social or political activity. They are the *raison d'être* of virtue and excellence, the ultimate test of human endeavor, the sole criterion of social progress.

In stating that Gandhi rejected the sharp dichotomy between ends and means, it is obviously not suggested that the distinction is entirely false and useless. Surely, everyone (including Gandhi) would agree that it is often possible to distinguish between ends and means, and also useful to do so. The distinction is most easily made when we are considering some particular purpose that a man might have in mind before embarking on a specific action. But if, like Bentham, we say that what a man wants is to get or to maximize "happiness," then it becomes much more difficult to make a clear distinction between the end (the greatest happiness) and all the various things said to be means to it. For a man's conception of happiness depends largely upon his desiring the things said to be means to it. It happens to be true that the things usually held up as supreme ends of human endeavor (happiness, freedom, welfare, etc.) are empty notions, apart from the things said to be means to them. We must distinguish between men's goals and their principles or the rules they accept. Sometimes, of course, their goal is to inculcate a principle or to observe it themselves or to get others to do so, but they have many other goals. But it seems to be more realistic to think of men as having a variety of goals, some of which matter more than others, than to think of them as having a supreme goal to which all others are subordinate, either as means to it or being willingly sacrificed whenever they conflict with it. The distinction between ends and means becomes misleading and dangerous when we dogmatize that there is a single supreme good or even a fixed hierarchy of goodness. Such dogmatism can have no place in the Gandhian dialectic, in which there is a dynamic fusion of *theoria* and *praxis* through the continual determination of the ends by the means.

Gandhi did not lay down the law for all men or impose on nature a rigid, teleological pattern of his own. He merely argued from the proposition that all men have some idea of truth (*satya*) but no adequate conception of Absolute Truth (*Sat*), to the prescription that society should regard the pursuit of *satya* as a common end. He further pointed out that in seeking the truth, we cannot help being true to our "real" natures (identical with that of all others) and this means exemplifying a measure of nonviolence in our attitudes and relations toward others. It is possible (though questionable) for people to argue that the unhappiness of some is required to maximize collective happiness, that individual citizens have to be coerced for the sake of general freedom, that the maintenance of public virtue sometimes requires subjects to choose (or support) privately corrupt but efficient and outwardly respectable rulers. It would, however, be difficult to contend that the collective pursuit of truth is compatible with the adoption of dishonest devices or the condoning of untruth. This could be advanced if a preordained, collectivist conception of truth were imposed on the members of a society. A dogmatic ideology may be propagated by dishonest and ruthless methods. *Asatya* necessitates *himsa*.

Gandhi explicitly believed that no person or group could speak in the name of *Sat* or Absolute Truth for the very reason that all are entitled to their relative truths, to *satya* as it appears to different people. As truth in this conception is identical with integrity (fidelity to one's own conscience), Gandhi could claim that no man can pursue greater integrity as an end by adopting means involving a sacrifice of the integrity he already has. The test of one's immediate moral integrity is nonviolence; it is a test of one's genuineness in the pursuit of truth (i.e., of intellectual integrity) through one's actions in the midst of society. If we understand the concept of *satya* and accept its pursuit as a common end, we cannot make a hard-and-fast distinction between this end and the means toward it that we employ. On the other hand, it is particularly if we regard the promotion of happiness as the whole duty of man that we become careless about the means and violate the "laws of morality." "The consequences of this line of thinking are writ large on the history of Europe," said Gandhi in his introduction to his paraphrase of Ruskin's *Unto This Last*. For Gandhi the *polis* is nothing more or less than the domain in which all men are free to gain skill in the art of action and learn how to exemplify *satya* and *ahimsa;* the arena in which both the individual quest could be furthered and the social virtues displayed among the masses of citizens in a climate of tolerance and civility; a morally progressive society in which neither the State nor any social organization is allowed to flout with impunity the sacred principle that every man is entitled to his relative truth and no one can claim the right to coerce another, to treat him as a means to his own end.

14

ASSESSMENT

I have not conceived my mission to be that of a knight-errant wandering everywhere to deliver people from difficult situations. My humble occupation has been to show people how they solve their own difficulties. . . . . My work will be finished if I succeed in carrying conviction to the human family, that every man or woman, however weak in body, is the guardian of his or her self-respect and liberty.

MAHATMA GANDHI

Political thinkers have usually operated on two different levels. They have been concerned with what they regarded as the vital problem of their epoch, the pressing need of their generation. In this sense, a political theorist is to some extent *engagé*; his doctrines and concepts seem to be propagandist devices; his writing appears to be a tract for the time. Even Plato, Aquinas and Spinoza, who viewed political society *sub specie aeternitatis*, addressed themselves to one or more of the issues agitating their contemporaries. At another level, the greatest thinkers were committed to lessening the gap between the possibilities grasped through political imagination, or a larger vision of life, and social realities. At least, they had some view, explicit or implicit, of the relation between the ends of human existence and the goals of political activity. Even thinkers who claimed to be concerned to describe the facts often disguised their preferences or presuppositions as purely empirical generalizations. On the other hand, classical political thought, especially in India, was unashamedly concerned to derive political conclusions and social norms from shared moral values and metaphysical beliefs. On the whole, what is common to the older and the more modern tradition of political thought is a preoccupation with the role of authority and the basis of social consensus, with the standpoint of the ruler rather than of the rebel.

In assessing the thought of Gandhi, it is essential to see that he was mainly a political moralist who wrote from the standpoint of the rebel, who did not concern himself with the ethical and practical problems facing men in authority. The significance of his conceptual formulations is necessarily limited by this fact. He was a man of action rather than an abstract theorist, and he had far more to say about the moral problems facing the citizen than about the tasks and purposes of government. It would be wrong, however, to assert that he was mainly concerned with resistance to authority or with problems at the fringe of political life. He tried to apply his basic concepts of *satya* and *ahimsa* to a variety of practical matters —the relations between capital and labor, the decentralization of political and economic power, social inequalities and different types of exploitation, the connection between individual liberty and national independence, the promotion of collective welfare and village self-government, attitudes toward work and the problem of full employment, the alienation of the intelligentsia and the universal obligation of manual labor, the problems of educational and social reconstruction.

If we take into account the entire body of Gandhi's prolific writings, it would be impossible to conclude that he was an essentially negative thinker. No assessment of Gandhi as a thinker would be complete or just without adequate consideration of his practical recommendations concerning the many problems facing Indian society. His ideas have considerable relevance to the societies of the future, even if his measures cannot be regarded as valid or feasible in differing conditions. Behind Gandhi's practical proposals there lay a vision, roughly sketched rather than worked out in detail, of a reconstructed polity and a regenerated society in which the pursuit of *satya* and the development of *ahimsa* are carried to their fullest fruition. His political vision was ultimately based upon the classical Indian myth of *Rama Rajya*, the ideal polity, ascribed to *Satya Yuga* or *Krita Yuga*, the Golden Age lost in the mists of antiquity and prehistory. Gandhi's active political imagination took him at times entirely out of the region of existing realities into the realm of utopian fantasy, the anarchist's paradise and the City of God.

Gandhi's practical proposals cannot be examined without full consideration of the Indian context in which they were formulated. Such a study would affect our view of the range of his moral and political thought. It would not, however, modify our assessment of the most significant element in his thought—his concern with a universal political ethic founded upon his concepts of *satya* and *ahimsa*. He was led to this concern with a political ethic by the problems he faced as a man seeking to become a saint while never ceasing to be a politician. Although his thinking as a political moralist was not dictated by mere expediency, his formulation of his views was at times colored by his missionary fervor and his role as a political propagandist. He did not, however, function only on the level of practical exhortation. He was also deeply concerned to transcend the limitations of time and space and to view political society *sub specie aeternitatis* in the classical tradition of political thought. He was much more *engagé*, far more committed and active than most political thinkers, but he was no less inspired than the greatest thinkers by a coherent and exalted conception of the ends of human activity, man's place in the cosmos and the moral responsibilities of the citizen. A careful study of Gandhi's writings shows that he cannot simply be regarded as a politician and a saint. He has certainly given greater thought and written more concerning "metapolitics" or "pre-political" matters than any other politician or saint, or any other political thinker in the twentieth century.

Gandhi's standpoint as a political moralist, as brought out in the preceding chapters, may be summed up as follows. Early in life, he reacted strongly against modern civilization and saw a contradiction between our deepest moral values as individuals and the materialistic criteria by which we tend to judge our institutions and our collective progress. He thought that the "sickness" of modern civilization is reflected in our "soulless" politics, owing to a segregation between religion and politics and the prevalent doctrine of double standards. He redefined both "religion" and "politics" so as to emphasize the distinction between sectarian beliefs and religious commitment, between power politics and *sattvic* or "pure" politics. Politics is corrupted by power-seeking and it could be purified by introducing the monastic ideal into the sphere of political activity and social service. All men must come to accept certain moral values as absolute, especially truth and nonviolence. At least, some men must pledge themselves by vows to upholding these absolute values in public life. The reason for such drastic remedies is that human nature is so constituted that it must either soar or sink, and it will increasingly connive at untruth and violence if the quest for self-perfection is abandoned. Individuals should not abdicate from social responsibilities in their quest for personal salvation. It is possible to combine an appeal to conscience with heroic action in the midst of society, to yoke freedom with commitment.

Gandhi proclaimed *satya* as the supreme moral value and the common end of human endeavor. He stressed action as the means to *satya* and distinguished between absolute and relative truth. He also declared *ahimsa* to be the only valid basis of all political and social conduct. He distinguished between the acceptance of *ahimsa* as a creed and as a policy, regarded some violence as unavoidable, and held that it is possible and necessary for the State and all social institutions to reduce progressively their reliance upon coercion. He further regarded *ahimsa* as the necessary means to the pursuit of *satya* in personal and social life. He also pointed out that we cannot make a hard-and-fast distinction between the means and the end, and we must not merely reject the doctrine that the end justifies the means, but also come to regard the purity of the means we employ as all-important. The individual always retains his moral authority in relation to the State, and while he must actively support the laws of the State and serve the needs of society, he must be ready to offer nonviolent resistance to unjust laws or an iniquitous system as well as to social abuses. This requires the readiness to suffer the consequences of resistance to injustice and untruth. The doctrine of *satyagraha* lays down the qualifications required by a *satyagrahi*, the criteria needed to distinguish between *satyagraha* and its abuse (*duragraha*), and the prerequisites for the legitimate application of appropriate modes of *satyagraha,* especially of civil disobedience and non-cooperation.

In the last analysis, Gandhi's political ethic rests upon his metaphysical presuppositions, which introduce a strong subjectivist element into his basic concepts, as well as a sustaining conviction that the morally right must necessarily be the most effective course of conduct in the long run. Those who reject Gandhi's presuppositions may come to regard all his views as questionable and unrealistic. Even those who share his presuppositions and overlook the ambiguities in his formulation of basic concepts, could point to the practical difficulties and dangers implicit in their unqualified application by the great majority of men. It is, further, possible to hold that the consequences of an uncritical adoption of Gandhi's attitudes to politics and society could be very different from what he intended.

It is not surprising that a saint or a moralist should react as Gandhi did to the social institutions and the political methods of modern civilization. It would be tempting but unworthy to respond to his moral indictment by dismissing him as a "reactionary" or a latter-day Puritan or a moral fanatic. Even if we think that his attack was intemperate and exaggerated, we could safely concede its value as a corrective to complacency. The difficulty with such indictments lies deeper. As a passionate moral reformer, Gandhi intended his attack to arouse people, especially in India, from their

uncritical acceptance of all that goes by the name of "moderniza-
tion" and "progress." Is there not, however, a danger that such attacks on modern civilization could and do produce two undesirable
consequences? Given Gandhi's own moral diagnosis of modern
man, only a few are likely to respond to his indictment with moral
earnestness and reformist zeal. Such people may come to enjoy
the luxury of moral indignation over contemporary institutions
without even trying to set the moral example that Gandhi gave to
his fellow men. This could lead to much frustration on their part,
as well as considerable annoyance among those who do not share
their views and resent the plane of false moral superiority from
which they are delivered. Secondly, and even more important, a
moral indictment such as Gandhi's could undermine the prevailing
loyalty to imperfect institutions among people who are not morally
prepared to follow Gandhi's positive injunctions or the example he
set. This difficulty is particularly important at a time when defeatism is more common than complacency. It is easier to encourage the defeatism of the weak than to disturb the complacency of
the strong, especially when the social structure is relatively stable.

The same point holds, but even more sharply, in regard to
Gandhi's stress on "pure" politics. In appealing for greater involvement in political activity which is untainted by power-seeking,
Gandhi may unintentionally be responsible for "apolitical" attitudes, for political disengagement by morally worthy people. Furthermore, the attempt to introduce religion (in its finer forms) into
politics may merely result in the exploitation of religious emotions
(of the baser varieties) by unscrupulous politicians. One of the
consequences of Gandhi's importation of the religious spirit, which
he exemplified in its exalted sense, into Indian politics was the increased stimulation of religious fanaticism by petty politicians
among Hindus as well as Moslems. On the whole, those in the West
who have emphasized religion in politics—thinkers like de Maistre
or Maurras—have been identified with authoritarian attitudes. Tolerance and civility came to be generally stressed in Europe at the
very time when politics became secular in tone and vocabulary.

Similarly, the taking of vows, despite all the precaution which
Gandhi stressed, by people who are not ready to carry them out,
would merely result in greater cynicism than existed before. In

India today, the wearing of a "Gandhi cap" evokes suspicion rather than respect. This may well reflect the instinctive suspicion of idealism in a corrupt and cynical age. In our century we can see all too clearly how easily and often the best becomes the enemy of the good. Similarly, the appeal to conscience commands respect in the case of rare individuals, but the very word loses its significance when it is overemployed. Gladstone may have been a man of conscience but his opponents could not help their amusement or annoyance at what they termed his "salamander conscience."

We can see this difficulty even more strikingly in regard to the heroic ideal. At its best, it is indeed admirable, and even today there is spontaneous appreciation everywhere for genuine instances of individual heroism in personal life or in arduous public sports. In politics, however, appeals to heroism often sound too fascistic, at the worst, or too smug, at the least, for our comfort. They serve their purpose in wartime or in periods of national crisis, but in more normal times they sound either hollow or dangerous. Repeated references to heroism even in support of deserving causes are self-defeating.

The distinction between absolute and relative truth is important and useful, but in practice people may come to hold to what they call relative truths with considerable dogmatism and inflexibility. If no man can ever possess absolute truth, by its very definition, the pursuit of relative truth by all men may be marked by conflicting views regarding the relative respect that must be shown to various relative truths. It is very difficult for most human beings to adhere firmly to their relative truths without bringing their feelings into it. The ideal of detachment, much stressed in India, is admirable in itself, but if most men could come to show it there would be no reason to respect it as much as we now do.

The difficulty in regard to the concept of *ahimsa* is that it appears too all-embracing and too demanding in its reference to thought, word and deed for it to be meaningfully employed. Further, the creed of *ahimsa* requires so exacting a discipline that it might seem safer to avoid the term altogether in politics than to encourage people to set themselves so high a standard that they are unable to take difficult decisions involving a choice of relative evils. The same objection could be raised, but even more strongly, in regard to *satyagraha*. Only a very few people seem to be capable of taking upon themselves considerable suffering in support of a worthy cause without becoming embittered in the process. The doctrine of *satyagraha* demands such a high standard of compliance with the laws of the community—compliance out of the highest motives, without a trace of fear or self-interest—that very few people would really qualify for its exercise.

Altogether, all these objections to the practical adoption of the Gandhian standpoint in politics turn upon assumptions about human nature. Even if we do not presuppose the unverifiable notion of the constancy of human nature, why should we expect that human beings would change more readily in response to the doctrines of Gandhi than they have been able to do in the past as a result of the exhortations of the religious prophets? Gandhian concepts have nothing in common with the Buchmanite or evangelical notion of a sudden transformation of human nature, but is there not a danger in practice that the doctrines of Gandhi could degenerate into some form of Buchmanism? Gandhi himself told Dr. Buchman once that his experience in his *ashram*s showed him that changes in human nature are harder to come by than Buchman thought. In any case, does Gandhi's political ethic merely amount to a renewed attempt at moral exhortation? Was Gandhi ignoring the weaknesses of the flesh, which are important factors in politics, in stressing the willingness of the spirit, which may be very necessary in mysticism? Did the saint in Gandhi prevent him from becoming a sage, in the Indian tradition? Was he too good a man to be politically or spiritually wise?

All these questions may be raised even by those who sympathize with Gandhi's standpoint. In the eyes of those who are positively unsympathetic to his views, such objections could be made the basis of the claim that Gandhi was a failure as a thinker and perhaps even as a saint. On the other hand, several Indian mystics, like Ramana Maharshi, thought that Gandhi was a good man who sacrificed his spiritual development by taking on too great, too Atlas-like, a burden upon himself. Such a line of reasoning could be reinforced by using Max Weber's distinction between the mystic and the ascetic. The ascetic, in this view, makes what the mystic would regard as the mistake of recognizing the corruption of the world but continuing to dabble in worldliness. The mystic may have chosen what seems to be the easier way, but the ascetic may actually come to harm others by his self-righteousness and obstinacy.

Gandhi's standpoint could also be criticized by employing a totally different line of attack. It is possible to rid his concepts of their religious overtones and to dilute them so as to make them correspond to the essentials of good liberal doctrine. One could then argue that what is valuable in the Gandhian standpoint amounts to no more than liberal truisms in an inflated religious language. The jargon may serve its purpose among illiterate, devout peasants, but we should not let it conceal the commonsensical and unoriginal nature of the Gandhian attitudes.

All the above criticisms—from pragmatic, mystical or liberal viewpoints—contain an element of truth but they ignore a very vital consideration. While the best may often be the enemy of the good, an appeal to the best may be the only way, in certain circumstances, of arresting a rapid moral decline or even of securing some good. The distinction between guilt and shame is relevant in this connection. In societies which give importance to the notions of sin and guilt, a general awareness of human weakness could result in the common attempt to establish minimum standards below which people usually do not fall. The reasons for such compliance may be frankly mixed—based in part upon presumed or actual self-interest, in part upon the competitive spirit and in part upon the pleasure in self-approbation which Hume stressed. These minimum standards could be justified both by the argument from survival and collective or long-term self-interest (notions that are not free from difficulties) *and* by the appeal to supernatural sanctions or some transcendental concept. It is then possible to argue as Hume did that the latter argument is based on a convenient fiction and that the effective factor is self-interest. Men may come to believe this and to distrust every form of high-mindedness, while zealous in the performance of the duties of their station.

In such societies there is no need to set extremely high standards, while it is possible for minimum standards to be maintained. The appeal to higher than normal standards may be made only at times of exceptional crisis. Even this may be no more than raising temporarily the minimum standards that men feel entitled to expect of each other. Normally, there would be reliable conventions that would prevent politics from becoming too impure or corrupt, while no one would be particularly bothered about raising it to an impossibly high level of purity. It is enough if people in public life silently cherish religious values, and it would be improper for them to bandy about religious terms in everyday politics. Politicians must be seen to be people who will not obviously misuse their position for personal advantage or too crudely seek power. They must be relied upon to keep their word in the normal way, and to respect their legal or ceremonial oaths. There is no need for them to take vows or publicly abjure all private property. They may be expected to refrain from conduct which offends their conscience but they may not talk much about "conscience." They may do heroic deeds while seeming to take them in their stride as though they were part of their essential obligations. They will avoid untruths though they might be rather hypocritical. They will regret the use of force, though they have no qualms about it in instances that are generally regarded as requiring such use. In such societies some men may be willing to suffer for their beliefs and even go to prison, while hating the thought of being regarded as rare martyrs. The authorities will put them in jail as a matter of course but avoid exulting in their action or appearing insensitive to the resister's appeal to his conscience. Altogether, in such societies men may seek to improve themselves morally without any wish to become more perfect.

On the other hand, there may be societies in which notions of shame and perfectibility, rather than guilt and sin, may be deeply rooted. The heroic ideal may be kept alive by national folklore. Men may respect goodness more than anything else and may respond to it even if they feel no compunction about falling below minimum standards. They may expect so much morally from their leaders that those who are found wanting by these very high standards may be deeply distrusted and may become responsible for the rapid spread of cynicism and demoralization. There is no need to elaborate on this model; the details can be filled in. In such societies the Gandhian standpoint may produce more results than mere appeals to commonsense and duty.

It is not suggested that India necessarily corresponds to the latter model. In a sense, the country had become so demoralized when Gandhi entered the political scene that the traditional notion of "shame" as well as the Western notion of "guilt" were inoperative. His heroic appeal to the forgotten language of tradition produced results—but not for long, as he discovered to his cost. Also, Gandhi had become imbued with Christian notions of sin and guilt while he was also filled with traditional Indian notions of shame and perfectibility.[1] By the end of his life, his faith in the readiness of the Indian people in regard to *ahimsa* was profoundly shattered and he began to feel that his ideas might have a better chance in other parts of the world.

It would, in fact, be wrong to suggest that the Gandhian standpoint was culture-bound and applicable only in India. Several elements in his doctrine are already precious in the West—the reduction of *himsa* in particular spheres (capital punishment, cruelty to animals, nationalist support of violence used against a hostile power in peace time) as well as the use of certain techniques of mild *satyagraha*—and they are more respected today than in his lifetime. This is not to say that these are signs of the spread of Gandhian ideas, but rather that in some ways the soil has already been more prepared for their absorption by the West than in the new climate of opinion in post-Gandhian India. Appeals to a mere sense of duty are losing their former force with the decline of conventional religions, and even the notions of sin and guilt are weaker than before. On the other hand, the ideal of heroic action and self-denial is coming to have a new significance in countries which have to find new forms of expression for the missionary zeal fostered by messianic religions and spent in empire-building.

Gandhi's fascination as a thinker lies in his inward battle between two opposing attitudes—the Tolstoyan socialist belief that the Kingdom of Heaven is attainable on earth and the Dostoevskian mystical conviction that it can never be materialized. The modern Hindu standpoint has generally been anti-utopian: *Rama Rajya* lies in the bygone *Satya Yuga*, and *Kali Yuga* is the age of unavoidable coercion. Gandhi began by challenging this view under the influence of Tolstoy, but he ended his life with more of a Dostoevskian pessimism. This does not mean that he abandoned either his imaginative, Utopian, political vision or what he called his practical idealism embodied in concrete programs of immediate action. He did not feel that he was wrong to *urge* men to set themselves, as he did in his own life, seemingly impossible standards, but he came closer to seeing that it is wrong to *expect* them to do so. In July 1947, six months before his assassination, he felt that he had been betrayed by the Congress leaders and let down by many of his countrymen. But he did not blame them for not living up to standards that he had set them but which they never chose or really accepted for themselves.

"Euclidean" models—of the *satyagrahi*, of a society based upon *satya* and *ahimsa*, of *Rama Rajya*—are not without their value in political theory, but they must not be mistaken for definitely realizable concretions. In Santayana's apt words:

> Ideal society belongs entirely to this realm of kindly illusion, for it is the society of symbols. Whenever religion, art, or science presents us with an image or a formula, involving no matter how momentous a truth, there is something delusive in the representation. It needs translation into the detailed experience which it sums up in our own past or prophecies elsewhere. This eventual change in form, far from nullifying our knowledge, can alone legitimize it. . . . And yet there is another aspect to the matter. Symbols are presences, and they are those particularly congenial presences which we have inwardly evoked and cast in a form intelligible and familiar to human thinking. Their function is to give flat experience a rational perspective, translating the general flux into stable objects and making it representable in human discourse. They are therefore precious, not only for their representative or practical value, implying useful adjustments to the environing world, but even more, sometimes, for their immediate or aesthetic power, for their kinship to the spirit they enlighten and exercise.[2]

Gandhi's concepts of *satya, ahimsa* and *satyagraha*, of *tapas* and, above all, of the *satyagrahi,* are such ideal constructions—"Euclidean" models as he himself called them. They do involve a "momentous truth," but they are also deceptive representations, in a sense. In constructing these, Gandhi was in the oldest political tradition that goes back to classical Chinese and Indian thinkers, and to Plato in the West. They could serve in the serious task of civic education (*paideia*) provided they are not taken to represent decisively the political realities of the future. Gandhi's literalness in regard to his own creations was characteristic of his tenacity as a politician, his single-mindedness as a saint, and his severity as an ascetic. His understandable zeal in this respect does not detract from the universal import of his political ethic. Every society must choose its own mode of transmission of this ethic into the detailed experience which it sums up in its past. All moral advance is continuous with past efforts to lead the good life, and must respect the quintessential goodness of classical traditions which have come to be drained of their vitality. There is no secular or sectarian guarantee of social survival or cultural self-renewal. In seeing beyond the confinements of past creeds and present *isms*, Gandhi drew from the reservoirs of the untapped moral energies of mankind, and pointed to the spiritual foundations of the civilization of the future.

ABBREVIATIONS USED IN NOTES

ABP   *Amrita Bazaar Patrika* (daily newspaper), Allahabad.

AO   *Ashram Observances in Action,* Navajivan, 1932 (translated by V. G. Desai).

CWMG   *The Collected Works of Mahatma Gandhi,* edited by K. Swaminathan, Navajivan, 1958-.

DD   *The Diary of Mahadev Desai,* Navajivan, 1953. All references are to volume 1, translated by V. G. Desai.

M   D. G. Tendulkar, *Mahatma* (in eight volumes). All references are to the original edition, V. K. Jhaveri and D. G. Tendulkar, 1951-54.

ER   *Ethical Religion (Niti Dharma),* Ganesan, 1922 (translated by Rama Iyer).

GOT   *Gandhian Outlook and Techniques,* Govt. of India, 1953.

H   *Harijan* (weekly paper), Navajivan, 1932-1948.

HS   *Hind Swaraj,* Navajivan, 1938.

IO   *Indian Opinion* (weekly paper), Natal, South Africa, 1903-14.

SMET   *The Story of My Experiments with Truth* (translated by Mahadev Desai, originally published in two volumes in 1927 and 1929). All references are to the one-volume edition, Navajivan, 1956.

SSA   *Satyagraha in South Africa,* 1928 (translated by V. G. Desai). All references are to the second edition, Navajivan, 1950.

SWMG   *Speeches and Writings of Mahatma Gandhi,* Natesan, 1934. All references are to the fourth edition, except when specific mention is made of the second or third edition.

YI   *Young India* (weekly paper), Navajivan, 1919-32.

YM   *From Yeravda Mandir,* Navajivan, 1932 (translated by V. G. Desai).

NOTES

1
INTRODUCTION

1. John Wyllie, *India at the Parting of the Ways*, Lincoln Williams, 1934, p. 9.
2. M. N. Roy, *Problem of Freedom*, Renaissance, 1945, pp. 28-33; *New Humanism*, Renaissance, 1947, pp. 34-47.
3. *YI*, January 1927, October 1936, October 1925, October 1921.
4. *YI*, May 1920.
5. *YI*, November 1928.
6. *YI*, September 1926.
7. Reginald Reynolds, *To Live in Mankind*, Andre Deutsch, 1951, p. 132.
8. P. Spear, *India*, University of Michigan Press, 1961, p. 359.
9. Quoted in *Light of India*, ed. M. S. Deshpande, p. 277.
10. In *Mahatma Gandhi*, ed. S. Radhakrishnan, Allen & Unwin, 1951, pp. 280-81.
11. W. H. G. Holmes, *The Twofold Gandhi*, Mowbray, 1952, p. 5.
12. George Orwell, *A Collection of Essays*, Anchor, 1954, p. 180.
13. Gilbert Murray in *Talking of Gandhiji*, Orient Longmans, 1957, p. 12.
14. M. R. Jayakar in *Talking of Gandhiji*, p. 14.
15. *Young India*, vol. II, Ganesan, p. 568.
16. *YI*, March 1925.
17. *YI*, March 1927.
18. *YI*, February 1930.
19. *Ibid*.
20. *H*, November 1933.
21. *SWMG*, Natesan, 1934, p. 531.

22. *SWMG,* Natesan, 1918, 2d ed., p. xxiv.
23. At twenty-five he held the Secretaryship of the Natal Indian Congress which he founded—the closest he came to holding any political office, apart from presiding over the Belgaum Congress in 1924.
24. It is significant that Philip Spratt, who wrote the best Marxist account of Gandhi, readily conceded Gandhi's "impartiality" and that there was no "insincerity or vulgar opportunism" in him (*Gandhism,* Huxley Press, 1939, pp. 112, 172). Indian Communists have been less generous, Namboodiripad even less so than Hiren Mukherjee. Regarding the radical change in Soviet views of Gandhi, see K. Tidmarsh's paper in *South Asian Studies,* Chatto & Windus, 1960.
25. *H,* March 1946.
26. This has been widely but wrongly regarded as a book written entirely by Gandhi. It was a paraphrase in Gujarati of a book by Salter, an American. Gandhi's version is actually the notes made from talks he gave, modeled on Salter's book.
27. *H,* March 1940.
28. *H,* May 1947.
29. *H,* September 1939.
30. In a conversation with the author in 1958.
31. *DD,* Navajivan, 1953, pp. 37-38.
32. *SWMG,* 2d ed., pp. 112-13.
33. *Ibid.,* pp. 126-27.
34. *Ibid.*
35. *DD,* p. 38.
36. *SWMG,* 2d ed., pp. 126-27.
37. *M,* V. K. Jhaveri, 1954, vol. 1, pp. 35-36.
38. *SMET,* Navajivan, 1956, p. 46 (he could not recall the correct title of Bentham's essay).
39. *M,* vol. 2, p. 147.
40. *Ibid.,* pp. 197-98.
41. *Ibid.,* p. 308.
42. *M,* vol. 3, p. 357.
43. *M,* vol. 4, p. 236.
44. *Ibid.,* p. 383.
45. *M,* vol. 6, p. 293.
46. *M,* vol. 7, p. 36.
47. *YI,* September 1928.
48. *YI,* November 1925.

49. *Talking of Gandhiji,* p. 15.
50. *DD,* p. 109.
51. J. J. Doke, *M. K. Gandhi,* Natesan, 1909, p. 34.
52. *SMET,* p. 299.
53. *SMET,* p. 265.
54. *DD,* p. 279.
55. *CWMG,* Navajivan, 1958, vol. 1, pp. 139, 165-67.
56. *M,* vol. 1, p. 86; Fischer's *Life,* Jonathan Cape, 1951, p. 469.
57. J. J. Doke, *M. K. Gandhi,* p. 142.
58. "Mahatma Gandhi—Political Philosopher," *Political Studies,* Oxford, February 1960.

2
THE INDICTMENT
OF MODERN CIVILIZATION

1. *Reflections on "Hind Swaraj,"* Bombay, Theosophy Co., 1948, p. 45.
2. Letter to Satish Babu, November 1929, and Mahadev Desai's preface to *Hind Swaraj,* Navajivan, 1938, pp. v-vi.
3. *M,* V. K. Jhaveri, 1954, vol. 1, p. 147.
4. *CWMG,* Navajivan, vol. 10, pp. 6-7.
5. *CWMG,* vol. 1, pp. 247-48, 279-80.
6. *CWMG,* vol. 3, p. 415.
7. It has been suggested that Gandhi might have been influenced by Plato's criticism of doctors and lawyers in the *Republic,* which he perhaps read at the same time as he was translating the *Apology* into Gujarati.
8. *The Sane Society,* Fawcett, 1955, p. 15.
9. *CWMG,* vol. 10, pp. 20-21.
10. *Ibid.,* p. 16.
11. See, for example, the special number of *The Twentieth Century* on "Who Governs Britain?", 1957.
12. *M,* vol. 2, p. 61.
13. *Lucifer,* May 1891.
14. *CWMG,* vol. 10, p. 35.
15. Frederick Soddy in *Reflections on "Hind Swaraj,"* p. 7.
16. G. D. H. Cole in *Reflections on "Hind Swaraj,"* p. 17.
17. Hugh I'A. Fausset in *Reflections on "Hind Swaraj,"* p. 51.
18. Gerald Heard in *Reflections on "Hind Swaraj,"* p. 61.
19. *Reflections on "Hind Swaraj,"* p. 31.

20. *Ibid.*, pp. 17-23.
21. George Catlin, *In the Path of Mahatma Gandhi*, Macdonald, 1948, pp. 141, 245.
22. Gandhi wrote this 30,000-word tract from November 13 to 22, 1909, on his return voyage from England to South Africa on the steamer's stationery. He wrote about fifty pages with his left hand because his right hand was exhausted (*M*, vol. 1, p. 105).
23. *CWMG*, vol. 10, p. 21.
24. *CWMG*, vol. 9, p. 40.
25. Letter to Albert West, January 12, 1910 (*CWMG*, vol. 10, p. 127).
26. Letter to a Friend in India, 1910 (*M*, vol. 1, p. 107).
27. *M*, vol. 2, p. 337.
28. *CWMG*, vol. 10, p. 37.
29. *L'Amy des Femmes ou Traité de la Civilisation*, 1766, Archives Nationales, Paris.
30. *YI*, May 1927.
31. *YI*, October 1931.
32. *YI*, September 1925.
33. *SWMG*, Natesan, 1936, 4th ed., p. 1042.

3
THE PURIFICATION
OF POLITICS

1. The substitution of the cenobitic life for the eremetic life of the solitary anchorite was justified by St. Basil and St. Benedict in the West. Further, Franciscan monasticism stressed poverty whereas Benedictine monasticism emphasized simplicity.
2. *M*, V. K. Jhaveri, 1954, vol. 2, p. 337.
3. *Ibid.*, p. 483.
4. *SWMG*, Natesan, 1934, 4th ed., p. 315.
5. *Ibid.*
6. *Ibid.*, p. 296.
7. *SMET*, Navajivan, 1956, p. 504.
8. *M*, vol. 3, p. 144.
9. *Ibid.*, pp. 155-56.
10. *M*, vol. 4, p. 53.
11. *Ibid.*, p. 190.
12. *Ibid.*, pp. 387-88.
13. *Ibid.*, p. 190.

14. *M*, vol. 7, p. 254.
15. *M*, vol. 6, p. 23.
16. *YI*, May 1920.
17. *The Portable Thoreau*, Viking, 1947, p. 654.
18. *YI*, July 1931.
19. *H*, February 1947; *M*, vol. 7, p. 254.
20. *H*, February 1940.
21. *YI*, May 1920.
22. *HS*, Navajivan, 1938, p. 49.
23. *M*, vol. 7, p. 314.
24. Pyarelal, *Mahatma Gandhi—The Last Phase*, Navajivan, 1956, vol. 1, p. 195.
25. Emerson, *The Complete Essays and Writings*, Random House, 1940, p. 422.
26. *Ibid.*
27. *YI*, April 1920.
28. J. J. Doke, *M. K. Gandhi*, Natesan, 1909, p. 7.
29. *The Spirit and Form of Indian Polity*, Arya, 1947, p. 8.
30. *M*, vol. 5, p. 296.
31. *H*, September 1936.
32. Archbishop Temple, *The Kingdom of God*, Macmillan, 1914, p. 84.
33. Kant, *Eternal Peace*, trans. W. Hastie, World Peace Foundation, Boston, 1914, p. 163.
34. *ER*, Ganesan, 1922, p. 43.
35. *Ibid.*, p. 36.
36. Swami Vivekananda, *"Karma Yoga," Speeches & Writings of Swami Vivekananda*, Natesan, 1934.
37. Shri Aurobindo, *The Ideal of the Karmayogin*, Aurobindo Ashram Press, 1950.
38. *DD*, June 30, 1932, Navajivan, 1953, p. 207.
39. *YI*, January 1920.
40. *Ibid.*
41. M. R. Jayakar, *The Story of My Life*, vol. 1, p. 387.
42. R. Duncan, *Selected Writings of Mahatma Gandhi*, Faber & Faber, 1951, p. 21.
43. M. R. Jayakar, *The Story of My Life*, Asia Publishing House, 1958, vol. 1, p. 387.
44. The word "sattvic" is the anglicized adjective derived from the Sanskrit term *sattva*, which means "truth," "goodness," "purity."
45. *M*, vol. 6, p. 340.

46. *Ibid.*
47. *YI,* January 1925.
48. *M,* vol. 8, pp. 278-80.
49. *Ibid.*
50. J. D. B. Miller, *Politicians,* Inaugural Lecture, University of Leicester Press, 1960.
51. *Ibid.*
52. Meinecke, *Machiavellianism,* trans. Scott, Routledge & Kegan Paul, 1957, p. 10.
53. *Moral Man and Immoral Society,* Scribner's, 1936, pp. 258, 270-71.
54. T. D. Weldon, in *The Vocabulary of Politics,* Penguin, 1953, has contended that the supposed theoretical difference between morals and politics is religious in origin.
55. L. T. Hobhouse, *Democracy and Reaction,* Fisher Unwin, 1904, pp. 128-29, a book highly commended in *Indian Opinion.*
56. A. W. Adkins, *Merit and Responsibility,* Oxford, 1960, p. 91.

4
THE NEED FOR ABSOLUTE
VALUES AND FOR VOWS

1. *ER,* Ganesan, 1922, p. 38.
2. *Ibid.,* p. 43.
3. *Ibid.,* p. 59.
4. *DD,* August 1932, Navajivan, 1953, p. 305.
5. Bishop Butler, *Fifteen Sermons,* G. Bell and Sons, Ltd., 1949 ed.
6. *YI,* March 1928.
7. *YI,* September 1929.
8. *The Gita According to Gandhi,* Navajivan, 1946, p. 200.
9. Shukla, *More Conversations of Gandhiji,* Vora, 1950.
10. *YI,* March 1922.
11. *H,* April 1934.
12. Letter to the Reverend Boyd Tucker, March 12, 1928.
13. *YI,* August 1929.
14. *H,* August 1940.
15. *H,* May 1936.
16. *YI,* September 1921.
17. *YI,* October 1928.
18. *H,* September 1940.
19. *YI,* January 1921.
20. *ER,* p. 36.

21. *YI,* January 1925.
22. *M,* vol. 4, V. K. Jhaveri, 1954, p. 198.
23. *H,* September 1939.
24. *Ibid.*
25. Letter to G. D. Birla, July 22, 1927.
26. Letter to Puratan Buch, July 24, 1932.
27. *SMET,* Navajivan, 1956, p. 242.
28. *H,* August 1939.
29. *YI,* October 1928.
30. *H,* November 1939.
31. *YI,* October 1926.
32. *The Portable Thoreau,* Viking, 1947, p. 644.
33. "The Statesman's Manual" (1816) in *Political Tracts of Wordsworth, Coleridge and Shelley,* Cambridge University Press, 1953, p. 35.
34. *YI,* August 1929.
35. *YI,* January 1919.
36. *YI,* June 1919.
37. *YI,* October 1925.
38. *SMET,* p. 207.
39. *H,* November 1936.
40. Letter from C. F. Andrews, date unknown (1920?).
41. *Gandhi Marg,* April 1959 (reprint).
42. *Ibid.*
43. Gandhi's letter to J. C. Kumarappa, *Gandhi Marg,* April 1959 (reprint).
44. *Ibid.*
45. *YM,* p. 49.
46. *Ibid.,* p. 51.
47. V. M. Bedekar, "The *Vrata* in Ancient Indian Culture," *Gandhi Marg,* October 1960.
48. Emile Durkheim, *Professional Ethics and Civic Morals,* trans. C. Brookfield, Routledge & Kegan Paul, 1957, p. 186.
49. Hume, *Treatise of Human Nature,* bk. III, pt. II, sec. V, Oxford, 1888.
50. *Ibid.*
51. *Ibid.*
52. *Ibid.*
53. Proudhon, *Idée générale de la révolution au XIXᵉ siècle,* Paris, 1851, p. 235.
54. *Ibid.,* pp. 235-36.

5
HUMAN NATURE, PROGRESS
AND PERFECTIBILITY

1. See Gilbert Ryle, *Dilemmas,* Cambridge University Press, 1954, pp. 64-65.
2. *H,* October 1938.
3. *YI,* July 1921.
4. *SMET,* Navajivan, 1956, p. 317.
5. *YM,* Navajivan, 1932, p. 81.
6. *ER,* Ganesan, 1922, p. 56.
7. *H,* April 1938.
8. *H,* January 1935.
9. *H,* August 1940.
10. *ABP,* August 1934.
11. *YI,* September 1924.
12. *H,* April 1938.
13. *DD,* Navajivan, 1953, p. 247 (Vinoba Bhave has stressed this element of *Samattva* in Gandhi's thought).
14. *YI,* December 1924.
15. *YI,* July 1926.
16. The suppressed premise here is that all men are the same in essence.
17. *YI,* July 1926.
18. *DD,* p. 252.
19. *YI,* December 1924.
20. *ER,* p. 55.
21. *Gandhiji's Correspondence with the Government,* 1942-44, Navajivan, 1945, p. 69.
22. *YI,* November 1931.
23. *M,* V. K. Jhaveri, 1954, vol. 4, p. 353.
24. *H,* November 1938.
25. *H,* May 1936.
26. *SMET,* p. 337.
27. *H,* August 1936.
28. *DD,* p. 113.
29. *YI,* October 1928.
30. *M,* vol. 4, p. 13.
31. *H,* June 1935.
32. *H,* April 1936.
33. *M,* vol. 4, p. 76.

34. *H*, March 1936.
35. *M*, vol. 7, p. 267.
36. *H*, June 1936.
37. *M*, vol. 7, p. 43.
38. *M*, vol. 7, pp. 86-87.
39. *M*, vol. 5, p. 17.
40. *YI*, December 1926.
41. *YI*, February 1927.
42. *SMET*, p. 216.
43. *YI*, October 1931.
44. *H*, October 1938.
45. *H*, November 1938.
46. *SMET*, p. 276.
47. *M*, vol. 4, pp. 110-11.
48. *SWMG*, Natesan, 1934, 4th ed., p. 363.
49. *H*, September 1939.
50. *YI*, January 1921.
51. *YI*, July 1920.
52. *H*, December 1947.
53. *M*, vol. 7, p. 475.
54. *H*, December 1937.
55. *YI*, March 1922.
56. *H*, October 1934.
57. *H*, June 1942.
58. *H*, August 1940.
59. Pyarelal, *Mahatma Gandhi, The Last Phase*, Navajivan, 1958, vol. 2, p. 303.
60. *Ibid.*, p. 202.
61. *Ibid.*
62. *M*, vol. 4, p. 13.
63. *H*, November 1947.
64. *M*, vol. 4, April 1938, p. 296.
65. *H*, May 1940.
66. *YI*, March 1931.
67. *H*, April 1937.
68. *M*, vol. 5, August 1940, pp. 392-93.
69. *YI*, vol. 3, Ganesan.
70. *H*, June 1935.
71. *H*, August 1940.
72. *H*, March 1936.
73. *SSA*, Navajivan, 1950, p. 212.

74. *M,* vol. 7, April 1946, p. 103.
75. *YI,* September 1925.
76. *H,* June 1935.
77. Pyarelal, *Mahatma Gandhi, The Last Phase,* vol. 2, p. 137.
78. *Ibid.*
79. Sushila Nayyar, *Bapu Ki Karavas Kahani* (Hindi), p. 152. Also, *Hindustan Times,* April 1950.
80. Pyarelal, *Mahatma Gandhi, The Last Phase,* vol. 2, p. 139.
81. *Ibid.*
82. *Ibid.*
83. Sushila Nayyar, *Bapu Ki Karavas Kahani* (Hindi) p. 155.
84. *Ibid.,* p. 152.
85. Pyarelal, *Mahatma Gandhi, The Last Phase,* vol. 2, p. 138.
86. Cardinal Newman, *Parochial and Plain Sermons,* V, Longmans Green, 1874-1921, p. 172.
87. *Ibid.*
88. He was not a teleologist in the sense that man can know the purpose of every creature or ascribe ends *a priori* to all human beings.
89. Shukla, *Conversations of Gandhi,* November 1933, Vora, 1949, p. 28.
90. *YI,* October 1924.
91. Pyarelal, *Mahatma Gandhi, The Last Phase,* vol. 2, p. 138.
92. *Outlines of a Philosophy of the History of Man,* trans. T. O. Churchill, Hansard, 1800, p. 467.
93. *Dr. Zhivago,* trans. Max Hayward, Collins & Harvill, 1958, p. 117.
94. *YI,* September 1926.
95. *YI,* November 1931.
96. *HS,* Navajivan, 1938, p. 130.
97. Shukla, *Conversations of Gandhi,* September 1933, p. 9.
98. Helvetius, *De L'Esprit,* Durand, 1758, vol. 1, pp. 170-71.
99. Turgot, *Oeuvres,* 1913-23, vol. 1, p. 277.
100. *YI,* February 1922.
101. Godwin, *An Enquiry Concerning Political Justice,* Robinson, 1793, vol. 2, p. 866.
102. *Ibid.,* vol. 1, p. 93.
103. *The Voice of the Silence,* trans. H. P. Blavatsky, Theosophy Co., 1928, p. 29.
104. Letter to Carl Heath, December 1934.
105. *YI,* September 1926.
106. *YI,* October 1931.

107. *The Dhammapada,* trans. Max Muller, Oxford, 1881, ch. 2.
108. *YM,* 1930, p. 47.
109. *YM,* pp. 47-48.
110. *Modern Review,* October 1935.

6
INDIVIDUAL CONSCIENCE
AND HEROISM IN SOCIETY

1. *YI,* November 1924.
2. *H,* February 1942.
3. *Ibid.*
4. *H,* May 1939.
5. *DD,* Navajivan, 1953, p. 284.
6. *M,* V. K. Jhaveri, 1954, vol. 5, p. 11.
7. *Ibid.*
8. *M,* vol. 7, p. 365.
9. *M,* vol. 7, p. 255.
10. Duncan, *Preface to Selected Writings of Mahatma Gandhi,* Faber & Faber, 1951, p. 14.
11. Pyarelal, *Mahatma Gandhi, The Last Phase,* Navajivan, 1958, vol. 2, p. 323.
12. *IO,* June 1908.
13. *M,* vol. 8, p. 11.
14. *The Rebel* (English translation), Hamish Hamilton, 1953, pp. 19-20.
15. Shukla, *More Conversations of Gandhiji,* Vora, 1950.
16. *YI,* March 1919.
17. *YI,* December 1921.
18. *YI,* March 1922.
19. *YI,* August 1921.
20. *Ibid.*
21. *Ibid.*
22. *Ibid.*
23. *Ibid.*
24. *YI,* January 1927.
25. *YI,* April 1931.
26. Carleton Washburne, *Remakers of Mankind,* John Day, 1932, pp. 104-5.
27. Gora, *An Atheist with Gandhi,* Navajivan, 1951, pp. 30-31.
28. Pyarelal, *Mahatma Gandhi, The Last Phase,* vol. 1, p. 225.
29. *Ibid.,* p. 198.

400 *Notes*

30. Lord Acton, *Additional Manuscripts*, 5395, The British Museum.
31. *The Hibbert Journal*, Oxford, 1914.
32. Xenophon, *Apology*, 11.
33. Plutarch, *De Genio Socratis*, 588 B-E.
34. Apuleius, *De Deo Socratis*, XVII, 157; XIX, 162-3.
35. *The Leader*, December 1916.
36. *YI*, August 1920.
37. Pyarelal, *The Epic Fast*, Navajivan, 1932, p. 34.
38. *YI*, December 1925.
39. *Ibid.*
40. *H*, July 1933.
41. *The Bombay Chronicle*, November 1932.
42. *Ibid.*
43. Lord Acton, *Lectures on Modern History*, Macmillan, 1950, pp. 31-32.
44. Lord Acton, *Additional Manuscripts*, 5395.
45. Stephen, *Science of Ethics*, Smith, Elder & Co., 1907, pp. 249-51.
46. *M*, vol. 2, p. 61.
47. *SWMG*, Natesan, 1934, p. 218.
48. Thomas Carlyle, *Heroes and Hero-Worship*, Cassell, 1908, p. 121.
49. *Ibid.*, p. 197.
50. *Ibid.*, p. 198.
51. *Ibid.*, p. 200.
52. *Ibid.*, p. 220.
53. *YI*, March 1922.
54. *YI*, June 1929.
55. *YI*, July 1931.
56. *SWMG*, pp. 386-87.
57. *H*, August 1940.
58. *Ibid.*
59. *DD*, p. 262.
60. *M*, vol. 4, p. 188.
61. *YI*, July 1921.
62. *YI*, June 1924.
63. *YI*, September 1921.
64. *Ibid.*
65. *YI*, December 1921.
66. Mitchison, *The Moral Basis of Politics*, Constable, 1938, p. 288.
67. *De Josepho*, cc. xxii-xxiv.
68. *Leadership and Political Institutions in India*, ed. Richard Park and Irene Tinker, Oxford, 1959, p. 295.

69. *YI*, April 1925.
70. *YI*, November 1929.
71. *YI*, September 1920.
72. *Ibid.*
73. *YI*, November 1930.
74. *YI*, September 1924.
75. *H*, March 1939.
76. *H*, April 1946.

7
SATYA
ABSOLUTE AND RELATIVE TRUTH

1. *YM*, Navajivan, 1932, ch. 1.
2. *SMET*, Navajivan, 1956, p. 34.
3. Monier-Williams, *Sanskrit-English Dictionary*, Oxford, 1899.
4. *Ibid.*
5. Shukla, *Conversations of Gandhiji*, Vora, 1949, p. 35.
6. *SMET*, p. 504.
7. *YM*, p. 2.
8. *CMG*, p. 36.
9. *YI*, December 1921.
10. *YI*, November 1921.
11. *YI*, December 1924.
12. *YI*, October 1928.
13. *DD*, Navajivan, 1953, July 9, 1832, p. 218.
14. *DD*, July 24, 1932, p. 250.
15. *DD*, April 8, 1932, p. 61.
16. Shukla, *Conversations of Gandhiji*, p. 36.
17. Gora, *An Atheist with Gandhi*, Navajivan, 1951, p. 48.
18. *A History of Western Philosophy*, Allen & Unwin, 1948, p. 848.
19. *H*, July 1947.
20. *To a Gandhian Capitalist*, Hind Kitabs, 1951, pp. 49-50.
21. *SWMG*, Natesan, 1934, p. 379.
22. *Ibid.*, p. 380.
23. *YI*, October 1920.
24. *YI*, December 1921.
25. *YI*, May 1925.
26. *H*, February 1942.
27. *YM*, p. 5.
28. *YI*, July 1931.

29. Shukla, *Conversations of Gandhiji*, p. 37.
30. *YI*, December 1931.
31. *Ibid.*
32. *YI*, November 1919.
33. Letter to the Reverend Boyd Tucker, September 1928.
34. *Mahatma Gandhi*, Ganesh, 1921, p. 245.
35. Letter to Mirabehn, February 6, 1947.
36. *H*, April 1946.
37. Letter to Herlekar, May 1920.
38. *YI*, September 1925.
39. *M*, V. K. Jhaveri, 1954, vol. 2, p. 410.
40. *Ibid.*, p. 450.
41. Pyarelal, *Mahatma Gandhi, The Last Phase*, Navajivan, 1958, vol. 1, p. 423.
42. *Ibid.*, p. 339.
43. *Ibid.*, p. 423.
44. *CWMG*, Navajivan, 1958- vol. 2, pp. 102-3.
45. *M*, vol. 6, p. 371.
46. *SWMG*, p. 417.
47. *Ibid.*, p. 419.
48. *M*, vol. 6, p. 300.
49. *SMET*, p. 350.
50. *M*, vol. 3, p. 184.
51. *Ibid.*, p. 365.
52. *Ibid.*, p. 359.
53. *Ibid.*, pp. 359-60.
54. *YM*, p. 51.
55. *HS*, Navajivan, 1938, p. 146.
56. *M*, vol. 8, p. 298.
57. *M*, vol. 7, p. 87.
58. *Ibid.*, p. 149.
59. *YI*, September 1925.
60. *H*, March 1940.
61. *YI*, September 1925.
62. *SMET*, p. 62.
63. *Ibid.*, p. 201.
64. *DD*, July 10, 1932, pp. 222-23.
65. *DD*, July 24, 1932, p. 249.
66. *M*, vol. 5, p. 304.
67. *Ibid.*, p. 380.
68. *M*, vol. 2, p. 450.

69. *M,* vol. 3, p. 363.
70. *Ibid.,* p. 330.
71. *YI,* March 1920.
72. Address in Bombay, May 18, 1924.
73. Letter to A. A. Paul, March 15, 1924.
74. Letter to M. Pratap, March 15, 1924.
75. *YI,* December 1921.
76. *YI,* June 1925.
77. *YI,* January 1932.
78. *HS,* pp. 33-34.
79. Gora, *An Atheist with Gandhi,* p. 46.
80. *DD,* July 24, 1931, p. 251.
81. Letter to Robert Armstrong, July 1925.
82. *M,* vol. 2, p. 249.
83. *SMET,* p. 16.
84. *YI,* June 1925.
85. *H,* March 1936.
86. *GOT,* Govt. of India, 1953, p. 12.
87. *YI,* February 1922.
88. *YI,* March 1922.
89. *H,* November 1949.
90. *SMET,* p. 345.
91. *YI,* December 1920.
92. *H,* December 1938.
93. *YI,* July 1931.
94. *H,* September 1936.

8

AHIMSA

NONVIOLENCE AS A CREED AND A POLICY

1. Edward Thompson in *Mahatma Gandhi: Essays and Reflections,* 2d ed., edited by S. Radhakrishnan, Allen & Unwin, 1949, p. 298.
2. Monier-Williams, *Sanskrit-English Dictionary,* Oxford, 1899.
3. *Purushartha-Siddhyupaya,* edited by A. Prasada, *The Sacred Books of the Jainas* (vol. IV), Central Jaina Publishing House, 1933.
4. *M,* V. K. Jhaveri, 1954, vol. 4, p. 168.
5. *YI,* November 1925.
6. *M,* vol. 2, pp. 418-19.
7. Letter in *Modern Review,* October 1916.

8. *H*, February 1946.
9. *YM*, Navajivan, 1932, p. 7.
10. *AO*, Navajivan, 1932, p. 40.
11. *YI*, March 1922.
12. *H*, September 1939.
13. *M*, vol. 4, p. 352.
14. *H*, May 1939.
15. *H*, June 1946.
16. *AO*, p. 45.
17. *M*, vol. 2, pp. 410-11.
18. *Ibid.*, p. 309.
19. *AO*, p. 45.
20. *DD*, Navajivan, 1953, p. 110.
21. *Ibid.*, p. 109.
22. *Ibid.*, p. 110.
23. *YI*, November 1928.
24. *M*, vol. 5, p. 5.
25. *M*, vol. 4, p. 159.
26. *YI*, October 1925.
27. *YI*, August 1926.
28. K. G. Mashruwalla, *Practical Non-Violence*, Navajivan, 1946, pp. 5-6.
29. *YI*, October 1925.
30. *Modern Review*, October 1916.
31. *HS*, Navajivan, 1938, p. 177.
32. *HS*, p. 139.
33. *M*, vol. 5, pp. 177-78.
34. *M*, vol. 2, pp. 175-76.
35. *M*, vol. 5, pp. 160-61.
36. *H*, May 1939.
37. *M*, vol. 8, p. 226.
38. *YI*, June 1921.
39. *H*, May 1946.
40. *Ibid.*
41. *H*, March 1939.
42. *H*, September 1936.
43. *H*, May 1938.
44. *M*, vol. 6, p. 33.
45. *Ibid.*
46. *YI*, February 1925.
47. *M*, vol. 8, p. 43.

48. *Non-Violence in Peace and War,* Navajivan, 1949, vol. 2, p. 201.
49. *M,* vol. 6, p. 145.
50. *H,* May 1940.
51. *H,* July 1940.
52. *Ibid.*
53. *H,* July 1940 (two articles).
54. *Ibid.*
55. *Ibid.*
56. *M,* vol. 5, p. 5.
57. *Fights, Games and Debates,* University of Michigan Press, 1960.
58. *H,* March 1940.
59. *YI,* December 1926.
60. *M,* vol. 5, pp. 209-10.
61. *AO,* p. 133.
62. Letter to Jayakar, March 1922.
63. *M,* vol. 5, p. 263.
64. *YI,* August 1920.
65. *M,* vol. 5, p. 97.
66. *YI,* August 1920.
67. Letter, March 1922.
68. *H,* April 1946.
69. *H,* December 1947.
70. *ABP,* August 1934.
71. E.g., Canon Shepherd's *We say "No"* or Max Plowman's *The Faith Called Pacifism.*
72. E.g., Aldous Huxley's *Ends and Means* and even to some extent Richard Gregg's *The Power of Non-Violence.*
73. *M,* vol. 6, p. 48.
74. *Ibid.*
75. Gandhi belonged to the *bania* merchant caste.
76. *M,* vol. 6, p. 48.
77. *H,* July 1947.
78. *H,* October 1935.
79. *SMET,* Navajivan, 1956, p. 504.
80. *M,* vol. 5, pp. 153-54.
81. *H,* September 1936.
82. *IO,* 1914.
83. *M,* vol. 2, p. 423.
84. *AO,* p. 45.
85. *M,* vol. 4, p. 39.
86. *YI,* October 1926.

87. *H*, July 1940.
88. *YI*, April 1928.
89. *H*, November 1938.
90. *H*, July 1935.
91. *YI*, April 1925.
92. *M*, vol. 2, p. 10.
93. *H*, September 1946.
94. *H*, October 1936.
95. *H*, November 1938.
96. *HS*, Chapter 16.
97. *M*, vol. 4, p. 173.
98. *YI*, April 1925.
99. *YI*, December 1924.
100. *YI*, May 1926.
101. *H*, August 1947.
102. *H*, June 1940.
103. *Ibid.*
104. *YI*, April 1926.
105. *YI*, February 1925.
106. *H*, July 1940.
107. *H*, August 1940.
108. *H*, October 1946.
109. Letter to C. F. Andrews, August 1919.
110. *HS*, p. 110.
111. *Ibid.*, p. 139.
112. *Modern Review*, October 1916.
113. *YI*, August 1920.
114. *Modern Review*, October 1916.
115. *H*, April 1946.
116. *Ibid.*
117. *CWMG*, Navajivan, 1958-, vol. 3, p. 222.
118. *M*, vol. 3, p. 4.
119. *M*, vol. 5, p. 308.
120. *M*, vol. 6, p. 145.
121. *Ibid.*
122. *YI*, October 1921.
123. *YI*, June 1927.
124. *M*, vol. 7, p. 77.
125. Letter to Satish Babu, November 1929.
126. Letter from Sabarmati Jail, March 1922.
127. *H*, July 1947.

128. *M*, vol. 8, pp. 338-39.
129. *YI*, December 1931.
130. *H*, February 1940.
131. *H*, July 1940.
132. *YI*, January 1922.
133. *H*, October 1938.
134. *H*, August 1960.
135. *H*, October 1939.
136. *M*, vol. 4, p. 361.
137. *H*, June 1938.
138. *YI*, December 1931.
139. *YI*, November 1925.
140. *YI*, January 1930.
141. *H*, October 1936.
142. *H*, April 1942.
143. *H*, July 1940.
144. *M*, vol. 5, p. 16.
145. *SMET*, p. 349.
146. *Ibid.*
147. *True Hinduism*, First Steps in the Yoga of Action, by Rama Prasad, Vasanta Press, 1909, p. 103.
148. *M*, vol. 1, p. 285.
149. *M*, vol. 2, p. 421.
150. *Ibid.*
151. *H*, September 1938.
152. *M*, vol. 4, p. 170.
153. *H*, June 1946.
154. *HS*, pp. 125-26.
155. *YI*, November 1926.
156. Note on Council Entry, 1924.
157. *M*, vol. 4, p. 7.
158. *YI*, April 1929.
159. R. W. Scott, *Social Ethics in Modern Hinduism*, Y.M.C.A. Publishing House, 1953, p. 101.
160. Letter to K. G. Mashruwalla, July 1947.
161. *M*, vol. 5, pp. 390-93.
162. *Ibid.*
163. *YI*, June 1919.
164. *H*, September 1946.
165. *Ibid.*
166. *H*, October 1935.

167. *H*, March 1936.
168. *Ibid.*
169. *H*, October 1938.
170. Letter to S. E. Stokes, March 1924.
171. *M*, vol. 5, p. 194.
172. *H*, March 1947.
173. Letter to P. D. Gupta, November 1926.
174. *Ibid.*, p. 344.
175. Letter to Raihana Tyabji, October 1929.
176. *M*, vol. 7, p. 379.
177. *M*, vol. 5, p. 348.
178. Letter to S. E. Stokes, March 1924.
179. *H*, June 1947.
180. *Ibid.*
181. *H*, February 1939.
182. Albert Schweitzer, *Indian Thought and Its Development*, Hodder & Stoughton, 1936, p. 231.
183. *H*, February 1939.
184. J. H. Qureshi, *The Religion of Peace*, Khwaja Hasan Niami, 1930, p. 58.
185. John Rae, "Children and the Myths of War," *The Listener*, August 17, 1961.
186. *Ibid.*
187. *Ibid.*
188. *M*, vol. 7, p. 466.
189. Janko Lavrin, *Tolstoy—An Approach*, Methuen, 1948, p. 29.

9
SATYA AND *AHIMSA*
THE RELATION BETWEEN TRUTH AND NON-VIOLENCE

1. H. L. A. Hart, *The Concept of Law*, Oxford, 1961, pp. 85, 167, 176.
2. *H*, July 1940.
3. Letter to a Burmese friend, 1919.
4. R. K. Prabhu, *This Was Bapu*, Navajivan, 1954, p. 102.
5. Speech, September 1929.
6. Speech, November 1, 1921.
7. *M*, V. K. Jhaveri, 1954, vol. 8, p. 157.
8. *YI*, November 1925.
9. Mirabehn, *Gleanings*, Navajivan, 1949, p. 19.

10. *YM,* Navajivan, 1932, pp. 8-9.
11. *DD,* Navajivan, 1953, June 18, 1932, 177.
12. Letter to Esther Faering, June 1917, *My Dear Child,* Navajivan, 1956, p. 14.
13. *Ibid.,* August 5, 1932, p. 271.
14. *To a Gandhian Capitalist,* Hind Kitabs, 1951, p. 49.
15. Kant, *On a Supposed Right To Tell Lies from Benevolent Motives* (trans. Abbott's).
16. Letter to P. D. Gupta, November 1926.
17. *YM,* pp. 5-6.
18. *SMET,* Navajivan, 1956, p. 504.
19. Letter to Basil Matthews, June 1927.
20. Letter to Clara Alias, February 1926.
21. *YI,* January 1920.
22. *HS,* Navajivan, 1938, Chapter 16.
23. Letter to the Akali Sikhs, 1924.
24. *M,* vol. 1, p. 209.
25. *M,* vol. 7, p. 236.
26. *Gandhi Marg,* October 1957.
27. Letter to Carl Heath, April 1941.
28. *YI,* September 1928.
29. *Vimalakirti Nirdesa Sutra,* Routledge & Kegan Paul, 1973.
30. *SMET,* p. xii.
31. *Ibid.,* pp. 503-4.
32. *YI,* April 1924.
33. *YI,* November 1924.
34. *To a Gandhian Capitalist,* p. 51.
35. *Ibid.,* p. 50.
36. *YI,* December 1920.
37. *YI,* November 1925.
38. *YI,* June 1922.
39. *YI,* October 1926.
40. *YM,* p. 3.
41. *H,* August 1939.
42. Kierkegaard, *Christian Discourses,* Oxford, 1961, p. 114.
43. *Ibid.,* pp. 156-57.
44. St. Thomas Aquinas, *Summa Theologia,* I. lxxix. II
45. *The Stoic and Epicurean Philosophers,* edited by W. J. Oates, Random House, 1940.
46. Hooker, *Of the Laws of Ecclesiastical Policy,* I. vii 7.
47. Jeremy Taylor, *Sermons,* 1864, p. 85.

48. Whichcot, *Moral and Religious Aphorisms,* Salter, 1753, No. 925.
49. W. Haller, *The Rise of Puritanism,* Columbia University Press, 1938, p. 189.
50. Romila Thapar's trans. in *Asoka and the Decline of the Mauryas,* Oxford, 1961, p. 255.
51. *M,* vol. 2, p. 249.
52. *H,* May 1940.
53. *YI,* September 1926.
54. *YM,* pp. 39-40.
55. *YI,* February 1921.
56. *YI,* October 1921.
57. *YM,* p. 54.
58. *YI,* March 1925.
59. *YI,* January 1925.
60. *Ideology and Utopia,* Routledge & Kegan Paul, 1960, p. 54.
61. Speech in Noakhali, *Hindustan Standard,* December 4, 1946.
62. *YI,* September 1928.

10
SATYAGRAHA
ACTIVE AND PASSIVE RESISTANCE

1. *De La justice dans la revolution et dans l'eglise,* vol. III, Paris, 1858, p. 513.
2. It is interesting to recall in this connection Newman's remark of Gladstone—that he is anxious to give the State a conscience but even he cannot do so—indeed no one can.
3. *YI,* November 1928.
4. Interview with N. K. Bose, *Modern Review,* October 1935.
5. *Ibid.*
6. *YI,* July 1931.
7. *Modern Review,* October 1935.
8. *YI,* October 1919.
9. *YI,* January 1927.
10. *Ibid.*
11. *YI,* July 1926.
12. *Ibid.*
13. *Ibid.*
14. *YI,* January 1925.
15. *YI,* March 1930.
16. *Ibid.*

17. P. Sitaramayya, *The History of the Indian National Congress,* Padma Publications, 1946, vol. 1, p. 649.
18. *Ibid.*
19. *Ibid.*
20. The right of resistance to tyranny was championed by Bhishma and Bamadeva. Passive resistance was practiced in different ways —notably *dharana, hartal* and *deshatyaga.*
21. I am using this distinction between guilt and shame as originally employed by the anthropologist, Ruth Benedict.
22. *The Doctrine of Passive Resistance,* Aurobindo Ashram, 1948, p. 12.
23. *Ibid.*
24. P. C. Ray, *The Life of C. R. Das,* appendix D, Oxford, 1927, p. 257.
25. *Henry Thoreau,* The Liberal Arts Press, 1952, pp. 11-14.
26. *Ibid.,* p. 24.
27. *Ibid.,* p. 32.
28. *Lectures on the Principles of Political Obligation,* Longmans, 1941, p. 150.
29. *SSA,* Navajivan, 1950, p. 109.
30. *Ibid.,* p. 232.
31. R. R. Diwakar, *Satyagraha: The Power of Truth,* p. 2.
32. *YI,* March 1925.
33. J. J. Doke, *M. K. Gandhi,* Natesan, 1909, p. 134.
34. *YI,* March 1921.
35. *H,* March 1948.
36. J. J. Doke, *M. K. Gandhi,* p. 135.
37. *SWMG,* Natesan, 2d ed., p. 132.
38. *HS,* Navajivan, 1938, pp. 131-32.
39. *Ibid.,* pp. 138-39.
40. *Indian Review,* December 1909.
41. *SSA,* pp. 113-14.
42. *YI,* November 1919.
43. Letter to Wattenberg, 1926.
44. Letter to the Reverend Boyd Tucker, February 1928.
45. Letter to Madame Privat, December 1947.
46. *YI,* March 1921.
47. *Ibid.*
48. *Ibid.*
49. *YI,* July 1928.
50. *YI,* December 1921.

51. *A Pilgrimage for Peace*, Navajivan, 1950, p. 88.
52. *YI*, October 1921.
53. *YI*, January 1922.
54. *Ibid.*
55. *YI*, November 1921.
56. *YI*, October 1921.
57. *YI*, January 1922.
58. *YI*, February 1922.
59. *YI*, September 1919.
60. *YI*, January 1922.
61. *YI*, April 1926.
62. *YI*, August 1921.
63. *YI*, January 1920.
64. *YI*, August 1921.
65. *YI*, March 1930.
66. *YI*, April 1930.
67. *YI*, March 1930.
68. *YI*, October 1921.
69. *YI*, June 1921.
70. *Ibid.*
71. *YI*, August 1920.
72. *YI*, June 1921.
73. *YI*, April 1924.
74. *YI*, February 1921.
75. *YI*, December 1920.
76. *YI*, June 1920.
77. *YI*, February 1922.
78. *M*, V. K. Jhaveri, 1954, vol. 1, pp. 261-62.
79. *YI*, March 1922.
80. *YI*, January 1920.
81. *YI*, August 1929.
82. *Ibid.*
83. *YI*, March 1925.
84. *India's Case for* Swaraj, Yeshanand & Co., 1932, p. 369.
85. *H*, January 1942.
86. *YI*, October 1927.
87. *H*, August 1946.
88. *YI*, September 1924.
89. *YI*, March 1925.
90. *YI*, June 1924.
91. *YI*, April 1931.

92. *YI*, June 1920.
93. *Ibid.*
94. *YI*, February 1925.
95. *YI*, June 1925.
96. *YI*, March 1931.
97. *Ibid.*
98. *IO*, June 1909.
99. *YI*, March 1931.
100. *YI*, April 1930.
101. *H*, April 1939.
102. *H*, September 1938.
103. *YI*, July 1931.

11
THE SCOPE AND
SIGNIFICANCE OF *SATYAGRAHA*

1. *YI*, November 1919.
2. *YI*, June 1920.
3. *YI*, November 1919.
4. *Ibid.*
5. *IO*, 1914 (article reprinted in *YI*, November 1927).
6. *Ibid.*
7. *H*, March 1946.
8. *YI*, June 1925.
9. *H*, February 1939.
10. *Ibid.*
11. *H*, March 1946.
12. *H*, June 1939.
13. *YI*, April 1921.
14. *Ibid.*
15. *YI*, October 1925.
16. *YI*, September 1928.
17. *H*, April 1931.
18. *H*, March 1939.
19. *YI*, January 1925.
20. *Ibid.*
21. *Ibid.*
22. *YI*, August 1921.
23. *YI*, October 1921.
24. *YI*, January 1921.

25. *YI*, September 1926.
26. *SSA*, Navajivan, 1950, pp. 232-33.
27. *YI*, January 1921.
28. *YI*, June 1924, February 1930.
29. *H*, June 1939.
30. *H*, October 1940.
31. *H*, June 1939.
32. *YI*, March 1930.
33. *Ibid.*
34. *YI*, September 1921.
35. *ABP*, August 1934.
36. *H*, March 1939.
37. *YI*, February 1922.
38. *YI*, January 1922.
39. *YI*, November 1921.
40. *Ibid.*
41. *Ibid.*
42. *YI*, November 1921.
43. *YI*, January 1920.
44. *YI*, August 1920.
45. *YI*, February 1921.
46. For an early sign of doubt regarding strikes, see *IO*, July 1913, and for concern regarding boycott, see letter to C. Vijayaraghavachariar, March 1924.
47. *YI*, April 1931.
48. *H*, June 1939.
49. *YI*, January 1922.
50. *Ibid.*
51. *YI*, January 1925.
52. *YI*, August 1928.
53. *H*, June 1939.
54. *YI*, July 1931.
55. Preface, 2d ed., *Constructive Programme*, Navajivan, 1945.
56. *H*, February 1948.
57. *H*, April 1939.
58. *YI*, March 1921.
59. *SSA*, pp. 208-9.
60. See W. K. Hancock, *Studies in War and Peace*, Cambridge University Press, 1961, pp. 74-75.
61. In a tape recorded interview with the author.
62. See Pyarelal, *Mahatma Gandhi, The Last Phase*, Navajivan, 1958.
63. *SSA*, p. 206.

64. *YI*, September 1926.
65. *YI*, January 1929.
66. *YI*, November 1921.
67. *YI*, January 1922.
68. *H*, April 1933.
69. *H*, January 1940.
70. *YI*, July 1927.
71. *Bombay Chronicle*, August 1942.
72. *YI*, June 1924.
73. *H*, April 1940.
74. *YI*, February 1930.
75. *SSA*, pp. 159, 332-33.
76. *A Pilgrimage for Peace*, Navajivan, 1950, p. 77.
77. *H*, March 1939.
78. *Ibid.*
79. *YI*, April 1921.
80. *YI*, December 1920.
81. *SSA*, p. 329.
82. *Ibid.*, p. 272.
83. *Ibid.*, p. 326.
84. *YI*, December 1921.
85. *YI*, April 1924.
86. *Ibid.*
87. *YI*, September 1924.
88. *YI*, July 1924.
89. *YI*, September 1921.
90. *H*, August 1940.
91. *Ibid.*
92. *H*, May 1933.
93. *YI*, December 1921.
94. *SMET*, Navajivan, 1956, ch. xxxiii.
95. *YI*, August 1928.
96. *YI*, March 1931.
97. *YI*, February 1925.
98. *Changing India*, ed. Sovani and Dandekar, Asia Publishing House, 1961, ch. 4.
99. K. Santhanam, *Satyagraha and the State*, Asia Publishing House, 1960, pp. 67-68.
100. *Ibid.*, p. viii.
101. K. G. Mashruwalla has said that Gandhi would not sanction *satyagraha* in a democratic system (*Gandhi Vichara Dohana*).
102. *Gandhi Marg*, October 1957.

103. *YI*, January 1920.
104. *YI*, January 1930.
105. *H*, July 1946.
106. *SWMG*, Natesan, 1934, p. 465.
107. *YI*, July 1920.
108. *H*, April 1939.
109. "The Rationale of *Satyagraha*," *The Times of India*, September 1955.
110. *SSA*, p. 317.
111. *H*, November 1947.
112. *YI*, September 1927.
113. *SSA*, p. xi.
114. *Ibid.*, p. 188.
115. *YI*, July 1925.
116. *Ibid.*
117. *YI*, April 1920.
118. *YI*, April 1924.
119. Letter to L. W. Maffey, April 1919.
120. Letter from Annie Besant, May 1919.
121. *YI*, April 1931.
122. *Ibid.*
123. P. Spratt, *Gandhism*, Huxley Press, 1939, p. 68.
124. *YI*, March 1925.
125. *IO*, May 1910.
126. *Ibid.*
127. *Ibid.*
128. *Ibid.*
129. *YI*, August 1920.
130. W. H. Holmes, *The Two-Fold Gandhi*, Mowbray, 1952, pp. 87-88.
131. *Mahatma Gandhi*, ed. S. Radhakrishnan, Allen & Unwin, 1939, p. 158.
132. *The Catholic Worker*, February 1950.
133. *Moral Man and Immoral Society*, Scribner's, 1936, p. 242.
134. *Ibid.*, pp. 244-45.
135. *Ibid.*, p. 246.
136. See chapter on *Ahimsa*.
137. *H*, March 1939.
138. *Introduction to Non-Violence*, Pacific Research Bureau, Ithaca, 1944, p. 6.

139. *Non-Violent Coercion*, Century Co., 1923, p. 402.

140. *YI*, January 1920.

141. *Ibid.*

142. *YI*, December 1931.

143. *YI*, June 1921.

144. Gilbert Murray, *The Ordeal of This Generation*, Allen & Unwin, 1929, p. 210.

145. *The Cure of Souls*, Cambridge University Press, 1908, pp. 207-10.

146. Letter to Volkar, April 1919.

147. *YI*, November 1927.

148. *H*, March 1939.

149. *H*, June 1939.

150. *SSA*, pp. 297-98.

151. *H*, August 1940.

152. *H*, March 1939.

153. *YI*, September 1920.

154. *YI*, August 1920.

155. *SSA*, p. xiv.

156. J. J. Doke, *An Indian Patriot*, p. 138.

157. Preface, *Satyagraha—Its Technique and History* by R. R. Diwakar, Hind Kitabs, 1946.

158. *SSA*, p. 272.

159. *A Pilgrimage for Peace*, p. 56.

12
SWARAJ AND *SWADESHI*
SELF-RULE AND SELF-RELIANCE

1. *YI*, March 1931.

2. *H*, April 1936.

3. *H*, December 1938.

4. *H*, April 1940.

5. *YI*, March 1931.

6. *H*, June 1942.

7. *YI*, November 1928.

8. *YI*, January 1921.

9. *YI*, March 1929.

10. *SWMG*, Natesan, 1934, p. 409.

11. *H*, March 1939.

12. *YI*, December 1920.

13. *YI*, December 1927.
14. *SWMG*, 3rd ed., p. 245.
15. *H*, August 1940.
16. *YI*, December 1921.
17. *YI*, August 1925.
18. *YI*, January 1925.
19. *YI*, June 1924.
20. *YI*, November 1924.
21. *YI*, March 1931.
22. *YI*, March 1930.
23. *H*, June 1942.
24. *YI*, April 1931.
25. *Ibid.*
26. *YI*, July 1924.

13

MEANS AND ENDS IN POLITICS

1. *HS*, Navajivan, 1938, p. 115.
2. *YI*, December 1924.
3. *YI*, July 1924.
4. *ABP*, September 1933.
5. *YI*, July 1924.
6. *Man and the State*, Phoenix, 1961, p. 55.
7. See Edwyn Bevan's comparison between the *Gita* and Stoicism in *Stoics and Sceptics*, Oxford, 1913.
8. *H*, February 1937.
9. *M*, V. K. Jhaveri, 1954, vol. 7, p. 204.
10. *H*, July 1947.
11. *M*, vol. 7, p. 254.
12. Letter to Carl Heath, January 1941.

14

ASSESSMENT

1. See R. G. Shahani, *Mr. Gandhi*, Macmillan, 1961.
2. George Santayana, *Reason in Society*, Collier Books, 1952, p. 152.

BIBLIOGRAPHY

PRIMARY SOURCES

Correspondence

Letters from and to Gandhi at the Sabarmati Sangrahalaya, Ahmedabad.

Letters from and to Gandhi at the Gandhi Smarak Nidhi, New Delhi.

Letters from and to Gandhi at the Office of the Collected Works of Gandhi, New Delhi (Ministry of Information, Government of India).

Birla, G. D. *In the Shadow of the Mahatma*. Calcutta: Orient Longmans Ltd., 1953.

Jack, Homer (ed.). *The Gandhi Reader*. Bloomington: Indiana University Press, 1956.

Kalelkar, Kaka (ed.). *To a Gandhian Capitalist*. Bombay: Hind Kitabs Ltd., 1951.

Mira (ed.). *Bapu's Letters to Mira*. Ahmedabad: Navajivan, 1949.

Nag, Kalidas. *Tolstoy and Gandhi*. Patna: Pustak Bhandar, 1950.

Journals (Edited by Gandhi)

Indian Opinion, Natal, South Africa (1903-1914).

Young India, Ahmedabad, India (1919-1932).

Harijan, Ahmedabad, India (1933-1948).

Books and Collected Speeches and Writings by Gandhi

Ashram Observances in Action. Translated by V. G. Desai. Ahmedabad: Navajivan, 1932.

The Collected Works of Mahatma Gandhi. Ahmedabad: Ministry of Information and Broadcasting, Government of India, Navajivan, 1958-.

Conversations of Gandhiji. Edited by Chandrashankar Shukla. Bombay: Vora, 1949.

More Conversations of Gandhiji. Edited by Chandrashankar Shukla. Bombay: Vora, 1950.

Delhi Diary. Ahmedabad: Navajivan, 1948.

The Diary of Mahadev Desai. Translated by V. G. Desai. Ahmedabad: Navajivan, 1953, vol. 1.

Ethical Religion. Madras: Ganesan, 1922.

Hind Swaraj. Ahmedabad: Navajivan, 1938.

Satyagraha in South Africa. Translated by V. G. Desai. Ahmedabad: Navajivan, 1928.

The Speeches and Writings of Mahatma Gandhi. Second Edition. Madras: Natesan, 1918.

The Speeches and Writings of Mahatma Gandhi. Fourth Edition. Madras: Natesan, 1934.

The Story of My Experiments with Truth. Translated by Mahadev Desai. Ahmedabad: Navajivan, 1956.

From Yeravda Mandir. Translated by V. G. Desai. Ahmedabad: Navajivan, 1932.

SECONDARY SOURCES

Bondurant, Joan. *Conquest of Violence.* Berkeley: University of California Press, 1965.

Datta, D. M. *The Philosophy of Mahatma Gandhi.* Madison: University of Wisconsin Press, 1953.

Desai, Mahadev (ed.). *The Gita According to Gandhi.* Ahmedabad: Navajivan, 1946.

Dhawan, G. *The Political Philosophy of Mahatma Gandhi.* Ahmedabad: Navajivan, 1951.

Diwakar, R. R. *Satyagraha—Its Technique and Theory.* Bombay: Hind Kitabs, 1946.

Doke, J. J. *M. K. Gandhi—An Indian Patriot.* Madras: Natesan, 1909.

Fischer, Louis. *The Life of Mahatma Gandhi.* New York: Harper & Brothers, 1950.

Holmes, W. H. G. *The Twofold Gandhi.* London: Mowbray & Co. Ltd., 1952.

Husain, S. Abid. *The Way of Gandhi and Nehru.* London: Asia Publishing House, 1959.

Maurer, Herrymon. *Great Soul.* New York: Doubleday, 1948.

Namboodiripad, E. M. S. *The Mahatma and the Ism.* New Delhi: People's Publishing House, 1958.

Nanda, B. R. *Mahatma Gandhi*. London: Allen & Unwin, 1958.

Ostergaard, G., and M. Currell. *The Gentle Anarchists*. Oxford University Press, 1971.

Polak, H. S., Brailsford, H. N., and Lord Pethick-Lawrence. *Mahatma Gandhi*. London: Odhams Press, 1949.

Prabhu, R. K., and U. R. Rao. *The Mind of Mahatma Gandhi*. Ahmedabad: Navajivan, 1967.

Prasad, Rajendra. *At the Feet of Mahatma Gandhi*. Bombay: Hind Kitabs, 1955.

Pyarelal. *Mahatma Gandhi, The Last Phase*. 2 vols. Ahmedabad: Navajivan, 1958.

————. *Mahatma Gandhi, The Early Phase*. Ahmedabad: Navajivan, 1965.

Radhakrishnan, S. (ed.). *Mahatma Gandhi: Essays and Reflections on His Life and Work*. London: Allen & Unwin, 1939.

————. *Mahatma Gandhi—100 years*. New Delhi: Gandhi Peace Foundation, 1968.

Reflections on "Hind Swaraj" by Western Thinkers. Bombay: Theosophy Company, 1948.

Reynolds, Reginald. *To Live in Mankind—A Quest for Gandhi*. London: Andre Deutsch, 1951.

Rolland, Romain. *Mahatma Gandhi*. London: Allen & Unwin, 1924.

Rothermund, Indira. *The Philosophy of Restraint*. Bombay: Popular Prakashan, 1963.

Sheean, Vincent. *Lead Kindly Light*. New York: Random House, 1949.

Spratt, Philip. *Gandhism: An Analysis*. Madras: Huxley Press, 1939.

Tendulkar, D. G. *Mahatma: Life of Mohandas Karamchand Gandhi*. 8 vols. Bombay: V. K. Jhaveri and D. G. Tendulkar, 1951-54.

Watson, Francis, and Brown, Maurice (eds.). *Talking of Gandhiji*. Calcutta: Orient Longmans, 1957.

GLOSSARY

AND GUIDE TO PRONUNCIATION

abhaya	fearlessness, courage
adharma	amoral, unrighteous
advaita	non-duality, monism
āgraha	firmness of grasp
ahaṅkāra	egoism
ahiṁsa	non-injury, nonviolence, harmlessness; renunciation of the will to kill and of the intention to hurt; abstention from any hostile thought, word or act; non-coercion
anāsakti	selflessness; selfless action
anekānt, anekantavada	
	Jain doctrine of the many aspects ("not-one") of reality
artha	politics; *raison d'état;* interest, material welfare
asat	false, unreal; falsehood, untruth; dishonesty
āshrama, ashram	monastic ideal; a spiritual fellowship or community
ātmaguna	soul-qualities
attavādá	the heresy of separateness
avidyā	ignorance
baniā	trader; merchant class
bhakta	devotee
bhakti	devotion, faith
Brahmā	the creative *Logos*
brāhmana, brahmin	
	teacher, priest
buddhi	discrimination; moral perception

charkhā	spinning wheel
chelā	disciple
dandā	legitimate coercion
daridranārāyan	God as manifested in the poor and lowly
darshan	vision; presence
dāsa	servant
dayā	mercy, pity
devatā	genius or overbrooding spirit personal to each man
dharma	duty, righteousness, moral law; social and personal morality; natural law, natural obligation
dharmakshetra	righteous struggle
dharmayuddha	righteous struggle
dhr	(root of *dharma*), to sustain or uphold
dhurna	holding out by sitting in a hunger strike
duragraha	persistence in wrong-doing
goondā	rowdy
grah	(root of *graha*), to seize, to grasp, to get hold of; to grapple with
grāma rājya	village autonomy; rural democracy
guru	spiritual preceptor and guide
harijan	"people of the Lord," formerly "untouchables"
hartāl	boycott, strike; cessation of work
himsā	injury, violence
Īshvara	eternal Ruler; controller of *maya*
Kali Yuga	age of darkness
kāma	desire, pleasure; human affections and happiness
Karma, karma	Moral Law; law of ethical causation and moral retribution; causality; action
karma yoga	spiritual realization through social action
karma yogi(n)	a religious man of action
karunā	compassion
khādi	hand-spun cloth
Krita Yuga	Golden Age
kriya yoga	yoga of action
kshatra	temporal power
kshatriya	doer; warrior

kurukshetra	earthly battlefield
lokasangraha	welfare of the whole world
Mahātma	great soul
mahāvrata	great vow
mantra	incantation
māyā	illusion; appearance
moha	delusion or glamour
moksha	liberation, emancipation, enlightenment, bliss; spiritual freedom and redemption, salvation
muc	(root of *moksha*), to set free, release; let go, deliver
muni	sage
nai talim	new (basic) education
nīti	political skill or craft
nivritti	cycle of withdrawal, disappearance; completion, repose, discontinuance of worldly acts or emotion
niyoga	law or prescription
paramārthasatya	highest of human ends
parartha	unselfishness
phalechcha	desire for the consequence
prakriti	matter
prāna	vital energy
prasād	divine grace
pravritti	cycle of outgoing; involvement
preyas	what is pleasant
pūrna swaraj	total independence, complete self-rule
purusha	spirit
purushottama	perfect man, universal man
rāj	rule
rājadharma	royal duty, regal obligations
rajas	passion; restlessnesss
Rāma Rājya	Golden Age; ideal polity
rishi	seer
rta	order, equilibrium, harmony of nature; moral order of the cosmos; moral interdependence
sacchakriya	act of truth
sadāgraha	firmness in a good cause

sādhaka	accomplisher
sādhana	discipline; practical means for the attainment of the goal of self-transformation
sādhu	ascetic, recluse
samattva	similitude
*samskāra*s	acquired tendencies of thought and character
sangh	fellowship, association
sannyāsa	renunciation of actions
sannyāsi	a monk or man of renunciation
sarvodaya	social good, public interest; universal welfare
SAT	absolute archetypal Reality; Eternal Truth
sat	abiding, actual, right; self-existent essence; as anything really is or ought to be
sattva	truth, goodness; purity
satyā	truth; real, existent; valid; sincere, pure; effectual
satyadhriti	adhering firmly to truth
satyāgraha	nonviolent resistance; a relentless search for truth and a determination to reach truth; truth-force or soul-force; holding on to truth
satyāgraha sangha	nonviolent assembly or corps
satyāgrahi	one who offers *satyagraha*
satyam eva jayate	truth alone triumphs
Satya Yuga	the Golden Age
shāstri	theologian; scholar
sreyas	what is salutary or superior
svasamvedya	known only through itself
svatantra	autonomous
swadeshi	self-sufficiency, self-reliance; patriotism
swarāj	freedom; self-rule, disciplined rule from within; political independence
syādvāda	Jain doctrine of the possibility of only relative predication
tamas	inertia; chaos; darkness
tanhā	will to live; driving force behind physical survival and bodily attachment
tapas	moral fervor; self-suffering; specific austerities and prolonged contemplation; that which burns up impurities; purificatory action; austerities, penance; warmth, heat
tapascharyā	meditation and austerities

vidhi	moral imperative; conscience
vīrya	dauntless energy
vitaraga	free from attachment, detachment
vrata	vow; a solemn resolve or spiritual decision; divine will or command
yajna (yagna)	sacrifice
yama	a spiritual exercise or self-imposed disciplinary rule or restraint
yoga	spiritual discipline; union with the divine; skill in action

INDEX

(Page references in bold face designate extensive discussion.)

Absolute, The, 63, 163
Absolutes, 156, 242-43, 252, 366
Absolutism, political, 258, 264
Absolutist(s), 21, 44, 48, 81, 196, 210, 225
Act(s), 52, 116, 119, 174, 248, 361
Action, 45, 64-66, 69-70, 108, 114-15, 119, 152-54, 181, 236-37, 249, 267, 360-61
Acton, Lord, 19, 44, 53, 125, 130, 245
Advaita, 91
Agathos, the, 145
Agnostics, 156
Agraha, 269-70
Agreement, 73
Ahimsa, 21, **178-222,** 224-34, 237-39, 249-50, 252, 301, 333-34
see also Nonviolence
Ajgaonkar, 52
Akrasia, 69
Alienation, 27, 32, 123-24, 168, 369
Allegiance, 257, 265
Altar to Truth, 153
Analogy of Religion, The (Butler), 16, 64, 120

Anarchist(s), 20, 44, 84, 85, 137, 191, 199, 219-20, 254, 258, 276, 325, 330, 346, 365, 375
Anarchistic, 146, 189
Anarchy, 187, 269, 276, 277, 282, 305, 316
  enlightened, 254
Anasakti, 182
Anaxagoras, 153
Andrews, C. F., 6, 75-76
Anekantavada, 247-48
Anselm, St., 240
Antigone, 134, 259
Antiphon, 153
Apathy, 32, 39, 85, 166, 360
Apology (Plato), 10, 124, 269
Appeasement, at Munich, 203
Apprehension, degrees of, 152
Approximations to Absolute Truth, 159
*Apta*s, 132
Apuleius, 127
Aquinas, St. Thomas, 19, 38, 46, 58, 153, 170, 218-19, 242, 374
Archetype(s), 163, 260, 339
Areopagitica (Milton), 244

Arete, 145
Aristotle, 38, 54, 58, 61, 152
Arjun, 200
Army, 142
    nonviolent, 186-88, 203
Arnold, Edwin, 15
Artha, 58, 67, 150
Aryan heroes, 176
Asat(ya), 151, 226, 366, 371
    see also Untruth
Ascesis, 236
Ascetic, 5, 236, 380-81, 385
Asceticism, 70
Ashram(s), 5, 10, 14, 41, 52, 75,
    187, 299, 380
Ashrama ideal, 41
Ashtasahasri (Vidyadandi), 131
Asian societies, 28
Asoka, 47, 185, 245-46
Assassin, political, 199-200
Assassination(s), 191, 262, 364
Association, 44, 168
Assumptions, 88, 163
Atheism, 127
Atheist, 124, 156
Athenians, 127
Athens, 125, 269
Atonement, 135, 139, 302
Attavada, 181, 226
Augustine, St., 46, 88, 156, 174,
    218-19, 242
Augustinian, 46, 58, 103
Augustinianism, 89
Aurobindo, 16, 17, 47, 49, 261-63
Authenticity, 69, 75, 85, 253
Authoritarian regime, 199
Authoritarian State, 255-56
Authority, 149, 150, 173-74, 189,
    225, 244, 252-53, 256, 259-60,
    265, 322, 332, 346, 356, 374
Autobiography of Gandhi, 6, 14, 40,
    237
Autonomy, 104, 114, 123, 133, 173-
    74, 235, 346, 351
Avidya, 162

Awareness, 100, 104, 176, 362
Axioms of the creed of nonviolence,
    193-94
Azad, Maulana, 202

Bajaj, Jamnalal, 229
Bakunin, Mikhail, 119, 220
Bamadeva, 260
Bana, 50
Bania, 193, 405
Barth, Hans, 149
Baxter, Richard, 244
Becket, St. Thomas à, 126
Belief, 161, 169
Belinsky, V. G., 30
Benda, Julien, 369
Benedict, Ruth, 411
Benevolence, 182-83
    universal, 106, 222
Benevolent man, 183
Bentham, Jeremy, 15-16, 17, 85, 123,
    130, 159, 253, 365, 369
Benthamites, 365, 367
Besant, Annie, 20, 325
Bhagavad Gita, 10, 14, 15, 16, 19,
    49, 51, 59, 65, 71, 80, 92, 93,
    108, 110, 135, 138, 179, 182,
    184, 238, 270, 330, 341, 363, 417
*Bhakta*s, 132
Bhakti, 158
    saints, 4
    see also Devotion
Bharve, S. G., 318
Bhave, Vinoba, 10, 232, 326, 396
Bhishma, 179, 226, 260, 270
Bible, 179
    New Testament, 15, 16, 75, 270,
        274, 330
    Old Testament, 75, 240-41
    Sermon on the Mount, 219, 270
Bismarck, Otto von, 137
Blanqui, Louis, 44
Blavatsky, H. P., 20, 28, 398
Body politic, 259, 279
    see also Polity

Bonald, Vicomte de, 43
Bondurant, Joan, 141
Book of Enoch, 240
Bose, Subhas, 17
Bourgeois, 27, 34, 168, 258, 350
Boycott, 262-63, 281, 303, 348, 414
Bradlaugh, Charles, 124
Brahma, 157
Brahmin, 47, 107, 138, 140
Brotherhood, 200, 221-22
Brotherhood of Man, 20
Browne, Sir Thomas, 113
Bruno, Giordano, 127
Buchman, Dr. Frank, 380
Buddha, Gautama, 4, 49, 50, 80, 98, 110, 166, 197, 215-16, 226, 235
Buddhi, 343
Buddhism, Buddhist(s), 13, 20, 67, 108, 150, 179, 181, 221, 225-26, 235-37, 245
Bunyan, John, 282
Burke, Edmund, 222, 258
Burns, Delisle, 29
Butler, Bishop, 16, 64-65, 120, 129

Callicles, 137
Calvin, John, 240
Cambridge Platonists, 243
Camus, Albert, 118, 251
Cant, 28, 168
Capitalism, 30, 34-36, 258
Caritas, 46
Carlyle, Thomas, 14, 15, 18, 135-37
Carpenter, Edward, 15, 25
Cartesian standpoint, 152, 174
Case, C. M., 334
Caste, 40, 52, 75, 80, 405
Catharsis in politics, 139
Chandavarkar, Sir Narayan, 330
Charisma, 8, 140
Charismatic leader, 5, 56
Charity, 180-82, 243, 248
*Charvaka*s, 132
Chesterton, G. K., 9
Children, 121, 216-17, 233, 294, 355

Choice, 68
Christians, Christianity, 20, 77, 110, 131, 218, 221, 228, 240-42, 264, 273, 330, 383
see also Jesus Christ
Church, 44, 77, 218
and State, 46-47, 235
Cicero, 153-54
Citizen, 43, 55, 252-60, 266-68, 278, 376
Civic education, 384-85
Civil disobedience, 141, 191, 275-82, 305, 307, 312, 315, 377
"Civil Disobedience" (Thoreau), 266-69, 275
Civil religion, 43-44
Civil resistance, *see* Resistance
Civility, 175, 231, 234, 235, 239-50, 276, 278, 296, 378
Civilization, 23-36, 38, 190, 252, 272, 293, 328, 376-78
of future, 385
"Civilization, the Death of Art and Beauty" (Blavatsky), 28
Civilized man, 32-33
Civitas dei and *civitas terrena*, 46
Class
conflict, 258
structure, 57
Classless society, 99
Cleanthes, 148
Clement of Alexandria, 218
Cobbett, William, 5, 27
Coercion, 50, 54, 57, 64, 104, 121, 149, 185-86, 189-90, 207, 209, 220-21, 265, 283, 293, 312, 318, 330-35, 344, 360, 376-77
Coexistence, 231, 234, 244
Cole, G. D. H., 29
Coleridge, S. T., 46, 72
Collective responsibility, 139, 256, 320
Collective will, 84
Commitment, 45, 64-68, 71, 73, 147, 296, 376

Common End, 370-71, 376
Common Good, 58, 67, 116, 231, 302, 306, 318
Communion, 154
 mystical, 151, 176
Communism, Communist, 34-36
Communist Manifesto, The (Marx), 30, 266
Community, 40, 45, 68-69, 92, 121, 124, 130, 134, 142, 168-69, 191, 295, 346-47, 351, 358, 361, 380
Compacts, 84-85
Compassion, 205, 215, 236-37
Competition, 26, 34, 140, 272
Complacency, 126, 377-78
Compromise, 47-48, 56, 66, 97, 164-65, 170, 176, 204, 303, 308-9, 314, 342
Comte, Auguste, 13, 105, 156
Concentration, 154, 363
Concord, 219, 245-46, 280
Concordia, 218
Condorcet, Marquis de, 33-34
Conflict(s), 56, 103, 123, 147, 168-70, 175, 178, 181, 189, 231, 234, 285, 360
 between *artha* and *dharma,* 50
 of claims of duty, 65, 127, 206
 between morals and politics, 48, 122
 of truthfulness and charity, 223
Conscience, 6, 32, 58, 65, 85, 118-34, 139, 144, 159, 223, 246, 252-53, 261, 266-68, 271, 278-79, 286, 299, 301, 308-9, 316, 320, 371, 379, 382, 410
Conscientious man, 121, 252
Conscientious objector, 216, 278, 338
Consciousness
 false, 168
 real, 221
 universal, 151
Conscription, 202-3
Consecration, 84
Consensus, 69, 189, 299, 360

Consent, 104, 189, 209, 255, 258-59, 264
Consistency, 8, 12, 13, 64, 65, 75-76, 332
Constant, Benjamin, 130, 229-30
Constantine, 218
Constitutionalism, 258, 276
Constitutionalist, 300, 318
Constructive Programme, 55, 186-87, 301, 306-7, 338, 369
Contemplation, 45, 71, 92, 108, 110, 145, 165
Contemplative, 147
Contracts, 81ff.
Contradiction(s), 7, 9, 33, 82, 376
Conversion, 139, 182-83, 185-86, 209, 246, 333
Conviction(s), 18, 33, 71, 122, 161, 176, 196, 233, 250, 368
Corruption, 7, 23, 46, 96, 141, 294
Cosmic order, 100, 150-51, 176, 352; *see also* Ṛta
Cosmopolitanism, 336
Courage, 69, 72, 136-38, 168, 173, 191, 196, 199, 216, 232, 271-72, 293, 297
Cowardice, 158, 164, 201, 204, 214
Credibility, 69
Crimes, 287, 361
Crito, 269
Cromwell, Oliver, 5, 44, 137, 243
Cunningham, The Reverend W., 337
Cycle
 the complete time, 100
 eternal, 211
 of outgoing (*pravritti*), 109
 of withdrawal (*nivritti*), 109
Cyclical view of history, 103-4
Cynics, 153

Daimon, 125, 127
Dalai Lama, 4, 305
Danda, 50, 54
Daniel, 271, 274, 282

Dante, 36, 136
Darwinian, 33, 90
Das, C. R., 263
Das Kapital (Marx), 17, 29
Davis, H. W. C., 113
Daya, 182
Death, 124, 163, 183, 232, 274, 312, 341
Deception, 190, 225, 232
Decision, 59-60, 154, 169, 361
De Deo Socratis (Apuleius), 127
Defeatism, 58, 378
De Genio Socratis (Plutarch), 127
Degrees of apprehension, 152
Degrees of truth and nonviolence, 148
De Josepho (Philo Judaeus), 140
Delphic Oracle, 125
Delusion, 25, 38
   see also Moha
Democracy, 27, 137, 141-43, 185-87, 215, 256, 258-59, 267, 284, 303, 310, 316-23, 346
Democritus, 153, 269
Demoralization, 215, 382
Demos, 286
Demou phatis, 145
De Officis (Cicero), 153
Depravity, 96
Depression, 161
Desai, Mahadev, 10, 155
Deshatyaga, 261
Detachment, 80, 81, 108, 135, 236, 379
Determinism, social, 115
Deussen, Paul, 131
Devata, 125
Devotion, 19, 157-58, 270
Dharma, 20, 47, 50, 54, 58, 67-68, 71, 79-80, 100, 115-16, 141, 150, 162, 176, 178, 225-26, 252-53
Dharmakshetra, 341
Dharmayuddha, 341
Dhebar, U. N., 321-22
Dhingra, 199

Dhurna, 261
Dialectic, 160, 358, 366, 370
Dialogue, 171, 245, 249
Dikaiosune, 134
Dike, 134
Diplomats, 28, 367
Discipline, 67, 80, 120-21, 129, 141, 159, 162-63, 165-66, 178, 181, 192-93, 277, 284, 288, 297-300, 314, 356
Discord, social, 168
Discours sur les sciences et les arts (Rousseau), 30
Discrimination, 68, 237
Disequilibrium, 23
Disinterested action, 81, 108
Disloyalty, 167, 257
Disobedience, 83, 257, 277, 312
   see also Civil disobedience
Disraeli, Benjamin, 58
Divine love, 182
Divine Reality, 156
Divine reason, 152
Divine right, 130
Doctrine(s)
   of *ahimsa,* 188-89, 210, 218, 247
   of *anekantavada* and *syadvada,* 247-48
   of collective responsibility, 256
   of dispassionate action, 110, 363
   of *karma,* 20
   of *maya,* 38
   of minimum State intervention, 254
   of *moksha* and *tapas,* 230
   of monism, 91-92, 234
   of non-possession, 111, 185-86
   of non-resistance, 218
   of nonviolence, 179
   of original goodness, 97-100
   of original sin, 97, 99
   of passive resistance, 260-69
   of perfectibility, 100, 105, 111
   of political obligation, 257
   of progress, 34-35, 38

Doctrine(s) (*Cont.*)
 of rebirth, 79, 100
 of *satyagraha,* 269-92, 294, 298, 377, 380
 of self-help, 94
 of sovereignty, 253
 that the end justifies the means, 364-68
 of tolerance, 241, 246-47
Dogmatism, 171, 173, 244, 249, 370, 379
Doke, The Reverend J. J., 9, 10, 19-20
Dostoevskian, 383
Doubt, philosophical, 25, 249
Doukhobors, 273, 305
Dreams, 127, 140
Drummond, Henry, 16
Du contrat social (Rousseau), 29, 43
Duragraha, 310-12, 315, 319, 335, 377
Durkheim, Emile, 57, 81, 121, 259
Duty, duties, 35, 45, 60, 65, 67, 71, 80, 109, 127, 131, 154, 158, 179, 218, 256-57, 266-67, 278-79, 282-84, 294, 308-9, 315, 321, 341
"Duty of Disloyalty, The" (Gandhi), 257
"Duty of Submission to Civil Government" (Paley), 266

Earnestness, 64, 153, 378
Eclecticism, 357
Education for Life (Armstrong), 17
Egoism, 40, 80, 115, 237
Egotism, 109, 126
Einstein, Albert, 4, 222
Elijah, 240-41
Emerson, R. W., 15, 18, 44-45, 64, 169
Encyclopaedists, 153, 287
End(s), 47, 50, 60, 66, 69-71, 116, 131, 140, 234, 250, 285, 360; and means, 162, 215, 224, 227-28, 230, 360-71
Energy, 6, 27, 92, 116, 151, 186, 200, 281, 306-7, 342-43, 351
Engels, Friedrich, 17, 365-66
Enlightenment, The, 98-99, 154
Environment, 32, 70, 89, 92, 94, 101, 118, 238
Epictetus, 218, 242
Equality, 136, 244, 250
Equilibrium, 31, 56, 98, 116, 173, 176, 225
Erasmus, 26, 219, 242
Error(s), 9, 38, 59, 99, 101, 105, 161, 169, 239, 248-49, 285, 305
Eternal concerns, 129
Eternal cycle, 211
Eternal laws, 259
Eternal principles, 71, 294, 308, 343
Eternal Reason, 153
Eternal truths, 45
Ethic(s), 42, 48, 63, 67, 71, 88, 150, 172, 220, 346, 348, 363, 367, 385
 see also Moral(s)
Ethical Religion (Gandhi), 10, 64, 70, 120
Euclid, 187, 204-5
Euclidean models, 384
Euripedes, 129
Europe, 198, 203, 212, 234, 236, 260, 264, 274, 344, 366, 371, 378
Evil, 38, 49, 56-57, 64, 70, 96, 98-99, 103-5, 116, 159, 162, 171, 202, 257, 282, 300, 312, 336
Evolution, 33, 100, 110, 160, 166, 176, 235, 294, 354, 356
Existentialists, 152, 154-55
Expediency, 40, 47-48, 77, 164, 167, 193, 197, 229, 267, 308, 360, 364, 375
Experiments, 6, 32, 35, 159-60, 214, 232, 234, 249, 324, 353-54

Exploitation, 60, 94, 98, 186, 208, 252, 254, 282, 374, 378

Failure, 170

Faith, 19, 25, 40, 41, 51, 98, 100, 124, 133, 141, 161, 163, 195-96, 203, 223, 239, 244, 250, 291, 313-14, 363

Falkland, Viscount, 244

Fallibility, 101, 160, 161, 244, 336

Falsehood, 151, 161
see also Asat(ya)

Family, 57, 294-95

Fanaticism, 147, 249

Fasting, 261, 304-5, 315, 333

Faust, Faustian, 110, 175

Fealty, 265

Fear, 34, 138, 175, 182, 189, 195, 200, 225, 230-31, 380

Fearlessness, 75, 138, 164, 180, 189, 199, 232, 250, 272
see also Courage

Feuerbach, Ludwig, 89

Fidelity, 63, 154, 224, 371

Fides, 154

Firmness, 269-70

Fischer, Louis, 20

Force, 104, 151, 179, 184-86, 189-90, 192, 194-95, 197-99, 201, 207, 209, 213, 215-16, 220, 222, 225, 227, 232, 267, 270, 273, 280, 292, 295, 317, 324, 327, 332-34, 342-43, 363-64, 382
see also Coercion *and* Soul-force

Formulations, 175

Fors Clavigera (Ruskin), 14, 36

Forster, E. M., 4

Fortitude, 293

Fortuna, 364

Fourier, Charles, 25, 33

Frailty, 96

Francis, St., 5, 181, 392

Fraud, 7, 175, 225, 232-33

Free man, 349

Free will, 130, 362

Freedom, 26, 53, 84, 104, 114, 132-33, 185, 231, 234-39, 241, 244, 247, 251, 307, 335, **346-51**, 355-56, 376

French Revolution, 15

Freud, Sigmund, 15, 222

Fromm, Eric, 26

Gadgil, N. V., 316

Gandhi, Maganlal, 269

Gandhi, Mohandas Karamchand (October 2, 1869-January 30, 1948)
on action, 66
and *advaita,* 91-92
approach to politics, 8, 41
approach to religion, 42
autobiography, 6, 14, 40, 237
and Bishop Butler, 64-65
and Madame Blavatsky, 28
on Bradlaugh, 124
and the Buddha, 49, 80, 98, 110, 215-16, 235, 363
and Carlyle, 135-36
change in methods, 287
charisma as leader, 8
compared with Godwin, 106
compared with Kant, 49
compared with Plato, 224
compared with Proudhon, 83-85
compared with Rousseau, 32
compared with Saint-Simon, 45-46
on compromise, 66
consistency of, 8, 13, 65
Constructive Programme, 55-56, 306-7
critics, 4, 7, 206, 325, 327-28, 330
dialectic, 160, 370
dilemma as politician, 192
as eclectic, 20
and Emerson, 44-45
on his errors, 9
Ethical Religion, 64
faith in the masses, 142-43

Gandhi, Mohandas Karamchand
    (October 2, 1869-January 30,
    1948) (*Cont.*)
  fascination as thinker, 383
  fasting, 304, 333
  favorite hymn, 228
  favorite *mantram,* 157
  followers, 21, 340
  and Gandhism, 12
  and *Gita,* 16, 19, 65, 80, 110, 135,
    179, 238, 363
  and Gokhale, 24
  Hind Swaraj, 26-30
  as Hindu, 20
  and Hobhouse, 60
  and Indian ethics, 67-68
  and Indian tradition, 47, 49, 70
  individualism, 115
  influences on, 14-16, 19, 24-25
  Inner Voice, 127-28
  integrity, 8-9
  inverse principle of progress, 33
  and the Jains, 52, 80
  as *karma yogi,* 9, 115, 135
  J. C. Kumarappa, 76-78
  last days, 53, 124, 212, 274
  on the Law of Karma, 71-72
  limitations, 61, 214, 358, 374
  on his Mahatmaship, 6
  and Marx, 12, 17, 30-31, 60, 154
  and Mazzini, 45, 154
  mission, 8, 373
  multiple roles, 5
  and Nehru, 170
  optimism, 95, 106-7
  as original thinker, 14, 17-18, 224
  participation in war, 204
  personality, 4-8
  political antagonists, 7, 308
  as political moralist, 48, 216
  as political thinker, 9-11, 13-14,
    19-21, 375-76, 383-85
  as politician, 6-8, 209, 308-9
  on power politics, 53
  practical intention, 81

  reaction to a fire in Paris, 25
  reading and study, 14-17
  on reincarnation, 100-101
  response to war camps, 200
  as revolutionary, 85, 118, 147-48,
    252-53
  and Ruskin, 10, 14-15
  as saint, 5-6
  as student of human nature, 90
  and Tagore, 28, 50, 132
  on theory and practice, 31, 66
  and Theosophy, 20
  and Thoreau, 72, 266-69
  and Tilak, 50-52
  and Tolstoy, 24-25, 31, 179
  on true morality, 64, 71
  as Victorian, 90
  view of logic and reason, 18-19
  view of moral pollution, 61
  vision, 134, 252, 358, 375
  on world poverty, 35
  writings, 10-14
Gandhian concepts, 5, 8-11, 13, 20-
    21, 179, 181, 245, 252, 301, 384
Gandhian dialectic, 160, 370
"Gandhism," 12-13, 24
Ganga (Ganges), 308
Garrison, Lloyd, 15, 16, 164, 336
Gautama, 68
Gentleness, 250, 296
Geometry, 71
Gita, Bhagavad, see Bhagavad Gita
Gita According to Gandhi (Desai),
    10
Gladstone, W. G., 379, 410
God, 6, 20, 35, 76-78, 84-85, 89-93,
    100-101, 103, 107, 110, 120,
    122, 124-25, 128-29, 133, 138-
    39, 144, 152, 155-57, 177, 221,
    227, 240-41, 259, 367
Godhead, 25
  and Truth, 124, 138, 155-58, 175,
    227, 237
Godliness, 124
Gods, 108, 125, 152

Godwin, William, 65, 87, 106, 155, 220
Goethe, J. W. von, 16, 110
Gokhale, B. G., 17, 18, 24, 287
Golden Age, 39, 50, 176, 190, 214, 375
Golden Rule, 171, 180, 184, 220-21, 246
Good, Goodness, 6, 11, 38-39, 42, 49, 58, 64, 67, 99, 106, 116, 206, 231, 242-44, 370, 382, 385
Goodwill, 180
Gorgias (Plato), 137
Government, 190, 241, 252-59, 262-63, 265-67, 282-83, 286, 294, 306, 316-21, 338, 346-47, 352-56, 368, 374; *see also* State
Grace, 20, 77, 99, 110.
Gradualist, 309, 323
Greatness, human, 136
Greece, Pythagorean, 89
Greek(s), 54, 103, 117-18, 135, 152-53, 172, 192, 346, 349
Green, T. H., 187, 267-69
Gregg, Richard, 405
Grey Eminence (Aldous Huxley), 42
Grotius, Hugo, 219
Growth, 31, 33, 59, 65, 68, 76, 77, 81, 160, 171, 195, 273, 283, 312, 314, 325-26, 346
Guilt *vs.* Shame, 261, 381, 411

Hamlet, 115, 145, 147
Hancock, W. K., 414
Happiness, 33, 43, 50, 109, 123, 148, 150, 287-88, 365, 369-71
Harischandra, 270, 290
Harmony, 165, 218-19, 252
Harmony of the Gospels (Tolstoy), 275
Harrington, James, 46
Hart, H. L. A., 224
Hartal, 261, 302
Hartmann, Eduard von, 290

Hatred, 200, 325
Heart, 18-19, 40, 45, 94, 96, 146, 155, 157, 169, 173, 195, 246, 248, 290
Heath, Carl, 5
Heavenly City, 174
Heber, Bishop, 261
Hebrew seers, 218
Hegel, G. W. F., 70, 103, 116-17, 125, 151, 174, 236
Helen of Troy, 102
Helvetius, 104
Hemachandra, 50
Heraclitus, 152
Herder, Johann von, 33, 103
Heresy, 169
Heretics, 248
Heroes and heroism, 83, 110, 133-39, 141-42, 144-46, 176, 182, 186, 200, 210, 214, 262, 270, 328, 340, 342, 382
Heroes and Hero-Worship (Carlyle), 135
Herzen, Aleksandr, 119, 140
Hierarchy, 57
of ends, 47, 68
Hijrat, 305
Himalayas, 73
Himsa, 178-79, 181, 186-90, 195-96, 201, 204-7, 211, 213, 229-32, 248, 255-56, 259, 330, 371
see also Violence
Hind Swaraj (Gandhi), 10, 24-32, 36, 232, 270-72, 327, 357, 361
Hindu Law (Mayne), 15
Hinduism, Hindu(s), 12, 13, 20, 42, 50, 52, 76, 90-91, 103, 131, 150, 155, 166, 169, 178-79, 200, 205, 211, 225, 234-35, 245, 304, 383
Historicism, 133, 136, 253, 369
History, 30-31, 68, 85, 101-6, 130, 133, 153, 163, 172, 201, 222, 354, 367, 371
Hitler, Adolf, 103, 136, 186, 197-98, 214

Hobbes, Hobbesian standpoint, 40, 54-55, 57, 88, 111, 116, 130, 163, 175, 219, 225, 258, 283
Hobhouse, L. T., 60
Holbach, Baron d', 53
Holmes, The Reverend W. H., 7
Homer, 61, 145
Homogenization, 358
Homonoia, 217
Honesty, 172, 298, 302, 311
Honor, 83, 134, 147, 277, 356
Hooker, Richard, 242
Housman, Laurence, 41
Hubris, 92, 116, 338
Huguenot, 265
Humanists, 26, 242
Humanity, 25, 31, 33, 45, 49, 67, 78, 80, 106, 109, 188, 238
see also Mankind
Human nature, 6, 74, 88-97, 106-7, 115, 123, 152, 211, 238, 293, 309, 313, 376, 380
Human relationships, 6, 36, 107
Hume, David, 61, 67, 82, 84, 85, 89, 136, 140, 183, 189, 381
Humility, 67, 109-10, 169, 173, 191, 228-29, 232, 265, 323
Hunger strike, 261
Husain, Dr. Zakir, 18
Huxley, Aldous, 42, 405
Hypnotism, 160, 221
Hypocrisy, 33, 142, 169, 201, 223
Hysteria, mass, 142

Ibsen, Henrik, 168
Ideal(s), 8, 28, 44, 51, 58, 66, 71, 76, 78, 97, 106, 111, 120, 135, 146, 178, 184, 210, 254, 270, 324, 331, 339, 353
Idealism, 165, 210, 379, 384
Ideologists, 230
Ideology, 101, 246-49, 370
Ignorance, 162, 226, 233, 235, 290
Illusion, 38, 150, 174
Ill-will, 180, 182, 198

Imagination, 144, 158, 210, 221, 303, 374-75
Immortality, 25, 91, 129, 195, 339
Imperative, moral, 131
Imperialism, 24, 27, 34, 336
Impersonality, 109
Impotence, 138, 222, 238
Impurity, 96, 235, 237-38
India, 4, 11, 89, 106, 122, 124-25, 132, 135, 140, 143-44, 167, 172, 179-80, 182, 201, 212-13, 234-36, 245-46, 260-62, 282, 319-20, 337, 347, 353, 357-58
Communists, 390
concepts, 179, 181
epics, 108, 135, 172, 179
Independence, 125, 355
intellectuals, 4, 9, 17
philosophers, 150-51
political thought, 47, 50, 213, 268, 347
politics, 180, 378
thinkers, classical, 13, 47, 55, 108, 118, 150, 384
tradition, 8, 18, 47, 49, 70, 107, 117, 135, 140, 148, 150-51, 158, 235, 246, 357, 380
Individual(s), 23, 31, 55, 67, 92, 114-17, 119, 121, 146, 168, 254-55, 259, 267-68, 272, 297, 316, 346, 353-54, 376
Individualism, 115, 117, 137, 235-36, 241
Individuality, 93, 116, 147, 254
Individuation, 133
Industrial laborers, 185
Industrial society, 27
Industrialization, 35
Inequality, 6, 186, 374
Inertia, 199
Inge, Dean, 223
Injustice, 252, 320, 336, 342
Inner Voice, 125-28, 215
Innocence, 96, 98, 180-81
Insecurity, 171, 249

Institutions, 27, 30, 32-33, 39,40, 44, 74, 114, 129, 142, 149, 167, 176, 187, 189, 209, 220, 254, 257-60, 366, 376, 378

Instrumentalist view of truth, 158

Integrity, 8-9, 48, 60, 111, 151, 167-68, 173, 224, 357, 371

Intellect, 137

Intention(s), 60, 76, 82, 89, 144, 159, 195, 218

Interest(s), 44, 46, 56, 60, 82, 123-24, 140-41, 170, 181, 184, 188, 205, 233-34, 249, 268, 346, 350

Intolerance, 169, 240, 246-48, 303, 314

Introduction to the Theory of Morals and Legislation (Bentham), 15-16

Intuition, 68, 143, 154, 174

Inwardness, 108-9, 111

Irenaeus, 218

Isaiah, 36

Ishvara, 155

Islam, 136, 241

Isms, 17, 385

Isopanishad, 12, 19

Ivan the Fool (Tolstoy), 202

Jainism, 18, 20, 52, 71, 80, 108, 132, 150, 178-79, 181, 221, 225-26, 247

James, William, 16, 60, 168-69

Janaka, 49

Jaspers, Karl, 174

Jesuits, 367

Jesus Christ, 4, 36, 77, 78, 218, 271, 273, 274-75, 290, 328

Jews, 17, 152, 218, 240

Jewish Contribution to Civilization, The (Roth), 17

Jinasena, 50, 53

Jnaneshwar, 16

Joan, St., 5, 126-27

Jones, Stanley, 5

Joseph, 140

Joshua, Rabbi, 241

Jowett, Benjamin, 58

Judaism, 241

Justice, 134, 154, 176, 229, 256, 266, 357, 363

Kali Yuga, 39, 50, 94, 104, 110, 134, 214, 383

Kallenbach, Hermann, 279

Kama, 67, 93, 108, 150, 226

Kant, Kantian standpoint, 33, 48-49, 61, 69, 71-72, 88, 96, 104, 106, 115, 129, 130, 151, 175-76, 219, 229-30, 259

Karma, 31, 71-72, 104, 108, 221, 236, 256, 361-62, 367-68

Karma Yoga, 9, 49, 115, 135, 174, 236

Kaushik, 66

Kautilya, 4, 13, 50, 54-56, 58, 179, 364-67

Kern, Fritz, 264

Key to Theosophy, The (Blavatsky), 15

Kierkegaard, Søren, 154, 238-39, 287, 345

Kingdom
  of God, 284
  of Heaven, 39, 45, 134-35, 237-39, 383
  of Truth, 290
  of Universal Peace, 218

Kingdom of God Is Within You, The (Tolstoy), 14, 179, 221

Kingsford, Anna, 20

Koran, 15, 20, 179

Krishna, 5, 50, 110, 213

Kropotkin, Prince Peter, 220

Kshatriya, 47, 140, 145

Kumarappa, J. C., 75-78

Laertes, Diogenes, 148

Lajpat Rai, Lala, 6-7

Lammenais, Hugues de, 43-44

Lao Tzu, 359
Law(s), 28, 83-84, 117, 120, 134, 153, 155-58, 174, 252, 257-60, 263-69, 271-72, 275, 282, 294-95, 316, 318, 377, 380
Law of Progression, 308
Leader(s), 56, 68, 72, 81, 86, 126, 139-44, 166, 217, 221, 280, 299, 304, 314, 347, 366, 382
Legalist, 343
Legitimacy, 49-50, 190, 219, 252, 268, 309, 346
Lenin, V. I., 5, 30, 168, 365-66
L'Homme révolté (Camus), 118, 251
Liberty, 101, 122, 129, 255, 317, 346, 350-51, 354, 373-74
"Liberty, Equality, Fraternity," 212
"Life Without Principle" (Thoreau), 72
Light of Asia, The (Arnold), 15
Ligt, The Reverend B. de, 203, 208
Locke, Lockean standpoint, 56, 88, 122-23, 175, 189
Logic, 18-19, 95
Logos, 129, 156, 249
Lokasangraha, 67
Love, 45, 53, 96, 104, 110-11, 166, 179-80, 182, 184, 195, 200, 204, 211, 215, 219-21, 227, 238, 247, 269-70, 279-80, 288, 294, 312, 327, 340, 366
Loyalty, 72, 118, 167, 204, 255, 257-58, 270, 296, 320, 337
Luther, Martin, 130

Machiavelli, Machiavellian standpoint, 40, 46, 54-55, 364-65, 368
Machinery, 34-36
Magic, 151, 290
Mahabharata, 16, 66, 75, 135, 179, 213, 226, 260-61
Maine, Sir Henry, 25

Maistre, Joseph de, 43-44, 99, 219, 258, 378
Maitland, Edward, 20
Majority, 141-43, 221, 266, 272, 303, 316, 318, 357
Man, 25, 71, 152, 157, 169, 211, 248, 272; *see also* Human nature
Mankind, 41, 48, 90-95, 102, 104, 118, 124, 180, 211-12, 234, 249-50, 366, 385
see also Humanity
Manliness, 94
Mannheim, Karl, 248
Mantra, 12
Manu, 179
Maoism, 358
Marcel, Gabriel, 63
Maritain, Jacques, 293, 363
Marriage, 74, 78
Martyrdom, Martyr(s), 29, 111, 124, 126, 141, 143, 146, 214, 218, 316, 339-40, 342, 344
Marx, Karl, 4, 5, 12, 17, 29-33, 60, 88, 99, 101-2, 105, 106, 130, 154, 168, 222, 236, 287
Marxism, Marxist(s), 12, 13, 17, 101-2, 114, 193, 258, 266, 285, 350, 358, 365
Mashruwalla, K. G., 183, 342, 415
Mass
  civil disobedience, 279-84
  hysteria, 142
  politics, 357
  satyagraha, 297, 299
  society, 158, 174, 259
Masses, 4, 8, 35, 40, 43, 135, 137, 139-44, 145-46, 166, 185, 191-92, 209, 212-13, 266, 272, 279-84, 297, 299, 305, 356, 365, 366, 369, 371
Materialism, 28, 31, 39, 44
Maturity, 68, 133, 346
Maurras, Charles, 58, 378
Maxim(s), 50, 58, 66, 181, 184, 226, 253, 364

Mazzini, Giuseppe, 5, 15, 30-31, 44-45, 154
Means and ends, 60, 162, 215, 224, 227-28, 230, 360-71
Meditation, introspective, 302
Mehta, Jamshed, 325
Meinecke, Friedrich, 57
Meliorism, 147
Mencius, 97, 221
Messianism, 147
Metaphysic(al), 69, 108, 117, 172, 176, 225, 231, 243, 290-91, 361-62, 374
Meta-politics, 46, 376
Method(s), 162, 271, 281, 295, 297, 300-301, 310, 326-27
Middle Ages, 264-65
Mikhailovsky, N. K., 142
Mill, J. S., 88, 130, 351
Mill, James, 130
Milton, John, 36, 242
Mind, 96, 106, 159, 272
Minority, 142, 195, 221, 272, 303
Mirabai, 340
Mirabeau, Marquis de, 35
Mitchison, Naomi, 139
Modern civilization, *see* Civilization
Moira, 134
Moksha, 13, 20, 50, 67, 150, 165, 178, 234-39, 245, 353
Monads, 105
Monasticism, 48, 80, 376, 392
Monism, 20, 91
Monists, 153
Monotheists, 153
Montaigne, Michel de, 243
Montesquieu, Baron de, 56, 222
Moore, Arthur, 330
Moral authority, 67, 71, 126, 130-31, 173, 255-56, 260, 377
Moral commitment, 64-68
Moral force and power, 213, 222, 342-43
Moral growth, 31, 33, 59, 65, 68, 76-77, 81, 160, 171, 346

Moral law, 20, 31, 71-72, 109, 155, 162, 176, 195, 214, 225, 362, 365
Moral obligation, 130-31, 260, 349
Moral principles, 70-71, 184, 229
Moral values, 6, 9, 40, 57, 69, 72, 254, 374, 376
Moralist, 18, 48-49, 216, 231, 343
Morality, 26, 35, 42-43, 48-50, 55, 59-60, 64, 71, 75, 100, 134, 153, 157, 184, 239, 252, 255, 259-60
Morals, 6, 10, 27, 33, 35-36, 40, 43, 54, 59, 65-71, 77, 93, 96, 98, 104, 122, 126, 133, 144, 169, 173, 181, 198, 202, 210, 216, 256, 259, 323, 333, 343, 362, 367, 377, 378, 380, 385
Morals and Politics, *see* Politics and Morals
Morley, Lord, 223, 280
Morris-Jones, W. H., 21, 391
Motive, 64, 96, 159, 198, 279, 296, 311
Mo-Tze, 221-22
Mountbatten, Lord, 308
Movement(s), 57, 116, 142, 148, 155, 280, 282, 284, 297, 356-57
Murder in the Cathedral (T. S. Eliot), 126
Murray, Gilbert, 126, 337
Murry, J. Middleton, 24
Mussolini, Benito, 137, 197, 336
Mystical
    communion, 150-52, 176
    conviction, 383
    vision, 174
    standpoint, 227
Mystics, 126, 182, 228, 339, 383
Myth(s), 90, 108, 139, 172, 216-17, 375

Nachiketas, 213
Naoroji, Dadhabai, 25, 347
Napoleon, 103, 137

Nationalism, 241-42
Natural Law, 16, 58, 151, 153-54, 176, 204, 210, 214, 219, 224-25, 242, 253, 263-65, 295
Natural Law in the Spiritual World (Drummond), 16
Natural obligations, 115
Natural rights, 115, 278, 351, 353-54
Nature, 89, 117, 119, 152-54, 156, 219, 232, 234, 252
Necessita, 364
Need(s), 33, 55, 60, 79, 140, 168
Nehru, Jawaharlal, 17, 170, 308, 358
Nehru, Motilal, 208
Neo-Stoicism, 243
Newman, Cardinal, 44, 102-3, 228
Niebuhr, Reinhold, 58, 330-31, 333
Nietzsche, Friedrich, 60, 118, 154, 192
Niti, 58
Nivritti, 109, 235-36
Niyoga, 132
Non-coercion, 189
Non-cooperation, 202, 275, 281-85, 294, 302, 315, 320-21, 325, 330, 337, 341, 352, 377
Non-possession, 75, 111, 185-86, 206
Non-resistance, 218, 328, 330
Non-retaliation, 270, 285
Nonviolence, 101, 135, 165, 177-222, 223-50, 276-77, 288, 295, 299, 306
Nordau, Max, 15, 25
Nordic sagas, 264
Norm(s), 64, 83, 249, 254, 374
Nous, noetic, 343
Nuremberg trials, 260

Oath(s), 74, 81, 165, 382
Obedience, 120, 127, 152, 261-64, 268, 275-77, 284, 296-97, 321
see also Disobedience
Obligation(s), 49, 80, 82-84, 123, 130-31, 134, 176, 184, 218, 244-45, 252, 255-60, 263-68, 278, 349, 382
Oneness of life, nature and man-kind, 97, 106, 182, 184, 232-34
Opinion, public, 117, 120-21, 141, 145, 217, 222, 271, 277, 286-87, 290, 292, 296, 329, 343
Oppression, 255, 262
Optimism, 33, 38, 88, 95-96, 106, 161, 170, 215, 242
Oracle, Delphic, 125
Organization(s), 43, 45, 81, 139, 142, 167-68, 357, 366, 369, 371
Origen, 218
Original goodness, doctrine of, 97-99
Original sin, doctrine of, 97
Orwell, George, 7
Ownership, 254

Pacifist(s), 178, 192-93, 202-3, 210, 218, 231, 365
Paideia, 385
Paley, William, 266
Palingenesis, 106
Paracharaxis, 153
Paramarthasatya, 150
Parartha, 183
Pareto, Vilfredo, 139
Parmenides, 151
Partial truth, 250
Participation, 55, 81, 203-4, 208, 346, 357, 366
Parties, 45, 116, 167, 203
Partisanship, 244
Pascal, Blaise, 170, 222
Passion(s), 35, 70, 105, 109, 117, 172-73, 226
Passive resistance, 260-75, 327-29, 337-38
Passivity, 215, 238, 245-46
Pasternak, Boris, 87, 103
Patanjali, 9, 15, 77, 80, 178, 205, 213
Pathfinders, 139

Path of action, 110, 135
   see also Karma Yoga
Patience, 124, 265, 293, 303
Patriotism, 167, 213, 217, 347-48
Paul, St., 36, 44, 182
Paullin, Theodore, 334
Peace, 187, 202-3, 208, 218-19, 239, 269, 294, 304, 363
Peasants, 185, 199
Péguy, Charles, 34, 37
Pelagian(ism), 38, 89
Penance, 91, 235, 239, 301, 304
Penn, William, 129
Perfect love, 111, 200
Perfect man, 16
Perfectibility, 87, 88, 99-101, 103, 105-7, 123, 174, 382-83
Perfection, 49, 72, 87, 101, 103, 105, 123, 138, 195, 225, 376
Persuasion, 50, 140, 184, 209, 223, 286
Pessimism, 26, 38, 61, 88, 106, 287, 383
Pethick-Lawrence, Lord, 7, 124, 308-9
Philo Judaeus, 140, 241
Pico della Mirandola, 248
Pilgrimage, 165
Pisistratus, 44
Planners, 365
Plato, Platonic standpoint, 4, 10, 15, 16, 19, 24, 44, 54, 61, 88, 119, 124-25, 134, 137, 141, 152, 163, 174, 224, 346, 384, 391
Pleasure principle, 85
Pledge, 73-76, 81-83, 164-65, 302
Plotinus, 156
Plowman, Max, 405
Plutarch, 127, 136
Plutarchian hero, 339
Polak, H. S. L., 8, 10, 31, 279
Policy, 172, 192-93, 196-99, 217, 274, 285
Polis, 371
   see also Polity

Political ethic(s), 19-21, 40, 47-49, 58, 60-61, 176, 225, 367, 369, 375, 380, 385
Political life, 6-8, 19-21, 27, 32, 39-42, 45-49, 57, 60-61, 68-69, 116, 140, 143, 149, 173, 189-90, 199, 209-10, 216, 222, 224, 233-34, 239, 246-47, 249, 252-54, 256-59, 261, 263, 265-68, 283-85, 287-89, 291, 294-95, 301, 309, 325, 328-32, 360, 364, 368, 375, 378, 383
Political moralist, 48-49, 216, 374, 376
Political theory, 149, 346, 374-75, 384
Political thinkers, 4-5, 38, 88, 224, 283, 360, 374-75
Politician(s), 41, 48, 72, 114, 144, 161, 168, 170, 209-10, 217, 375-76, 382
Politics, 36, 56, 68, 72-73, 146, 161, 167-73, 184, 239, 252, 256, 286, 308-9, 332-33, 339, 365, 369, 376, 378-80, 382
Politics and morals, 58-61, 227, 231, 252-69, 282-89
Politics and religion, 38-53, 58, 239-50, 264, 289-91, 338
Polity, 179, 346, 348, 375
   see also Body politic
Pollution, 61
Polybius, 54, 56
Populists, 56, 368
Positivism, legal, 253, 266
Potency of *tapas,* 144
Potentia, 222
Poverty, 35, 41, 57, 340, 392
Power, 28-9, 39-42, 44, 52-57, 72, 79, 94, 116, 126, 129, 137, 140-41, 143-44, 171, 184-85, 188, 192, 194, 196, 198, 202, 205, 222, 236, 242-44, 254-56, 259-60, 265-66, 284, 294, 332, 360, 364, 366, 382

Power politics, 40, 42, 52, 53, 57, 98, 185, 188, 369, 376
Pragmatism, 368
Pragmatist, 309, 363
Prahlad, 270, 339
Prakriti, 102, 108
Prana, 343
Pravritti, 109, 235-36
Pressure, 198, 209, 248-49, 292, 333-34, 364
Presupposition(s), 13, 19-21, 29, 158, 170, 172, 196, 210, 212-14, 216, 230, 239, 289, 296-97, 332, 360, 374, 377
Preyas, 47, 165
Pride, 227, 232, 244
Principle(s), 8, 29, 41, 44-45, 47-48, 52, 60, 65, 69-72, 78-79, 94, 138, 154, 157, 184, 189, 191, 203, 219, 222, 224, 227, 249, 267, 271, 273, 291, 294, 364, 370
Probation, 25, 94
Progress, 25, 33-34, 38, 66, 78, 100, 104-5, 142, 145, 171, 211, 219-21, 228, 233, 239, 255, 308, 354, 362, 369, 376, 378
Promise(s), 77, 79, 81-83, 154
Propaganda, 161, 166, 212-13, 217, 246, 284, 303
Property, 39, 179, 186, 356, 382
Prophet(s), 36, 72, 170, 178, 216, 332, 339, 380
Protagoras, 117
Proudhon, P. J., 44, 83-85, 220, 252-53
Prudence, 48-9, 189, 242, 261, 364
Psyche, 343
Psychology, 61, 88, 249, 361-62
Public, 43, 54, 73, 118, 120-22, 145, 149, 217, 222, 268, 271, 277, 286-87, 292, 296, 370, 376
Punishment, 51, 53, 189, 219-21, 274, 277
Pure politics, 50, 376, 378

Purification, 49, 64, 184, 234-39, 279, 284, 289-90
Puritanism, political, 59
Puritans, 129, 265
Purity, 20, 64, 96, 172-73, 195, 215, 220, 224-25, 229, 362, 377, 382
Purusha, 102, 109
Purushottama, 16, 117
Pyrrho, 243
Pythagoras, 152
Pythagoreans, 153

Qualities of Nature, 16
Quest, 59, 156, 158, 250, 371, 376
Quixote, Don, 115, 147

Rae, John, 216-17
Raison d'état, 47, 58, 319, 321-22, 337, 343, 347, 364
Rajadharma, 50, 260
Rajchandra, Kavi, 15
Rama, 5, 49, 77, 134, 213, 270
Rama Rajya, 39, 134, 283, 375, 383-84
Ramana Maharshi, 212, 380
Ramayana, 15, 75, 135, 145, 213
Ranade, Mahadev, 17, 38
Rapaport, Anatol, 188
Ratio, 153
  recta, 242
Rationality, 99-100
Rationalization, 165, 366
Ravana, 77, 213
Reason, 18, 32-33, 70, 94, 99, 107, 119, 129, 152-53, 156, 180, 192, 215, 220, 229, 244, 250, 263, 267, 287-89
Rebel(s), 30, 118, 132, 134, 190, 251, 265, 374
Rebellion, 118, 132, 134, 265, 267, 269, 279, 299, 324
Rebirth, 79, 100, 106, 140, 171, 214
Reform, 41, 45, 85, 113, 272

Reformation, The, 235, 241
Reformer(s), 5, 69, 75, 80, 107, 134, 216, 290, 325, 342, 377
Reincarnation, *see* Rebirth
Relative truth(s), 149, 158-59, 162, 229, 233-34, 239, 249, 371, 376, 379
Reliability, total, 164
Religion(s), 26, 28, 40-47, 50-51, 138, 166, 238, 240-41, 245-47, 259, 272, 291, 338, 368, 376
Religion and Politics, *see* Politics and Religion
Renaissance, 235, 242-43
Renouvier, Charles, 34
Renunciation, 80, 90, 93
Resistance, 116, 208, 220-24, 252, 260-82, 285, 291, 297, 313, 320, 338
Resister(s), 262-82, 300, 328-29
Respect, 259, 262, 265-66, 269, 276, 278, 282, 285-86, 308
Responsibility, 60, 68, 139, 173, 256, 258, 267, 283, 320, 351, 354, 376
Revolt, 262, 265, 267-68, 307
Revolution(s), 85, 105, 136, 212, 220, 263, 266-67, 269, 271, 296, 323, 342
Revolutionary, 30, 48, 69, 111, 114, 143, 146-47, 167, 198, 338, 365
Reynolds, Reginald, 6, 9
Richelieu, Cardinal, 58
Rights, 45, 47, 115-16, 224, 229, 236, 251, 256-58, 260-68, 271, 276, 278-79, 280, 283-84, 297, 343, 350, 354
Rishi, 93
Ritual, 82
Role(s), 140, 141, 146, 177, 255, 268
Rolland, Romain, 5, 21
Rousseau, Jean Jacques, 4, 5, 14, 19, 29, 30, 32, 43-44, 55, 106, 115, 121, 129-30, 185, 189, 236, 258

Roy, M. N., 17
Roy, Ram Mohan, 20
Rta, 47, 79, 100, 116, 151, 176, 225, 339, 368
Rule, Ruler, 252, 254, 258, 260-61, 264, 265-66, 286, 294
Rules, 64, 69, 74, 100, 133, 153, 157, 246, 259, 267, 275-76, 278, 298
Ruskin, John, 10, 14, 15, 18, 19, 24, 30, 36, 371
Russell, Bertrand, 151, 156

Sacchakriya, 176
Sacrifice, 83, 139-41, 144, 165, 195, 213, 220, 271, 314, 336, 342, 351
Sadhana, 107
Sage, 8, 236, 261, 380
Saint, 48, 143, 146-47, 165, 210, 328, 339, 375-76, 380
Saint-Simon, Comte de, 4, 30, 45-46, 49, 106, 219
Salvation, 81, 111, 235, 238-39; *see also Moksha*
*Samskara*s, 98, 100
Sanction(s), 47, 69, 84-85, 117, 131, 176, 179, 252-53, 255, 265-66, 275-76, 286, 303, 381
Sanctity, 122-23, 151, 164-65, 174, 184, 195
Santayana, G., 384
Santhanam, K., 316-17
Sarvodaya, 252, 268, 337
Sat, 150-51, 155, 176, 225-27, 370
Satan, 77, 159, 167, 240, 342
Sattvic politics, 52
Satya, 149-76, 223-50, 252-55, 258-60, 268-69, 283, 285-86, 301, 336, 339, 384; *see also* Truth
Satya Yuga, 50, 214, 375
Satyagraha, 251-92, 293-344, 377
Satyagraha in South Africa (Gandhi), 10, 272, 310

Satyagrahi, 135, 145, 273-74, 278, 286-88, 290-91, 298, 301, 308, 311-12, 322-23, 335, 339-40, 343

Schweitzer, Albert, 215

"Second birth," 182-83

Sect, Sectarian, 3, 12, 42-43, 245-46

Secular(ization), 47, 235, 243, 329

Seeker, 156, 163, 174, 228, 231, 233-34, 239, 243, 246, 249-50

Seer(s), 93, 132, 140

Self-awareness, 176, 311, 351, 356-57

Self-criticism, 165, 310, 311, 344, 357

Self-deception, 9, 57, 126, 137, 192, 204

Self-defense, 187, 197, 201, 284

Self-denial, 57, 74, 80, 336, 383

Self-determination, 106, 347, 354

Self-discipline, 68, 73-75, 166, 288, 314, 356

Self-discovery, 116, 352

Self-examination, 9, 69, 139, 213, 302, 311

Self-government, 320, 346-47, 353-56

Self-interest, 50, 158, 206, 233, 308, 364, 380-81

Self-knowledge, 123, 236

Selflessness, 182, 236

Self-purification, 45, 49, 73, 127, 194, 213, 279, 288, 302, 304, 328, 340, 352, 357

Self-respect, 187, 207, 278, 344, 355-57, 373

Self-restraint, 75, 148, 182, 205, 235, 277, 349, 354, 357

Self-restraint versus Self-indulgence (Gandhi), 10

Self-rule, 94, 254, 292, 306, 346-58

Self-sacrifice, 139, 271, 297, 304, 314-15

Self-suffering, 158, 180, 183, 237, 278-82, 286, 289-90, 293-94,

301, 312, 315, 328-29, 333-34, 338-39

Service, 49, 80-81, 86, 93-94, 109, 111, 122, 139, 143, 167, 238, 255, 351

Setalvad, Sir Chimanlal, 159-60

Sexby, Colonel, 364

Sexual morality, 10

Shamalbhatta, 179

Shame, 261, 381-83

Shankara, 16

Shaw, G. B., 16, 126

Shelley, P. B., 132

Shepherd, Canon, 405

Silence, 164, 173, 230

Simplicity, 113, 173, 392

Sin, 38, 78, 97, 181, 206, 257, 382-83

Sincerity, 49, 113, 136, 297

Sinha, Justice B. P., 317-18

Sisson, Professor Charles, 14

Sita, 181

Skepticism, 169, 171, 243-45

Smith, Adam, 16, 119, 134, 144

Smuts, General, 7, 280, 308

Social action, 140, 246, 249, 281, 288

Social conformity, 123

Social conscience, 122-23

Social contract, 84, 258

Social harmony, 140

Social reform(s), 41, 45, 69, 306

Social values, 118

Social work, 237, 297, 299, 307

Socialism, 19, 322, 363

Socialism and War (Lenin), 365

Society, 27, 39-40, 44, 73, 114-19, 134, 140, 155, 167, 186, 202, 204-5, 211, 215-17, 219-21, 223-25, 229, 235-36, 239-40, 243-49, 252, 255, 258-60, 268, 283, 306, 312, 316, 319, 322, 346-47, 351, 370-71, 381-82, 384

Socinians, 241

Socrates, 4, 32, 120, 124-27, 129,

242, 259, 269, 271, 274, 339-40

Socratic standpoint, 118-19, 154, 249, 338

Soldier, 73, 200, 300

Solidarity, 93, 124, 236, 244

Solitude, 168, 346-47

Somadeva, 50

Sophists, 117, 153

Sophocles, 129

Sorel, Georges, 139, 190, 192, 220, 225, 233

Soul, 25, 49, 68, 104-5, 116-17, 127-29, 131, 138, 147, 173, 175, 196, 211-12, 236, 238, 242, 244, 253-55, 257, 271, 291

Soul-force, 104, 109, 157, 184-85, 232, 270-71, 295, 302, 325, 339

South Africa, 9, 20, 24-25, 32, 45, 107, 120, 126, 269-70, 279-80, 287, 310, 324, 326-27, 340

Sovereignty, 84, 94, 130, 253, 258-59, 265-66

Spencer, Herbert, 115

Spinoza, Benedict de, 4, 31, 93, 374

Spirit, 47, 52, 101-2, 104, 109, 206, 211, 232, 380

Spiritual(ity), 35, 47, 52, 57, 64, 101, 148, 175, 176, 211, 214-15, 220, 235, 238, 247, 261, 281, 288, 293, 327, 330

Spratt, Philip, 193, 326

Sreyas, 47, 165

Stalin, J. V., 197, 214, 367-68

Standards, 58-61, 145, 381, 384

Stanhope, Major-General, 263

State, 43-47, 53, 55-57, 58, 83-4, 114-17, 122, 124, 129, 141, 149, 174, 185-86, 189, 220, 235, 252-61, 264-69, 275-78, 281-96, 300, 346-47, 350, 371, 377, 410

Statesman, 48, 140

Stephen, Justice, 257

Stephen, Leslie, 130

Stirner, Max, 220

Stockmann, Dr., 168

Stoicism, Stoic(s), 19, 31, 39, 69, 91-92, 94, 119, 129, 148, 152-53, 156, 172, 218, 241-42, 346, 417

Story of a Satyagrahi, The (Gandhi), 10, 120, 269

Strength, 39, 79, 144, 147, 191, 272-73, 279, 310, 344, 353

Strike(s), 261, 302, 304

Suffering(s), 143, 148, 180, 183, 217-18, 232, 235-39, 264, 271, 273-74, 278-79, 283, 287-90, 293-94, 296-97, 299, 301, 312-13, 315, 328, 334, 343, 380

Suffragettes, 270, 273

Suicide, 214

Sukra, 13, 261

Summum bonum, 72, 164, 238

Sun, 73, 78-79, 91, 151, 161-63, 314

Sunyata, 236

Svasamvedya, 131

Svatantra, 131

Swadeshi, 75, 94, 265, 336-37, 347-48, 357-58

Swaraj, 185, 292, 305, 345-58

Syadvada, 247-48

Symbols, 384

Symmachus, Quintus, 240

Sympathy, 218, 221, 248-49

Synesius, 156

Systems, 175, 260

Tactics, 52, 261-62, 273, 307, 326, 335

Tagore, Rabindrinath, 17, 28, 38, 50, 55, 132, 282, 336-37, 358

Tanha, 200-201

Tapas, 144, 158, 213, 234-39, 252, 281-82, 286, 289-90, 301, 306, 333-34, 339

Tawney, R. H., 26, 30

Taylor, Jeremy, 243

Teleologist, 68, 103, 105, 369, 398

Temple, Archbishop, 48

Tertullian, 264

Tertz, Abram, 367

Their Morals and Ours (Trotsky), 366

Themis, 134

Theoria and *praxis,* 370

Theory and practice, 31-32

Theosophy, 15, 20

Theresa, St., 126

Thomists, 172

Thoreau, Henry David, 5, 15, 18, 19, 25, 42, 72, 155, 254, 266-70, 275, 305

Thucydides, 269

Tiberius, 218

Tibet, 214

Tilak, Lokamanya, 16, 17, 38, 50-52, 58, 347

Time, 100, 362

Tolerance, 157, 206, 231, 233-35, 239-50, 296, 335, 378

Toleration, 218, 241, 245-46, 296

Tolstoy, Count Leo, 5, 14, 15, 18, 19, 24-26, 30, 31, 164, 179, 202-3, 220-22, 270, 275, 324, 328, 383

Torah, 240

Toynbee, Arnold, 177

Transubstantiation, 82, 84

Tree
  banyan, 285
  upas, 28-29

Trotsky, Leon, 366-67

Trust, 79, 83-84, 109, 153, 256, 282, 313

Truth, 28, 41, 70, 75, 138, **149-76**, **223-50**, 269-72, 274, 279, 285-86, 288, 291, 340, 366, 369-70, 376, 379
  see also Absolute, Relative Truths, *Sat and Satya*

Turgenev, Ivan, 115, 119, 147, 221

Turgot, Baron, 33, 104-5

Twain, Mark, 164

Tyranny, 135, 222, 231, 257, 260, 265, 272, 281, 335, 364

Ultimate authority, 150, 225

Ultimate end, 250

Ultimate values, 118-19

Unconditional, the, 63

United States
  colonists, 262-63
  Negroes, 212, 327
  public life, 368

Unity, 45, 93, 325

Universality, 20, 93, 109, 117, 151, 154, 270, 278, 295-96, 309, 340, 345, 358, 366, 375

Unto This Last (Ruskin), 10, 14, 371

Untruth, 28, 41, 152, 160-62, 171, 175, 229, 232, 278, 302, 313, 366-67, 370
  see also Asat(ya)

Upanishads, 12, 15, 16, 47, 108, 172, 225

Utilitarian(ism), 16, 67, 75, 81, 83, 172, 190-91, 287, 302, 329, 346, 350, 363

Vaishnava, 20, 155

Value(s), 6, 27, 34, 40, 44, 63, 64, 67-73, 83, 118-19, 132, 147, 225, 249, 258, 293, 342, 361, 374, 376, 382

Vedanta, 20, 69

Vedas, 79, 108, 117, 151

Veracity, 152, 176, 246

Vico, Giambattista, 153-54, 225

Vidhi, 131

Vidyadandi, 131

Violence, 34, 90-91, 129, 136, 147, 171, 177-81, 184, 190-212, 218-22, 224, 226-27, 229-33, 243-45, 247, 249-50, 254, 263, 270-72, 276, 279-86, 289, 296, 299, 303, 305, 312, 314, 324, 330, 367, 383
  see also Himsa

Virtu, 364-65

Virtue(s), 64-65, 68-69, 71, 92-93, 113, 119-20, 137-38, 141, 147-48, 178, 184, 189, 364, 369
Virya, 138
Vision, 160, 216-17, 232, 246-48, 252, 284, 298, 341, 375
Vital energy, 342-43
Vitaraga, 93, 182
Vivekanada, Swami, 38, 49-50
Voltaire, 25, 106
Vow(s), 5, 41, 73-81, 164-67, 193, 272, 376, 378
Vrata, 77, 79-80, 165

Wallace, Henry, 15, 33
Walpole, Horace, 263
War(s), 102-3, 162, 194, 200, 202-4, 208, 216-18, 222, 245, 267, 287, 363, 365-66
Warfare, 293, 299
Watergate scandal, 368
Weakness, 96, 181, 274, 281, 284, 313
Wealth of Nations, The (Adam Smith), 16
Weber, Max, 380
Weil, Simone, 23, 154
Weldon, T. D., 394
Welfare, 57, 67, 90, 92, 111, 130, 150, 370, 374
West, Albert, 10, 31-32

Whiggery, 162, 171-72
Wickedness, 183
Wilfulness, 121
Will(s), 26, 39, 69, 75, 79, 81, 82-85, 94, 96, 106, 111, 116, 119, 128, 130-31, 147, 178, 184-86, 189, 191, 193, 201, 206, 221, 242, 248, 255, 257, 300, 343, 355, 360
Wisdom, 8, 70, 152, 237, 274, 278, 303, 310
Women, 5, 17, 27, 217, 270, 272-73
Words, 82, 249
Wordsworth, William, 124
Worship, 138, 155
Wybergh, 327-30

Xenophobia, 357
Xenophon, 400

Yajna, 165, 213
Yama, 77
Yevtushenko, Yevgeny, 367
Yoga, 178, 205, 236
  see also Karma Yoga
Yoga Sutra, 9, 77, 80, 213

Zeno, 218
Zero, 93, 116, 194
Zeus, 134, 218
  city of, 92